LONDON REVIEW OF BOOKS
AN INCOMPLETE HISTORY

London Review of Books
An Incomplete History

ff

First published in 2019
by Faber & Faber Limited
Bloomsbury House
74-77 Great Russell Street
London WC1B 3DA

Typeset by LRB (London) Limited
The text is set in FF Quadraat
Printed and bound in Slovenia by DZS-Grafik d.o.o.

A CIP record for this book
is available from the British Library

ISBN 978-0-571-35804-5

MIX
Paper from
responsible sources
FSC® C112556

10 9 8 7 6 5 4 3 2 1

Contents

Introduction
Mary-Kay Wilmers

'The *London Review of Books* is something new,' Karl Miller, the paper's first editor, announced in its first issue. 'This, for the first time, is it.' The issue was dated 25 October 1979.* Forty years on, I'm not sure that I any longer know in what its newness consisted except that it was to come out not once a week like the *New Statesman* or once a month like *Encounter* but once every two weeks. And it felt sorry for itself: that definitely was new. 'We were not long in discovering where we could least expect to gain attention,' Karl reflected when the LRB was up and running.

He liked to talk about the LRB and he liked to say it wasn't getting its due, and most of all he liked to say it in the LRB because that was in some sense his home and had been from the start. It was founded by the *New York Review of Books*, for which he sometimes wrote. He was among friends, though he didn't see it that way.

At the beginning of the summer a labour dispute at the *Times* brought publication of the Thomson Newspapers to a halt. As well as the main paper, the TLS, the educational supplements and the *Sunday Times* all disappeared from view. I was an editor at the TLS when that happened and had no reason to complain: for me, being paid to stay at home was a treat. But if you were an academic and had just written your first book, or a publisher who'd committed more money than you had to a work of scholarship that only the TLS was likely to review, or you just liked the TLS, you'd have reason enough to regret its absence.

Fifteen years earlier something similar had happened at the *New York Times*. An industrial dispute led to the paper's closure and with it that of the weekend *Book Review*. The closure was brief – just under four months. But had it not happened there might never have been a *New York Review of Books*, or a *London Review of Books*. Readers had been complaining for years about the 'vapidity' of the *Times Book Review*. 'A universal, if somewhat lobotomised, accommod-

ation reigns,' Elizabeth Hardwick noted in an essay in *Harper's* in 1959: 'A book,' she wrote,' is born into a puddle of treacle; the brine of hostile criticism is only a memory.' When the first issue of the *New York Review of Books* came out four years later (Hardwick was one of its founders) the *New Yorker* said it 'was the best first issue of any paper ever'. Evidently the treacle hadn't quite drained away.

In Britain meanwhile things were stagnant. Six months after the dispute began and with no sign of anyone coming to the rescue, Frank Kermode wrote a piece in the *Observer* 'on behalf of all the new books that don't get reviewed'. All the new books with one exception. *The Genesis of Secrecy*, Frank's book on the interpretation of narrative, came out that year. Was it one of the hapless new books he had in mind? Maybe but maybe not: 'Unlike most authors I find that the date of publication invariably coincides with the moment when my loathing for my book reaches its maximum intensity.' I imagine there were days when he felt like that about his book and days when he didn't – his arguments were rarely straightforward and all the better for that – but I'm quite sure he meant what he went on to say about the strengths of the TLS and the spinelessness of its readers.

It was the NYRB that took note of Frank's complaint and chivalrously stepped in: 'chivalrously' because, created in the NYRB's image, the LRB could hardly fail to become its rival, and looking back now I wonder why the *New York Review* didn't see the danger ahead. The relationship between the two papers was, to use Karl's word, 'marsupial': the *London Review* modestly tucked away – hidden from view? – inside the *New York Review*. The wedding announcement too had been puzzlingly low-key, positioned with a wounding absence of fanfare at the foot of page 22 of the new joint paper. Has it taken me forty years to see that Karl's self-pity wasn't entirely misplaced?

The divorce, when it came in May 1980, was friendly enough. They didn't order us to close down, but they might have been pleased had we done so. Our existence, they said, was damaging theirs. I don't imagine that we were stealing their readers or their advertisers – they had so many more of

---

* I had been part of the paper since the summer, as had Susannah Clapp and Peter Campbell. The three of us had worked together at the 'Listener' in the 1960s when Karl was its editor.

each – but good writers are thin on the ground and we didn't like their using ours any more than they liked our using theirs.

By the time the dispute with the unions was settled, there had been two issues of the LRB. The first sold an impressive 18,000 copies; but when the second was in the shops so too was the TLS and the figure was nearer 3000. We couldn't be sure that Karl wouldn't close the paper – he often threatened to do so when things weren't going his way – so when potential advertisers asked questions about our circulation we said 'around 15,000' and hoped to leave it at that. Forty years later our circulation is more than 76,000 and because it's ABC-rated advertisers would know if we were fibbing. And so would the TLS.

★

I'm writing this on 24 March 2019, five days before it was decreed that Britain would leave the European Union, although we didn't. (Now we're not due to leave until Halloween.) It's a game we play in tandem with the government, whoever's in charge. Thus our very first issue – reprinted now to mark our 40th anniversary – includes a piece by the Cambridge economist Wynne Godley urging the government to leave the EU while at the same time 'strongly' supporting our continuing membership. Among other pieces in that first issue there's a review by John Bayley of *Darkness Visible*, William Golding's new novel; there are poems by Ted Hughes and Seamus Heaney; there's a piece criticising government policy on the universities – nothing new there – by Ralf Dahrendorf, the director of the LSE, and, in the guise of a review of the new Arden edition of *A Midsummer Night's Dream*, a magnificent piece by William Empson in which he calculates the speed at which Puck would have had to travel to 'put a girdle round about the earth/in forty minutes'. The point I'm trying to make is that what was a good issue forty years ago would be an equally good issue now.

The LRB, you could say, occupies a privileged position: unsparing in its criticism of Y's policies and X's book, it receives few criticisms in return. 'The style of a writer,' Cyril Connolly said in *Enemies of Promise*, 'is conditioned by his conception of the reader and varies according to whether he is writing for himself or for his friends, his teachers or his God, for an educated upper class, a wanting to be educated lower class or a hostile jury.' There are ten of us on the editorial floor of the LRB and we are all fact-checkers and subeditors. That is how we spend most of the day and I doubt that there are many places in the world where a medium-size book review is given so much time and attention. Some contributors are grateful, some are furious, and there are still a few who send in their articles as they might send in their laundry, as if, like washing and ironing, it's someone else's job, usually a woman's, to correct the spelling, put in the punctuation and tidy up the grammar.

Some readers call for more reviews ('Call yourself a review of books?'); others don't like our attitude to Israel; but mostly we are criticised for the disproportion between the number of pieces by women and the number of pieces by men in any given issue. We're working on it but progress is very slow and many women would say that saying that isn't good enough. That in fact it's insulting.

Karl Miller retired in 1992 and died 22 years later, but I don't think the paper that comes out now is very different from the one that came out then; certainly it wasn't my intention to change it. On the other hand I don't feel sorry for myself, or for the paper, in the way Karl did. Why would I? The world is so much more friendly to us, so much more tolerant and ready to praise than it was then. Forty years ago a paper like ours with a small circulation, academic interests and a leftish point of view was condescended to and often mocked. Now the LRB is described as a 'legendary paper' – people must have got used to it.

The Scariest Room in London

Andrew O'Hagan

Before I'd even met a literary editor, I knew they were central to the kinds of world that interested me: I would seek out their journals and spend summers over their back issues. The magazine I arrived at in the early 1990s was in Tavistock Square in London. Located on the site of the house Dickens lived in during the 1850s, the office, at the top of many stairs, was like something from the scraggier end of *Sketches by Boz*. Great heaps of papers on filing cabinets, packets of proofs and marked galleys on the tables, old issues, bound volumes, letters and manuscripts. There were corners soft with Jiffy bags and pots sharp with scalpels. Fags in stuffed ashtrays and tomes in grey mailbags. The *London Review of Books*, by then my favourite mag, was a child of the *Listener*, and its editors worked together in one room with not much air and no computers. I'd applied for the job of editorial assistant after seeing an advert in an issue of the paper I bought at Brighton station. The issue featured a cover drawing by Bruno Schulz and contained about a dozen essays, one by John Bayley on Graham Greene, one by Frank Kermode on Virginia Woolf, and something by Asa Briggs on the history of the pencil.

The man upstairs looked like Horatio Sparkins. 'Decidedly the most gentleman-like young man I ever saw,' Dickens wrote. 'Was he a surgeon, a contributor to the magazines, a writer of fashionable novels, or an artist?' He was, as a matter of fact, Inigo Thomas, one of the assistant editors, wearing a huge blue jumper and smoking a cigarette that caused curlicues of smoke to appear through its holes. 'You're here for the interview,' he said, kicking shut the door to the editorial office. 'Just a sec. A few things going on.' It seemed that the editors were having an argument and tempers were raised. I didn't think anything of it: great papers are made from strong personalities, and I knew about life on the old *Edinburgh Review*, and I imagined – quite fairly, as it turned out – that the paper spun on the notion that nothing is simply one thing.

They took me on and I never left. I wasn't into football, but if I had been it would have been like signing for Celtic. Jock Stein once said that the happiest Celtic player was really, with one or two adjustments, the perfect fan, and the two things are inseparable when it comes to literary magazines.

You love the magazine you're writing for and you want it to win the league. There are tribulations, of course, but what you remember are the thrilling fixtures, the goals and the misses, not the shouting matches back in the dressing room. Michael Neve once described that Tavistock Square office as 'the scariest room in London', and there were times, back then, when the struggle to get the paper out could feel like Entebbe at the time of the raid, though it was also the funniest place I'd ever spent time in.

The editor, Karl Miller, had two jobs: this job and his job as a professor of English at University College London, Northcliffe Professor to be precise, in honour of the newspaper magnate. He would cross to us from the UCL English Department off Gower Street, often arriving at the office with some absurd observation about life in the outside world. After the great storm of 1987 he told Christopher Hitchens, who was calling from Los Angeles, that he'd 'walked to work through squares in which every second tree was on its knees'. Not all funny people encourage other people to say funny things – or like it when they do. Karl was at his best when making common cause with his colleagues against difficult contributors. Such and such 'was a home-breaker of the most disagreeably high-minded kind'. Somebody else was 'mentally low-grade' and 'as a Lazarus pretty arthritic'. Some days he seemed like a Scottish schoolmaster ruing the day he'd stepped into the classroom. A famous poet was like 'some kid battering on his plate with a spoon'. A hero of postmodernism 'exuded human falsity'. A well-known novelist was 'nice from afar, but far from nice', and once, when the phone rang, Karl shouted: 'If that's Frank Kermode, don't answer it!' A recently applauded young writer was advised to count his blessings: 'The world lies at your feet, I should let it stay there for a while.' He gave the impression that the paper was a matter of life and death, only more important. 'We're keeping abreast of the latest frenzies,' he said with a sigh, and the paper's habit of staying abreast of the frenzies, while remaining detached from them, became its character.

I can't speak for the paper, I can only speak of it, and I'm probably too close to it to argue for its qualities, but not for nothing has the LRB become the bestselling literary journal in Europe. People forget how criticised it was in the early days, by literary hacksaws and jackdaws and Auberon Waughs, for trying to be good and for taking the positions it took, but the struggle was real enough, especially for the founding editors. Karl, Mary-Kay Wilmers and Susannah Clapp worked hard against some fascinating odds and in what the editor of the *New York Review of Books*, Robert Silvers, called 'rough conditions' (see Nicholas Spice's letter to the landlord about a leaking roof). A paper had to be made from scratch, and the spirit of invention, astringency and critical freedom, abroad in the paper to this day, wasn't forged from any obviously available tradition, nor by a high-minded committee with a strong business plan. The paper wouldn't have happened without Karl but it wouldn't have developed without Mary-Kay, and the central story of the *London Review of Books* lies there.

Demands on writers (and on letter-writers: see Karl's changes and additions to one written by the former prime minister James Callaghan) were high from the start. There are friendships that lead to confidences, and confidences that lead to writing (see Susannah's letter from Bruce Chatwin). There is evidence of reluctance here and there – see David Cornwell's, a.k.a. John le Carré's, masterstroke of self-consciousness, or Philip Larkin's fears that poetry has given up on him. There is evidence of inspired noticing (Mary-Kay's letter about Kim Philby) or inspired negligence (my letter to Irvine Welsh). In my time working at the office, it was a fairly regular occurrence for readers to phone with an objection. ('Thank Christ we're not in charge of a nuclear submarine,' Karl said.) Every time we published a piece by Edward Said there would be a passing shower of cancelled subscriptions. It was all part of the hurly-burly. This has become much worse since the internet: people can now form an international pitchfork-rabble, not necessarily by reading what you wrote, but by not reading it and believing your detractors, whose message is more to their taste. Over the course of forty years, many of the contributors vented their own despair. Frank Kermode got very antsy when Al Alvarez's book about divorce was reviewed by Alvarez's ex-wife. Another delight here is to see Isaiah Berlin in subscription-cancelling mood, accusing the paper of using only 'zealots when writing about the Middle East'. Events surrounding 9/11 provoked similar responses. In the latter case, the editors published sentences that smashed a few taboos about America, or about the West, and the letters page, always edited in favour of the critics, became a leading forum of debate about the attacks.

Taking care of people's writing, shaping it for the magazine, eliciting the best, gaining the true measure of the piece, making changes, planning an issue, choosing a cover, maintaining your writers' confidence, maintaining your own confidence, challenging your readers' expectations, forming a tone, remaining independent, writing a heading, mending a fence, having an idea, having another idea, drawing on your experience, standing back when you should, taking a punt, defending what you believe in, valuing what you publish, and making the magazine reach further than any

other – all these are the responsibilities of editors. When the *LRB* was invented, nobody was sure it would last a year, but it has blossomed in a garden of worries about the culture dumbing down. To those who care for it the *London Review* is a national treasure. It opposes certainty, it favours ambivalence, it knocks back group-think and the pride of the elect, and wherever possible it finds the world more questionable than the world finds itself.

In the right hands, editing is a kind of autobiography. William Shawn's *New Yorker*, for all his discretion, was powerfully a work by William Shawn; he was present everywhere and visible nowhere, like Flaubert's idea of the perfect novelist. Nothing in the *LRB* is ever not personal, but nothing is shouted out. Mary-Kay encouraged Christopher Hitchens to write about subjects far and wide. It was her idea to have John Lanchester write about banks, and to have Jenny Diski write about everything under the sun, and to persuade Alan Bennett to release his yearly bundle of prose.

I've always considered Mary-Kay's editorial manner to be inseparable from the things she says and the way she says them. 'All men are Idi Amin,' she told an expert on the failures of feminism. 'Marriages end, but divorces never do,' she said to a member of the editorial board. A sign in her handwriting was tacked above the sink in the office. It said: 'Please wash your cup. There's nobody who doesn't resent doing other people's washing up.' Each of these statements was like a heading, or a book title, or a manifesto, and I'd be pleased if they could be included in *Hart's Rules* as examples of editorial mindfulness. She has what John Lanchester called 'a Russian horror of clarity'. She believes that people who think in black and white are usually wrong, and has been the guardian of the paper's subjectivity for forty years.

The spirit of elucidation wants courage for a friend. Thus, the young Tony Blair was invited to explain New Labour before it was a thing. Thus, Hilary Mantel was invited to devote a LRB Winter Lecture to the new royals, and Mearsheimer and Walt were encouraged to submit their findings about the Israel lobby. Eliot Weinberger built his magnificent piece about Iraq and Tom Crewe was encouraged to tackle Aids. It has been a mainstay in the collective mind of the *London Review* that critical writing depends not on a zeal to rebuke but on a willingness to open your mind, to investigate thoroughly, and to believe that culture and politics – high and low, explicit and hidden – have a great deal to do with each other. Examining Corbyn and the press requires guts as well as a willingness to resist the home comforts of wishful thinking.

A magazine's character is a concordance of its editorial urges, its carefulness, its curiosity and its long-shots. Writers who were once essential to a paper can disappear, due to a falling off or a falling out, or because the writer didn't like a review of their book, or because the writer decided he didn't need the editor or the editor decided she didn't need the writer. The point is that magazines are human organisms. If they sometimes fail to reach their goals, well, people do, and societies do, and the effort to get it right might seem like a relentless deflection of getting it wrong. There are people who rely on the *LRB*, and people who rely on not liking it, and that is probably the way it should be. In a world of debatable facts – or warring lies – it is good to know a paper that is willing to go in for what Joseph Mitchell, speaking about his own magazine, once called 'wild exactitude'. That doesn't mean always being right, but it does signal an ambition to publish the sort of writing that will prove imaginative in the avoidance of being obvious. The *London Review* has spent decades spreading doubt about official versions – about the Falklands War, about the Guildford Four, about September 11 – and maybe its time has arrived. It is not enough for a paper to gather facts, even supposing they are facts: it must discover where these facts come from, and how they come, and to whose gain. A side benefit of such a publication is that it will sometimes meet with Coleridge's notion of a writer's task, 'to disimprison the soul of fact'.

'That's all fine,' Mary-Kay might say, 'but do you have to put it up on stilts? And do we have to use words like "disimprison"?'

When the paper moved to Little Russell Street, many years ago, it found itself across the road from St George's Bloomsbury, Hawksmoor's bizarre confection, where any day of the week you can observe a unicorn climbing the steeple. Happily adjacent, the *London Review* began to grow. It did this editorially, by taking a greater interest in international politics, by publishing more memoir and reportage, and by a willingness to be the paper of discord. It also took flight as a digital entity and developed in a way that carried its stories over the rooftops. A book such as the one you're holding can't show the achievements in publishing, marketing, digital development, advertising and subscriptions. But all agree: it is the writing it publishes that is the heart of the *London Review*. The editors don't go in much for hearts, and Jean McNicol, handy with the blue pencil for nearly thirty years, is hovering, so I won't go on, except to say that for many of us – fans and players – the fun of the magazine has been like the motion of life.

Editorial Note

Most of the archive of the *London Review of Books* is, somewhat surprisingly, in Austin, at the Harry Ransom Center at the University of Texas: we've been sending it there since the mid-1990s. The rest resides in other research libraries – notably Emory's collection of Karl Miller's correspondence, and the Frank Kermode papers at Princeton – but also in folders and shoeboxes in attics all over London, in forgotten drawers at our office in Bloomsbury, and in the memories of writers and editors and designers, many of whom have worked for the paper since the very beginning, forty years ago: some undoubtedly correct, some intriguingly contradictory.

Tracing a history of the LRB through the artefacts that we were able to unearth, and the box-files of documents that colleagues brought in – sometimes retracting permission for their use, on reflection, a couple of days later – was always going to result in an incomplete account. As one lacuna was filled, we became aware of two more.

This volume – or scrapbook, as Mary-Kay Wilmers prefers to call it – is, as much as anything, an attempt to accept the impossibility of assembling a complete history. In some cases, extracts have been edited for clarity, and they don't always begin at the beginning – a list of links to the original pieces can be found at lrb.me/incompletehistory. All covers featured in the book were designed by Peter Campbell, unless otherwise stated. There are no doubt baffling inclusions and unforgivable omissions throughout, and we apologise for having somehow managed to create an illustrated history in which every other image is, in fact, yet another chunk of text.

Sam Kinchin-Smith

1979-81

For the First Time

The London Review
OF BOOKS

Volume 1, Number 1   *25 October 1979*

'Darkness Visible' is William Golding's first novel for twelve years: John Bayley thinks it is his best, and thinks of him as a magician

Borges has written (and it is certainly true of Borges) that the writer is like a member of a primitive tribe who suddenly starts making unfamiliar noises and waving his arms about in strange new rituals. The others gather round to look. Often they soon get bored and wander off, but sometimes they become hypnotised, remain spellbound until the rite comes to an end, adopt it as a part of tribal behaviour.

A simple analogy, but it does fit some novelists and tale-tellers, preoccupied in the midst of us with their homespun magic. They are not modish, not part of any literary establishment. Nor is there anything of the showman about them: Dickens was a magician in another sense, the sense that goes with the melodrama and music hall, and tribal magicians are not creators as Dickens and Hardy were. They do not invent a whole natural world of their own in which the client can lead a solitary life; their appeal has something communal, as the Borges image suggests, and the shareability of a cult. A largely Anglo-Saxon phenomenon, with a suggestion of Beowulf about it (another of the Borges admirations), and *The Lord of the Rings* as one of its longer, more popular texts. America lacks this type of magician – the shamans there are grander, more worldly, more pretentious – and the German-style version of Hesse or Grass is too instinctively metaphysical, not homespun enough. Richard Hughes was one of our most effective local magicians; John Fowles has become one; William Golding has had the status a long time.

His new novel* confirms him as a master craftsman in his particular sort of magic. It is beautifully constructed, it grips the reader – so much so that its effectiveness gives it the air, a little disturbingly, of being closer to one of those rather different pieces of master-craft by Graham Greene or Le Carré than to its own progenitors. But this resemblance is no bad sign. It indicates change and maturity, a greater toughness and naturalness. In fact, this seems to me Golding's best book yet, compounding and refining the virtues of *The Lord of the Flies*, *Pincher Martin* and *Free Fall*, and avoiding the weaknesses of *The Spire* – that all too Shavian exercise in the medieval picturesque – and the rather nervelessly genteel social reminiscence of *The Pyramid*, Golding's last novel, now 12 years old.

The weakness of *The Pyramid* has been turned in some measure into the strength of *Darkness Visible*. Its meticulous, uneasy

*Darkness Visible. Faber, 256 pp., £4.95.

kinds of social questioning, seeming there consciously muted and damped down, have now found a new kind of certainty and force. *The Pyramid* was a depressing book: *Darkness Visible* is in a sense a hopeless one, but far from depressing.

> ... yet from those flames
> No light, but rather darkness visible
> Served only to discover sights of woe,
> Regions of sorrow, doleful shades, where peace
> And rest can never dwell.

Milton's lines were presumably very much in Mr Golding's mind. His narrative begins in the Blitz, when the firemen manning a pump see a burnt child approaching them down a burning street. The creature is eventually reconstituted after long spells in hospital, sent

Faces from the autumn publishing lists. Marc will draw regularly for the 'London Review', in which Clive James will be writing about Bernard Levin's essays and John Vincent about Jeremy Thorpe.

to school, found a sort of job in a moribund hardware emporium. No one knows where he comes from; he fits in nowhere; he seems barely to belong to the human race. His scarred appearance is so repulsive that he is disliked all the more by those who show him charity, because their principles compel them not to turn their heads away. At school, a master who loves boys is accidentally exposed by him, which results in dismissal and imprisonment, while the boy the master loves is found dead after falling off the roof.

Matty, the name given the misfit, is deeply but confusedly troubled by these events. He discovers the Bible: he goes to Australia. After various jobs and difficulties he comes back, still trying to find out who he is, and what he is *for*. He keeps a diary, and becomes convinced

that angels of a kind are giving him commands and leading him towards some event. He gets a menial job at a posh private school where the well-brought-up little boys take a polite but wholly natural interest in his disfigurements. This makes him love them. He still mourns for the fate of Mr. Pedigree, who couldn't bear him. He sees two angelically beautiful small girls looking into a bookseller's window, and he prays for them also.

At this point Part I ends. Part II takes up the life of the little girls, twins: Toni, the odd dreamy one, and Sophy, with whose consciousness we are in touch. Their divorced father is vaguely distinguished and well-off, a chess and music critic; they live with grans, mistresses, au pairs. Golding's brilliance at conveying the consciousness of the young has never been more exact, but to what purpose? We apprehend through a growing and repulsive sense of tedium, tedium conveyed (as it might be in Gogol, who ends a story with the words: 'Things are tedious in this world, gentlemen') through a narrative grip and persuasiveness which is the very reverse of tedious. Neither hell nor heaven lies about the infancy of these two, but something worse. What is it for? The reader's first reaction is to feel that here is magic turned inside out; that, although wonderfully under control, the novel has joined the ranks of those numerous other more or less modern novels whose pride and purpose seems to consist in establishing the dullness of experience, its inherent squishiness, its *nausée*.

Not so, however. There is a reason why growth in this case is the growth of absence, non-feeling. At seventeen or so Toni leaves home and becomes, by easy stages – overland to Afghanistan, conferences in Cuba – a presumptive terrorist. Piqued into competition, Sophy joins the criminal classes via a series of hitch-hiking experiences, deliberately incurred. The twins, 'everything to each other', have felt too little for hatred or love. They come together again as the novel gathers itself carefully together and pours itself over the edge of an effective climax: the school, hostages, fire, and Matty, seeking to save, vanishing into it as he had emerged from it at the beginning. The end, which succeeds the climax and brings Mr Pedigree back, is extremely moving.

Reaction afterwards, though, may be disappointment at what seems the patness of the fable: terrorists, hostages, the emptiness of evil, all things running down into aimlessness. It is an odd thing, certainly, that any novel today which tries to make use of what seems the all-important topicality risks the

Intent

The *London Review of Books* was founded in 1979, during a lock-out at the *Times*, which prevented, among other things, the publication of the *Times Literary Supplement*. The first issues were funded, published by – and appeared within – the *New York Review of Books*. 'It is a pleasure to be able to say,' Karl Miller wrote in the longhand draft of his 'statement of policy or intent', 'that this is the first journal I have worked on of which no one is in a position to say it is not nearly as good as it used to be.' The sentence didn't make it into the version published in the first issue of the LRB. Miller had been a student at Edinburgh High School in the 1940s and knew all about the journals of the Scottish Enlightenment, but this excised sentence caught the central excitement of the project now beginning: the *London Review* would be 'something new'.

His statement only gestures – with some diffidence – at what the paper might decide to stand for (social democracy) and oppose ('the elimination of the author from his work'). It would take a number of issues, even a number of years, for the paper really to declare its purpose, not in manifestos but through the writers it commissioned, through what they said when questions were asked of them, through the care with which their work was edited and their pieces assembled. The way readers perceived the paper's politics would change, its approach to literary theory would shift, but it would always cling to another of Miller's principles: it would remain 'separate and independent', not automatically conforming to established opinion but making up its own mind.

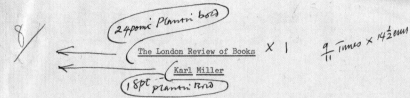

First page of the typescript of Karl Miller's 'statement of policy or intent', published in the issue of 25 October 1979

Karl Miller's notebook containing the first draft of
his statement

Possibilities

Karl Miller relied on what he called his 'jotters' – the term used by Scottish schoolchildren for exercise books – for most of his career. In them he'd write first drafts of pieces, plan editorial projects, and enthusiastically glue newspaper clippings, ideas for cover photographs and other miscellaneous documents. Lists of pieces commissioned for the first issues of the LRB, as well as proposed page layouts and a draft of his piece on the editorial principles of the paper, are contained in one such notebook, and the tables of contents for every issue Miller edited until he left the paper in 1992 are laid out in a series of five jotters, interspersed with copies of advertising rate cards, lists of possible contributors (with some names thoroughly scored out) and subjects, cover captions and so forth. Once an issue went to press, he would glue the final table of contents over the handwritten early versions.

Peter Campbell designed the layout of the LRB and chose the fonts and type sizes detailed on the typed sheet Karl Miller stuck into his notebook (shown overleaf). The designer and publisher Julian Rothenstein and his wife, Hiang Kee, were responsible for the paste-up of the first few issues. Rothenstein and Karl Miller's wife, Jane, herself a contributor to the LRB, remember a makeshift spirit inhabiting the Millers' house in Chelsea and Hiang's flat in the paper's first months: planning and proofing sessions on the kitchen floor; cow gum and long galleys from the typesetter; Karl turning up in an immaculate black suit to complain about a word that had been split in the wrong place.

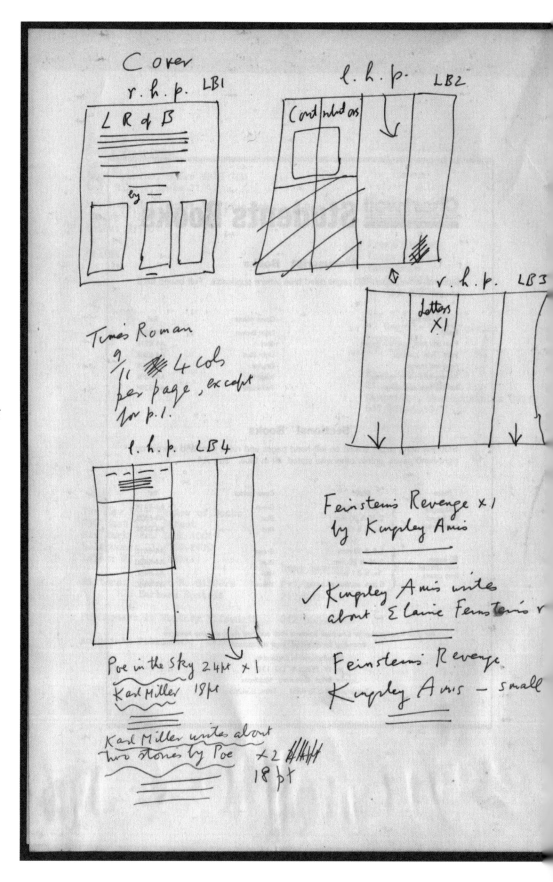

Two pages from Karl Miller's notebook containing plans for the paper

total   words

16 pp ~~editorial~~ . 15,000 / every 2 weeks .
10 reviews an issue at £75 each . 10 pp
editorial . Cd . go up to 20 pp total . Computer
typesetting (Compugraphic), offset printing at

          Bucks Free Press

25 October   30 hours of
          setting for NYR
(on-sale date 11 Oct.)

1. Frank Kermode on millenarianism : reviewed
                NYR
2. Stuart Hampshire on Mary Midgeley's <u>Beast</u>
            <u>and Man</u>
3. Seamus Heaney on <u>The Year of the French</u>
4. Karl Miller on V.S. Naipaul's <u>The Bend in the</u>
            <u>River</u>
5. Francis Wyndham on the world of Heathcote
            Williams
6. Tony Tanner on Conrad (Frederick Karl)
7. Emma Tennant on Frederick Forsyth
8. Editorial Statement   Poem
9. Ralph Dahrendorf on the univers. Seamus Heaney
    010 / 41834 9134 - dies
10. Phillip Whitehead on socialism 11. Roy Jenkins
              on Harold
              Wilson

Possibilities   5. Phillip Whitehead 12. Peter
1. Roy Jenkins on   on Benn   Medawar
  Europe: East Hendred 253 = 023588253 on Popper
        721 5262
2. Garrett Fitzgerald
  on Ireland 6. Boxer, Kitaj ! (62 or 4)
        Campbell, [set at]
3. Leavis and <u>Scrutiny</u> Peter Blake
  (~~T. Wright~~)   7. Emma Rothschild on the coming
              crisis
4. ~~Letters~~ (of Advice): 8. Ricks on
 ~~Steiner~~, Amis, Sutherland, Rosenthal, Heaney
 ~~Haycraft~~, Brophy 9. Bayley on
            Golding

Contributors to the first issue, whose contents can be seen sketched out in Miller's jotter (on the preceding page), included Stuart Hampshire, Seamus Heaney, Frank Kermode, William Empson and Emma Rothschild. Early issues covered D.H. Lawrence, Malthus, the state of the universities, Collins dictionary, Northern Ireland, Trotsky, Germaine Greer, sociobiology, linguistic philosophy, deserts, mountains, the Booker Prize, Charles II and Jilly Cooper. Of the possible writers, poets and artists listed here, many became regular contributors to the paper, some exceedingly prolific: Alan Bennett has appeared 78 times (and counting); John Sutherland 137; John Bayley 177.

Two pages from Karl Miller's notebook containing a list of possible contributors and design specifications for the new paper.

FORMAT

1. The first question is whether the format should be same as the New York Review, with a different logo and a body type slightly different at 9/11 point. Or whether it should be different, but not very different. These notes assume the second course.

2. Each issue of the London Review to read continuously from beginning to end. No article to be presented differently from the others. But the Letters section calls for a separate arrangement. The first review should start on p.1, heading across 3 columns. The first page should have 3 columns, the others 4. The first review should have its publication details footnoted, as should any subsequent articles which are not formal reviews. Formal reviews to have publication details listed at the head, across 1 column or across two. Articles will mostly run from 1000 to 1500 words.

3. Display type at the head of articles should be organised as follows.
Either: Salim and Yvette   24 pt
                                       bold
                 Karl Miller   18 pt bold centred

Or: Karl Miller writes   18 pt bold x two columns,
                 about V. S. Naipaul's   range from left to right
                 new novel

Headings to be short or long, brief or explanatory. Long articles will have spaces between sections from time to time, with occasional use of sectional numbers.

4. In addition to reviews, there will be occasional opinion pieces and descriptive pieces. These will be subject to the same lay-out as reviews. Poems will be used to hold the page.

5. No single satirical artist will be responsible for illustrations. A team of artists will contribute drawings which will either support articles or stand on their own. No regular use of historical material. Illustrations from the books reviewed will be used if strongly apposite.

A Short Tradition of Caricature

Roger Law and Peter Fluck were the creators of the satirical TV show *Spitting Image*. The *LRB* followed their advice and used 'intelligent and critical drawings to complement the opinions and reviews' for its first year or two. The cartoonist Mark Boxer, founding editor of the *Sunday Times* colour supplement and, after his spell contributing to the *LRB*, editor of *Tatler*, was a friend of Karl Miller's. He was often on the tail of his many friends, caricaturing them in his drawings, not always to their liking. The *LRB* published Boxer's drawings of Clive James, A.J.P. Taylor, F.R. Leavis (wearing a doublet), Margaret Drabble, Ted Hughes, Barbara Castle, David Owen and Shirley Williams, Graham Greene, Seamus Heaney, Germaine Greer as the Venus de Milo, and, in the first ever issue, Jeremy Thorpe, Harold Wilson and Bernard Levin, as well as V.S. Naipaul, looking like a yogi in a loincloth.

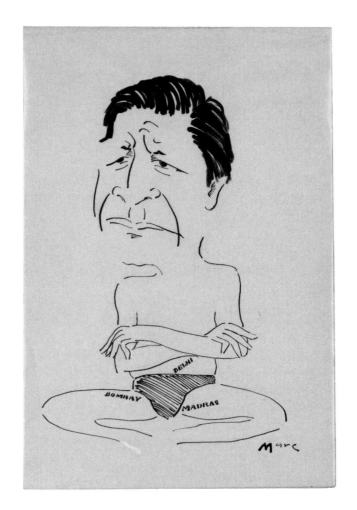

Mark Boxer's caricatures of V.S. Naipaul and, below, Jeremy Thorpe, Harold Wilson and Bernard Levin, published in the issue of 25 October 1979

Sent. telegram asking to 17 Aug.
ning. 12·45.
S.

not in phone book
under either name.

Roger Law and Peter Fluck
Victoria Hall,
Victoria Street,
Cambridge.

August 2 1979.

Dear Frank Kermode,

Here are the proposals that you asked for.

The New York Review of Books has a casual appearance which we like. We propose a format for the London Review that is basically similar but is distinguished from the N.Y.R. by the use of a different body type and subheadings.

The consistent style of the N.Y.R. has much to do with the use of David Levines caricatures and Grandvilles fantasies. The London Review will not find a European equivalent to David Levine and it would be a mistake to try. We suggest that it could be helped to achieve its own personality within the pages of the N.Y.R. by using intelligent and critical drawings to complement the opinions and reviews. England and Europe have a wealth of illustrators and caricaturists working now who would welcome the opportunity to work for the London Review. Europe also has a long tradition of caricature, and much of this work is now available out of copyright - see attached list.

In these ways the London Review could be made distictive and yet complementary.

We would be happy to help with the dummy.

Yours

Roger
Peter Fluck

Letter from Roger Law and Peter Fluck to
Frank Kermode, 2 August 1979

Refusing Your Entreaties

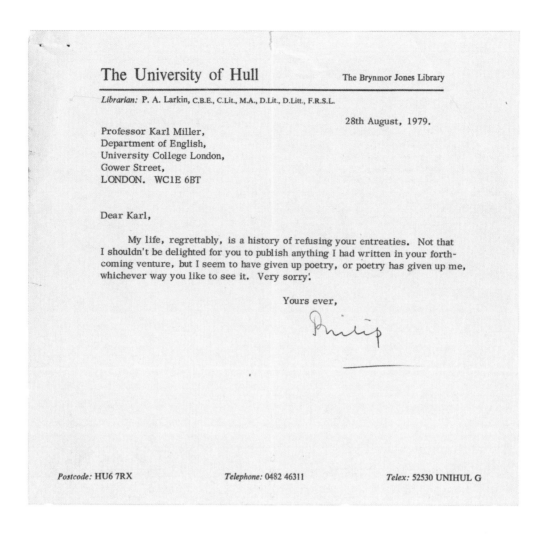

No good writer dislikes being asked to write, but saying no to things is, unfortunately, a crucial part of what makes them good. Spurned approaches could be encouraging – 'I would love to,' Beryl Bainbridge wrote – or hilariously po-faced (John le Carré, a.k.a. David Cornwell, complaining about 'the minefields of the London literary scene') or bracingly honest about the impossibility of contributing. 'To all intents I have given up reviewing,' Graham Greene wrote from Antibes, 'and it would need an undiscovered novel of Evelyn Waugh's to stir me into action.' Extremely good writers never quite say no while saying no; they could almost be saying yes. 'We can certainly talk about it next year or the year after,' Norman Mailer wrote. He thought he might have met Karl Miller in England at the Ayerses, he couldn't quite remember, but what he did remember was Christopher Ricks's praise of *The Execut-ioner's Song* in an early issue of the *LRB*. Ricks, Mailer told me, had used the phrase 'Mailer writes like an angel' – actually that phrase isn't in the piece, though it planted itself for ever in Mailer's mind. When my American publisher sent him my novel *Be Near Me*, Mailer wrote back, saying, ahem, 'O'Hagan writes like an angel.' Joan Didion, who reviewed Mailer's book in the *New York Times* – she said it was 'absolutely aston-ishing' – was asked many years later by Mary-Kay Wilmers to write about Jane Miller's book on old age. 'I can't do it be-cause I'm working on something that may or may not touch on the same territory,' Didion wrote back.

I once asked the Glaswegian James Kelman to write about British prisons. He was perfectly nice about it, the subject interested him, but he left a firm enough impression that he could never write for a paper with London in the title. Philip Larkin, who recalls in one of his published letters being pulled out of a conference to take a telephone call from Karl Miller asking him to 'add' books to a review he was writing for the *Listener*, which Karl edited at the time, wrote to the *LRB* to say: 'I seem to have given up poetry, or poetry has given up me.' He'd also given up being dragged to the phone. The philosopher Karl Popper had his assistant at the LSE write to say Popper didn't write reviews, though he would 'be interested to know if you have published any reviews of his own books'.

'I would like to write something,' Gore Vidal said. 'But maybe later, when the chrysanthemums come out.'

Andrew O'Hagan

DAVID CORNWELL

Mary-Kay Wilmers
New York Review of Books
c/o Dillon's University Bookshop Ltd
1 Malet Street
London WC1   27th November, 1979.

Dear Mary-Kay,

It was kind of you to ask me to review the Cheever, and
thank you for sending the book. It is a little difficult
for me to explain why I have decided not to review it, but
I surely owe you an explanation. I don't think very fast
on the telephone, but afterwards it occurred to me all too
clearly that I had almost by mistake agreed to depart from
a firm principle which I made when I first became a full-
time novelist - namely, never to get involved in the London
reviewing scene, never to confuse the production industry
with the service industry. Reviewing for the New York Times
is something remote. But reviewing for London literary
journals immediately involves me in a kind of partisanship
which I find very difficult to live with so long as I remain
in England. I think Cheever is a magnificent story-teller,
but I know that when I say that in the context of a London
literary journal, I appear to be making a case for narrative
writers like myself to the detriment of more fashionable
trends. I think he is better at English prose than anybody
practicing in this country, but this is a view which takes
on a quite disproportionate significance when I say it here.

I suppose what I am saying really is that I find the business
of being a successful English novelist living in England hard
enough already - there is nothing quite like the flak of home
guns - without walking into the minefields of the London
literary scene as well. Sorry.

Best,

David

Left, letter from Philip Larkin to Karl Miller,
28 August 1979; above, letter from David Cornwell
to Mary-Kay Wilmers, 27 November 1979

A Writer Responds

Letter from V.S. Pritchett to Karl Miller,
8 October 1979

V.S. Pritchett, the eminent short story writer and critic, wrote a handful of pieces for the *LRB* in the early 1980s and was a member of the paper's editorial board until his death in 1997, at the age of 96. In this letter, written after the publication of the first issue of the *LRB*, he praises Brigid Brophy's plea for 'justice for fiction', complaining that it is generally dealt with in the 'most perfunctory way', and singling out Karl Miller – who wrote about V.S. Naipaul in that first issue – for 'according the profession a dignity that, elsewhere, is just chatted away'.

Transcription:

Dear Karl,

I must say at once, what a really brilliant first number of the *London Review* you have produced. It stuns me with its excellent writing and criticism which one has missed for so long. Empson was a delight, so witty are his ingenious spiders' webs, Bayley so penetrating on Golding, and yourself really unsurpassed on Naipaul, so full of meat. And Wynne Godley so intelligent in his analysis of the Common Market troubles – I like a pill of politics; it does my rather constipated political bowels good. I still have to read Frank's piece, but I am looking forward to a couple of hours with his mysteries.

I thought Brigid Brophy's plea for fictioneers very timely, for really we entertainers are disgracefully treated by English reviewers. We are dealt with in a most perfunctory way. And that brings me to the point I have often thought of when reading you on contemporary novelists: you are easily the most responsive and thoughtful critic of interesting novelists, writing today. And you set a standard for which all of us are grateful. How rare it is nowadays to find a reviewer of novels, really bothering to see what the wretched novelist is trying to say; treating him or her with sympathy and according the profession a dignity that, elsewhere, is just chatted away.

In short, congratulations, dear Karl,

VSP

Big Beasts

'Russell and Wittgenstein and Heidegger and Sartre are dead,' Richard Rorty declares at the top of his piece on Foucault in 1981, 'and it looks as if there are no great philosophers left alive.' The age of the big beasts is over. Doubtless it seems this way to each new generation. A philosopher writing in the LRB today might lament the passing not only of Foucault and his Parisian colleagues, but also of the mid 20th-century generation of British and American philosophers, several of whom – Stuart Hampshire, Jerry Fodor, Thomas Nagel, Hilary Putnam, Bernard Williams and Rorty himself – wrote regularly in the LRB from its inception. They reviewed the work of contemporary eminences: Kripke, Quine, Rawls, Derrida. They wrote about each other: Williams on Rorty, Hampshire on Williams; Williams, Rorty and Fodor (twice) on Putnam. And occasionally they chose the LRB as a place to publish original work; in his only contribution to the paper, a two-part essay published in 1998, Derek Parfit tried to answer the question: 'Why does the Universe exist?' It can sometimes seem that today's big beasts are less willing than their forebears to engage with each other, or with the fundamental questions of their discipline, in public. Or perhaps the degree of specialisation in philosophy is now such they can't see a way to do it in language that the rest of us would understand.

Beyond Nietzsche and Marx

Richard Rorty

FOUCAULT offers the two things which people want from a philosopher: a view about what values to place on current knowledge-claims, and hints about how to change the world. More specifically, he combines a sceptical judgment about the nature of science with concrete suggestions about how power might be taken from those who presently possess it. His view of knowledge derives from Nietzsche. His view of power derives from Marx. But he uses each of these men to criticise the other. The common complaint about Nietzsche is that he offers no social hope, no sense of human community. The common complaint about Marx is that he is in bondage to simple-minded 19th-century ideas about philosophy as 'science', that Marxist theory is a hindrance to Marxist practice. People who like Nietzsche on the subject of knowledge are embarrassed by Nietzsche on power. People who like Marx's analysis of power-relations in modern society are embarrassed by his pretentions to methodological and epistemological theory. Foucault offers one a chance to be as sceptical about science and philosophy (and 'theory' generally) as Nietzsche, while being as socially concerned and politically-minded as Marx.

If Foucault can bring this off, he will have worked a combination which no other important philosopher of our century (except Dewey) has managed. Russell had both epistemological and social concerns, but the two had nothing in particular to do with each other. In this, he resembled most academic philosophers: e.g. Husserl and Quine. Wittgenstein and Heidegger resembled Nietzsche and Kierkegaard in thinking mostly about other philosophers. They spent their lives detecting the self-deceptions into which their predecessors had fallen, in diagnosing their spurious claims to philosophical knowledge. This left them little time, or inclination, to speak to, or about, society. Sartre tried to combine the kind of writing about other philosophers which exposes their self-deceptions with the kind of writing which mobilises men and women to create a better world. But his attempt failed. The more Sartre used themes from his early 'existentialist' writings to recast Marxist analyses in a new jargon, the better straightforward, old-fashioned Marxism looked. The more he tried to associate particular political initiatives with an overall philosophical view, the more he seemed merely a knee-jerk revolutionary, able to offer a fast philosophical apology for anything which might hurt the French bourgeoisie.

Foucault's attempt to get philosophy and politics together is much more wary, complicated and generally intelligent than Sartre's . . . If we drop 'existentialism' (not to mention 'phenomenology' and 'structuralism') from our vocabulary, we shall be able to see the mainstream of 'Continental' philosophical thought more clearly. We shall see it as an attempt to draw the consequences of Nietzsche's claim that faith in 'science' is as hopeless as faith in God – that both are forms of 'the longest lie'. The two most powerful of such attempts are those of Heidegger and Foucault.

Heidegger shrugged off Husserl and academic philosophy fairly quickly, and Foucault seems never to have taken either seriously – nor, for that matter, to have paid much attention to Heidegger. Like Heidegger's, however, his work divides into a pre-Nietzschean and post-Nietzschean period – or, more exactly, an early period in which Nietzsche is not an important figure, and a later one in which finding the right response to Nietzsche becomes all-important. Foucault's early writings – including the 1967 book which made him famous, *The Order of Things* – were histories of institutions, disciplines and vocabularies. They pointed a philosophical moral: that what counts as 'science' and as 'rationality' is a matter of rather suddenly formed 'grids', ways of ordering things. In these books, he showed us how what counted as 'medicine', 'disease', 'madness', 'logic', 'history', and the like, changed in startling ways at various periods. He was trying to exhibit the radical contingency of the concepts used at a given time, the looseness of fit between what went on and what people said and did about it.

Princeton University DEPARTMENT OF PHILOSOPHY
1879 HALL
PRINCETON, NEW JERSEY 08544

14 January 1981

Ms. Mary-Kay Wilmers
LONDON REVIEW OF BOOKS
6A Bedford Square
London WC1 B3RA
ENGLAND

Dear Ms. Wilmers,

I'm very sorry to be sending this review some two months after the date ~~on~~ for which you requested it. I had a terrible time getting my thoughts on Foucault in order. He's one of those people who never quite fits within the terms in which one has begun to describe him.

The review may also be too long for your purposes, and thus may require some editing. You might want to start with the quotations, of which I perhaps have too many. I thought they would be helpful in giving people an idea of what Foucault was up to, but I may have overdone it.

Sincerely yours,

Richard Rorty

Richard Rorty

+ Maxine Berg's & Mandelma's reprints for box on the 17th-c social class bk.

Letter from Richard Rorty to Mary-Kay Wilmers, 14 January 1981

A Reader Responds

M.F. Golinsky wasn't the only reader to complain about the density of the *LRB*'s layout in its first years. 'This is terrible,' C. Maynard wrote in 1979. 'Every time I open the pages of the *London Review*, my eyes swim and I feel distinctively down at the mouth. Couldn't you make a slight concession to what the human eye can and cannot do with endless columns of text?'

Nowadays, a page like the one Golinsky complained about would be broken up with an advert, a poem, a picture, a short piece in a box or at the very least a couple of drop caps. All of this is more straightforward now that the paper uses a desktop publishing program. Before 1990, pieces were edited by us, sent to Red Lion typesetters and returned as proofs, set in columns of the right width and in the fonts used by the paper. These proofs would then be corrected (marked in different colours for the setters' mistakes and the paper's changes, which we had to pay for), as the process began to prepare the paper for the printer every fortnight.

Bryony Dalefield, who has done the *LRB* paste-up since the start of 1982, explains how it worked: I would be given a layout, with the order of the pieces hand-sketched by Karl Miller on an A4 template which gave a miniature version of each two-page spread. From that plan I'd make a full-size layout, two pages side by side on an A2 sheet, by cutting up the proofs sent back from the typesetters, sticking them with cow gum to the layout sheet, leaving any overmatter flapping off the bottom of the page. Susannah Clapp would photocopy these pages, wrestling, with much swearing, to fit them on the photocopier. The pieces were then read again, with the aim of fitting them to the page and dealing with widows and orphans (single lines at the top or bottom of a column).

The amended copy went back to the typesetters and was returned in the form of rolled scrolls of photographic paper, which were pasted onto a new set of A2 sheets. Adverts were pasted in at this point, and lines around boxes (the Diary, poems and sometimes adverts) were ruled with a pen. All this was done on a drawing table with parallel motion and a T square. (To make sure I was pasting the strips of text in the right order, I had more or less read all the articles by the time I had done all this.) More changes would then be sent off to the typesetters and would come back as a corrected line or lines, which I would cut out and paste in. At the final stage I would make text changes myself with a scalpel. Rephrasings, typos, bad word-splits or unsatisfactory inter-word spacing over several lines meant I had to cut out with a scalpel single characters in a word, then remake the word and evenly respace all the words in the line or lines. I would have beside me (and all over me by the end of the day) a sticky salad of words and single letters ready to arrange into replacement text. Old artwork was cannibalised to find an uppercase 'Z' in Plantin bold, or for something to fashion an accent as yet unavailable to the typesetters.

The man from the printers would arrive at 5 p.m. on press day, his van parked on double yellow lines, all urgency as a shield against our asking for a few minutes more, then disappear down the stairs with the maroon artwork folder, tied with a black ribbon, under his arm.

LONDON W 8
01-938 1675

28th January, 1981.

The Editor
London Review of Books
6a Bedford Square
London WC1B 3RA

Dear Sir,

I am a journalist working and living in London, and I subscribed to the "London Review of Books" in order to learn something about literature and books. My attempts are severely limited by your extraordinary lack of sensible layout. Can you really read p. 18 in your last issue (22 January-4 February) with pleasure ? I cannot. It is dull, without any subtitle or any illustration. Ms Mitchinson's talent is totally lost through the unimaginative presentation. If you cannot manage to improve this style (which is very easily done), I will seriously question my subscription renewal.

Yours faithfully,

M. F. Golinsky (Ms)

Marshall does not consider, in his analysis of the ethic shown in much of the legislation, is that the people who passed it in many cases did absolutely nothing to bring it into action. No locality can, for instance, be found impressing vagrants at its own cost into manufactories, and no industry took advantage of this subsidised but otherwise unattractive labour-force. When noblemen or merchant burgesses took off their Parliamentary robes and became potential ratepayers or employers, they could see that such legislation was impractical.

Dr Marshall makes a thorough investigation into one industrial enterprise set up to take advantage of the wide economic privileges offered in 1681, the Newmills Cloth Manufactory outside Haddington. We have no record of the religious views of the directors, though it can be assumed that they were normal conformists, but their business decisions are shown to be fully in line with the capitalist ethos. Profit was systematically pursued, workers encouraged by financial incentives to be careful and industrious; pay was based on piece work and bonuses, unprofitable lines were closed down and the workers in them dismissed; capital as it accumulated – and it is an essential part of the Weberian thesis that it should accumulate – was used to enlarge the enterprise. Dr Marshall cannot, of course, tell how far the work-force accepted the economic ethos of the company. Probably it did not. Well into the 19th century workers in this part of Scotland can be seen to have resisted economic incentives in favour of the traditional concept of a reasonable day's work. In this enterprise, discipline problems, particularly theft of materials, led the managers to consider having their own prison for offenders. One is reminded that it was the recalcitrance of miners to their employers which led to the introduction of the thumbscrew to Scotland. The Newmills managers exploited their legal privileges to prevent other businesses poaching their skilled labour, and used the system of certificates set up by the Calvinist Church to check on the moral character of workers. These points are offered as part of the capitalist ethos.

The picture of a modern capitalist outfit is confirmed by many details. The company even had its slush fund: bribes, in the form of beaver hats, coats and riding cloth, were given to regimental officers to persuade them to use the company's cloth for uniforms. More seriously, Dr Marshall contrasts the rational policy of expansion by reinvestment of profits with the simple impulse of financial greed which can provide tycoons in any society. His argument would be stronger if he could show that the company used modern accounting methods – it does not appear that it knew of double entry, though this had existed since the 14th century – and that it envisaged a system in which the enterprise would be able to dispense with legal privileges and stand up to foreign competition. In fact, when trade with England was freed by the Act of Union, the Manufactory was still too weak to survive.

The author's grasp of the 17th century is not as sure as one would like. He implies that it was Scottish protectionism which created protectionism in other countries, stating that the Act of 1681, which gave almost every conceivable privilege to Scottish manufactories, 'was responsible for the closing of almost all foreign markets'. Attention to the policy of the English Parliaments after 1660, or to Colbert's, would show that here he has got things the wrong way round. Scottish protectionism was an ineffective response to a world of closing markets. The attitude to labour poaching which he regards as capitalist was a principle of the guilds, which made their members take oaths against it. He underestimates the Calvinism of the Anglican Church in the 17th century, overestimates the expansionist attitudes of Scottish coal-owners and is far too sure that 17th-century church discipline actually did get everyone to church (on the few occasions on which numbers can be checked they are markedly deficient). The main theme of the book, that Scottish manufacturers held by the principles of expansionist capitalism, is, in his chosen instance, proved, though his explanation of why this led to so little general economic growth is inadequate.

A theme which Dr Marshall does not take up, but might consider, is the method by which the Calvinist clergy of the 17th century did eventually achieve the modernisation of Scottish society. The morality of the Reformed Kirk was a punitive one: offences were specific and should be drastically punished, preferably by death. For this reason, the King was always at odds with the clergy over the treatment of offenders. Scottish society was still, at the beginning of the 17th century, based on kinship and lordship, and the policy of the Crown was, of necessity, to settle issues and disputes by bargains and compromises between the heads of the great houses. The forces of law and order were hamstrung by the need for such compromise. But after the Great Rebellion and the disasters of Whig rule and the Interregnum, all this changed. The nobility had learned discipline from the Whig dictatorship, but preferred that it should be exercised by the Crown. It accepted the authority of the central government as part of the terms by which it was itself restored in 1660. The economic development which was so conspicuous in the 18th century relied on the stabilisation and modernisation of society which was the achievement of this period. Dr Marshall might consider whether these changes did not owe more to the Judaic intransigence of the clergy in the 1630s and 1640s than to the Calvinist ethic as expressed in economic terms.

Bruce Lenman's book on the Jacobite risings sets out to show, not only that Scottish history is more than the study of a few dramatic episodes strongly coloured by royal personalities (the rule of Mary Queen of Scots, the Forty-Five), but also that the stream of Jacobite sentiment, intrigue and effort is more complex than has traditionally been allowed. Scottish Jacobite episodes have frequently been offered to the public either as stirring narrative or as detailed family historiography. This book is neither. It is not to be recommended as narrative, for whenever a clear and dramatic story-line is called for the call is ignored. The author seems to think that that aspect has already been provided. He may well be right. It is the why and wherefore of Jacobitism, the external setting that made its aims and plots at times realistic, the complicated bundle of national or dynastic prejudices and loyalties and the counteracting squabbles and personal vendettas of members of the upper class, particularly the landed class of Scotland, which are the stuff of this book.

Behind it lies not only a wide reading of both obvious and obscure secondary material but a detailed acquaintance with particular manuscript collections which give depth to Mr Lenman's view of Scottish society. Customs records illustrate the deeply-held Scottish prejudices against paying realistically for the benefits of government. Judicial records, particularly those of the jurisdictions in private hands, show what a long way the Scotland of the early 18th century had to go to be a modern state. And the archives of Blair Atholl illustrate the diversities of allegiance within a dominant family strategically placed between Highland and Lowland society, anxious to assuage social and national prejudices and yet to get the best out of the English connection.

Mr Lenman's appreciation of the complexity of the motives of those who, for one reason or another, played or worked at Jacobitism is lively and alert. His evaluation of the 18th-century Whig hegemony is, by contrast, distinctly crude. He overrates the effectiveness of the central government when it set out to act unscrupulously, as well as the frequency with which it did so. His view of Whig politicians as corrupt and self-seeking is fair enough, but he does not allow enough for the fact that the preservation of personal power over large areas of territory, certainly an aim of those who opposed Whiggery, could be just as unpleasant and ruthless as the cultivation of power based on money. Whig society was open at the top, 'like the Ritz'. Traditional society was not. I am not sure why one should feel tender towards the latter and denigrate the former for this. In any case, when a Scottish historian sets out to complain of the brutal use of force in 18th-century England, he should bear in mind that that society was not as bloodthirsty as the rule of the Covenant had been in 17th-century Scotland.

The author's wayward mixture of insight and opacity leads him to assert that 18th and 20th-century British societies were both 'patronage-ridden' – a coupling which adds nothing to our understanding of either. But it also produces an enlightened comment on personalities: Walpole 'closely resembled some 20th-century Prime Ministers in that he was a curiously isolated sort of figure, with no serious political ideology, sustaining himself on a combination of the arrogance of office and a deep sense of his own inherent reasonableness and rationality'. All of us can put at least one modern name to this description. Another insight in this book, of a non-parochial nature, is the appreciation of the international setting. After 1716, Jacobitism could not hope to win without powerful foreign backing, so an evaluation of its chances involves understanding the problems and aims of Cardinal Fleury and Elizabeth Farnese. Even though the exploration of English Jacobitism in this book is superficial, the European dimension makes it a great deal more than the exploration of an anachronistic quirk of Scottish history.

It is natural that this book, while ostensibly 'British' in coverage, should give much more attention to Scotland than to England, for it was in Scotland that Jacobitism was, at least for a short time, a serious alternative to Whig rule, that it received support from sections of society outside the landowning class, and that most of the real fighting took place. Of course, since 1603 any major political transference of power had to be effective in both countries, and so English Jacobitism, less widespread than Scottish though no less deeply held, in many cases, was vital to success. For this reason, the only important Jacobite rising was the Fifteen. The Jacobite refusal under Claverhouse to co-operate with Williamite supremacy was, as Lenman asserts, 'merely the dying spasm of an abandoned political order'. Given the readiness of the English to do without James II and the passivity of those few sections of English society not happy at the Revolution, it was on its own. The Claverhouse rebellion embodied features, all the same, that were to become peculiarly Jacobite: a personal inability to work within the new political structure, an exalted conception of hereditary right which meant that the royal claim to inheritance was merely a larger manifestation of the property consciousness of landed society, and a reliance on the dissatisfaction of the clans of the south-west Highlands at a political settlement in which the imperialist house of Argyll had a dominant share. But the Fifteen brought together a much more serious repertoire of motives.

There was the total lack of 'charisma' in the Hanoverian monarch. True, James VIII had little enough of this himself, but he had an honest, gloomy incompetence which roused protective instincts. There is the perceptive comment of Fletcher of Saltoun on his stupidities that he was 'taking all the pains to ruine his owen affairs; which convinces everybody who formerly did not believe it that he is of the Family.' In the other line, Stewart family features, the Stewart mixture of intellect and tactlessness, seem to have descended to the Electress Sophia but then to have died out. There was the support obtained from Roman Catholicism in Lancashire, from bankruptcy in Northumberland. There were the justifiable grievances among the Episcopalians in north-east Scotland, and the more general and equally justified sense of national outrage in Scotland as a whole produced by the shabby backtracking on the explicit and implicit promises of the Union bargain by post-Union Parliaments. Altogether in 1715 there was a powerful mixture of opposition, and very little positive enthusiasm for Hanover with which to resist it. Unfortunately for the Stewarts, in the two areas where serious campaigning was called for, Lancashire and central Scotland, the military leadership was totally incompetent. After that, Jacobitism waned rapidly in England. The combination of Walpole's unscrupulousness, changes in the diplomatic setting, and the disunity of the few active Jacobites, ran the movement into the ground. All that survived in the 1720s were the people who adopted the label as a form of self-assertion (Sir John Hyde Cotton of Madingley is an obvious example), men who had absolutely no intention of risking so much as a farthing on the cause; and those who, like William Shippen, used it as a title for their disgust at the mechanisms and ethos of Whig rule and who would have found a Stewart regime equally distasteful. But in Scotland Jacobitism survived as a sentiment and a base for intrigue and as a sense that the whole question of the dominant regime was still open, in spite of the disasters in England and in Europe. The main task of the book is to explore this fact.

One important reason was the failure of disciplinary action after the Fifteen. In England the Government had had to call off any large-scale programme of executions because the populace, perfectly prepared to have men hung for theft, felt that treason was a more venial crime. In Scotland, physical personal retribution was only a token show. The more serious policy of property confiscation ran up against a silent conspiracy. Judges, lawyers, families, tenants and neighbours all united to make it impossible. Even where estates could be confiscated, various manoeuvres meant that the profits from them could be retained in 'suitable' hands. Debt was part of the normal climate of landed society, so those with claims against forfeited estates obtained recognition, and the accredited claims could be bought up like any other paper security. The end result, for instance, of the confiscation of the lands of the Jacobite Mackenzie of Applecross was the accumulation of claims against them in the hands of Mackenzie of Kinchulladrum. Was it any real change? Elsewhere bullying of the tenantry in the interests of exiled Jacobite landowners meant there were no rents to collect.

But the survival of Jacobitism in Scotland, particularly in the north-east, was based on more than the immunity resulting from the cohesiveness of Scottish society. This book attempts to explain Jacobitism as a personal force driving individuals into actions likely to be dangerous or costly. Partly this happened because Scotland had experienced in the 17th century a development in church organisation which fitted badly into her traditional social order, and was particularly unacceptable in those parts of the country where the social order was least modernised. Traditional views of lordship and dependency still survived in the north-east. Officially they were expected to co-exist with a church organisation rabidly independent of lay power; hostile to the exercise of patronage and held together by a strong professional ethos. The Presbyterian Church of Scotland was not, of course, nearly as anti-Erastian as it proclaimed, but its official statements denied the sort of society which had prevailed throughout the country in the early 17th century, and still survived in Aberdeenshire. The north had been losing out to the central valley of Scotland in wealth and political leadership for at least two centuries, and its adherence to episcopacy and Jacobitism was evidence of a deep-seated protest at this cumulative failure. In southern Scotland landed society managed both to co-operate with and to control the Presbyterian Church, and to retain enough residual lordship to give it hegemony over the peasantry and social dominance over the merchant class. It was not, in the long run, irrational that the failure of the Forty-Five rebellion should be followed by the destruction of the most conspicuous surviving remnant of feudal lordship, the heritable jurisdictions, but landed society in the south could maintain its dominance without this feature.

Jacobitism in the Highlands was haphazard in distribution and much more haphazardly adhered to than in the north-east. Various leading Jacobite chiefs ran with both hare and hounds, and some had to make hurried and difficult decisions in the summer of 1745. Mr Lenman shows that there was no simple link between economic backwardness and political conservatism. Lochiel the younger was a ruthless exploiter of the resources of his clan lands, Mackintosh of Borlum an enthusiast for the most basic features of improvement.

*Left, letter to the editor from M.F. Golinsky,
28 January 1981; above, page 18, 22 January 1981*

A Dose of Salts

Angela Carter's first piece for the *LRB* was on Bertolucci's 1979 movie *La Luna*: 'I've been asking myself what Jocasta thought about that unpleasant business at Thebes for a long time now.' Her last contribution appeared in 1991, less than a year before she died. Reviewing Iain Sinclair's *Downriver*, she evoked her experience of a bifurcated London, reflected on time and the novel – and defined windmills as 'the herbivores of the energy world'.

In the days before email, the lost-in-the-post excuse for late filing was popular. Angela took another route: 'I went deaf & I trod on a rabid squirrel & All has been Hell.' In 1980: 'I was overcome with wild, weary anger at the spectacle of the criminals, psychotics & retards whom Reagan has appointed to man the ship of the States & could not lend my mind to Sloane Rangers.' In those typewriter years she would often, as in the letter opposite, draw a wavy line – the printer's instruction for bold type – underneath a heading or her signature.

She wrote for the *LRB* about the ANC, fashion, Christina Stead, Louise Brooks. In 1980 she wrote about Colette, and a dinner party at which 'babbling away to *les gars* . . . [she] offered De Beauvoir only the meagre attention of an occasional, piercing stare.' And she wrote expansively about food: her chosen book for *Desert Island Discs*, which she didn't have a chance to record, was the *Larousse gastronomique*. She examined 'that godless vegetable' the potato and identified writers for whom 'cookery is what the open road was to Cobbett'. In 1985, discussing Elizabeth David's *An Omelette and a Glass of Wine* and the *Official Foodie Handbook*, she laid into 'piggery triumphant' and the new 'mincing and finicking obsession with food'. She also mentioned the Ethiopian famine. Accused on the letters page of 'self-righteous priggery', she sent a riposte from America in the form of a postcard. The picture showed a recipe for a terrifying scarlet chili. Her message ran: 'Carter's reply to her critics! Texas chili, it goes through you like a dose of salts. I would like to forcefeed it to that drivelling wimp . . . preferably through his back passage.'

Susannah Clapp

MARY-KAY WILMERS: THREE WITCHES

London Review OF BOOKS

VOLUME 5 NUMBER 4 3 MARCH TO 16 MARCH 1983 60P

GAMES PLAYED BY ANGELA CARTER

~~Even~~ After all these years, De Beauvoir still appears to be
proud that only Sartre achieved higher marks in those first exams
than she. What would have happened, one wonders, if she had ~~kixgxmx~~
come top? What would it have done to Sartre? Merely to think of
it makes the mind reel. *Only love can make you proud to be an also-rans*

But Colette simply did not believe that women <u>were</u> the second
sex. One of Goudeket's anecdotes from her declining years is very
revealing. He carried her in her wheelchair into a holiday hotel;
the lobby filled with applauding, ~~abxxx~~ cheering fans; she was
a national institution in France, after all. Colette ~~was~~ (*appeared to be*) *∞*
touched. 'They've remembered me from last year.' This isn't
modesty, though ~~Goudek~~ Goudeket pretends to think so. It's irony, *I hope,*
because, if it isn't irony, then what is it? What monstrous vanity would
think it was perfectly natural for a little old lady to recieve
a tumultuous welcome from her hotel staff? Of course she didn't
believe she was really famous, towards the end. She knew she
wasn't famous <u>enough</u>. These are not the ~~feelings~~ *passions* of a woman who
knows her place.

1208

~~But to believe women are stronger, tougher, more clever, more~~
~~beautiful, more capable than men~~

← Nevertheless,
~~But~~ to believe women are not the second sex is to deny a whole
area of social reality, however inspiriting the toughness and
resilience of Colette and most of her heroines may be, ~~espeGzxl~~
especially after the revival of the wet and spineless woman-as-
hero which graced the Seventies. (The zomboid creatures in
Joan Didion's novels, for example; the resurrected dippy dames
of Jean Rhys, so many of whom might have had ~~walk-on parts in~~
~~Colette's own music hall stories.)~~ pathetic walk-on parts in
Colette's own stories of Paris in the Twenties.) Colette celebrated
the status quo of femininity, not only ~~xxx~~ it's ~~phymx~~ physical
glamour but it's capacity to subvert and withstand the boredom of
patriarchy. This makes her an ambivalent ally to the Woman's
Movement. She is like certain shop-~~xGx~~ stewards who devote so
much time to getting up management's nose that they lose sight of
the great goals of socialism.

Brixton in Flames

April 17   41 Arlington Avenue
                                            Providence R.I.02906

MK - ?

Susannah Clapp
London Review of Books
Bedford Square
and etc.

Dear Susannah,

Herewith the Poe piece. It's really an extended piece of literary
criticism, unless that sounds too tongue in cheek. I rather like it,
although there are probably one or two more grues and shivers to be
inserted before I'm completely satisfied... however. As it turns out,
the story you saw referred to in the GRANTA ad. is not this one
but a wolf-child story - yet another wolf-child story - and Buford's
connection with the BOSTON REVIEW has been severed, so, if you at all
fancy this one, feel free.

I've recieved a copy of the Lorna Tracey stories from Virago, now, by
the way; they've used a quote from me on the cover. Is it still ethical
to review it and, if so, how much and by when?

Only another week of classes. Only another eight weeks of the U.S.A.
Every night, on television, they show Brixton in flames and I wonder if
I will have a home to go back to. It's taken several days for the media
here to actually getting around to suggest that the riots might have something
to do with the/government's proposed racist legislation but - I think they
            U.K.
liked the idea that, all over the world, black folks enjoyed to riot in
the spring spring, and did not want to advertise the notion it might be more
than a seasonal celebration. Anyway, it ought to bring Thatcher down but
it won't, it will bring Ted Knight down. Oh, god, oh, god.   Yes. I have
been worrying about the Homeland. You bet.

E.P. T hompson is addressing a No Nukes rally here next week. What with one
thing and another, the feeling that I've been through all this before p.t.o.

Letter from Angela Carter to Susannah Clapp,
17 April 1981

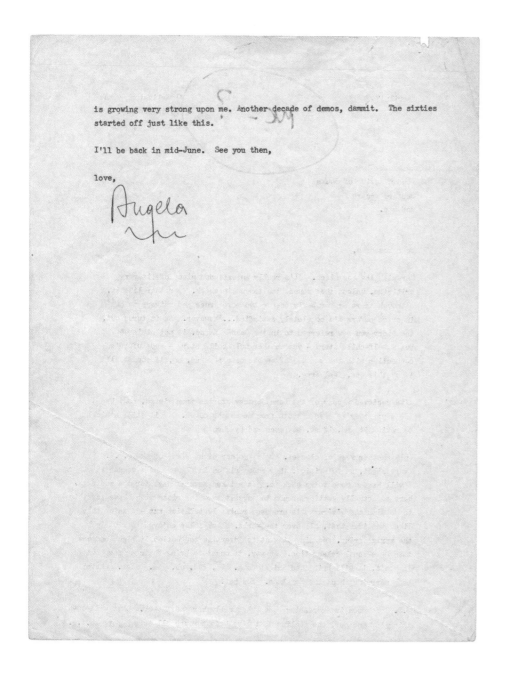

is growing very strong upon me. Another decade of demos, dammit. The sixties
started off just like this.

I'll be back in mid-June. See you then,

love,

Angela

The Brixton riots of April 1981, which
Angela Carter discusses in her letter,
took place after a police operation
aimed at reducing street crime resulted
in almost a thousand predominantly
black people being stopped and
searched over a period of five days. One
man, who'd been stabbed, was taken to
hospital by the police, but the rumour
went around that he had been killed as
a result of 'police brutality', helping
precipitate the riots. The LRB cover here
shows the Brixton riots of September
1985, which began after a botched raid
aimed at arresting a young black man
led to the shooting by the police of his
mother.

Carter was teaching in the US in 1981,
but usually lived in South London, not
far from Brixton; Ted Knight was the
Labour leader of the local council. He
was forced to resign not in 1981, but in
1984, after Lambeth Council refused to
set a budget complying with spending
limits set by the Thatcher government.
As Carter predicted, the 1980s was
'another decade of demos' – anti-
apartheid, CND, the miners' strike and
Wapping, where Rupert Murdoch had
sacked the print workers at the *Times*
– rounded off, in March 1990, by the
poll tax demo. Images depicting unrest
during the miners' strike, the Wapping
dispute and the poll tax protest also
appeared on LRB covers.

Music, Football and Sex

In the late 1960s and early 1970s the BBC music division – and, in particular, Radio 3 – was not afraid to invite its listeners into intellectually challenging territory that would be considered out of bounds today. One of the leading critics and commentators engaged by the BBC was Hans Keller, who grew up in Vienna, emigrating to Britain in 1938. He trained as a professional violin and viola player, but found his true métier as a writer and broadcaster about music. He wrote frequently for the BBC magazine the *Listener* in the early 1970s, when Karl Miller was its editor and Mary-Kay Wilmers his deputy, and they brought him along to the *LRB*, to which he contributed a number of characteristically feisty essays about music, football and sex in the early years of the paper, as well as a number of combative letters to the editors. 'Dear Hans,' Miller wrote to him in 1980, 'Every day I find a large accumulation of letters of contention and complaint addressed to me. Most of them are from you.' Keller died in 1985; he was pictured posthumously on the cover of the *LRB* in 1987, to accompany a piece by Donald Mitchell.

Left, Hans Keller on the cover of the issue of
3 September 1987; above, letter from Hans Keller to
Karl Miller, 16 February 1981

London Review of Books

[Annotation top left, by Keller:] I profoundly apologize: I had no idea it was under 2000. Had I been aware, I'd never have asked my question.

6 A Bedford Square, London W C I B 3 R A. Telephone 01-631 0884
Advertising and Distribution 01-580 3401

[Annotation top right, by Keller:] Really? I'd say that on the contrary, & LRB apart, the more go under, the better.

Hans Keller
Summer School of Music
Dartington Hall
Totnes   South Devon TQ9 6EJ

28 7 81

Dear Hans,

It seemed simplest (and most economical) to return the typescript for your first emendation. *[Annotation:]* Indeed: attached. Thank you. 10 words (1+9) did it.

Your question about the football fee is easily answered. We pay £100 for 2000 words (and more): under 2000 we pay under £100. I know that to people who write for other papers our fees don't always seem generous: but papers like people have to survive. Would you feel better if you knew how much we pay ourselves not for writing (we don't pay ourselves anything for that) but for working 12 hours a day? Two things were different when Karl first talked to you about fees: a.the paper wasn't independent; b. we didn't know how much it cost simply to get a paper out.

[Annotation:] I see: thank you.

Yours ever,

Mary-Kay

PS Is the Simpson material to follow the Hopkins - or vice versa?

[Annotation, by Keller:] Either works, but ideally, the answer to your first question is yes.

[Annotation bottom right, by Keller:] No: what difference does that make? We all — I mean, people like you & me — pay ourselves little or nothing for certain jobs (teaching intense but uncompensating talent in my case), & we all have to make sure to stay alive nevertheless — especially since these jobs tend to take a lot of time.

*Letter from Mary-Kay Wilmers to Hans Keller,
with annotations by Keller, 28 July 1981*

Difficulties

Mary-Kay Wilmers writes: One can find all sorts of reasons for the split with the *New York Review* but in reality there was one large one: what Eric Hobsbawm in a letter reproduced later in this book called 'the logic of publicity and sales' – see Bob Silvers's letter overleaf. Silvers was more straightforward than Karl (most people were), and Karl had a sense of irony and the possibility of failure, which the Americans involved in the negotiations found unhelpful. Besides, the *LRB* was exerting pressure on many of the same contributors as Silvers wished to publish, and the combined sales weren't proving very exciting. In any event, after a few issues in the kangaroo's pouch, and a degree of 'worry and tension' about accumulating debts, the *LRB* was pushed out. I had just been given some money. I was furious; I didn't want it. I didn't want to be that person. So I found a use for it.

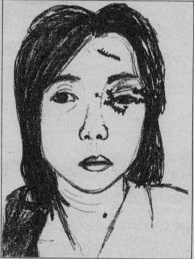

The London Review
OF BOOKS

Volume 2, Number 4 — 6 March 1980

What's wrong with Britain
David Marquand

'Self-portrait, following a car accident, by Hiang Kee. Further studies by her, done, like this one, in the Nelson Ward of the West Norwich Hospital, appear on a later page

Editor: Karl Miller. Deputy Editor: Mary-Kay Wilmers. Assistant Editor: Susannah Clapp. Advertising Manager: Michael Richards. Design: Peter Campbell.
Editorial Board: Stuart Hampshire, Frank Kermode, V.S. Pritchett, Emma Rothschild.

Contents

The London Review of Books, 6 March 1980 1

Front page of the issue of 6 March 1980, with a self-portrait by Hiang Kee, after she and her husband, Julian Rothenstein – the 'paste-up pair' Karl Miller refers to in his letter opposite – were involved in a car accident on a country lane in Norfolk

Professor Karl Miller   25 January 1980
Department of English

Dear Bob,

I think it would be as well if I were to tell you that
we are experiencing great difficulty at present in keeping
the paper going. I will run over the main features of that
difficulty: this might serve, at least, as a way of briefing
you against the arrival of Peter Campbell in New York.

Over the last few weeks three of the small staff have
been injured in accidents. The paste-up pair are still out
of the reckoning as a result of a car crash, and with
Campbell's departure abroad, we are now moving to a stand-in
paste-up man for the forthcoming issue.

I have now learned indirectly from the Fitzgeralds that
the office which we were expecting to move into any day now
has fallen through.

Fitz has given me no information about circulation
since Issue 2. A week or so ago he told me that he was
completing a breakdown for dispatch to New York. I have
no idea, therefore, what the position is. The advertising
position deteriorated, as you know, over Christmas. It is
now picking up again, but the position there certainly
requires to be assessed before long.

My own feeling is that the editorial content is reasonably
good, perhaps as good as it could be expected in the circumstances, and there is a fair amount of word-of-mouth testimony
in corroboration of that. Against this must be set the
undoubted fact that the availability of the paper is not at
all what it should be. We are continually oppressed by
complaints about the difficulty of ever getting it in shops.
I realize that this constitutes an old story by now. But
the editorial people on the paper are cast down by it. We
have come to feel that no matter how hard we try, we are
bound to be presented, sooner or later, with the view that,
in the light of failures in respect of circulation and
advertising, we are not doing well enough. It would be
true to say that we have done the best we could editorially,
and could hardly have done more.

Mr Robert Silvers,
New York Review of Books,
250 West 57th St.,
New York, NY 10019, USA.

Letter from Karl Miller to Robert Silvers,
25 January 1980

The New York Review of Books

250 West Fifty-Seventh Street
New York City, New York 10019
PLaza 7-8070

25 February 1980

Dear Karl,

On February 4 the air messenger delivered here your letter
dated January 25 about the London Review. I've wanted to
answer it but practically each day has brought up some
new development. As I write now Whitney is again about to
meet with Robert Wilmers, but I wanted to write out some points that
have been accumulating during all the worry and tension of the
last weeks.

Just at the time of Peter Campbell's visit here last month
we were confronted by reports that were very discouraging to
us, far worse than we'd expected, and made us see that we could
not go on as before. Whitney had received these reports just before
Peter Campbell arrived and, in retrospect, it seems unfortunate
that Peter gave a quick account of our reaction to these reports
by telephone before Whitney himself could summarize them in a
letter and say why we didn't feel we could continue, as he
did a few days later.

This was a terribly hard decision for all of us. We never
expected the London Review to make much profit; we would have
been very glad if it had broken even, or shown a reasonable
prospect of doing so, during the first year. In December there
seemed some reason to be encouraged. The reports of newsstand
sales showed the combined NYR and LRB were selling some 4500
copies more than the NYR alone had sold previously. Whatever
the failings of newsstand distribution, it was clear that the

First and last pages of a letter from Robert Silvers to
Karl Miller, 25 February 1980

give up control of the UK edition of the paper; so long as
the new paper is inserted in the NYR, matters of printing,
distribution, advertising,etc. would affect our entire UK
and European edition, and we would have to be able to make
decisions about them. As I write, it still isn't clear what
can or will be worked out. We've intensely appreciated what
you've been trying to do, and how hard it has been, and
whatever happens you can trust us to do our best to be as
helpful and as open about it as anyone in our situation
could be.

                    Yours ever,

                    Bob

P.S. After I wrote this we finally arrived at a new plan
      by which the LRB will be issued separately within a
      few months by a newly formed company. There will,
      I think, be many advantages to this, particularly
      in giving the paper a better chance to sell on news-
      stands. We're all strongly hoping that the general
      approach we discussed with Robert Wilmers can now
      be worked out.

A Small Paper

The ninth issue of 1980, dated 15 May, contained a piece by Karl Miller which informed the paper's readers that, from the next issue, 'we shall be coming out on our own, twice a month.'

London Review of Books: Separate Publication

Karl Miller

THE first issue of the *London Review of Books* appeared on 27 September last year, and the present issue is the 14th we have produced. The journal was started when some newspapers were in abeyance, and others had taken to cutting back on the space allowed for the discussion of books. Publishing houses were rumoured to be in financial difficulty – such as Penguin – and Collins were presently said to have become 'over-heated' in Australia. Publishers were felt to be peculiarly exposed to the fortunes of the economy, and the country, for all its oil rigs, was felt to be keeling over. It is still felt to be keeling. But the absent newspapers have resumed. Publishing houses have righted themselves. And it is also the case that the whole British rig has yet to descend into the North Sea.

So far, the *London Review of Books*, while editorially separate, has appeared within the *New York Review of Books*. This was always seen as a temporary arrangement, and it is soon to cease. With effect from the issue which goes on sale on 22 May – two issues from now, that is to say – we shall be coming out on our own, twice a month. The *New York Review* will be represented on the board of the company which has been formed for this purpose. But from now on the *London Review* will not only be edited in Britain: it will be British-controlled. Subscribers in Britain and Europe will continue to receive both papers, and when subscriptions come up for renewal, they will be invited to resubscribe to one or the other, or to both.

I am not trying to make us sound like ICI or Courtaulds. We are, and shall remain, a small paper. Perhaps it needn't be explained that we are not so much interested in expansion and profit as in being a place where good writers can be published, and new books examined and evoked. We started at short notice – a month's notice, to be exact – and with a part-time editorial staff of four we have had to improvise our way through the difficulties which any small paper is certain to meet. The response we have had from writers has been very good, though we were not long in discovering where we could least expect to gain attention: of those who have refused to write, or who have promised and failed to deliver, almost all have been MPs. For our first six months, the circulation has stood at around the 15,000 mark.

Many of our readers are outside the university fold, and we are pleased about that. We will continue to review academic books, but are keen to reach that wider community of informed and interested readers which used to be among this country's claims to fame and which can't have melted into the sea. We mean to extend our subject matter when the paper separates: there will be more in the way of argument and reporting, more pictures, and some fiction.

The university fold is sometimes said to be devoted to the business of structuralism, semiology, post-structuralism, deconstruction. Whether or not this is true, it has been clear, over the past six months, that the subject is second only to Marxism as a source of new titles in the higher publishing. There are publishers who are now pouring out, at a quite astonishing rate, titles which contain the word 'language' or the word 'structure', with the word 'revolution' frequently subjoined.

Britain makes no films to speak of any more: but it maintains, not only a national Film Institute, but also, in magazines, manuals and manifestos, a busy structuralist critique of the medium. Structuralism is the philosophy of those in the universities and thereabouts who are not philosophers; it is the philosophy of English departments and teacher-training institutes throughout the English-speaking world. The propagation and diffusion of these ideas would be a matter worth serious study, but it is not one that will figure, for a long time if ever, among the flow of new titles.

5.

of publications.   The new point of view can be appointed to posts.- [There

on the shelf, awaiting review, sits A Structuralist Reading of Charlotte Brontë,

and the rest of the... ⊙

Deconstruction and D.H.Lawrence,   A writer in the American magazine Commentary,

Michael Vannoy Adams, ~~has this to say on the subject:~~ *gives this account of some of the arguments in Gerald Graff's book, Literature Against Itself:*

Pl. indent at 8/10 pt →

NP   [It seems *, then,* that

promotion.   There is

'for prof

which has been put to w

their professional usefulness

omit it from any assess

~~and diffusion of these~~

thriving discourse whic

ssion and retreat can

~~construction and indif~~

and diffusion of these

both   *of desires and disd*

treat. It is a thriv

that of the designedly

have travelled further

The deconstructionists render literature invalid or ineffectual by default; they deprive literature of the relevance it ought, by all rights, to have, and they reduce criticism from a serious and influential discipline to a frivolous and inconsequential—and quite expendable—exercise. Why, then, have they captured the English departments of so many universities and become so dominant on the academic landscape? Graff offers an economic explanation. He says that sheer quantity of output, not quality, is the way to tenure and promotion in the university today. For English departments to insist on a real standard of excellence in literary criticism would be comparable to the American economy's returning to the gold standard: the effect would be the immediate collapse of the system"—the academic system depending as it does on mass production (publish-or-perish). Hence the urgency to produce new (not stricter) methods of literary criticism, which produce different (not truer) interpretations, which produce more (not better) publications. According to Graff, the deconstruction of texts is make-work, a mere game that critics now play when the "explication of many authors and works seems to have reached the point of saturation" ⊙

ad to publication and to

turalism

s not the only set of ideas

d be wrong to ████

governed the transmission

doubtful how far the

equivocal stance of aggre

where mere humble mis—

unites

~~together~~ aggression and re-

bewilder; its popularity is

perfectly true that its ideas

(likely) een

~~ossible~~ in the days when they

(so to speak,)

were first identified, it is also true that, at the last count, only two MPs in the

the general reader does not know about it ⊢

#

Page from the typescript of Karl Miller's piece on the 'separate publication' of the 'LRB', published in the issue of 15 May 1980

I Shall Not

ANTONIA FRASER BY MARC

London Review
OF BOOKS

6A Bedford Square, London WC1B 3RA. Telephone 01-631 0884
Advertising and Distribution 01-580 3401

Dear New York Review Subscriber,

It all started during the 1979 London <u>Times</u> strike when Frank Kermode, writing in the <u>Observer</u>, called for a new book review in the UK — one that would not only fill the vaccuum created by the disappearance of the <u>Times Literary Supplement</u> but would also bring new vitality to British literary and intellectual life.

The response from prominent authors and publishers was immediate and enthusiastic: <u>The London Review of Books</u> was launched.

First published in the marsupial pouch of <u>The New York Review</u> (which began in similar circumstances during <u>The New York Times</u> strike in 1963), <u>The London Review of Books</u> has since established itself as an independent cultural and intellectual journal.

As a reader of both magazines, the summary of events recounted above must be familiar to you. Your subscription to <u>The London Review of Books</u>, however, will expire in 3 months, and we would like to take this opportunity to invite you to renew.

If we receive your renewal instructions promptly, you will not miss a single issue of this new journal, <u>The London Review of Books</u>: featuring major reviews and essays by William Empson, Antonia Fraser, Brigid Brophy, V.S. Pritchett, Emma Rothschild, A.J. Ayer, Martin Amis, P.B. Medawar, and Mary McCarthy, to mention only a few. A subscription form is enclosed for your convenience.

We look forward to hearing from you.

Yours sincerely,

Karl Miller

Karl Miller
Editor

OVER

EDITOR: Karl Miller DEPUTY EDITOR: Mary-Kay Wilmers ASSISTANT EDITOR: Susannah Clapp
PUBLISHER: Alan Smythe ADVERTISING AND PUBLICITY MANAGER: Michael Richards DISTRIBUTION: Susan Bosanko
EDITORIAL BOARD: Ian Hamilton, Stuart Hampshire, Frank Kermode, V. S. Pritchett, Emma Rothschild

Published by LRB Limited, registered in England at the above address No 1485413

Above, subscription renewal letter from 1981;
opposite, note from Martha McCulloch to Karl
Miller, written on the back of the renewal letter,
20 March 1981

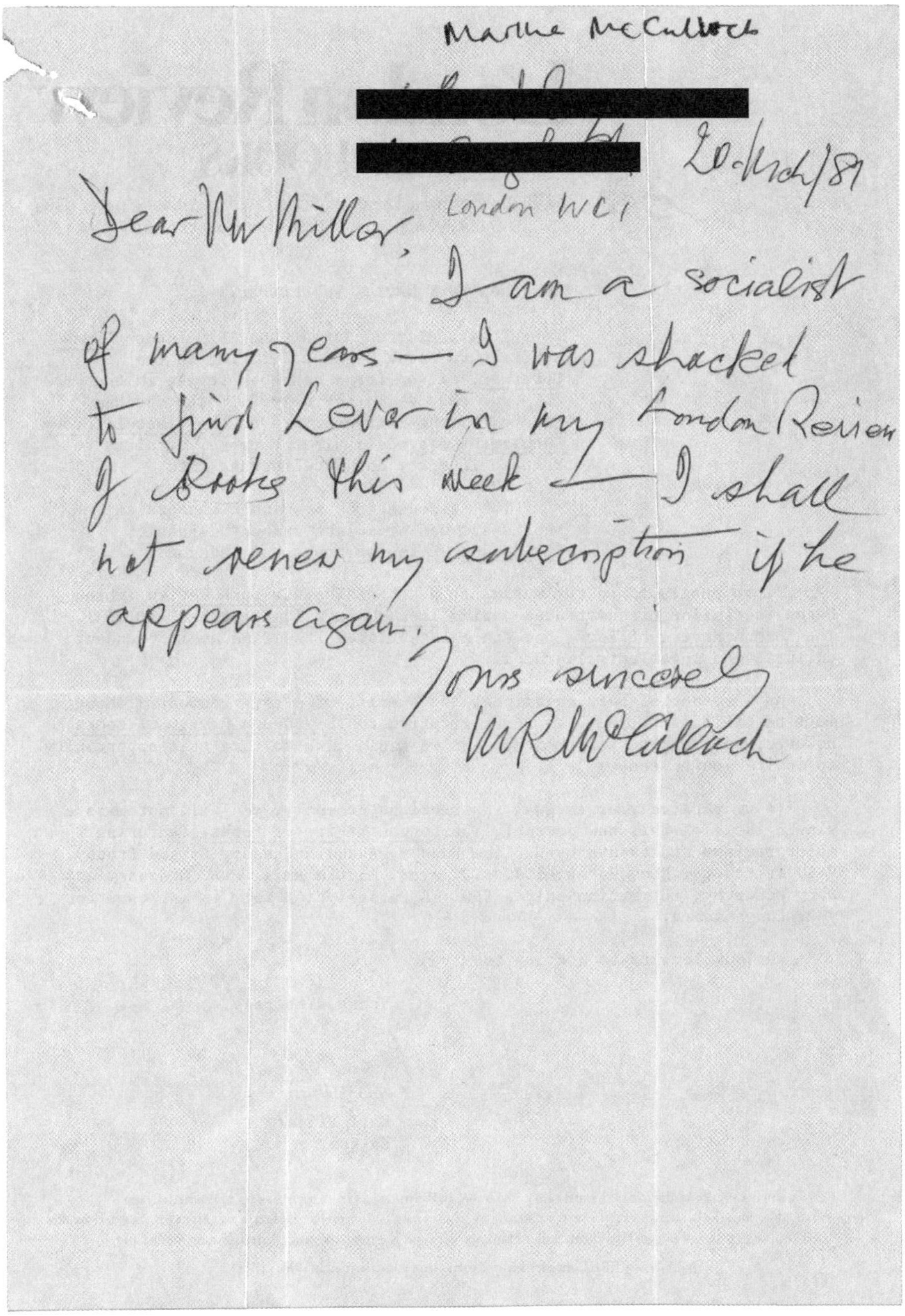

Handwritten letter:

Martha McCulloch

▬▬▬▬▬▬

▬▬▬▬▬ 20 March/81

London WC1

Dear Mr Miller,

I am a socialist of many years — I was shocked to find Lever in my London Review of Books this week — I shall not renew my subscription if he appears again.

Yours sincerely
M R McCulloch

'Subscribers in Britain and Europe will continue to receive both papers,' Karl Miller wrote when the LRB split from the NYRB, 'and when subscriptions come up for renewal, they will be invited to resubscribe to one or the other, or to both.' At least one subscriber saw the invitation to renew as an opportunity to send the editor some feedback. Miller responded in withering tones: 'Dear Mrs McCulloch, I'm sorry you feel the way you do. I am a lifelong socialist myself and so is Harold Lever. Socialists should support the principle of free debate.' The piece by Lever, a former Labour cabinet minister, had criticised proposed changes to the party's constitution that weakened the power of MPs, blaming them on a coalition of 'left-wingers and recently arrived extremists'. The SDP was founded in March 1981, the same month Lever's piece was published.

Transcription:

Dear Mr Miller,

I am a socialist of many years – I was shocked to find Lever in my *London Review of Books* this week – I shall not renew my subscription if he appears again.

Yours sincerely,
Martha McCulloch

1982-89
One of the Few Good Things

CHRISTMAS BOOKS

London Review
OF BOOKS

VOLUME 11 NUMBER 23   7 DECEMBER 1989   £1.40   US & CANADA $2

A Note of Confidence

Memorandum : for discussion on Monday 20 dec. at 3 p.m.

In the 3 months since the last LRB business report, events have shown that the note of confidence struck in it was not altogether unjustified. The financial position of the paper will probably be better at the end of March than predicted in the budget. Administrative improvements have continued apace. Some savings have been made (e.g. on libel insurance, postage, petty cash expenditure). Bad debts and unclaimed VAT are now being collected. Some promotional activities have gone ahead as planned

Despite all this, and the fact that there are now more people working full-time on the business side of the paper, LRB's commercial performance is sluggish and unexciting. Proper forward planning and cost control does not exist. Advertising revenue has stagnated at an unacceptably low level and is still made up almost wholly of book advertisements. Newstand circulation is only creeping up. Subscription levels are barely holding steady. Promotions have been haphazardly planned and hastily executed. Record keeping is rudimentary. In other words, LRB Ltd. is still an unsophisticated commercial animal with serious developmental problems. If the loss is reduced this year, it will be mainly the result of increased efficiency not increased sales. The underlying rate of growth in circulation and revenue is static. Our health this year is merely relative to last year's disease. We are still dangerously unprepared for blows of fate : if book advertising slumped, January renewals were unexpectedly low, Camden City rates rose sharply, and/or the Arts Council decided to withdraw its grant (to name a few possiblities), we would be powerless to hold the situation steady. The slide would begin.

First and last pages of a memorandum by
Nicholas Spice, 17 December 1982

(12).

It is the business manager's considered opinion that
if these changes are not accepted and put into
effect as soon as possible, ~~LRB~~ the London Review
of Books will ultimately fold. It may anyway,
but this would hasten it.

If, on the other hand, we accept these changes,
there's a good chance we may grow from strength
to strength. At least we will know we did
what we could. Growing from strength to strength
is much more fun than standing still and
getting anxious

Nicky Spice.
17.12.82

Nicholas Spice writes: From its first issue, the LRB knew exactly what kind of magazine it wanted to be and how to be it. Surefooted editorially, in its early years it stumbled as a business – badly short of knowledge, experience and staff. The fact that in June 1982 the LRB appointed me as its first full-time publisher, although I had no track record in magazine publishing, was perhaps a symptom of this imbalance between editorial and business nous; it was certainly an act of faith. For all the self-assurance of my December 1982 memorandum excerpted here, the LRB as a business continued to explore blind alleys for a while yet. Following the common practice among literary magazines of overstating readership, Karl Miller had announced in the first independent issue of the LRB that its circulation was 15,000 – it was nearer 5000. In the spring of 1984, as we got the hang of circulation marketing, the numbers began to rise, and they have continued to rise every year (bar one) since then. In 1994, the LRB joined ABC (Audit Bureau of Circulation) and returned a figure of 18,400 for the year. The figure for 2018 was 75,725.

Inventories

In its first 18 months, with only half a dozen staff, the LRB occupied a room above Dillons University Bookshop on the corner of Malet Street – now a branch of Waterstones. This had the advantage of proximity to Karl Miller's professorial office at University College London. In 1981, the team moved to an attic office at 6a Bedford Square, at that time a shabby building in the middle of an elegant Georgian terrace (now an expensively refurbished PR agency). As the letter to the landlord's agent on the opposite page suggests, conditions were not palatial. There was no central heating and no thought for health and safety: on one occasion someone left a two-bar electric fire trained on a table leg overnight. But, with three rooms, it was an advance on Malet Street. The door to the offices was not robust and one night an opportunistic thief smashed his way in through the central panel. Arriving for work the next morning, Karl Miller, never one to be distracted from the editorial task, climbed through the jagged hole and went to his desk without comment.

Between 1984 and 1994, the paper had offices in the BMA building on Tavistock Square, overlooking Upper Woburn Place just at the spot where the number 30 bus was blown up in the terrorist attacks of 7 July 2005. Since 1994, the paper's offices have been at 28 Little Russell Street, where, now with forty members of staff, it occupies three floors opposite Hawksmoor's St George's Church, Bloomsbury.

Items to be purchased WHEN WE MOVE to 6a Bedford Square,WC1

1. Typewriter(s?)--
2. Desks-- 3? ------------------------
3. Table(s) ---
4. Chairs---
5. Waste paper dustbins-----------------------------
6. Book case
7. ash trays
8. Kettle
9. Fire(s)
9. Crockery..at least 6 cups/mugs..
10. Box of tissues

Note check whether telephone directories belong to Dillons or us before we go, if not ours contact GPO.

Inventory of items to be bought before the paper's move to Bedford Square

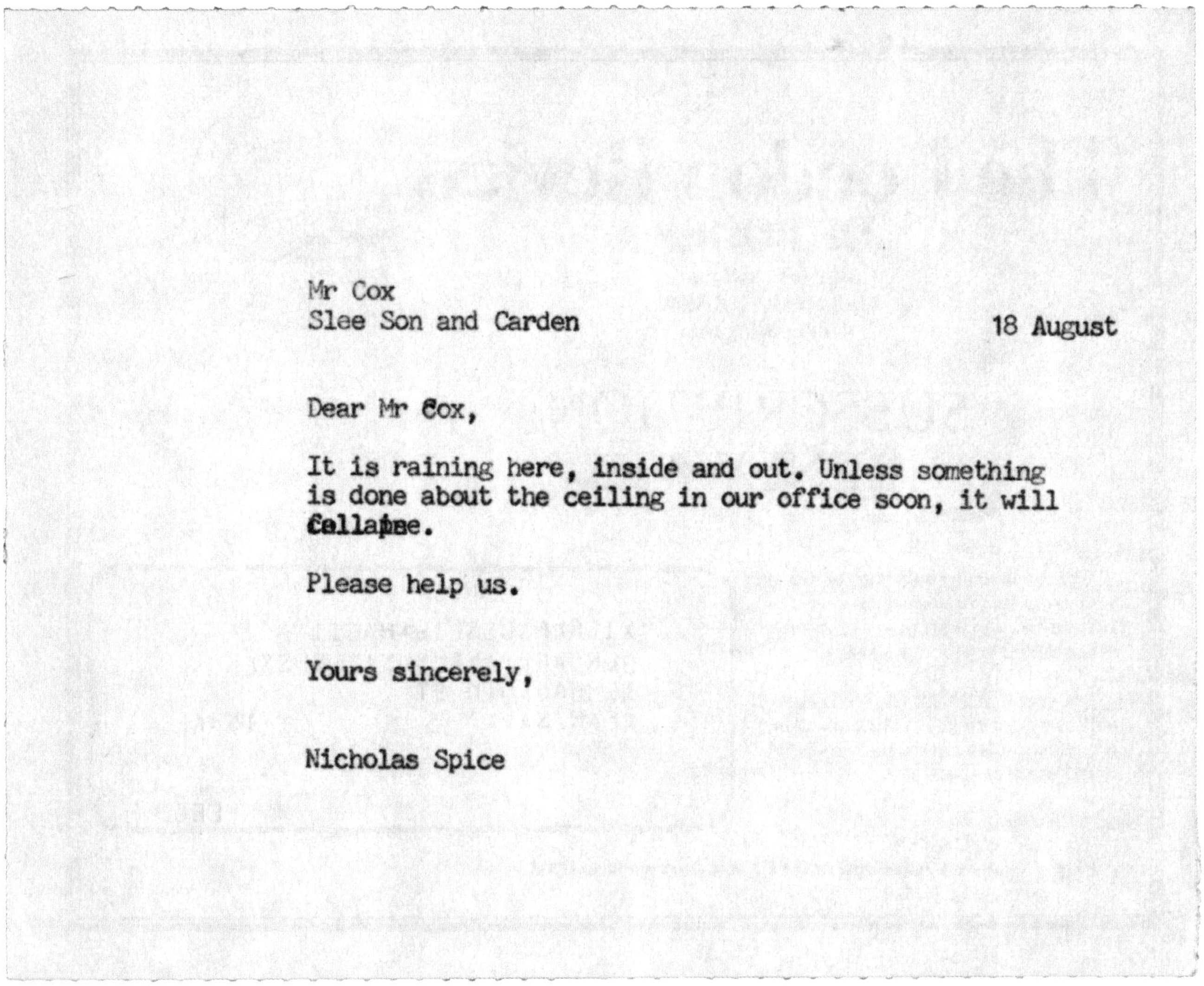

Mr Cox
Slee Son and Carden   18 August

Dear Mr Cox,

It is raining here, inside and out. Unless something
is done about the ceiling in our office soon, it will
collapse.

Please help us.

Yours sincerely,

Nicholas Spice

Letter from Nicholas Spice to Slee, Son and Carden,
18 August 1982

Two Thousand Pounds

Mary-Kay Wilmers writes: Matthew Evans was my colleague at Faber in the 1960s. We were both young and recent arrivals. We did our work quite seriously, but we also had a good time, especially at the Frankfurt book fair, where Matthew used to speak quite solemnly to foreign publishers and make faces as soon as they turned their backs. In time he became the managing director of Faber and everyone took him very seriously, not that he did himself. I wouldn't have had any compunction about asking him to commit to some advertising. I suppose it was quite like him to ask exactly how much and rather like me not to beat about the bush.

Charles Monteith, Chairman. Matthew Evans, Managing Director.
T. E. Faber. A. T. G. Pocock.
Rosemary Goad. Giles de la Mare. G. W. Taylor.
Secretary: J. D. F. Nichols

FABER AND FABER LTD

PUBLISHERS

3 Queen Square, London WC1N 3AU   Fabbaf London WC1   01-278 6881
Telex: 299633 (FABER G)

ME/CMW

10th November 1981

Ms Mary-Kay Wilmers,
London Review of Books,
6A Bedford Square,
London WC1B 3RA

Dear Mary-Kay,

I'm sorry I've been slow in coming back to you on your letter about support for LRB. Before I come back to you with a figure, may I put the question back to you the other way round. How much would you expect a firm like Fabers to commit themselves to?

Yours,

Matthew Evans

Registered Office as above.   Registered in England.   No. 944703

Letter from Matthew Evans to Mary-Kay Wilmers, 10 November 1981

London Review of Books

6 A Bedford Square, London w c 1 B 3 R A. Telephone 01-631 0884
Advertising and Distribution 01-580 3401

Matthew Evans
Faber and Faber Ltd
3 Queen Square
WC1N 3AU   13 11 81

Dear Matthew

Two thousand pounds.

Yours

Mary-Kay

EDITOR : Karl Miller DEPUTY EDITOR : Mary-Kay Wilmers ASSISTANT EDITOR : Susannah Clapp
PUBLISHER : Alan Smythe ADVERTISING AND PUBLICITY MANAGER : Michael Richards DISTRIBUTION : Susan Bosanko
EDITORIAL BOARD : Ian Hamilton, Stuart Hampshire, Frank Kermode, V. S. Pritchett, Emma Rothschild

Published by LRB Limited, registered in England at the above address No 1485413

Letter from Mary-Kay Wilmers to Matthew Evans,
13 November 1981

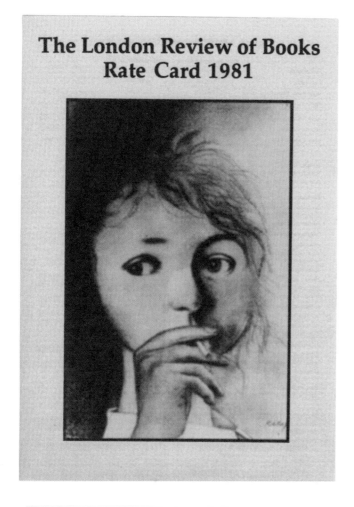

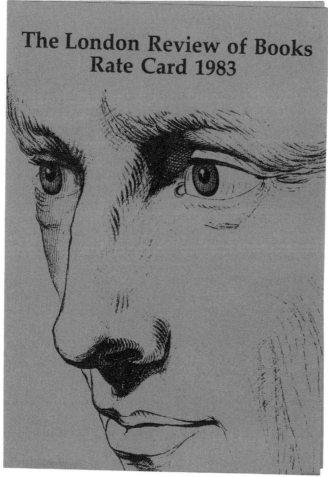

London Review of Books
RATE CARD 1985
PUBLISHING SCHEDULE AND PROMOTIONAL HIGHLIGHTS

London Review
OF BOOKS
PUBLISHING SCHEDULE AND PROMOTIONAL HIGHLIGHTS

London Review
OF BOOKS
PUBLISHING SCHEDULE AND PROMOTIONAL HIGHLIGHTS

London Review
OF BOOKS
PUBLISHING SCHEDULE AND PROMOTIONAL HIGHLIGHTS

"The London Review of Books is easily the liveliest literary journal in the country, and the only one I think of as essential reading." Salman Rushdie, 1987

Aarsleff v. Berlin

In 1981, Hans Aarsleff, a Danish historian of ideas, sent the LRB a critical assessment of Isaiah Berlin's essays on the philosopher Giambattista Vico. Karl Miller invited Berlin to respond 'to the foregoing criticisms of his work' in the same issue in which Aarsleff's piece would be published – the first and only time that a writer has been shown such deference in the history of the paper (so far). 'I enclose this vast counter-indictment, probably longer than the original article; but you did tell me not to worry about length (dangerous advice to someone like me),' Berlin wrote in his cover note. It was indeed longer than the original article. 'I realise these academic duels are a source of pure entertainment to the reader, who doesn't much care where the truth lies, and usually has no idea what it is all about, but enjoys the spectacle of academics hitting out at each other,' he went on. Berlin returned his payment, on the grounds that 'it was a favour to me that you printed so long a piece,' while noting he would be pleased to have the cheque back if it was thought he was being 'over-punctilious'. Miller didn't oblige.

Self-Amused
Adam Phillips

ISAIAH BERLIN was returning from Paris in 1952 when the aeroplane – 'it was an Air France: Air Chance is a better name' – 'caught fire and scenes of extraordinary panic occurred'. Berlin mentions this, jokily and in passing, in several letters, but Alice James, the wife of William James's son Billy, gets the full story of the disaster that didn't happen, at least to Berlin. 'I saw a thin flame crawling up the side of my window & decided that it would take at least ten minutes to reach me & there was, therefore, no reason for haste. I was, however, mistaken in this':

> The aeroplane was emptied amid screaming etc. I thought of little save how to save (a) my Abercrombie & Fitch new overcoat to which I felt devotion (b) a particularly neat small wireless set which I was bringing as a present to my parents. I therefore behaved with a false calm & as I imagined some detached dix-huitième observer of life might have behaved. But no sooner was I out & contemplating the burning wreck in a Gibbonian manner than I was screamed at by a loudspeaker: told not to be mad . . . & to run fast. It was only then that I observed that the other passengers were as specks in the distance & that I was alone in my distinguished detachment.

Noticing, in his self-amused way, that he was behaving rather oddly, both inside the plane and when he got out, Berlin was baffled by the choices he'd made. An interest in the costs of choice-making, in the losses that every decision involved, was one of the things that distinguished him from run-of-the-mill anti-determinists. But choices were always risky because preferences were always being sacrificed ('I thought of little save how to save'). In 'Two Concepts of Liberty', the inaugural lecture he gave in 1958 and one of the culminating achievements of the period covered by this second volume of letters, there is a well-known statement that sheds some light on this incident, the published work often being a better commentary on the letters than vice versa. 'If, as I believe, the ends of men are many, and not all of them are in principle compatible with each other, then the possibility of conflict – and of tragedy – can never wholly be eliminated from human life, either personal or social.' As it turned out, the emergency landing was more of a farce than a tragedy, and one of the many pleasures of these letters is Berlin's capacity for self-caricature, his sense of the ridiculous, his unrelishing of tragedy – his preference for the self-revealing situation over the getting of self-knowledge. What is striking in his description of the occasion is the lack of conflict, the apparent ease, the unflappableness with which he makes his choices, and that makes him obtrusively repeat himself; he behaved like 'some detached dix-huitième observer of life', he was alone in his 'distinguished detachment'. It was a false calm that kept him calm, but it worked.

As his strangely unguarded and un-self-regarding letters show, Berlin was never quite sure whether what was distinguished about him wasn't somehow false; whether his choices were always too easy; whether he used history to make masks for himself. Whether he was, in fact, a wildly emotional Russian Jew behaving with the eccentric composure of an imaginary Oxford don. As the letters make clear, he was troubled by the forms of ease his unease took. His detachment always puzzled him. He felt it to be at once a necessity and a self-estranging technique. Being able to be more English than the English while being self-evidently a foreigner put him at an odd angle to himself. When he married Aline Halban in 1956 after nearly thirty years of more or less celibate bachelorhood, he wrote to his friend Marion Frankfurter: 'Goodness me: I don't feel enormously real: I *suppose* it is all in order: I suppose it is right to embark on such critical courses with no sense of drama, like opening a window.'

BERLIN

OXFORD, OX3 9HU

TEL: OXFORD 61005

7 December 1981

Dear Karl,

Thank you ever so much for sending me £125, but I cannot
in conscience accept it: all I did was to defend myself against
a somewhat peculiar piece by my Danish acquaintance, which, had
it appeared in the form of a letter, you would not have been obliged to pay for - or, indeed, publish. It was a favour to me
that you printed so long a piece, even if, according to some,
this might have helped to sell an extra copy or two of the Review.
So how can I accept payment? Adding reward to favour? I return the cheque. If, of course, you think this over-punctilious,
or even silly, I should be glad to have it back, *rather than incur you*
the mildest raising of your eyebrow.

Yours ever,

Isaiah

Nov. 27 1981

Lloyds Bank Limited

17-9A.

LANGHAM PLACE BRANCH

324 REGENT STREET LONDON W1R 5AA

30-94-87

PAY Isaiah Berlin _____ OR ORDER

One hundred twenty-five pounds £ 125.

FOR L R B LIMITED

AUTH'D SIGNATORY

Letter from Isaiah Berlin to Karl Miller,
7 December 1981, returning a cheque

Falling Apart with Gaps

learn to swim is to acquire a technique for doing something whose nature we already grasp: we know what it is to swim, but do not yet know how to do it. To learn French is not to learn a technique for doing that of which we already know what it is to do it: someone who does not know French does not know what it is to speak French; he could, for example, be fooled by people speaking nonsense words with a French intonation. One can grasp what swimming is without grasping how it is done. But there is no saying what it is to speak French without saying how it is done, just as there is no saying what it is to play draughts without saying how it is done: that is why one cannot even try to speak French without having learned it, as a man who had never learned to swim might well try to do so. This fact may not justify us in supposing that to know a language is to be in a genuinely epistemic state: but one can hardly reject this contention without acknowledging, and attempting to account for, the fact which tempts us to advance it.

What is it, then, that Harris would desire of a 'demythologised' or 'integrational' linguistics? Such a linguistics would be, he says, 'an investigation of the renewal of language as a continuously creative process'. By this he means that it should not content itself with attempting to describe a language only as spoken at a particular time, as Saussure proposed, but should describe it as incorporating the possibility of 'what is traditionally classified as belonging to "language change"'. This last phrase is characteristic of the somewhat impressionistic style in which Harris often writes. What appears as a linguistic change from one standpoint will not count, from another standpoint, as involving any change in the language, but, say, as a widespread change of belief or of social convention: but there is no warrant to imply that there is no such thing as linguistic change by putting the phrase 'language change' in scare quotes, since, if there is not, then most of Europe and the Americas and much of India are still speaking Proto-Indo-European. Harris still intends a description of a language as it is at a certain time, but he wants the description to provide for the possibility of linguistic innovation without predicting what it will be.

Harris gives, in his last chapter, several entertaining examples of such innovation, beginning with the description of Mr Heath by the *Times* as 'a doorstep loser', which, as he remarks, involved no allusion to any propensity on Mr Heath's part to mislay doorsteps. He refers disparagingly to explanations of such innovatory uses by 'orthodox linguistics' which invoke a distinction between linguistic knowledge proper and pragmatic or other knowledge. We have, however, to ask whether a theory of the kind he desires would distinguish between innovatory and non-innovatory uses of language. If it did, it is hard to see how it would differ very sharply from the 'orthodox' approach he so unfavourably contrasts with it. If it did not, then it would surely be unable to recognise anything effected by the innovatory uses as involving change; and so, although it would have set the boundary between change and stasis at a different place, it would not have presented language as capable of evolving at all.

Harris wants a reformed, 'integrational' linguistics to take 'as its point of departure the individual linguistic act in its communicational setting': 'language,' he says, 'cannot be studied in isolation from the investigation of "rationality"'; when both are studied together, 'linguistic behaviour is . . . placed on a par with all other forms of voluntary human action.' It is unquestionably true that, in linguistic interchange, we are constantly guided by the same kind of evaluation of other people's motives and intentions as when we are concerned with non-linguistic behaviour; we rely on this to grasp the point of what other people say, why they take it as relevant, or perhaps are deliberately changing the subject, whether they are saying something by way of concession, or illustration, or corroboration, etc – in short, what they are driving at. For this reason, Martians who failed to recognise us as rational agents would not attain true comprehension of human speech. It in no way follows that we cannot separate out what is specific to the mastery of a particular language from what is essential to the understanding of all voluntary human action, including the use of language. Someone who does not know English very well may not understand the word 'doorstep' or the word 'loser'; or he may as yet be unaware of the rather loose manner in which, in English, it is permissible to use nouns as quasi-adjectives to qualify other nouns. But, if he knows all three, his failure to understand 'doorstep loser' will not testify to a defect in his knowledge of English; nor will his English teacher at any stage need to instruct him in principles that would enable him to understand the phrase, as opposed to background information about the practice of canvassing.

Remembering Teheran

How it hung
In the electrical loom
Of the Himalayas – I remember
The spectre of the rose.

All day the flag on the military camp flowed South.

In The Shah's Motel
The Manageress – a thunder-head Atossa – wept on her bed
Or struck awe. Tragic Persian
Quaked her bosoms – precarious balloons of water.
But still nothing worked.

Everything hung on a prayer, in the hanging dust.

With a splash of keys
She ripped through the lock, filled my room, sulphurous,
With plumbers –
Twelve year olds, kneeling to fathom
A pipeless tap sunk in a blank block wall.

. . .

I had a funny moment
Beside the dried-up river of boulders. A huddle of families
Were piling mulberries into large bowls, under limp, dusty leaves.
All the males, in their white shirts,
Drifted out towards me, hands hanging –

I could see the bad connections sparking inside their heads

As I picked my way through thistles
Among the dead-drop wells – open man-holes
Parched as snake-dens –

Later, three stoned-looking Mercedes,
Splitting with arms and faces, surfed past me
Warily over the bumpy sea of talc,
The uncials on their number-plates like fragments of scorpions.

. . .

I imagined all Persia
As a sacred scroll, humbled to powder
By the God-conducting scripts on it,
The lighting serifs of Zoroaster,

The primal cursive.

. . .

Goats, in charred rags,
Eyes and skulls
Adapted to sunstroke, woke me
Sunbathing among the moon-clinker.
When one of them slowly turned into a goat-herd

I knew I was in some ultimate century

And wrongly dressed.
All round me stood the peculiar thistles –
Desert-fanatics –
Politicos, in their zinc-blue combat issue –

Three-dimensional crystal-theorems
For a complete impaling of the given air –

Arsenals of pragmatic ideas –

I retreated to the Motel terrace, to loll there
And watch the officers half a mile away, exercising their obsolete horses.

A bleaching sun, violet-edged,
Played with the magnetic field of the mountains.

And prehistoric giant ants, long-shadowed outriders,
Cast in perfect metal (radiation-proof),
Galloped through the land lightly and unhindered,
Stormed my coffee saucer, testing the stain –

At sunset
The army flag rested for a few minutes
Then began to flow North.

. . .

I found a wriggle of water
That had somehow smuggled itself down
From the high Mother of Snows, halfway up the sky,
Spilling and scribbling its last inches to ease
A garden of pot-pourri, in a tindery shade of peach-boughs –

Its naked little current seemed almost dangerous

As the whole evening city
Sank in the muffled drumming
Of a subterranean furnace –

And over it
The desert's bloom of dust, the petroleum smog, the transistor commotion
Thickened a pinky-purple thunderlight.

The pollen of the thousands of years of voices,
Murmurous, radio-active, rubbing to flash-point –

Scintillating through the migraine,
The world-authority on Islamic art,
Sipping at a spoonful of yoghurt
And smiling at our smiles, described his dancing
Among self-beheaded dancers who went on dancing with their heads
(But only God, he said, can create a language).

Journalists proffered, on platters of silence,
Split noses, and sliced-off ears and lips –

. . .

At a giddy moment –
To the belly-dancer, the snakiest, loftiest beauty,
(Though she would not dance on my table or kiss me through her veil,
And though she made her request
Only through her demon-mask warrior drummer)
I composed a bouquet – a tropic, effulgent
Puff of publicity, in the style of Attar,

And watched myself translated by the drummer
Into her liquid
Lashing shadow – those arabesques of God,

That thorny fount.

Ted Hughes

Above, page 10, 19 August 1982; opposite, detail
from page 32, 26 April 2012

No One Could Relax around Jezebel
Anne Carson

Shame Stack

Shame requires
the eyes of others
unlike guilt. Eyes
of Elijah the Tishbite saw
in Jezebel a person with much
to be ashamed of. There is a link
between shame and mercy people who
lack the one lack the other. Psychoanalysts say
shame ruins your capacity for reverie by making cracks
in the mind where it is dangerous for thought to wander. In
the end Jezebel's own eunuchs throw her off the parapet. Her blood is on the wall and on the horses.

Stack of What Made Jezebel Jezebel

Adrenaline.
The threadlike pressure of small social conditions.
Her father his terrific purple eyebrows.
A historical mistrust felt by people in the west for
anything that comes from the east
or by people in the north for what comes from the
south and so on.
This streaming of existence within me (she said).
Again
the picking
of small stones
out
of
the rice.
Elijah's prophecy (her blood licked by dogs) which
it was.
The
gold smoke (her Buick) at dawn against a frozen
sun.

Cheapjack Stack

The Phoenicians were a commercial people, they
traded
metals,
weapons, ostrich eggs,
shoelaces, whistles, nuts, panthers, letters of the
alphab-
et.
They invented the alphabet.

They invented alphabetical order.

They used these inventions for commercial
transac-
tions
which
were
scribbled
on
the
backs
of
envelopes
and
vanished from history. From the Phoenicians the
Greeks
stole
the
alphabet,
added a few letters
and sat down to write the classics of Western civilisation.
Jezebel is filed between ice cream and karma.

Thunderstorm Stack

A bird flashed by as if mistaken
then it starts. We do not think speed
of life. We do not think why hate
Jezebel. We think who's that
throwing trees against the house.
Jezebel was a Phoenician.
Phoenician thunderstorms are dry
and frightening, they arrive one
inside the other as torqued ellipses.

'Poems will be used to hold the page,' Karl Miller wrote in his blueprint for the LRB. The first poem to appear in the paper was Ted Hughes's 'Night Arrival of Sea-Trout', wedged into the bottom left-hand corner of page 8 of the first issue, propping up Francis Wyndham's piece on Heathcote Williams. This sonnet about honeysuckle, foxglove and dogrose was exactly the thing to make up the shortfall. But poems weren't just fillers to be used when a piece was the wrong length or there weren't enough ads. In August 1982, the paper published Hughes's 'Remembering Teheran' in a box that took up most of a page. ('I like the way you print poems, in boxes with lots of decent white around them,' Les Murray wrote in 1990.) Hughes's letter (overleaf), responding to the proof he was sent of 'Remembering Teheran', begins with the objection that a title that is also a poem's first line shouldn't interruptingly be followed by the poet's name in 18-point type. He also points out that the removal of his five-dot ellipses between sections has imposed false unity on a poem that's structured – uncharacteristically – as a series of discrete snapshots of Teheran, which he visited in 1971. 'Dock the cost of the changes off the fee,' he told Miller.

The best verse is often the trickiest to accommodate. Jorie Graham felt that our first attempt at laying out 'On the Virtue of the Dead Tree' split the poem across pages at an awkward moment, creating 'formal melodrama that the poem cannot afford right there at a key turn and uptick in tone'. Her distinctive long lines can also pose a challenge: 'Tell your layout people they can move those inner margins (in this case way to the right) a tiny way back in towards the left – if that helps. Obviously the effect of the form has to stay the same but there is wiggle room, and I am open to all kinds of experiments'; then, more self-consciously: 'next book: haikus'. In July 2018, we published 'My Skin Is', Graham's response to the 'insanity' of Trump's America. 'My US publishers keep asking me why I give my best work to LRB,' she wrote, 'and I keep telling them it's because the LRB has the best readers, the best editors, and the best layout team. It is so rare for poetry to be given the space it needs to breathe in and in which to be "audible". We all know this is true . . .'

We don't always get it right. In April 2012, an Anne Carson poem broke up Jacqueline Rose's piece on Marilyn Monroe. Carson said 'how satisfying it was to see "Jezebel" pillowed by Marilyn on the page', but added that we'd messed up the layout: 'The poem was intended to be a single long shape, with sections moving from justified left to justified right in a sort of S curve, but it has been cut into two parallel chunks on the page, making the lineation and shapes look clumsy, irrational and unstable. Rats!'

Joanne O'Leary

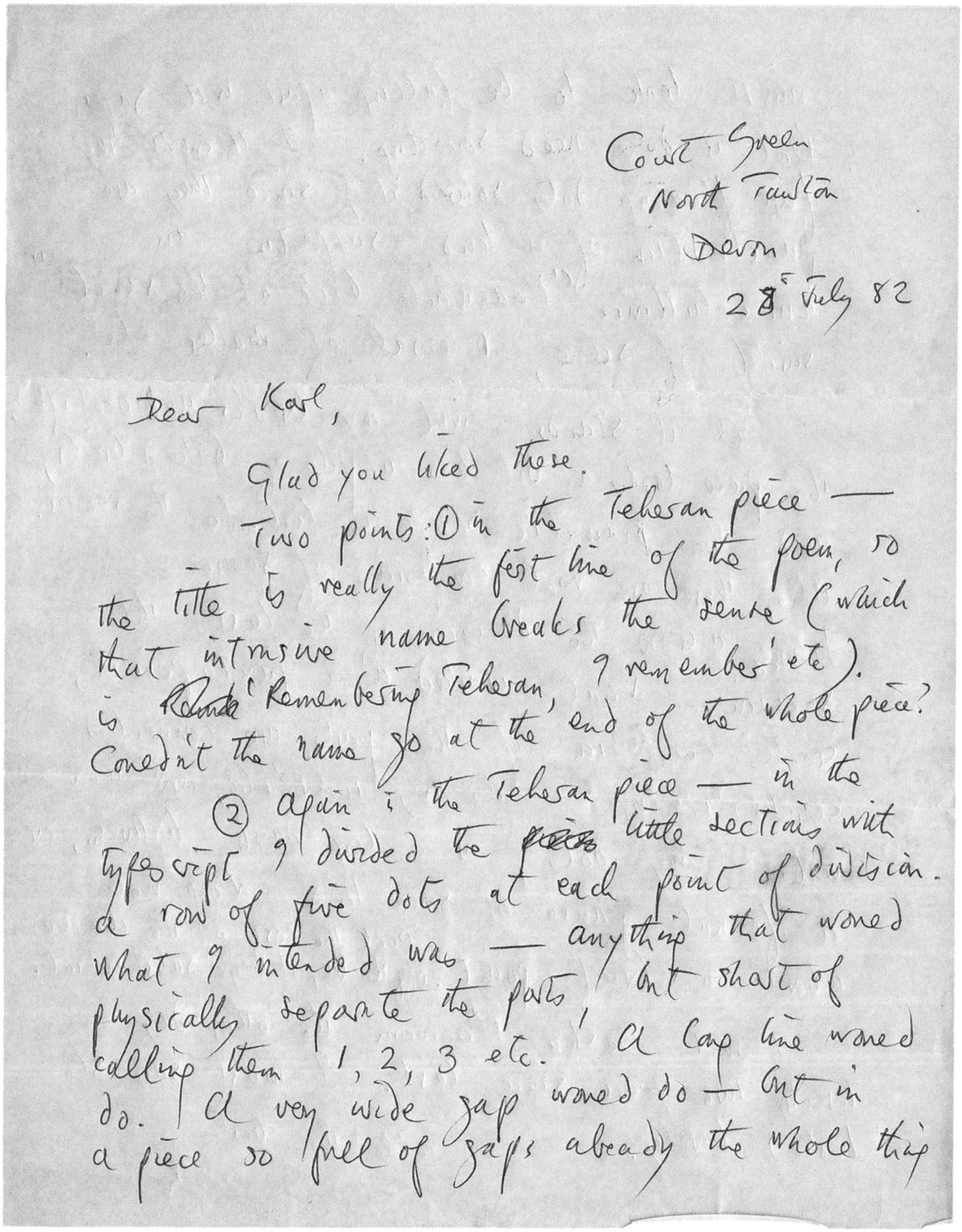

Court Green
North Tawton
Devon
28 July 82

Dear Karl,

Glad you liked these.
Two points: ① in the Teheran piece —
the title is really the first line of the poem, so
that intrusive name breaks the sense (which
is ~~Rememb~~ 'Remembering Teheran, I remember' etc).
Couldn't the name go at the end of the whole piece?
② again in the Teheran piece — in the
typescript I divided the ~~piece~~ little sections with
a row of five dots at each point of division.
What I intended was — anything that would
separate the parts, but short of
physically calling them 1, 2, 3 etc. A long line would
do. A very wide gap would do — but in
a piece so full of gaps already the whole thing

Letter from Ted Hughes to Karl Miller, 28 July 1982

might look to be falling apart with gaps.
But it does need something. I thought my
five floating dots solved it, since they are
punctuation of a kind suggesting an
anacoluthonic "Meanwhile back at the ranch"
switch of scene, renewal of matter etc,

As it stands, with my breaks unidentified,
the piece looks a bit like a pile of baked bricks,
and the dramatic shape is lost to the reader.
Also, there are real confusion of sense —
between across the division of the last three
sections. What worked as a juxtaposition,
creates confusion if the parts are connected
syntactically — as they inevitably are now
without my dots, or a long dash between, or
a formal pause of some kind. Long note
about a brief point. Dock the cost of the changes
off the fee, if they're substantial.

I met Sasha Moorsom the other day —
twenty two years since last. I must say she
looked lovely.   all the best
                                   Ted

Political Yah-Booh

Inigo Thomas writes: In 2003, by which time he was the longest serving MP, Tam Dalyell was thrown out of the chamber of the House of Commons for berating the front bench of his own party about the intelligence document known as the 'dodgy dossier', which gave Tony Blair the evidence he needed to go to war in Iraq.

Dalyell wrote 16 pieces for the LRB, several of them about the Falklands War of 1982, and in particular the sinking of the Argentine battleship, the *Belgrano*. In his view, the sinking was a war crime: the sailors were given no warning and had no chance to surrender or abandon ship. In 1991, we asked him to write about that year's war in Iraq. He rang the office to say he had finished his piece, and asked me whether I'd like to come and collect it – and have tea in the House of Commons dining room. Yes and yes, I must have said. He handed me the piece, which was handwritten on House of Commons notepaper – much like the page pictured here, from a piece we didn't publish.

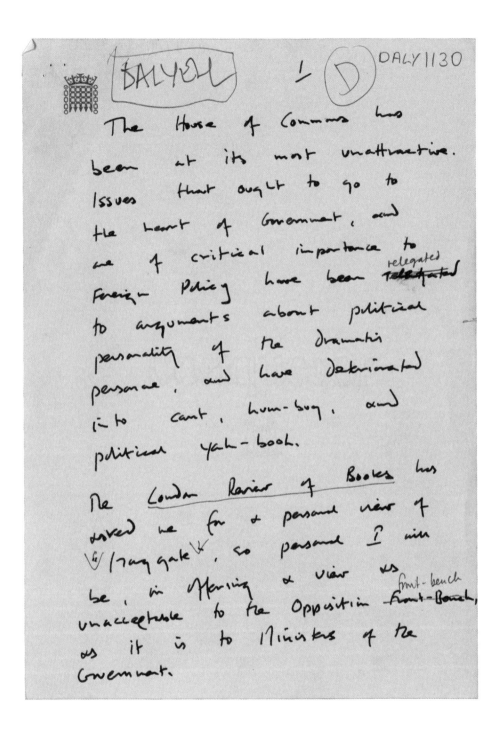

Transcription:

The House of Commons has been at its most unattractive. Issues that ought to go to the heart of Government, and are of critical importance to Foreign Policy have been relegated to arguments about political personality of the dramatis personae, and have deteriorated into cant, hum-bug and political yah-booh.

The *London Review of Books* has asked me for a personal view of 'Iraqgate', so personal I will be, in offering a view as unacceptable to the Opposition front-bench as it is to Ministers of the Government.

First page of a typescript by Tam Dalyell, 1992

A Falklands Polemic

Tam Dalyell

NEVER underestimate the importance of fortuitous timing in the development of events. Governments and nations can get onto a motorway, and then find to their alarm that they are on a journey on which they never intended to travel, but from which there is no acceptable exit. We are faced with a shooting war in the South Atlantic that few British politicians thought could, should or would occur.

One day, historians will put under the microscope the events of Friday, 2 April 1982. The full truth may never be revealed. Who telephoned whom, to say what? The apparent ephemeralities of that morning may never be identified. What is certain is that within minutes of the news of the Argentinian military aggression in the Falklands – otherwise known as the re-integration of the Malvinas – opposition leaders were being hounded for instant comment. Crucially, Labour's defence spokesman, John Silkin, went onto the important *World at One* radio programme, and seemed to commit the opposition to a belligerent reaction. Uncharacteristically, I leapt to my telephone to ask what was going on, and was calmed down by Anne Carleton, his long-term personal assistant, who told me that my alarums had been overtaken by events.

The mould was set. The prime minister guessed that she could count on the opposition's endorsing strong measures. Ironically, this is one of those rare occasions when an opposition, fifty parliamentary seats down, could have had a decisive influence on events. Without the imprimatur of the Labour shadow cabinet, and against the backcloth of a disunited nation, a task force could not have been proposed. Yet Labour had appeared to signal green, before there had been an opportunity for reflection within the shadow cabinet as a whole, let alone the parliamentary party, or the party in the country. Had the military occupation taken place on a Monday to Thursday when Parliament was sitting, I believe there might have been a different gut reaction. Once Michael Foot had struck an attitude, 'loyalty to Michael' became an element in a situation where the notion of actual gunfire in the South Atlantic was surrealist fantasy. People had some vague scenario, at worst, of a simple SAS operation, and, more generally, that, of course, a solution would be arrived at, long before any warship actually arrived in the South Atlantic. 'Thank God, we have plenty of time!'

On the government side, timing was also crucial. It so happened that the evening of Friday, 2 April, was the appointed date for a large number of Conservative constituency association annual general meetings. Normally, Tory MPs are allowed to 'get on with the job' rather than being held accountable as Labour MPs are supposed to be. (In practice, Constituency Labour Parties tend to take a generous view of their MPs' deviations, if they are thought to be serious, on policy matters.) On this occasion, a significant number of Tory MPs were goaded into extreme bellicosity by the fresh fury of their constituency party men, and particularly women. The Falklands, Belize, Gibraltar, Hong Kong are like some weird kind of umbilical cord with the end of the British Empire. Rage was further inflamed on the Conservative benches by what was perceived as either the incompetence or the perfidy of the Foreign Office in allowing the Falklands to be taken. The anti-Foreign Office attitude, constantly articulated by Enoch Powell, has been reinforced by the drip, drip, drip of anti-Foreign Office 'briefings' emanating from Downing Street. Many Tory MPs simply relished the humiliation of the Foreign Office. Whatever surmises are possible, the fact is that Conservative MPs created a hysterical mood when they returned hot-foot to the Commons for the debate of 3 April 1982, the like of which I have not witnessed in twenty years as an MP. The mechanics of that debate will be of lasting consequence.

Unprejudiced Reviewing

In 1982, the writer and critic Al Alvarez published a book called *Life after Marriage: Scenes from Divorce*. Noticing that the book made full reference to Alvarez's ex-wife, Ursula Creagh, in terms that could only be favourable to the author, the LRB sent her the book to review. Her piece was unsurprisingly hostile. Most readers loved the theatrics, and a woman being given the opportunity to answer a man's self-serving account of their relationship; others, like Frank Kermode, a member of the LRB's editorial board, felt this had been an 'extraordinary' decision for a journal 'which depends for its reputation on unprejudiced comment'. Karl Miller's reply was equally combative, but the disagreement was soon smoothed over.

First Chapters
Ursula Creagh

IN the first chapter of this book, a chapter which concerns the time of our marriage, Alvarez has cast me in a variety of roles, from Jungle Jane to Giant Sloth. It may come as a surprise to him to find me among his critics.

Life after Marriage follows much the same pattern as his bestselling *The Savage God: A Study of Suicide*. The personal bit, the friends, the literary figures. A formula that was perhaps worthy of repetition. The principal literary figure then in question was Sylvia Plath, a writer on whose work, and death, Alvarez became an authority. It was a very readable book and did much to awaken interest in Plath: but it also heralded the author's addiction to plangent autobiography. Over the years of his critical career Alvarez has expressed the belief that, in this century, true art is produced by those on the edge of sanity, or under severe pressure. By airing his own abortive suicide attempt in *The Savage God*, he seemed to me to be making an effort to join the club. His interest in the writings of the people concerned became of secondary importance. He turned sociologist, historian, psychologist and philosopher almost overnight, and moved a long way from his early, and serious, critical work.

If one sets aside the quotations with which the new book is embellished, Alvarez can now be said to have abandoned literature altogether. An account of his own unhappy first marriage dominates the field. After the initial shock, I found this bewildered me less than did the descriptions of the period surrounding his suicide attempt in the earlier book. From Scene One, where I am to be found complaining about the toast crusts while Alvarez is giving us 'And now good morrow to our waking souls,' it is clear that I am destined never to raise my insensitive head again as far as the readers of this book are concerned.

The publishers sent me the manuscript of this chapter (libel laws), and as a result some insults directed at myself, and at my 85-year-old father, were removed. But I cannot say that I think much of the chapter that survived these objections. After a separation of over twenty years and overtly friendly relations for at least the last eighteen, I am taken in hand for the magic formula. The fact that our marriage was a drab and commonplace failure like countless others was plainly quite unacceptable. No one was going to buy that book. He has done his best to enliven the drama with a series of contrasting images: 'he' is a clever young writer, an ambitious literary-critical young man, has a first-class degree, fellowships; 'she' appears to take no interest in his work, has never sat an exam in her life. 'He' has youthful sentimentality, romantic innocence, moral ambition, appreciates the beauties of nature; 'she' is taciturn, hates toast crusts, has fixed black rages and eyes like green stone. Even her own parents are wonderstruck that anyone should want to marry her; his parents dote on him. But above all he suffers. He is sensitive and she is not. 'There is,' Alvarez writes, 'even a certain status in being one of the world's walking wounded.

The shortcomings of Alvarez's semi-fictional method permeate this chapter, as they do the rest of the book. A principle of selection leads him to omit all too many things that would damage his thesis. His style is not what it was, but he can still handle words. Thus we hear that while he was teaching in America his wife 'left prematurely for England' (called away on business perhaps?), while he later 'upped and left her'. He uses the voice of the great to illustrate his feelings throughout. 'Nothing became him in his wife like the leaving of her.' The un-Shakespearean rhythm of this line is troubling in itself, and when we look at the phrase in *Macbeth* which he is parodying, and which refers to the death of the traitor Thane of Cawdor, the implication is fierce. And presumptuous. I do not recollect Alvarez leaving his wife with the same dignity that Cawdor left his life.

1 June,1982

The Editor,
London Review of Books

Dear Karl,

        I was amazed to see Ursula Creagh's review of Alvarez's
book in the new issue of the paper. I have nothing against Mrs.
Creagh and am not surprised that she dislikes the book, but it
seems extraordinary that she should have been asked to review it
in a journal which depends for its reputation on unprejudiced
comment. She is surely the last person in the world to provide it
in this instance. I think it would have been all right to publish
a letter from Mrs. Creagh in relation to a notice by someone else;
but to invite her to review the book was deliberately to solicit
the most hostile response to be had.

        You won't, I hope, take it amiss that a member of your
Editorial Board registers this objection, especially as he finds
himself in the unhappy position of seeming to endorse what he takes
to be a virtually inexcusable lapse. I daresay the other members
of the Board will have their own views of the matter, but I shall
send them copies of this letter to ensure that they are aware of
mine.

                                        Yours ever,

                                        Frank

                                        Frank Kermode

Letter from Frank Kermode to Karl Miller,
1 June 1982

London Review of Books

6 A Bedford Square, London W C I B 3 R A. Telephone 01-631 0884
Advertising and Distribution 01-580 3401

Frank Kermode
King's College
Cambridge   14 June

Dear Frank,

You have written to tell me that you find 'virtually
inexcusable' the decision to publish a discussion by
his first wife of Alvarez's new book. I have to say that
I do not seek to be excused by you, and that I would take
the same decision tomorrow if the matter came up again.

I do not believe in 'unprejudiced' reviewing - and I had
gathered from your wriiftngs that you didn't either. But
I do believe in accurate reviewing. You do not question
the accuracy of Mrs Creagh's discussion, and it may be
that you had not yet had the opportunity to read the book.
It was precisely because I had read Al's writings of
recent years that it seemed fitting to publish this
discussion. It expressed, not a hostility to Al personally,
though you may not believe that, but a disapproval of the
histrionically self-serving and tendentious character of
his recent work. It seems to me that we were entitled to
allow such feelings to influence the choice of reviewer.
It was not, as it happens, certain that Ursula Creagh's
account would prove as hostile as it did, despite the
falsehooods about her which had to be removed from the
manuscript, so I am informed, after legal representations:
it seems indeed that her review is less hostile than others
that have appeared. There is a cant which says that reviews,
at all times, and of all books, must be written by those
without personal knowledge of the author in question.
Reviewers are to be like judges. The rule, if it is a rule,
is broken constantly. But of course you know all this,
just as well as I know that a judicial aspiration of a
kind is appropriate in reviewing.

It follows that I think of you - without prejudice, so
to speak - as prejudiced here by virtue of your being a
friend of Al's. Perhaps, since this is the case, it
would have been sanguine to expect you to use your imagination
to the extent of seeing the point of such a discussion. I
do not say to you that the decision was positive, corrective
and considerate in its intent, though that is what I hope.
I will say to you that if it is all right for Al to publish
a book belittling his first wife, then it cannot be all
wrong and virtually inexcusable to publish an intelligent
discussion of the book by that first wife.

EDITOR : Karl Miller DEPUTY EDITOR : Mary-Kay Wilmers ASSISTANT EDITOR : Susannah Clapp
PUBLISHER : Alan Smythe ADVERTISING AND PUBLICITY MANAGER : Michael Richards DISTRIBUTION : Susan Bosanko
EDITORIAL BOARD : Ian Hamilton, Stuart Hampshire, Frank Kermode, V. S. Pritchett, Emma Rothschild

Published by LRB Limited, registered in England at the above address No 1485413

Letter from Karl Miller to Frank Kermode,
14 June 1982

London Review of Books

6 A Bedford Square, London W C I B 3 R A. Telephone 0 I-63 I 0884
Advertising and Distribution 0 I-580 340 I

Yours has been the only negative response to the review which has been volunteered so far (apart from Stuart's courteous objection, delivered in response to a copy of your letter to me). But I am well aware that I have not heard the last of this, and it is already apparent that at least one newspaper is soliciting shocked comment on hearing of your reaction. I feel that your best course would have been to publish a letter of disagreement in the paper, or to voice that disagreement at the editorial meeting which we intended to hold next week. Instead, you have sent a copy of your letter to the editorial advisers (some of whom, as you must surely have noticed, have shown no interest what ever in the editorial policy of the paper). It may be that you did this with the intention of creating a scandal and of injuring my authority as editor. You have sometimes given me the impression that you had little sense of the nervous wear and tear which it has cost us to make this paper, and that - apart from the matter of your articles - what most roused you were the occasions when you felt entitled to rebuke us. Your articles, to be sure, have been a very important matter indeed. I am fully conscious of the value of what you have written for us, and of the editorial guidance you have provided. I am grateful for this, and since I am grateful I am sad to think, and to say, that the time has come for us to have no more to do with one another, and to realise that you are likely to feel the same way.

Yours,
Karl

EDITOR : Karl Miller DEPUTY EDITOR : Mary-Kay Wilmers ASSISTANT EDITOR : Susannah Clapp
PUBLISHER : Alan Smythe ADVERTISING AND PUBLICITY MANAGER : Michael Richards DISTRIBUTION : Susan Bosanko
EDITORIAL BOARD : Ian Hamilton, Stuart Hampshire, Frank Kermode, V. S. Pritchett, Emma Rothschild

Published by LRB Limited, registered in England at the above address No 1485413

Addenda, Delenda, Corrigenda

Oliver Sacks had a longstanding relationship with the *LRB*, which had published him from the beginning (and from before the beginning in the *Listener*). He sent lots of different drafts of his pieces – 'addenda, delenda, corrigenda', as he put it in the letter opposite – and waited for a final version to emerge. In 1984, Michael Neve, a lecturer at the Wellcome Institute for the History of Medicine, was asked to write about Sacks's new book, *A Leg to Stand On*. The paper had published an early incarnation in 1982, a year or so before carrying the essay that was what Sacks called the 'starter' for *The Man Who Mistook His Wife for a Hat*. *A Leg to Stand On* began with an accident Sacks had on a mountain in Norway, after which he temporarily lost all movement in one of his legs. Neve wasn't persuaded by Sacks's account. 'Are you sure you want to go through with this?' Karl Miller asked Neve when he had finished reading the piece. Neve was sure. 'So what title are we to give it?' *A Leg to Stand On* gave Neve his inspiration: 'It's Got Bells On.' Sacks never wrote for the *LRB* again.

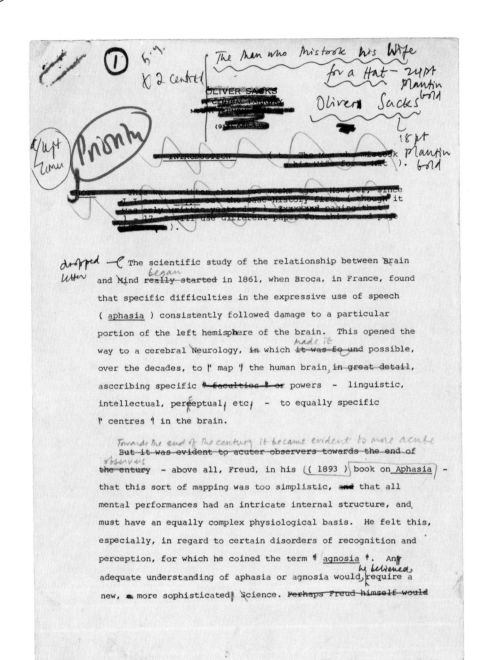

First page of the typescript of 'The Man Who Mistook His Wife for a Hat' by Oliver Sacks, published in the issue of 19 May 1983

OLIVER W. SACKS, M.D.

████████ ████████

████████ ████████

212-885-2068

PS " The Tourette Syndrome Association of England " is represented by Joan Wolfe, 734 High Street, Ilford, ESSEX. 1G3 8QY

Dear Mary Kay,

Let me get ██████ this off to you before I drive you (and myself) mad ... as I started doing (oh so long ago !) when writing The Great Awakening !

What I wrote last night is on ████ Horton Street notepaper, and consists of four double-spaced sheets (████ sides 1-8). I am sending this, and not laying hands on it. However I am also sending (on Beth Abraham paper) a couple of revisions I started to do -- one (in single space) of the beginning of the piece ; the other (double spaced) of its ending (which (ohm and a redraft of a para on side 6) I thought rather choppy in the original). However, I am almost devoid of judgement in regard to what I write -- so I will send you both the original and the revisions, leaving it entirely to you to pick what you please. I will not trouble you with more addenda, delenda, corrigenda, etc... nor further drafts, nor anything more ; but will wait with eagerness and equanimity for ████ some proofs to reach me...

I am very delighted and very grateful that you are taking the piece - as I was, so many years ago, with the- your

bringing out (in all senses) of my Listener article. I need such an article, as I needed that, as a sort of " starter " for a book on the subject... Somehow an article can breach the terrible wall of inhibition, and permit me the feeling that I can speak out and write...   And equally grateful for your splendid sensitive commonsense and knowledge of me (because I know I am almost impossible).

With all my thanks and fondest regards

Letter from Oliver Sacks to Mary-Kay Wilmers,
1981

A Subject Responds

In a piece published in 1983 on Martin Seymour-Smith's biography of Robert Graves, Paul Delany wrote that it would be hard to write a definitive study until 'Graves, and Laura (Riding) Jackson, are dead'. Within weeks, Laura Riding responded with a short letter to the editor complaining about Seymour-Smith's book and castigating 'ugly British reviewer behaviour'. She followed this up with a much longer letter in which she said that 'Seymour-Smith executes in his book a mission of his own of all-out vindictive defamation of me, distinct from Graves's plotting to cover the dishonesties he committed against our comradeship with ever greater and greater ones, ought to be perfectly plain to the moral intelligence of all readers of the book.' She continued at some length, describing Graves as a 'lout' who has 'awful elements in his moral interior'.

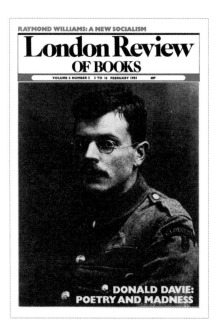

Queen Famine's Courtier
Paul Delany

LAURA (RIDING) JACKSON is, of course, no mean obstacle to gaining a clear and unobstructed view of Graves. Martin Seymour-Smith's first difficulty with her is that she is American: on the evidence of this book Americans are people he neither likes nor understands. His second is that she is Jewish, which he makes little of, despite the provocative comments of Gertrude Stein (printed by O'Prey): 'It was terribly important for you to have liked her; for your Jesus book, after all, she was Jew every single bit of her, but . . . she was the materialistic jew camouflaging her materialism by intellectualism.' Seymour-Smith does not treat Riding altogether ungenerously, and he shows due respect for her poetic talent: but he presents Graves's relation with her as a misguided episode, perhaps even a deluded one.

The reissue of Riding's *Progress of Stories* is a welcome reminder both of her literary gifts and of her ability to disconcert all who came within range of her exigent personality. 'I haven't any human sympathy,' one of her characters says, 'but I have instincts . . . When I write [my stories] I feel like an animal writing about people.' This is what gives her stories value: it is also what makes most of them tedious after the first few bright pages. Riding could always rivet attention to herself by her complete self-possession and disregard of rival wills ('There is nothing that pleases me so much as to have people agree with me'). But in the long run she consumed both her courtiers and her own gifts – ending up as 'Queen Famine', in Graves's deadly phrase.

Seymour-Smith's account of Graves's involvement with Riding in 1926-39 supplies new clues to the puzzle of how someone as turbulent as Graves could have fallen completely under Riding's sway. One of her attractions was her promise of control over time and change: 'bodies have had their day' was the kind of pronouncement she could get Graves to believe in. She appealed strongly to his streak of romantic masochism, playing on the sexual guilt and fear instilled in him by his puritan mother.

Considering Graves's obsession with the feminine, surely his mother deserves closer attention than she gets from Seymour-Smith. He drops a few hints about Graves's sexual eccentricities, but does not probe deeply into his emotional development. It is curious that when Riding became sexually infatuated with other men, in 1929 and 1939, Graves showed a childlike complaisance where one would expect him to have felt outrage and betrayal. In between, the celibacy which she enforced on him from about 1933 seemed to make the union closer, rather than undermining it.

Riding's power, one could argue, rested on her ability to exploit Graves's long-standing idée fixe about sex: that it was the most important thing in his life, but also something that someone else – his current Muse – should take responsibility for. This was an awkward rule for everyday life, but handy for writing love poetry, since the best poems of this kind are typically one-sided and obsessive, like Graves's. The Muse's function, for Graves, is to trigger the self-consuming mania craved by her poetic devotee; she is a neutral spirit, like that required by the Lover's counterpart, the alcoholic.

Certainly Riding's behaviour was often destructive or bizarre – she once went to the Dorchester nightclub wearing a tiara that spelled out her name in capital letters. But Graves himself was not a model of decorum; and Seymour-Smith's irritation with Riding's outrages upsets the balance of his book, especially when combined with his adulation of Beryl Graves. Though Seymour-Smith apparently detests T.S. Matthews, his *Under the Influence* (1978) gives a much more lively impression of Graves's domestic milieu in the 1930s. While it is true that Riding got Graves in trouble with the police and with almost everyone he knew, it was the kind of trouble he wanted, since it confirmed his inclination to leave England and set up a coterie existence at Deya. There is no evidence that she hindered Graves's development as a writer, or lowered the standard of his work.

(Riding Jackson)

Box 35 Wabasso Fla.
32970

June 1 1983

Mr. Karl Miller

The Editor
London Review of Books
6A Bedford Square
London WC1B 3RA

Mr. Miller!

I thank you for your prompt acknowledgement of the
piece of writing that I sent to you (and give thanks also for
the brief initial notice from Miss Nickles of my letter-
article's having reached your office).

How you have written, generally, cheers me. Power-structures
are such, of course, that the massive Hutchinson- Seymour-Smith and
reviewer-brotherhood combination has an impregnable force of
security against challenging of its defamations of myself -
where counteractive defence of myself against them , and any single
opportunity given me to attempt it, come into danger of punitive
revenge by the self-legalized denigrators. I have written letters on
some of the reviews of the book, books, published in England, but   d
only a brief onexxxxxx was printed in The Observer (and that subjected
to a joking title), and a medium-long one in The Timez Literary
Supplement (and I learned that this was effected by the grace of
Anthony Burgessxx,xx the TLS reviewer,xxand Martin Seymour-Smith, of
agreeing not to bring libel charges -- the latter given space along
with my letter for a letter in which he made insolently unsupported
denial of one of my points, and fatuous assertion of the utter accu-
ravy of the entire contents of his book). Not long ago the editor of
an English magazine who had himself written with confid ent expatiaiton
on Seymour-Smith's picturing of me agreed to consider a letter from
me on a review of the Hutchinson volumes highly assaultive of myself
(though protesting that he had thought to be of a high standard). He
wrote to me, on receiving my letter, submitted for publication, that
he had read it with great interezt, but could not publish it because
I had asked that no cuts be made in it. He did not advance uneasiness
as to the posibility of libel action, or use the term I have met with
in other responses of cowardice to letters of protest sent to editors
on the Hutchinson volumes: unsuitable. His was stylistically unadul-
terated cowardice.

You have honored me with unhesitant indication of a need of apprais-
ing the danger of libel-suit involvements if you publish the piece.
Whatever you decide, your honesty of statement and the courageous spirit
of your appraisal have given me an experience to prize, among the
many of morally shabby and I have had in connection with the Seymour-
Smith outrage (and its trailer-accompaniment).

With all-grateful feeling, I am

Laura Jackson

The London Diary

The first *LRB* Diary appeared in March 1982. Its author was the historian A.J.P. Taylor, whose contributor's note read: 'Alan Taylor's Diary inaugurates a regular feature of the paper. The Diaries will be by various hands. Clive James's will scan and will eventually compose a "Poem of the Year".' A.J.P. Taylor wrote 26 of them over the next four years or so. Most memorably, after a mental breakdown in 1984, he described the elaborate fantasies of an alternative life he'd experienced while in hospital. 'One day life will begin again for me,' he ended. 'I cannot say that I miss it very much.' Clive James's contributions constituted a history of 1982. Here are a couple of stanzas on the Falklands War from one of them:

> The war dance falters. Foam dries on the lips
> As word by drawn-out word the news comes through:
> The *Sheffield*, one of our most modern ships,
> A spanking, Sea Dart-armed type 42
> Destroyer built to wipe out radar blips,
> A Space Invaders expert's dream come true,
> Is hit. With what's so far an untold cost
> In lives. Has burned. Is given up for lost.
>
> An Etendard released an Exocet
> Which duly skimmed the waves as advertised.
> Our tabloids wring what mileage they can get
> Out of French perfidy, but undisguised
> Is their amazement such a classy jet
> Flown by these dagoes that they've patronised
> Should leave the runway, let alone deliver
> This thing so clever that it makes you shiver.

Every issue since March 1982 has contained a Diary. The only rule (not very strictly adhered to – readers complain) is that it should be written in the first person, or contain some element of personal experience. Later, in 2000, another new column, Short Cuts, was introduced as a place for responding to the present political moment (among other things).

Letters from A.J.P. Taylor to Karl Miller,
24 June and 1 July 1985

LONDON
NW5 1DN
01-485 1507

24 June 1985

Dear Karl,

Here is a rather ▨▨▨▨▨▨▨ belated contribution to the London Diary.   If it is a little short you cam restore the delated page 2..   I am quite pleased with what I have written.

Yours ever,

Alan

[1985]

LONDON   1 July
NW5 1DN
01-485 1507

Dear ▨▨▨▨ Karl,

I am glad you liked my diary entry.   I can never remember what I have written.   If you will return the ▨▨▨▨▨ three entries I sent to you I will▨▨▨▨▨▨▨▨▨▨▨ manufacture something more or at least I will try.   At present my mind is empty but it▨▨▨▨▨▨▨▨▨▨▨▨ usually fills up.

I have just acquired a grandson named Karl.

Yours ever,

Alan

Diary

A.J.P. Taylor

I T is some time since I wrote a diary here. It will be seen I have had plenty to write about. I should explain that there are two versions of a period of my life. One is the version of other people, a version which others try to impose upon me. The other is my own version, a version equally genuine and much more unusual.

According to others such as my doctors and the members of my family, I had a mental breakdown, was the victim of fantasies and never moved from the hospital bedroom except to have a bath and did not read even the newspaper. This version can be disregarded. According to my recollection, I had a life of adventure interrupted by periods of relaxation, and never encountered insoluble difficulties. Most of my life seems to have been passed in some part of the North of England and at different periods. My first stretch was in Roman Britain, when I lived in York and was afterwards stationed on the Wall. These experiences were very instructive to me as an historian.

The Romans did not remain long. Nor did I waste much time at the court of King Arthur. The outstanding figure of my attraction was the king, though I did not manage to encounter him often. This was the period when I spent most of my time on the Yorkshire moors. I got lost pretty often, though always rescued by other wanderers. Gradually I moved into a more civilised existence. The centre of my life was now Harrogate, a place I have never visited in my life. I had difficulties here obtaining regular copies of the Manchester *Guardian*, which did not surprise me at all. I also attended a very expensive luncheon party one Sunday in Harrogate given by my daughter Amelia, who is not in the habit of giving expensive luncheon parties.

I gradually resumed a family life. The principal figures in it were my mother and father, both of whom had, I thought, been dead for some time. My father had taken over a medieval monastery – was it Furness Abbey? – which he had transformed into a boarding-house for holidaymakers. My father was as delightful as ever and as efficient. I spent an occasional night with him during the summer. Though friendly, he never displayed much interest in my actitivies whatever they might be.

I sometimes went shopping with my mother in Manchester, a thing I had done often enough in real life. I found Kendal Milne a great obstacle against getting from one end of Manchester to another. One afternoon I encountered a birthday party given by some shop assistants. I wanted to get through, not to take part in it. My father took me out to his monastery, an event which somewhat puzzled me because in the general puzzle of my existence I was aware that I lived in the 18th century when motor cars did not exist. It also puzzled me that my hospital rooms were sometimes in London and sometimes in France, probably in Paris, though the nurses were always English. No one ever tried to explain to me where I was or what I was doing. It was a long period of bewilderment which I gradually accepted as one of total incomprehensibility. It then just disappeared along with the figures who populated it, including my father and mother. I was sorry to lose him, otherwise I did not worry.

In the last episode of my medical career some of it became clear to me. I recognised that I was in a hospital, though it was not clear to me where – probably London, though it might be somewhere in France. It was also clear to me that wherever it was it was difficult or impossible to get out of it. In the quiet of lunchtime I would pack a small bag and set off for the way out. Sooner or later a nurse would catch me and ask me where I was going. Patiently I would be led back to my own quarters without any explanation. I must have read something during this long and dreary period. But apart from the *Times* every morning, I can only remember reading *The Good Soldier Schweik* in its most extended edition – something over seven hundred pages. It is still an incomparable war book.

A drawing of A.J.P. Taylor by Mark Boxer on the cover of the issue of 8 November 1990

In November 1987, I wrote a Diary for the LRB about the hazard of literary prizes, the whimsical manner in which they are sometimes bestowed, and the varying qualifications of the judges. For instance, in 1972, the (then only three) Booker Prize judges were Cyril Connolly, George Steiner and Elizabeth Bowen; whereas fifteen years later, Trevor McDonald, by virtue of having written a biography of Viv Richards, was more 'literary' than at least one of the other judges. I concluded that, for shortlisted candidates, 'the only sensible attitude to the Booker is to treat it as posh bingo. It is El Gordo, the Fat One, the sudden jackpot that enriches the plodding Andalusian muleteer.'

No one disputed this view at the time, and I soon forgot that I had voiced it. The Booker went on its plush and mystifying way. I had been shortlisted first in 1984, and again in each of the subsequent three decades, the last time in 2011. By then, something had changed in the world of journalism: digitisation. The LRB archive had become freely searchable, and after nearly a quarter of a century my quip about 'posh bingo' suddenly resurfaced. So that's what he really thought about it! Happy to be shortlisted, but never taken it seriously! Bingo Barnes briefly became my nickname. I admit to having had a twinge that the 2011 judges might be adversely affected by such levity. I also reflected on the way a literary career often gets reduced in journalistic terms to one or two seemingly key questions. In my own case: 1. Are you and Martin Amis still talking? (yes); and 2. You called the Booker 'posh bingo', didn't you? (yes).

Prize night came round; to my equal pleasure and relief I won, thereby not turning into a version of five-time 'loser' Beryl Bainbridge (whose entire writing life was often simplified down into 'always the Booker bridesmaid, never the bride'). Twenty minutes after receiving the cheque, I was sitting next to Stella Rimington, chair of the judges, at a press conference. I was hardly unprepared for a question about Martin Amis. Or another about Posh Bingo. Wearily, I tried to explain one last time. It's like this: you start writing a novel, thinking of nothing else, not knowing when you will finish it, or if it will be any good; you have no idea who else in the Anglophone world is also writing a novel, how good it will be, and when it will be published; you also have no idea who the judges will be a year, or two, or three, ahead. What other sensible attitude to it all is there except that of the Andalusian muleteer? I had already – for at least the previous twenty minutes – been a considerable fan of Dame Stella; but my esteem was magnified when she leaned into her microphone and commented: 'That's all perfectly true.'

Julian Barnes

DIARY   — 24pt Rankin bad   (PRIORITY)   for this issue

BARNES - 1

In Madrid the other week ~~I was told~~ a literary journalist told me the following joke. ~~From a journalist on El País.~~ A man goes into a pet shop and sees three parrots side by side, ~~one~~ priced at $1000, ~~one at~~ $2000 and ~~one at~~ $3000. 'Why does that parrot cost $1000?' he asks the owner. 'Because it can recite the whole of the Bible in Spanish,' ~~is~~ comes the reply. 'And why does that one cost $2000?' 'Because it can recite recite the whole of the Bible in English and in Spanish.' 'And the one that costs $3000, what does he ~~say?~~ recite?' 'Oh, he ~~can't~~ ~~speak~~ doesn't say a word,' explains the pet shop ~~says the~~ owner: 'but the other two call him Maestro.'

This made me think, naturally enough, ~~of the case~~ of E.M. Forster; and then ~~also~~ of the fact that we were about the undergo the annual garrulity of the Booker Prize for Fiction. Would Forster have won the Booker? In 1905, when he published Where Angels Fear to Tread, he would have been up against ~~such varied contenders~~ not to mention more populist contenders like ~~as~~ Kipps, The Scarlet Pimpernel, and Mrs Humphry Ward's The Marriage of William Ashe. In 1910 Howard's End might have run into Clayhanger, ~~or~~ and (Wells again) The History of Mr Polly; ~~and~~ perhaps the Antipodean outsider Henry Handel Richardson ~~might~~ would have scooped it with The Getting of Wisdom. In 1924 ~~his~~ Forster's publishers might have thought they had a real chance with ~~Forster's~~ his big one, A Passage to India. ~~But it was a tough year: no Wells to dog him, at least, but~~ For once, Wells wasn't dogging him: but there was Maurice Baring's C, Ford's Some Do Not, Masefield's Sard Harker, Mottram's The Spanish Farm, plus various dangerous ~~floating outsiders~~ floaters like The Constant Nymph, The Inimitable Jeeves and even (if it was to be a year for the booksellers) Mary Webb's Precious Bane. ~~There are many barriers with these words.~~ ~~But it would be a mistake to look too closely~~ Still, the mistake, then as now, is to look at the books themselves. When literary editors pen ~~their~~ those overnight pieces on the Booker shortlist and lament the omissions - where was McEwan? where was Boyd? where was Amis? and the other Amis? - they are ~~looking at~~ examining the candidates (not all of whom they can possibly have read) rather than ~~the~~ the judges. If I were Mr Ron Pollard of Ladbrokes (whose odds have got a great deal meaner since the days when some of us cleaned up on Salman Rushdie at 14-1), I would ~~not even bother to read the~~ give only cursory attention to the books on

First page of the typescript of Julian Barnes's Diary,
published in the issue of 12 November 1987

All the Versuses of Life

Tony Harrison's *V.*, written after he visited his parents' grave and found the stone covered in graffiti, was first published in the *LRB*, in 1985. A review by Denis Donoghue of two volumes of Harrison's poems appeared in the next issue. Harrison complained to Karl Miller that he didn't understand the review. 'Getting understandable discussions of new poetry is becoming beyond me,' Miller replied. 'I cheer myself up by thinking that you will be sending some more of yours.' The most recent of them, 'Polygons', was published in 2015 as a two-page spread, just as *V.* had been thirty years before.

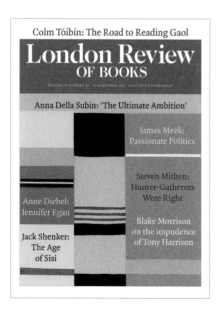

The Authentic Snarl

Blake Morrison

WHEN people are offended by brutally direct forms of writing, chances are it'll be the ideas they're objecting to as much as the words. That was certainly the case in the furore over Richard Eyre's film version of Tony Harrison's poem *V.* when it was shown on Channel Four with none of its expletives deleted. Campaigners against the film claimed to be horrified by its vulgar tongue but the vulgarity of the author's origins and politics were no less an issue. 'The riff-raff takes over,' the Tory MP Sir Gilbert Longden complained, while to his colleague Gerald Howarth it was a case of 'another probable Bolshie poet seeking to impose his frustrations on the rest of us'. Just as Harrison's English teacher wouldn't allow him to impose his low-life Yorkshire accent on Keats, so right-wing newspapers and Conservative MPs wanted to prevent him from upsetting viewers with rude words about class division, youth unemployment and the miners' strike.

In the film the poet plays himself – a bard among gravestones – with aplomb: if that English teacher had let his pupil speak more than four words he might have recognised Harrison's gift for performance. All his plays are in verse and much of his poetry is theatrical: *V.* is a dialogue between the poet and his alter ego, the skinhead who is his second skin, the lad on benefits he might have been if he hadn't had the benefits of an education. When Harrison mentions his poetry, his rival self, a graffiti artist, is scornful: 'Who needs/yer fucking poufy words. Ah write mi own./Ah've got mi work on show all over Leeds.' And when Harrison speculates that such graffiti are a cri de coeur, the response is contemptuous:

So what's a cri-de-coeur, cunt? Can't you speak
The language that yer mam spoke. Think of 'er!
Can yer only get yer tongue round fucking Greek?
Go and fuck yerself with cri-de-coeur!

Though a two-hander of sorts, a monologue disguised as a duologue, *V.* is also an elegy: for his parents, for childhood, for a time when gravestones weren't vandalised. Coleridge described elegy as 'a form of poetry natural to the reflective mind', with 'sorrow and love' its principal themes. The description fits Harrison's elegies, except that his disrupt the conventions of elegy, not just with the material they include – class, work, politics – but formally, through puns, dialect and hectic typography. Elegies are about loss but they're where Harrison found his true voice, grieving less for death than for the thwarted lives that precede it. Elegies are invariably pastoral but his are urban; *V.* doesn't come from a country churchyard but from a cemetery above a used-up pit. Elegies are supposed to be one-offs, like funeral addresses, but his are recurrent – *Continuous* is the title of one of his collections – and sometimes come in numbered parts and echo one another: his sonnet 'Divisions', for example (a quintessential Harrison title), includes the same props – skinhead haircuts, tattoos, football and aerosol-can graffiti – that later feature in *V.* Elegies look back but Harrison's also look forward: the first line of *V*, published in 1985, invokes the next millennium, now with us (in the poem Harrison imagines not making it past 2015). Elegies are sad and sometimes despairing but his are also angry: in *V.* he turns the anger on himself but closes the poem optimistically with the word UNITED and the 'v' of victory rather than the 'v' of versus.

Harrison's elegies are also acutely self-conscious. As well as the reflective mind, there's an eye on the mirror – and on the audience. Rather than pretending that we, as readers, have secretly gained access to the poet's private grief, his elegies remind us that they are public acts, or atefacts, and that he knows we're there: he watches himself watching us watching him. The laments for his parents are both heartfelt and heart-on-the-sleeve. 'I did then, and do now, choke back my tears,' he says in one poem.

*If mi mam's up there, don't want to meet 'er
listening to me list mi dirty deeds,
and 'ave to pipe up to St fucking Peter
ah've been on t'dole all mi life in fucking Leeds!*

*Then t'Alleluias stick in t'angels' gobs.
When dole-wallahs fuck off to the void
what 'll t'mason carve up for their jobs?
The cunts who lieth 'ere wor unemployed?*

*This lot worked at one job all life through.
Byron, 'Tanner', 'Lieth 'ere interred'
They'll chisel fucking poet when they do you
and that, yer cunt, 's a crude four-letter word.*

'Listen, cunt!' *I said,* 'before you start your jeering
the reason why I want this in a book
's to give ungrateful cunts like you a hearing!'
A book, yer stupid cunt, 's not worth a fuck!'

'The only reason why I write this poem at all
on yobs like you who do the dirt on death
's to give some higher meaning to your scrawl.'
Don't fucking bother, cunt! Don't waste your breath!'

'You piss-artist skinhead cunt, you wouldn't know
and it doesn't fucking matter if you do,
the skin and poet united fucking Rimbaud
but the *autre* that *je est* is fucking you.'

*Ah've told yer, no more Greek . . . That's yer last
    warning!
Ah'll boot yer fucking balls to Kingdom Come.
They'll find yer cold on t'grave tomorrer morning.
So don't speak Greek. Don't treat me like I'm dumb.*

'I've done my bits of mindless aggro too
not half a mile from where we're standing now.'
Yeah, ah bet yer wrote a poem, yer wanker you!
'No, shut yer gob a while. Ah'll tell yer 'ow . . .'

'Herman Darewski's band played operetta
with a wobbly soprano warbling. Just why
I made my mind up that I'd got to get her
with the fire hose I can't say, but I'll try.

It wasn't just the singing angered me.
At the same time half a crowd was jeering
as the smooth Hugh Gaitskell, our MP,
made promises the other half were cheering.

What I hated in those high soprano ranges
was uplift beyond all reason and control
and in a world where you say nothing changes
it seemed a sort of prick-tease of the soul.

I tell you when I heard high notes that rose
above Hugh Gaitskell's cool electioneering
straight from the warbling throat right up my nose
I had all your aggro in *my* jeering.

And I hit the fire extinguisher ON knob
and covered orchestra and audience with spray.
I could run as fast as you then. A good job!
They yelled 'damned vandal' after me that day . . .'

*And then yer saw the light and gave up 'eavy!
And knew a man's not how much he can sup . . .
Yer reward for growing up's this super-bevvy,
a meths and champagne punch in t'FA Cup.*

*Ah've 'eard all that from old farts past their prime.
'ow now yer live wi' all yer once detested . . .
Old farts with not much left 'll give me time.
Fuckers like that get folk like me arrested.*

*Covet not thy neighbour's wife, thy neighbour's riches.
Vicar and cop who say, to save our souls,
Get thee beHind me, Satan, drop their breeches
and get the Devil's dick right up their 'oles!*

It was more a *working* marriage that I'd meant,
a blend of masculine and feminine.
Ignoring me, he started looking, bent
on some more aerosolling, for his tin.

'It was more a *working* marriage that I mean!'
Fuck, and save mi soul, eh? That suits me.
Then as if I'd egged him on to be obscene
he added a middle slit to one daubed V.

*Don't talk to me of fucking representing
the class yer were born into any more.
Yer going to get 'urt and start resenting
it's not poetry we need in this class war.*

*Yer've given yerself toffee, cunt. Who needs
yer fucking poufy words. Ah write mi own.
Ah've got mi work on show all over Leeds
like this UNITED 'ere on some sod's stone.*

'OK!' (thinking I had him trapped) 'OK!'
'If you're so proud of it, then sign your name
when next you're full of HARP and armed with spray.,
next time you take this short cut from the game.'

He took the can, contemptuous, unhurried
and cleared the nozzle and prepared to sign
the UNITED sprayed where mam and dad were buried.
He aerosolled his name. And it was mine.

The boy footballers bawl *Here Comes the Bride*
and drifting blossoms fall onto my head.
One half of me 's alive but one half died
when the skin half sprayed my name among the dead.

Half versus half, the enemies within
the heart that can't be whole till they unite.
As I stoop to grab the crushed HARP lager tin
the day's already dusk, half dark, half light.

That UNITED that I'd wished onto the nation
or as reunion for dead parents soon recedes.
The word's once more a mindless desecration
by some HARPoholic yob supporting Leeds.

Almost the time for ghosts I'd better scram.
Though not given much to fears of spooky scaring
I don't fancy an encounter with my mam
playing Hamlet with me for this swearing.

Though I've a train to catch my step is slow.
I walk on the grass and graves with wary tread
over these subsidences, these shifts below
the life of Leeds supported by the dead.

Further underneath's that cavernous hollow
that makes the gravestones lean towards the town.
A matter of mere time and it will swallow
this place of rest and all the resters down.

I tell myself I've got, say, 30 years.
At 75 this place will suit me fine.
I've never feared the grave but what I fear's
that great worked-out black hollow under mine.

Not train departure time, and not Town Hall
with the great white clock face I can see,
coal, that began, with no man here at all,
as 300 million-year-old plant debris.

5 kids still play at making blossoms fall
and humming as they do *Here Comes the Bride.*
They never seem to tire of their ball
though I hear a woman's voice call one inside.

2 larking boys play bawdy bride and groom.
3 boys in Leeds strip la-la *Lohengrin.*
I hear them as I go through growing gloom
still years away from being skald or skin.

The ground's carpeted with petals as I throw
the aerosol, the HARP can, the cleared weeds
on top of dad's dead daffodils, then go,
with not one glance behind, away from Leeds.

The bus to the station's still the No 1
but goes by routes that I don't recognise.
I look out for known landmarks as the sun
reddens the swabs of cloud in darkening skies.

Home, home, home, to my woman as the red
darkens from a fresh blood to a dried.
Home, home to my woman, home to bed
where opposites seem sometimes unified.

A pensioner in turban taps his stick
along the pavement past the corner shop,
that sells samosas now, not beer on tick,
to the Kashmir Muslim Club that was the Co-op.

House after house FOR SALE where we'd played
                                                cricket
with white roses cut from flour-sacks on our caps,
with stumps chalked on the coal-grate for our wicket,
and every one bought now by 'coloured chaps',

dad's most liberal label as he felt
squeezed by the unfamiliar, and fear
of foreign food and faces, when he smelt
curry in the shop where he'd bought beer.

And growing frailer, 'wobbly on his pins',
the shops he felt familiar with withdrew
which meant much longer tiring treks for tins
that had a label on them that he knew.

And as the shops that stocked his favourites receded
whereas he'd fancied beans and popped next door,
he found that four long treks a week were needed
till he wondered what he bothered eating for.

The supermarket made him feel embarrassed.
Where people bought whole lambs for family freezers
he bought baked beans from check-out girls too harassed
to smile or swap a joke with sad old geezers.

But when he bought his cigs he'd have a chat,
his week's one conversation, truth to tell,
but time also came and put a stop to that
when old Wattsy got bought out by M. Patel.

And there, 'Time like an ever rolling stream' 's
what I once trilled behind that boarded front.
A 1000 ages made coal-bearing seams
and even more the hand that sprayed this CUNT

on both Methodist and C of E billboards
once divided in their fight for local souls.
Whichever house more truly was the Lord's
both's pews are filled with cut-price toilet rolls.

Home, home to my woman, never to return
till sexton or survivor has to cram
the bits of clinker scooped out of my urn
down through the rose-roots to my dad and mam.

Home, home to my woman, where the fire's lit
these still chilly mid-May evenings, home to you,
and perished vegetation from the pit
escaping insubstantial up the flue.

Listening to *Lulu*, in our hearth we burn,
as we hear the high Cs rise in stereo,
what was lush swamp club-moss and tree-fern
at least 300 million years ago.

Shilbottle cobbles, Alban Berg high D
lifted from a source that bears your name,
the one we hear decay, the one we see,
the fern from the foetid forest, as brief flame.

This world, with far too many people in,
starts on the TV logo as a taw,
then ping-pong, tennis, football; then one spin
to show us all, then shots of the Gulf War.

As the coal with reddish dust cools in the grate
on the late-night national news we see
police v. pickets at a coke-plant gate,
old violence and old disunity.

The map that's colour-coded Ulster/Eire's
flashed on again as almost every night.
Behind a tiny coffin with two bearers
men in masks with arms show off their might.

The day's last images recede to first a glow
and then a ball that shrinks back to blank screen.
Turning to love, and sleep's oblivion, I know
what the UNITED that the skin sprayed *has* to mean.

Hanging my clothes up, from my parka hood
may and apple petals, browned and creased,
fall onto the carpet and bring back the flood
of feelings their first falling had released.

I hear like ghosts from all Leeds matches humming
with one concerted voice the bride, the bride
I feel united to, *my* bride is coming
into the bedroom, naked, to my side.

The ones we choose to love become our anchor
when the hawser of the blood-tie's hacked, or frays.
But a voice that scorns chorales is yelling: *Wanker!*
It's the aerosolling skin I met today's.

My *alter ego* wouldn't want to know it,
his aerosol vocab would baulk at LOVE,
the skin's UNITED underwrites the poet,
the measures carved below the ones above.

I doubt if 30 years of bleak Leeds weather
and 30 falls of apple and of may
will erode the UNITED binding us together.
And now it's your decision: does it stay?

Next millennium you'll have to search quite hard
to find out where I'm buried but I'm near
the grave of haberdasher Appleyard,
the pile of HARPs, or some new neonned beer.

Find Byron, Wordsworth, or turn left between
one grave marked Broadbent, one marked
                                        Richardson.
Bring some solution with you that can clean
whatever new crude words have been sprayed on.

If love of art, or love, gives you affront
that the grave I'm in's graffitied then, maybe,
erase the more offensive FUCK and CUNT
but leave, with the worn UNITED, one small v.

Victory? For vast, slow, coal-creating forces
that hew the body's seams to get the soul.
Will Earth run out of her 'diurnal courses'
before repeating her creation of black coal?

But choose a day like I chose in mid-May
or earlier when apple and hawthorn tree,
no matter if boys boot their ball all day,
cling to their blossoms and won't shake them free.

If, having come this far, somebody reads
these verses, and he/she wants to understand,
face this grave on Beeston Hill, your back to Leeds,
and read the chiselled epitaph I've planned:

*Beneath your feet's a poet, then a pit.
Poetry supporter, if you're here to find
how poems can grow from (beat you to it!) SHIT
find the beef, the beer, the bread, then look behind.*

London Review of Books, 24 January 1985 13

Nice One, Ian

Diary

Ian Hamilton

Christopher Tayler writes: When the cash-strapped *New Review* went under in 1979, the LRB inherited some reference books and a scattering of office furniture. It also inherited the critical voice of the *New Review*'s much mythologised editor, Ian Hamilton, who was a very good friend of the paper and wrote regularly for it until his death in 2001. Hamilton, a gifted, terse and unprolific poet, had been known in the 1960s for his 'sizzling assassinations', as he termed Randall Jarrell's efforts in this direction, of those he saw as charlatans, slackers and phoners-in. His first piece for the paper made fun of C.P. Snow; another went a few rounds with Norman Mailer; and now and then he exhibited, not wholly without pride, the scars from his roughhousing days. (Donald Davie, Hamilton notes in one piece, wrote to an acolyte: 'Death to Ian Hamilton and all his works.') But asperity isn't the dominant flavour of his contributions, which give literary history the immediacy and humour of high-quality pub gossip. And he was alert to the poetry of pop culture. He wouldn't have minded if the poet laureateship had gone to Snoop Dogg, or even 'Snoop's dogg, should he possess one', and, as a lifelong Spurs fan, slipped a riff on the phrase 'Nice one, Cyril' into an assessment of Cyril Connolly's career.

TODAY, Live Soccer returns to 'our screens' after a six-month haggle between TV and the Football League. The jaunty build-up – our old buddy welcomed back, our prized weekend routines restored – ought to discover an answering jauntiness in us. It doesn't, though. How could it? After all, the last time most of us witnessed Live Soccer on TV it was Juventus versus Liverpool in Brussels.

On the night of the Brussels disaster, and for several days thereafter, my disposition was to defend 'the game' against sermonisers who seemed to be cashing in on what had happened: people who hated football anyway and wouldn't at all mind if it were blown away. I would point out to them that the set-up at the Heysel stadium was 'at least partly to blame', that you could go to football matches every week in England without running into any 'really bad' passages of violence. And yet there is this lingering unease, this feeling that 'business-as-usual' is being announced a bit too soon, a bit too eagerly.

At my own team, Spurs, the gates are down this year by some ten thousand – that's to say, 25 per cent – and they now stand at a lower average figure than at any time I can remember. The few stay-aways I've been able to consult all speak of something temporary, a mild dis-affection that will surely pass. It's not that they won't carry on preferring soccer to most other things. At the moment, though, the separation between it and those 'other things' doesn't feel quite so magically, or childishly, clear-cut as it did half a dozen months ago.

Out of habit, I battled my way to White Hart Lane on the first day of the season, expecting to savour the ten-year-old's sensations I've been savouring for thirty years . . . This August, though, the whole thing was quite different. Even before the game started, I felt sour, irritable, out-of-it – a bit *literary*, I suppose you could say. The yobs on the Shelf were grunting the same old thicko war-chants. A year ago, I might have smiled frostily and thought 'Ah, well . . .' This year, I felt the urge to climb up there and give them a quick blast of further educ-ation. And when the players trotted out,

peacocking in their new tans and hair-styles and waving to the yobs as if they liked them . . . it had to be confessed that, if you looked hard enough, there was something a bit yobbish about *them*, also. Even their new shirts – featuring a grotesque semiotic punch-up between Holstein and Hummel, and with just a touch of blouson at the shoulder – seem-ed to proclaim their dumb servitude to the bejewelled young directors who were even now filing into the West Stand. And just look at the West Stand – those glass-faced boxes in which, thanks to an urgent application to the local magis-trates, 'business parties' could escape the government's post-Brussels liquor ban. The game, the season, was kicking off, and here I was, longing to go home.

And so I did, and stayed there for three months. Until last week . . . I went again, this time to Highbury on New Year's Day, for Arsenal v. Spurs. Since this is the key grudge match of the year, I ought to have known better; on the other hand there was this feeling that the likes of Ardiles ought not to be neg-lected for too long. As it turned out, he played beautifully, and after about half an hour I was beginning to feel some of the old tension and contentment. Then Graham Roberts struck. With the ball nowhere in sight, Spurs's neanderthal defender followed through on Charlie Nicholas with such force that the Scot was hurtled over the groundside hoard-ings into about the fifth row of the con-crete enclosure. He was lucky to escape without a broken back. Within seconds of impact, as if some huge lever had been pulled, the Spurs fans lurched into song: 'There's only one Graham Roberts,' with accompanying solo barks of 'Kill him next time' and 'I hope the wanker's dead.' And this carried on for the next sixty or so minutes, swelling in volume and ferocity whenever Nicholas went near the ball – which wasn't often. At the whistle, Roberts showed his grat-itude by lingering on the pitch, his arms aloft: the bloodstained conqueror. So much, then, for aesthetics. And so much for my comeback. I just hope I feel better in time for the World Cup.

7 point caps

~~Ian Hamilton~~

8/10 pt.

Sir: The London Review doesn't have, or intend to seek, an Arts Council subsidy. This means that the envious, the indolent, the mischievous must, if they wish to be *am* damaging, take issue with the journal itself, and not with the way it is financed. Most writers believe that they are (or, given the chance, could be) terrific editors, and they are particularly contemptuous of the skills that go into par producing journals from which their own works are excluded. Arts Council grants, I've come to see, make it all too easy for the whimper of neglect to masquerade as public-spirited dismay. The London Review won't have to get annoyed about this kind of thing.

41   It will have other things to get annoyed about, but many of these can be seen as pretty well routine: the publishers will be cag*ey*, the librarians won't want to know, the backbiters will go on about elitism, metropolitant cliquishness, lack of compassion for the avant-garde, the sycophants will wait and see. The appalling thing about our 'literary culture' at the xxxxx moment is that a large section of its representatives seem to get more of a kick out ag of seeing things collapse than they do out of seeing them survive. Sooner or later (and I would like to think that (this) might be the moment) they must ask themselves if they really do want another serious reviewing journal; or if, in their heart of hearts, they prefer to xxx sit around complaining that they haven't got one.

Ian Hamilton →

Bold upper.

Roman

Miss Susanna Clapp   As from   ███████
The London Review.   ███████

Oxford OX9
6QS

13ᵗʰ June 1988

Dear Sirs,
        The article printed by you
and written by John Ryle begins ....
        This is hogwash. The word
AIDS is probably the cruellest silliest
neologism of our time.
        "Aid" means "help" "succour"
"comfort" _ yet with a hissing, sibilant
tacked on to it, it becomes a nightmare.
It should never be used in front of patients.
HIV virus (Human Immuno-defficiency
virus) is a perfectly easy name to live
with. A.I.D.S. causes panic & despair
_ has probably done more to facil.late
the spread of the disease than any
other factor.
        In France, not even M. Le Pen
could do much with Le S.I.D.A., he
had a go, but was made to look
totally ridiculous.   I

Letter to the editor from Bruce Chatwin,
13 June 1988 (continued overleaf)

Not Some Gay Götterdämmerung

In his letter to the LRB, Bruce Chatwin left it to the editors to supply the section of John Ryle's review of three books about Aids, published in May 1988, that had offended him. The opening paragraph began, 'There is no good news about Aids,' and continued: 'the majority of [HIV-infected individuals] – possibly all of them – will eventually develop Aids and die.' Chatwin's response, like Ryle's essay, is a product of its time: next to no progress had been made in finding a cure since the arrival of Aids at the start of the decade, and the death toll was ticking up, especially in Britain, where the epidemic was slower to take off than in the United States. But whereas Ryle prophesied that Aids, like other plagues, would leave behind 'a smaller, more resistant population' and gave the projected death rates for the year 2000, barring 'unprecedentedly rapid progress in the development of a vaccine', Chatwin was more optimistic, even foolishly so. It turned out he was right to stress that people could be HIV-positive for long periods without developing Aids and so shouldn't give up hope, and right to predict that a 'cure will be found' (though the 'cure', announced in 1996, suppresses the disease rather than eradicating it).

Chatwin died of Aids seven months after writing his letter. It's not just hindsight that makes it seem full of barely repressed frustration. But we know now what readers didn't know then: that Chatwin was infected. He never publicised his diagnosis; he told all but a few close friends that he was suffering from a strange disease previously only detected in ten Chinese peasants and the corpse of a killer whale, or one picked up from a Chinese egg. It's sad, though not unusual, that he felt unable to be honest, perhaps because he had never publicly admitted to his bisexuality, though that wasn't unusual either. His relationship with the truth became ever more ambiguous as his health deteriorated and his medication levels increased: he writes as a member of the Oxford Team for Research into Infectious Tropical Diseases, which didn't exist.

Tom Crewe

HIV is not some gay Gotterdamerung. It is another African virus, a very dangerous one, presenting the greatest challenge to medical science since tuberculosis, but one for which a cure will be found.

Any virus, be it measles, mumps or chicken-pox will create a "mirror image" of itself, known as an "antibody" which in time will stabilise the infected person.

That should be the pattern. But H IV. is a very slippery customer. There is no positive evidence of antibodies at work, only negative evidence that a great many infected people are alive. In one case in the U.S. an infected person suddenly became HIV negative.

We should, in fact, take Mr Ryle's own figures

At this moment, there are 800,000 infected persons in the United States, of whom 80,000 have died

That means nine survivors to one death.

II

This can mean one thing:
that some mechanism, pharmaceutical
or otherwise, is keeping them alive.
   One point cannot be emphasised
too strongly. An infected person
must never use anyone else's
tooth brush. We all have gingivitis
(bleeding gums) from time to time
+ this is a way of infecting another
person.
   What is so horrifying about Mr
Ryle's article is the callous cruelty
with which he condemns hundreds
of thousands of people to death.
   If a young man, who has just
been told that he is H.I.V. positive,
got hold of the article, the chances are he
might commit suicide. There have been many
such cases.
   Mr Ryle's article, written in a high
pontificatory tone, is a disgrace to your
columns.
                 Yours Bruce Chatwin
            sincerely
                          BRUCE CHATWIN
Member of the Oxford Team for Research
into Tropical + other Infectious Diseases
   Oxford University   III

New-Fangled Foreign Nonsense

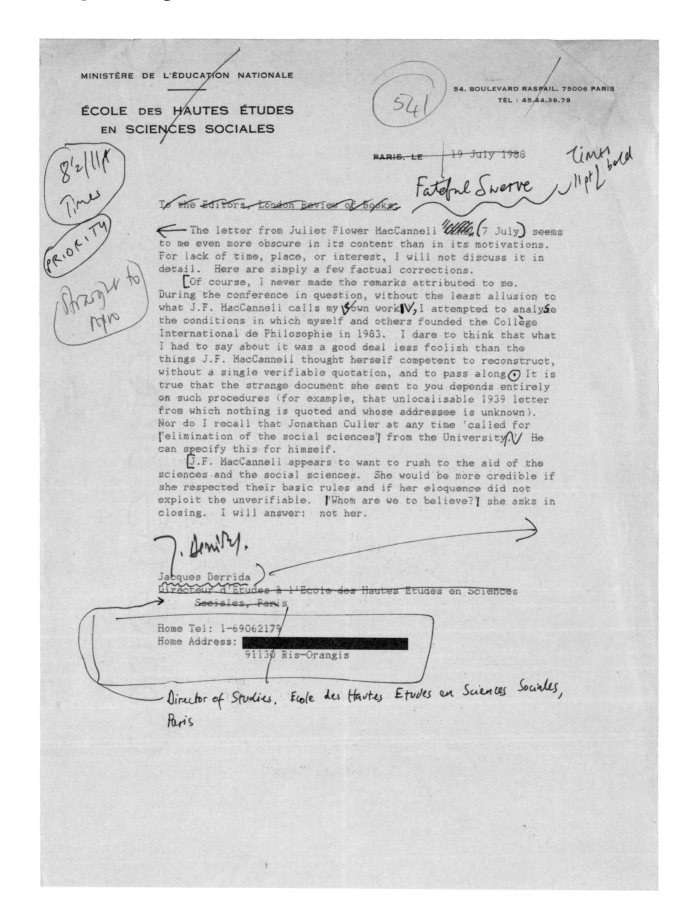

'Literary theory,' Frank Kermode remarked in the *LRB* of 7 May 1981, 'is somewhat bewilderingly in the news.' When the paper was established in 1979, with Kermode as one of its founding intelligences, the 'theory wars' were much on his mind. The open seminar he ran at University College London in the late 1960s and early 1970s had been the main channel through which fresh ideas from France – structuralism in particular, and subsequent developments in criticism (Barthes), philosophy (Derrida), psychoanalysis (Lacan), history (Foucault) and Marxism (Althusser) – were imported into the study of literature in Britain. In 1974 Kermode was appointed top dog in the English faculty at Cambridge, at a time when there were moves, partly inspired by the word from Paris, to shake up the undergraduate curriculum. Sides were taken, manifestos issued; the national papers made the most of the infighting. In Cambridge, matters came to a head – this was the 'news' Kermode was referring to – when one of the most energetic of the would-be revolutionaries, Colin MacCabe, was refused tenure. Kermode left for America shortly afterwards.

'It really takes an English reviewer,' Kermode, at his testiest, wrote later that year about the treatment in other papers of an inoffensive primer on structuralism by David Lodge, 'to suggest that this whole movement of thought . . . is a load of new-fangled foreign nonsense.' What were his colleagues fretting about? On the face of it, that if the militants had their way, the foundations of traditional literary interpretation would be torn up and abandoned. Karl Miller himself came out against the trend in his editorial statement in the first issue of the *LRB*: 'We are not in favour of the current fashion for the "deconstruction" of literary texts, for the elimination of the author from his work.' Whether or not that is indeed what 'deconstruction' entailed – John Sturrock, who later came to work for the paper, and, like Kermode, never allowed his curiosity about literary theory to disturb either his interpretative confidence or the limpidity of his prose, insisted in a letter to the *LRB* in 1980 that deconstruction did not 'evacuate meaning from the text . . . it adds to that meaning by showing at what point the writer has failed to be aware of his own presuppositions' – it can be conceded that no one starts a literary magazine with the idea of dismissing the author from the scene altogether.

In the event, the *LRB* published scores of articles about 'theory' during its first ten years. It is notable that most of the nuance and judicious writing is on the side of the open-minded – Kermode and Sturrock; Christopher Norris too – while the temper, the sneering and a casual way with the truth is all with the antis. They appear embattled, as the powers that be sometimes can appear when trouble stirs at the margins. A low point is reached in 1985 when two of the victors in the Cambridge fracas, Christopher Ricks and Eric Griffiths, are given the freedom, on facing pages, to gleefully tramp the dirt down – in Griffiths's case, in a piece as spiteful as it was unnecessary, on MacCabe himself. One has the sense, reading some of this stuff, that what really got at the

antis wasn't the threat to the status of the author, or to some cherished notion of truth in interpretation, but to the critic himself, and his freedom to respond to literature guided only by his own finer sensibility.

There was better to come. Literary theory was in the news again in 1987, when it was discovered that Paul de Man, the most fêted of all deconstructionist literary critics, had written antisemitic articles for a Nazi-supported newspaper during the Second World War. The antis were quick to seize the moment: it was surely unsurprising that an author wanting to relinquish responsibility for his own utterances would cleave to a theory that allowed him to do just that. Those arguments were not made in the *LRB*. Christopher Norris rose to the occasion, and Kermode rose even higher, with subtle meditations on the complexities of the relationship between writing and biography.

Eventually the fuss died down, and in universities literary theory was absorbed into the history of ideas in English that every first-year undergraduate takes on board. The *LRB* has continued, more sporadically, to carry writing about theory, though very little theoretical writing. (Pierre Bourdieu may have thought he had common cause with the *LRB* when he asked the paper to support *Liber* (see overleaf), but the only time he appeared in the magazine, in 1980, it was with a brisk note about Sartre that shared little with the densities of his most famous work, published the year before, *Distinction: A Social Critique of the Judgment of Taste*.) The *LRB* closed the book on the theory wars proper with a piece from John Sturrock in 1998 about Alan Sokal, a physics professor in the US who felt he had landed a knockout blow for the antis by sneaking his pastiche of postmodern jargon into an academic journal of cultural studies. On the contrary, John concluded, it was 'a hoax barely worth the perpetration'.

Paul Myerscough

CENTRE DE SOCIOLOGIE EUROPÉENNE

DU COLLÈGE DE FRANCE ET DE L'ÉCOLE DES HAUTES ÉTUDES EN SCIENCES SOCIALES

Paris, le 18 juillet 1991

Madame Mary Kay Wilmers
55 Gloucester Crescent

Londres NW1
Grande-Bretagne

Chère Mary Kay Wilmers,

Pardonnez-moi de faire ainsi irruption. Robbin Blackburn
m'a suggéré de prendre contact avec vous pour voir si vous
pourriez être intéressée par une publication éventuelle
(totale ou partielle) de Liber dans le London Review of Books.
Je ne voulais pas prendre contact avec vous avant de pouvoir
vous donner un exemple de ce que nous voulons faire : vous
trouverez ci-joint les épreuves.

Il va de soi que si vous étiez disposée à participer, nous
serions prêts à vous associer à la conception et à la
préparation des numéros.

Je suis à Paris jusqu'au lundi 22 juillet. Vous pouvez
m'appeler au téléphone soit chez moi (42.77.23.57), soit à mon
bureau, si vous voulez que nous ayons une discussion sur notre
possible collaboration.

Yours sincerely,

Pierre Bourdieu

52, RUE DU CARDINAL LEMOINE · 75231 PARIS DEDEX 05   TÉL. (1) 45 27 18 40
FAX (1) 44 27 18 52

Letter from Pierre Bourdieu to Mary-Kay Wilmers,
18 July 1991

Translation:

Dear Mary-Kay Wilmers,

Please excuse the unsolicited approach. Robin Blackburn suggested I get in touch to see if you might be interested in *Liber* possibly appearing (in part or in whole) inside the *London Review of Books*. I didn't want to write before I was able to give you a sense of what we want to do: you'll find examples attached.

It goes without saying that if you were interested, we would be happy for you to be involved in the planning and preparation of each issue.

I'm in Paris until Monday 22 July. You can call me at home or at my office if you'd like to discuss the idea of collaborating.

Yours sincerely,
Pierre Bourdieu

London Review of Books

Tavistock House South, Tavistock Square,
London WC1H 9JZ
Editorial: 071-388 6751   Advertising: 0359 42375
Distribution: 071-388 7487   Fax: 071-383 4792

Bord.

```
Pierre Bordieu,
Centre de Sociologie Europeenne,
Du College de France et de L'Ecole
des Hautes Etudes en Sciences Sociales,
52 Rue du Cardinal Lemoine - 75231,
Paris Dedex 05.

22 August 1991

Dear Pierre Bourdieu,

I am flattered by your suggestion that the LRB
should become the English component of Liber.
The idea that Liber represents is admirable and
editorially it would be a challenge.  However, I
must say straight out that we couldn't possibly
join you because we could not afford to.  We have
neither the human nor the financial resources to
take on something the size of Liber in addition to
what we do already; nor any plausible source of
subsidy.

I am sorry to decline your invitation so bluntly
but the reasons are compelling, as I'm sure you'll
understand.

With best wishes.

Yours sincerely



Mary-Kay Wilmers
```

Letter from Mary-Kay Wilmers to Pierre Bourdieu,
22 August 1991

Happy Accidents

John Lanchester writes: Now that files come into the LRB electronically and are typeset electronically, and spellchecking is a thing, typos, in the purest sense of spelling mistakes, are happily rare. People don't know just how much hand-to-hand combat was involved in keeping typos and similar mistakes out of print in the days when everything was typeset by hand. Just occasionally, though, the accidents would work out well. There were historic precedents for this. In Auden's 'Journey to Iceland', a typographical error created one of the poem's most memorable lines: 'the ports have names for the sea'. Auden had originally written 'poets' but he thought the typo was better, so he kept it. I read about that as a graduate student and always loved the romance of it, the serendipity – like the moment when Joyce was dictating *Finnegans Wake* to Beckett, and at one point said 'Come in,' and when Beckett read the passage back to Joyce he liked the effect so much that he retained it.

It was a great thrill to live through an LRB version of the same experience, courtesy of one of Hugo Williams's poems about Sunny Jim. Williams wrote that Jim 'rewinds his alarm clock for another working day'. A typesetter – in those days the process was done out-of-house – set that as 'reminds'. We sent the proof to Williams and corrected the mistake on our galleys, but then when the proof came back Williams had gone with 'reminds' and changed the rest of the line. Feeling a bit sheepish, I rang him up to apologise and explain that we would change it back, but he just laughed, said he'd realised what happened, but thought the idea of Jim reminding his alarm clock of work was so much in character that he wanted to keep it.

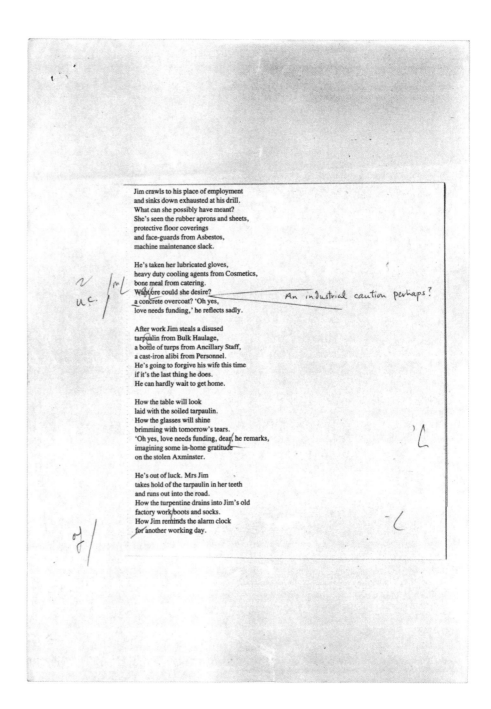

Marked-up proof of 'The Apotheosis of Sunny Jim' by Hugo Williams, published in the issue of 22 June 1989

█████████
London N1 8NW
25 5 07

Dear Mary-Kay,

        I took note of your comment about
the last line of my poem "As Good as New" which
you took last October. I realised that this was
a too personal reference and I am grateful to you
for pointing it out. I have now re-written the
end of the poem, which I enclose for your approval.

                Best wishes,

                    Hugo

                Hugo Williams

Well that's fine. It's
one we didn't take
when we published
his father poems
but it isn't enough
on its own; we could
ask for more?

Letter from Hugo Williams to Mary-Kay Wilmers,
25 May 2007

Unhappy Accidents

Andrew O'Hagan writes: 'While doing things, or in the interstices between doing things,' Paul Keegan wrote in his introduction to *The Psychopathology of Everyday Life*, 'we do other, less obvious things.' When the *LRB* doesn't like something, it can show it without showing it, and the results can be called accidents, or just editing. For instance, the paper now and then finds it difficult to like the last line of poems. They are often too 'last-line-y'; Karl Miller once told me they were 'unnecessarily plangent'. On one occasion he asked me to ring a young poet and tell him we liked his poem and wanted to publish it, but hated the last line. I remember it included the phrase 'the musak of the spheres'. The poet was outraged, but, desiring to be published, sniffed and told us to go ahead if we must. Patricia Beer, a contributor to the paper since its first issues, never forgot the mutilation of her poem 'Cockcrow'. She told me that seeing it on the page was one of the two worst things that ever happened to her, the other being the burning down of her thatched cottage in Devon.

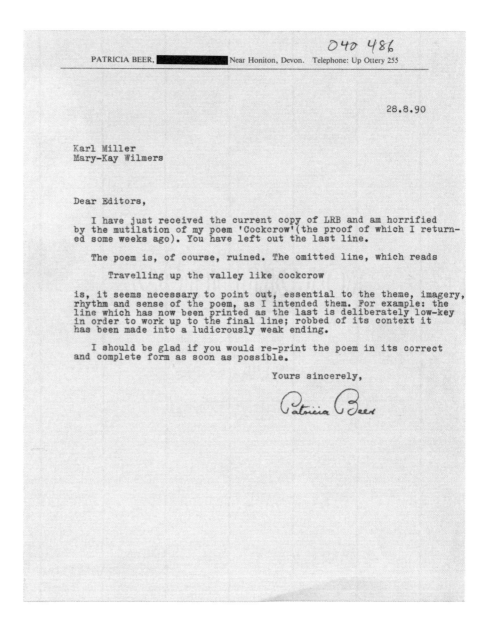

Letter from Patricia Beer to Karl Miller and Mary-Kay Wilmers, 28 August 1990

main theme of Heller's book – the fate of poetry and of the creative imagination in an age of prose – by briefly retracing its argument from Goethe through Nietzsche and Jacob Burckhardt to Rilke, Spengler, Karl Kraus and Kafka: and concluded by commending the book to 'everyone who cares for the survival of literature and of human values. The condition it describes is our condition, and I can think of no other modern book in which it is described so clearly.'

In the event, *The Disinherited Mind* turned out to be a critical landmark. It established or at least consolidated a canon of modern German literature; it helped to introduce this literature into many university courses from which it had so far been excluded; and it was one of the first books to succeed in overcoming an English-speaking public's understandable weariness with 'the German problem'. It made German and Austrian literary and philosophical thought available by means of a critical argument subtly balanced between the particular nature of that thought, and its roots in the European civilisation which Hitler's Germany had brought to the brink of destruction. Beginning with that book, and continued throughout Heller's many subsequent writings, goes his illuminating dialogue with Nietzsche: the present welcome collection of ten essays on this most literary of philosophers constitutes a sort of stock-taking of Heller's critical achievement over almost four decades.

The first essay sets out 'the importance of Nietzsche' as the anticipator, first analyst and critic of nihilism; and nihilism (seen as 'the state of human beings and societies faced with the total eclipse of all values') follows – Nietzsche and Heller say: follows necessarily – 'the death of God'. In his succinct account of Nietzsche's war on Christianity, Heller connects it with his radical questioning of 'the Truth'. What is at issue in Nietzsche's polemics is not our capacity to attain certain knowledge of our place in the total scheme of things: it is the value, purpose and uses of truth itself that are being queried. Heller then asks what if anything we can take to be Nietzsche's actual beliefs – the Superman? the Eternal Recurrence of the Same? the aesthetic validation of all existence as a game? – and he follows Nietzsche through the paradoxes and contradictions entailed by these 'beliefs', on the one hand, and his inveterate suspicion of all 'believers' and of the ideology of 'belief' itself, on the other. From this introductory essay (of 1965) we proceed to two studies from *The Disinherited Mind*, 'Nietzsche and Goethe' and 'Burckhardt and Nietzsche' – the two great minds whom Nietzsche admired and at the same time suspected of harbouring a tragic vision of the human predicament which they preferred not to disclose but to ignore or hide in their work. 'Nietzsche, the Teacher of "Free Spirits"' (1986) returns to the 'relativism of truth' as the penultimate step to nihilism, while 'Zarathustra's Three Metamorphoses' – the camel, the lion and the child – considers the poetic and autobiographical aspects of Nietzsche's imagery. 'Rilke and Nietzsche', the most accomplished chapter of *The Disinherited Mind*, contains an excursus on 'Belief and Poetry' in the form of a challenging discussion with T.S. Eliot and his notion of poetry as 'the emotional equivalent of thought'. This essay was among the first and remains the most illuminating of the many studies in which critics have portrayed Rilke as 'the poet of a world of which the philosopher is Nietzsche'. The predicament of this world of modernity is described, in traditional metaphysical terms, as 'the loss of significant external reality'. In such a world, Heller writes:

> Neither Rilke nor Nietzsche praises the praiseworthy. They praise. They do not believe the believable. They believe. And it is the praising and believing itself that becomes praiseworthy and believable in the act of worship.

And again:

> It is a world in which the order of correspondence is violently disturbed . . . Good does no good and evil no harm. Terror and bliss are one. Life and death are the same. Lovers seek separation, not union. All the sweetness of the visible world is stored in invisible hives.

In this portrait, which is both deeply sympathetic and critical, Rilke ('the St Francis of the Will to Power') is not just the poet of a *religio intransitiva*, he is (with Nietzsche's help) its philosopher and theologian, too.

Throughout these essays, then, Nietzsche is presented as the critic of traditional metaphysics, but also as the last great, albeit negative, metaphysician. True, in Nietzsche's *Nachlass* there are notes toward a philosophy of perspectivism – a philosophy of 'becoming' and 'being-in-relationships' – which point toward a relativist critique of the metaphysics of traditional ontology. In these notes 'truth' figures merely as a matter of perspective, and it isn't even 'subjective' because (as Heller writes) 'the concept of "subject" is not a "given"; it is itself an interpretative invention.' At this point, we are told, Nietzsche himself 'resolutely crosses the frontier of nihilism'. Heller doesn't question Nietzsche's inference from 'perspectivism' to 'nihilism', from 'there are no facts, only interpretations' to 'everything is permitted' and anything goes because the central authority and sanction behind all action and all intentions has gone. Seeing that Nietzsche anticipated in a general way some of the disasters of our century (and took some pleasure in doing so), his 'prophecies' may be read as confirmations that the inference is valid; and to anyone querying its validity, Heller is likely to reply: 'Looking around at the world we live in, what more by way of proof do you want?' But it is Nietzsche's premise that is questionable, if only because it doesn't obey his own relativist injunction. 'The truth' surely is that, with its heavy ontological load and its insistence on the compensational psychology of 'two worlds', Nietzsche's is a very North German view of Christianity.

With this weight of a 'tragic' or at all events catastrophic understanding of the world on his mind, why did Nietzsche continue to write? In the last essay of this book Heller answers the question by describing 'Nietzsche's Terrors: Time and the Inarticulate' (1985) – that is, his 'desire to escape from transience, oblivion' and to wrench experience from the abyss of silence. It is hard to think of a writer who is free from such a desire. In Nietzsche's case it is so strong that it carries him into a jungle of contradictions, from which Heller undertakes to rescue him: what matters about Nietzsche's views (he writes) is not their content but their quality, not their consistency but their 'rank', and the 'rank' or authenticity of those who hold them; and this curious opinion Heller attributes not just to Nietzsche but, less justifiably, to Ludwig Wittgenstein.

The 'and' in the titles of several of these essays has of course more than one meaning. 'Yeats and Nietzsche' (1969), on the poet's marginal notes in his copy of a Nietzsche anthology, is an outstandingly successful example of an 'and' that implies not just a comparison but a powerful influence. In one essay, though, it might with advantage have been replaced by 'or': in spite of some highly illuminating overlappings, 'Wittgenstein and Nietzsche' (1965) opens the view on two very different approaches to philosophy. To start with the 'family resemblances': both philosophers distrust 'categorical' certainties, and both have a genius for peering 'into the most unsuspected hiding places of error and fallacy'. They share an interest in the relationship of language and experience, though for Nietzsche (but not for Wittgenstein) it is one 'interest' among many. And both rebut the assertions of ontology (which for Nietzsche, though not for Wittgenstein, includes Christian 'ontology') by affirming that our existence in the world is to be understood not in the abstract isolation in which Idealist philosophers placed it, but contextually, as 'being-in-relationships'. But here, I think, we come to a difference that outweighs all resemblances. Even where Nietzsche avoids connecting the absence of categorical certainties with the descent into nihilism, he does little to suggest what an alternative 'philosophy of contexts' would be like. The later Wittgenstein, on the other hand, examines the many ways a language – the paradigm of contexts – actually functions, instancing the kind of certainties we live by: in all his philosophical writings after 1929 Wittgenstein looks at the ways we establish and sustain the meaningful experiences in which and by which we live. He neither seeks nor misses a transcendent Value outside the world, but shows the relationships of values to usage and usefulness, always on the assumption, which he shares with the poets, that there is only one language, 'the language of everyday'; and that 'if the words "language", "experience", "world" have a use, it must be as humble as the use of the words "table", "lamp, "door".'

Such arguments are of no interest to Nietzsche, and they don't thrill Heller either. He singles out for critical attention Wittgenstein's aperçu, 'To imagine a language is to imagine a form of life.' The attempt to describe such a form of life (Heller objects) 'sets a task that could not be fulfilled by a legion of Prousts or Wittgensteins: for what is the "form of life" which, in any one language, is shared by Goethe and Hitler. . . ?' Well, anyone who has waded through the morass of historical analyses which purport to show 'the straight line that leads from Luther (or Goethe, or Nietzsche) to Hitler' will agree with Heller's refusal to contemplate such a flagrant abstraction. But seen in its context, Wittgenstein's 'form of life' is not open to this interpretation. On the contrary, in the argument of which it is an integral part, image after image is arrayed to show that the phrase 'form of life' designates not a monolithic concept at all but a complex of family resemblances which have no common denominator and no single thing in common – a complex of relationships which is useful nevertheless, 'for a particular purpose', as an answer to a particular question. I cannot think of a question in answer to which a statement of what Goethe and Hitler have in common would make any tolerable sense. But there is nothing implausible about, say, a history of ideas describing a 'form of life' – a changing concept – which stretches throughout the hundred years from Goethe to Hitler, for, as Wittgenstein put it, 'we extend our concept . . . as in spinning a thread we twist fibre to fibre. And the strength of the thread does not reside in the fact that some one fibre runs through its whole length, but in the overlapping of many fibres.' And again: when Wittgenstein speaks of 'the ground of language', Heller suspects that the phrase betrays a metaphysical belief; he reads it as a 'transparent metaphor' through which a mystical light shines on a desolate landscape, whereas it is one more summary phrase for that multitude of customs, conventions and rules which it is the task of Wittgenstein's philosophy to submit to reasoned thought. Just as Kant made our experiences available to reason by analysing them as determined by the forms of perception, so Wittgenstein makes them available under the aspect of language. Making available is a task to try anybody's patience, and both Nietzsche and Wittgenstein are impatient philosophers. But there is a difference: Nietzsche's philosophy vaunts his impatience, much of his pathos derives from it, whereas the motivating force of Wittgenstein's philosophy is impatience subdued. Not all of Wittgenstein's reflections are free from the rhetoric of pathos, but his is (mainly) the pathos of the teacher, never that of the public arena. Free from the stridency of 'the death of God', his discourse has the virtue of accuracy. In the preface to *Philosophical Remarks* (1930) he writes: 'I would like to say that "this book is written to the glory of God" but that would today be an infamy, i.e. it would not be understood aright.'

Nietzsche's achievement, and the difficulties he bequeathes to his reader, are connected with his instinctive need to label every insight and every act of understanding with a value judgment. Thus error and misprision turn out to be the results of imperception, imperception blends with evasion, deceit of others and of self. Being aware of this tendency, Nietzsche seeks to free himself from it: sometimes by criticising it ironically as the disposition of a 'graceless, hundredweight spirit', at other times by writing with a lightness of touch and in a style of good humour which aspire to the condition of a lighthearted game, 'an innocence of becoming' symbolised by Heraclitus's image of the child playing cribbage with the Universe. Heller is at his best when sketching this process, and he also follows it part of the way. An abundance of insights derived from historical parallels and contrasts comes easily and naturally to him, and so does the play of paradox and irony: and these, in 'the profession of letters', amount to a rare grace. Quoting from *Beyond Good and Evil*, Heller provides a clue to his own undertaking. 'There are "scholarly men",' Nietzsche writes, with Burckhardt in mind, 'who make use of scholarliness because it gives them a serene façade, and because it suggests that the man is superficial: they wish that people should arrive at a wrong conclusion about them'; and in the same context Nietzsche mentions 'buffoonery' (*Narrheit*) as a possible disguise for 'desperate, all-too-certain knowledge'. 'Clearly,' Heller comments, Nietzsche 'meant himself, referring to his own display of paradoxical formulations, witty extravagances, provocative exaggerations'. Heller never plays the 'buffoon', nor does he wish to lead the reader to wrong conclusions. And yet there is a family likeness: his literary manner, too, conceals a dark vision of what the world has become since Nietzsche's time. If on a few occasions this style betrays signs of caprice, it also provides illumination by which to read our immediate past, and its traces in our present, illumination not always contained in critical writings which lack the wit to be capricious. Professor Heller's essays are themselves a part of the literature which is the subject-matter of most of them. 'The condition they describe,' Edwin Muir wrote, 'is our condition.' □

Cockcrow
Patricia Beer

Up at five o'clock on an August morning
We carry light luggage out of the house.
With heavy cases our children stoop.
Their children are winged
With small bright backpacks.

The sky is a shop window before opening-
time,
Goods shadowy as trees. But in a back room
And spreading, the light will soon come on.

We breathe cautiously in the untried air,
Talk warily at the centre of six fields.

And then comes cockcrow, swaggering up
Out of the valley. The invisible bird
Plumes himself. He was the one chosen
To nail good terrified Peter. He conquers
The dark with flying colours.

We wave our dear children and theirs
Into the growing light. We are old
And sleep late after bad nights.
We shall not hear the conquistador again
Till they visit us in another season.

Content over Style

The journalist and agitator Paul Foot wrote more than sixty pieces for the LRB. The first, in 1984, was on the power of the tobacco companies; the last, in 2004, a couple of months before he died, on the shortcomings of the 1832 Reform Act. Mary-Kay Wilmers, who had known him since they were at university, wrote in a short piece published in the paper after his death that 'he even included a standard *Socialist Worker* harangue in every piece he sent us, for the sheer pleasure of watching us take it out.' He might have denied that he enjoyed seeing his pieces topped and tailed, stripped of their rousing introductions and perorations, of their stock adjectives (you can see in the piece of copy opposite that a 'dreadful murder' has had its adjective cut), but as long as his story remained intact he didn't mind too much. There are some writers whose pieces disappear when you start to edit them, but Foot's were a triumph of content over style. He wrote in a hurry – there was always a column due or a meeting to speak at – but he knew his material: miscarriages of justice, political scandals and the illicit wars carried out by what we probably didn't let him call the 'ruling class'.

Accidents

Paul Foot

WHEN something awful or unexpected happens in public affairs, we are usually referred to the 'cock-up theory of history'. This is preferred by realists to the 'conspiracy theory of history'. That strange or shocking events should be ascribed to mistakes, accidents or coincidences is very much more comforting than the notion that they are part of some sinister plot. Take the example, familiar to readers of this paper, of Hilda Murrell. In 1984, Miss Murrell, a 72-year-old rose specialist who lived in Shrewsbury, was taken out of her house in her own car, driven to a field outside the town and systematically, apparently ritualistically, stabbed. She was left unconscious in the field, where she died of exposure. The Shrewsbury police announced that the murder was the result of a burglary gone wrong. Their suspect, they were convinced, was a 'common burglar'. He had, we were told, been surprised by Miss Murrell returning to her home, and had panicked. This was perhaps the first common burglar in the history of petty crime who 'panicked' in such a way that he took his victim out of the house, where he and she were relatively unobserved, and in broad daylight drove her through crowded streets to a place where he carried out a ritual murder. There were those at the time who challenged the police assumptions. There were even some conspiracists who observed that Hilda Murrell had been an objector to the proposed new nuclear power station at Sizewell; that the surveillance of all such objectors had been put out to contract by a high-powered London security firm; and that the contract had been won by an Essex private detective, Victor Norris, whose main credentials were that he was a Satanist, a fascist, and had been sent not long previously to prison for six years for hiring out his own small daughters for the sexual gratification of his associates. Norris wasn't Hilda Murrell's murderer – who, everyone agrees, was a man half his age – but the choice of someone like him to carry out this kind of surveillance is an interesting indication of the characteristics required of a nuclear spy.

With the help of the *Daily Mail*, the realists – or 'cock-up' theorists – prevailed in the argument over the Hilda Murrell murder. In the end, most people were inclined to adjudge it beyond belief that an old woman should have been so foully murdered as part of a conspiracy about a nuclear power station on the other side of Britain. The police relentlessly pursued the 'common burglar' theory. They rounded up all the common burglars in the area and questioned them. They pursued the matter with 'the utmost rigour' – and never even came up with a suspect.

If something so extraordinary happens once, most people will think it a cock-up or an accident or a coincidence. But what if something rather like that happens again? What if William McRae, a radical Glasgow solicitor, and a prominent objector to the dumping of nuclear waste in the Galloway hills, is found shot dead in his car with the revolver some twenty yards away in a stream? Are we to assume, as the authorities in Scotland did, that the solicitor had shot himself? How did he manage to hurl the gun that distance before his (instant) death? 'There are no circumstances to justify a public inquiry,' said the procurator fiscal. And thanks to the rather quaint Scottish habit of not holding inquests, there was no inquiry of any kind into this strange death.

What about Vera Baird? She was the lawyer acting for LAND, Lincolnshire against Nuclear Dumping, which campaigned against the proposed NIREX site at Killingholme. Her car was broken into and her confidential papers stolen. Or Debbie Ladley. She was 18, a nanny, and she had given some help to LAND. In *Britain's Nuclear Nightmare* James Cutler and Robert Edwards record: 'On 29 September 1986, she was hanging out her washing in her garden at Stragglethorpe near Fulbeck. A man grabbed her from behind by the throat and banged her head against the wall. She suffered a fractured wrist, a cracked rib and injuries to the face.' The men muttered threats which can only have been connected with her anti-nuclear work.

~~BRITAIN'S NUCLEAR~~ ~~Nightmare~~
~~by JAMES CUTLER and BOB EDWARDS~~ · ~~Spear Books~~

(1

titles:
dropped
letter
Nuclear
Poison
Bucket of
Blood

— (When~~ever~~ something ~~quite~~ awful or unexpected happens ~~peter~~
~~xtxcxnxmxkxy~~ in public affairs, ~~we are totally assured that it is the fault of~~ we are ~~nearly~~ usually

released to
the 'cock-up theory of history'. This ~~'cock-up theory'~~ is ~~always~~ is ~~generally~~

preferred by realists to the ~~more unusual~~ 'conspiracy theory of

history'. That strange or shocking events should be ascribed to

mistakes, accidents or coincidences is very much more comforting

than the notion that ~~there is perhaps some~~ they are part of some sinister plot. Take the

~~xxxxxxxxxxxxxxxxxxxxxxx~~

~~et out. It is also very much more exciting.~~

Consider a

~~Here is~~ an example ~~instance~~ — ~~Hilda~~ *Miss* Hilda Murrell, In 1984, a 72-year-old rose specialist

, familiar
to readers
of this
paper, of
Hilda
Murrell.

who lived in Shrewsbury was taken out of her house in her own car

driven to a field outside the town and systematically, apparently

ritualistically, stabbed. She was left unconscious in the field,

where she died of exposure.

The Shrewsbury police announced *shortly afterward that the* ~~very soon after this~~

~~dreadul~~ murder ~~that it~~ was the result of a burglary that had gone

wrong. Their suspect, they were convinced, was a 'common burglar'.

He had, we were told, been surprised by ~~Miss~~ *Miss* Murrell returning to

her home, and had ~~blank~~ panicked.

First page of the typescript for 'Accidents' by Paul Foot,
published in the issue of 4 August 1988

-15-

that the peoples of Western Europe, with their deep differences and distinctiveness, and with their fear for their survival alongside competing cultures and peoples had chosen the wrong path to preserve and protect their differences. They had pursued confrontation which led them into many bloody conflicts with those whom they distrusted. The results would have been ruinous for Europe as a whole.

After 1945, led by men of vision, they tried a new way. They sat down with former enemies to hammer out agreed institutions which settled relationships and preserved difference. No one would have believed in 1945 that by 1992 they would be moving towards the United States of Europe, with the Germans still German and the French still French. One thing is certain: they would never have achieved it had they continued to dwell on the past and call up the ghosts of the past. That approach would have led, as it always had done and as it does in Ireland, to conflict in every generation. Can we in Ireland not learn the same lesson? Can we not sit down with former enemies, with those whom we distrust, and hammer out institutions which will settle our relationships and preserve our differences?

Is it too much to ask that we invest in the future for a change. For we haven't finished with our anniversaries. Very substantial ghosts of the past loom in the 300th anniversaries of 1689 and 1690 - the Siege of Derry and the Battle of the Boyne. In addition to our own local quarrel, those dates were symbolic of a wider and deeper European quarrel. That quarrel has long been laid to rest in Europe. So have subsequent and more bitter ones.

The question we face is, Will these anniversaries reinforce our spirit of confrontation, or will we commemorate them as divisions of the past by laying to rest the ancient quarrel that continues to disfigure us as a people?

Final page from the typescript of John Hume's piece on the 'end of the Unionist veto in Ulster', published in the issue of 2 February 1989

A Suitable Question for a Referendum

Europe was not an idea that played well with the British left when the paper tackled the subject in its inaugural issue, with a piece by the economist Wynne Godley. Godley favoured Britain's membership of the EEC for 'political and cultural reasons', but he couldn't reconcile the cost of UK membership with his continentalism. He was writing at a moment when UK transfers to the Common Market had spiked, having gone from 0.1 per cent of UK 'national income' to 0.5 per cent in a few years. In 1984 Thatcher's rebate left the UK feeling pleased with itself – and her – but Britain was still a grudging net contributor, rummaging in its pockets. The electorate and the government were looking west, transfixed by Reagan's supply-side miracle: deregulation, competition, low taxation, and – ipso facto – wealth and property for all.

Increasingly, Brussels was facing in the same direction. But for the Northern Irish politician John Hume, leader of the SDLP, writing about Ireland in 1989 in the piece whose ending is shown here, the drift to economic liberalism – at the expense of Europe's 'social model' – was a secondary issue. For Hume, the European ideal had produced half a century of peace among its members, and was now the best hope for an end to the Troubles. 'No one would have believed in 1945,' he wrote, 'that [we] would be moving towards the United States of Europe, with the Germans still German and the French still French.'

Not many believed it in 1996, when Perry Anderson described the EU as 'a more or less unfathomable mystery to all but a handful of those who, to their bemusement, have recently become its citizens'. He foresaw 'an extraordinary conjunction of divergent movements in the coming years: the passage to a European monetary union; the return of Germany to continental hegemony; and the competition among ex-communist countries for entry'. Europe's future

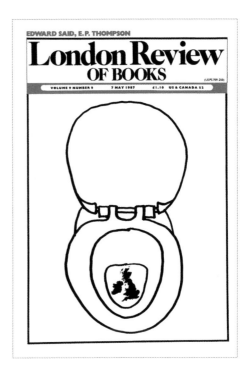

was one of 'radical indeterminacy': enlargement, after all, would either unravel the institutional fabric of the Union or force its hand, with bona fide federation the only way to settle its unwieldy contradictions.

'Europe,' Helen Thompson wrote in 2018, 'is the heir of competing civilisations, none of which can provide a coherent answer as to where the continent begins and ends or what values count as "European".' By then, Greece had been humiliated by Germany's finance minister and Britain had voted to leave. The EU, Thompson decided, had no foreign policy, and was riven with internal faultlines. That was the least of it. Europe had yet to find a 'form of language' that would give it meaning as a political community whose authority 'can rest on popular consent'. Remainers in the UK clung on bravely. 'I voted Remain because I am, by temperament, a leaver,' Nicholas Spice wrote in 2019. 'My wife, who is German, already has permanent right to remain (that's to say, "leave to remain") and my son has dual nationality. I associate my Remain vote with my tendency to claustrophobia: I like to know how I can get out.'

Jeremy Harding

EXTRACT FROM VOL. 18 NO. 1 · 4 JANUARY 1996

Under the Sign of the Interim

Perry Anderson

THE institutional upshot of European integration is a customs union with a quasi-executive of supranational cast, without any machinery to enforce its decisions; a quasi-legislature of inter-governmental ministerial sessions, shielded from any national oversight, operating as a kind of upper chamber; a quasi-supreme court that acts as if it were the guardian of a constitution which does not exist; and a pseudo-legislative lower chamber, in the form of a largely impotent parliament that is nevertheless the only elective body, theoretically accountable to the peoples of Europe. All of this superimposed on a dozen or so nation-states, determining their own fiscal, social, military and foreign policies. Up to the end of the 1980s the sum of these arrangements, born under the sign of the interim and the makeshift, had nevertheless acquired a respectable aura of inertia.

In the 1990s, however, three momentous changes loom over the political landscape in which this complex is set. The disappearance of the Soviet bloc, the reunification of Germany and the Treaty of Maastricht have set processes in motion whose scale can only be compared to the end of the war. Together, they mean that the European Union is likely to be the theatre of an extraordinary conjunction of divergent movements in the coming years: the passage to a European monetary union; the return of Germany to continental hegemony; and the competition among ex-communist countries for entry. Can any predictions be made about the kinds of outcome that might emerge from a metabolism of such magnitude?

At this historical crossroads it is worth thinking back to the work of Monnet and his circle. Historically, state-construction has proceeded along three main lines. One is a gradual, unplanned, organic growth of governmental authority and territory, such as occurred in – let us say – late medieval France or early modern Austria, whose architects had little or no idea of long-term objectives at all. A second path is conscious imitation of pre-existing models, of a kind that first really emerges in Europe in the 18th century, with the emulation of French Absolutism by its Prussian or Piedmontese counterparts. A third and historically still later path was deliberate revolutionary innovation: the creation of completely new state forms in a very compressed period of time, under the pressure either of popular upheavals like the American or Russian Revolutions, or elite drives like the Meiji Restoration in Japan.

The process of statecraft set in train by the projectors of a federal Europe – the Burkean term of alarm can be taken as homage – departed from all these paths. It was without historical precedent. For its origins were very deliberately designed, but they were neither imitative of anything else nor total in scope; while the goals at which it aimed were not proximate but very distant. This was an entirely novel combination: a style of political construction that was highly voluntarist, yet pragmatically piecemeal – and yet vaultingly long-range. Relying on what he called a 'dynamic disequilibrium', Monnet's strategy was an incremental totalisation, en route to a hitherto unexampled objective – a democratic supranational federation. The implications of his undertaking did not escape him. 'We are starting a process of continuous reform,' he wrote, 'which can shape tomorrow's world more lastingly than the principles of revolution so widespread outside the West.' It is one of the great merits of François Duchêne's biography of Monnet that it seeks so intelligently to take the measure of this innovation, which he calls – by contrast with conquest, adjustment or upheaval – 'that rarest of all phenomena in history, a studied change of regime'. This is a striking formula. Yet there is at once a certain overstatement and understatement in it. The changes were more improvised than studied; but at stake was more than a regime.

LONDON NW3 6AX
071-435 2381

23-01-96

Dear Sirs,

Would Perry Anderson care
to distil his splendid article into
a suitable question for a referendum?

Yours faithfully,

[signature]

A.D. MICHAELS.

Letter to the editor from A.D. Michaels,
23 January 1996

Priority for the next issue

The Lady in the Van

Alan Bennett

824

THE LADY IN THE VAN

dropped
Letter C

'I ran into a snake this afternoon,' Miss Shepherd said. 'It was
coming up Parkway. It was a long, grey snake, a boa constrictor
possibly, it looked poisonous. It was keeping close to the wall and
seemed to know its way. I've a feeling it may have been heading
for the van.' I *was* relieved that on this occasion she *didn't*
demand that I ring the police, as she regularly *did* if anything
out of the ordinary occurs. Perhaps this *was* too out of the ordinary
(though it turn*ed* out the pet shop in Parkway *had been* broken into *the* last
previous night so she may have seen a snake). She brought her mug over
and I make her a drink which she *took* back to the van. 'I thought
I'd better tell you,' she *said*, 'just to be on the safe side. I've
had some close shaves with snakes.'

This encounter with the putative boa constrictor was in the summer
of 1971 when Miss Shepherd and her van had for some months been at
a permanent halt opposite my house in Camden Town. I had first
come across her a few years *before that*, stood by her van,
stalled as usual near the convent at the top of the street. The
convent (which was to have a subsequent career as the Japanese School)
was a gaunt reformatory-like building that housed a dwindling garrison
of aged nuns and was notable for a striking crucifix attached to the
wall overlooking the traffic lights. There was something about the
position of Christ, pressing himself against the grim pebbledash beneath
the barred windows of *the convent* that called up visions of the
Stalag and the searchlight and which had caused us to dub him 'The
Christ of Colditz'. Miss Shepherd, not looking un-crucified herself, was
standing by her vehicle in an attitude with which I was to become very
familiar, left arm extended with the palm flat against the side of the
van indicating ownership, the right arm summoning anyone who was fool
enough to take notice of her, on this occasion me. Nearly six foot,
she was a commanding figure and would have been more so had she not
been kitted out in greasy raincoat, orange skirt, Ben Hogan golfing cap
and carpet slippers. She would be going on sixty at this time.

She must have prevailed on me to push the van as far as Albany
Street, though I recall nothing of the exchange. What I do remember as
I trundled the van across Gloucester Bridge was being overtaken by
two policemen in a panda car and thinking that, as the van was certainly
holding up the traffic, they might have leant a hand. They were wiser than
I knew. The other feature of this first run-in with Miss Shepherd

Photocopied pages of Alan Bennett's 'The Lady in
the Van' typescript (with editorial annotations),
published in the issue of 26 October 1989

sorry the van's in such a state. I haven't been able to do any 29
spring cleaning.' ~~~~~~ #

⌐In the interval between Miss Shepherd's death and her
funeral a week later I found out more about her life than I had in
twenty years. She had indeed driven ambulances during the war and was
either blown up or narrowly escaped death when a bomb exploded nearby.
I'm not sure that her eccentricity, ~~bordering on mild schizophrenia~~, can
be put down to this any more than to the legend, mentioned by one of the
nuns, that it was ~~death~~ the death of her fiancé in this incident that
'tipped her over '. It would be comforting to think that it is love, or
the death of it, that unbalances the mind, but I think her early attempts
to become a nun and her repeated failures ('too argumentative,' one of
the sisters said) point to a personality that must already have been ~~~~
quite awkward when she was a girl. After the war she spent some time
in mental hospitals but regularly absconded ~~and~~ finally remaining at
large long enough to establish her competence to live unsupervised.

The turning-point in her life ~~came some after arising~~
came when she was involved in ~~another accident~~ an accident when a
motor-cyclist crashed into the side of her van. If her other vans were
any guide, this one, too, would only have been insured in heaven so it's
not surprising she left the scene of the accident ('skedaddled,' she would
have said) without giving her name or address. The motor-cyclist
subsequently died so that, while blameless in the accident, by leaving
the scene of it she had committed a criminal offence, ~~so that now~~ The
police mounted a search for her. Having already changed her first name
when she became a novice, she now changed her second name, and calling
herself Shepherd, made her way back to Camden Town and the vicinity of
the convent where she had taken her first vows. And though she had little
to do with the nuns or they with her, she was never to stray far from the
convent for the rest of her life.
All this I ~~learned~~ learned in the ten days between her death and ~~th~~
her funeral . It was as if she were a character in Dickens whose history
has to be revealed in the general setting. to-rights before the happy
ever after. ~~Hers was a turbulent history, a tale of escape and flight,~~
~~death and concealed identity. By comparison my own life looks tame. So~~
~~that even at the finish I feel she has had the last laugh.~~

Dizzy Blonds Like Me

I have written for the London Review of Books on and off since it first appeared in 1979; occasional book reviews and, more regularly, a Diary.

In many ways it isn't a particularly English paper; it's not gossipy, cosy or cliquey; nor, unlike the New York Review of Books, with which it shares some of its contributors, is it snobbish, saved by a welcome streak of silliness, which surfaces in the letters column and the occasional editorial comment. (Nothing could be less silly than the letters to the NYRB.)

Nor does the LRB feel that it has to be breathlessly up to date in the manner of the serious Sundays, though it must be gratifying that other newspapers regularly see fit to pick up its controversies and reprint its contributions. Some of its most valuable contributors, though, remain firmly un-picked up, as ever since its inception the LRB has maintained a consistently radical stance on politics and social affairs. It's one of the few publications that hasn't got shallower or gone deliberately downmarket over the years, its only concession to reader-friendliness Peter Campbell's delightful covers.

There's no similar journal on the right, unless one thinks of the Spectator (which I try not to do). In contrast to the unfevered tones of the LRB, the Spectator seems to be written by the kinds of candidate who often used to win scholarships at Oxford and Cambridge, provocative, flashy, determined at all costs to catch the examiner's eye. The LRB is made of sterner stuff.

Of course, writing for it I would say all this, wouldn't I? I do have beefs. It's fond of football, which is a pity. I wish the Diary was more of a genuine diary and so a bit chattier; I wish the political stuff made more concessions to dizzy blonds like me; it could 'lighten up' as they say nowadays, the writers allow themselves the odd joke. Still I know that every fortnight when I see it lying on the mat I cheer up and am grateful for it.

Alan Bennett, writing in July 1996

May it go on and on and on

The *LRB* first appeared in 1979, the year Thatcher and the Ayatollah Khomeini came to power. Khomeini died in 1989; Thatcher was forced to resign in 1990, leaving the *LRB* the sole survivor of what Graham Martin describes opposite as the 'awful decade of the 1980s'. By the end of 1989 its circulation was 12,000 copies.

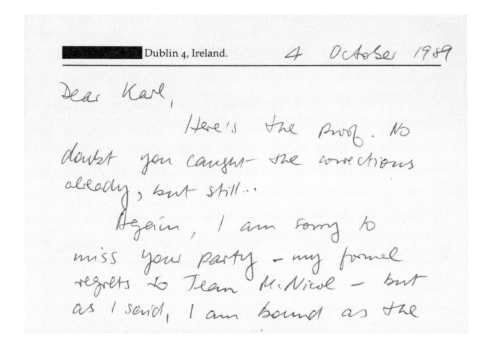

Transcription:

Dear Karl,

Here's the proof. No doubt you caught the corrections already, but still . . .

Again, I am sorry to miss your party – my formal regrets to Jean McNicol – but as I said, I am bound as the newest fellow (even as a 'supernumerary non-stipendiary' one) at Magdalen to speak at their Restoration dinner. An ironical duty: the dinner commemorates the college's resistance to the imposition of a Papist president by James II, and the glorious relief brought by William. I shall have to speak a work for the Jacobites. Have a good time on the night.

Seamus

Note from Seamus Heaney to Karl Miller,
4 October 1989

THE OPEN UNIVERSITY

The Open University
Walton Hall
Milton Keynes
MK7 6AA

Telephone: Milton Keynes 652092 (Direct Line)
Milton Keynes 74066 (Switchboard)

Department of Literature
Professor Graham Martin

18 October 89.

Dear Karl,

A couple of Sundays ago, there was a celebratory piece about you and LRB in The Correspondent noting the tenth anniversary of the periodical. I was very delighted to read it, and also to see the pic of KM, both arms outstretched into a kind of semi-circle. I thought this welcoming gesture coupled wiith your direct and critical gaze very well chosen. It depicted the two most admirable things about LRB: its impressive subject range and its demanding standard.

have/   What I'd like to add is that your achievement with LRB is one of the few really good things that/happened in this awful decade of the 80's. I admire it enormously.

You won't want me to add 'may it go on for ever', but nevertheless, may it gone and on and on.

My own little theory about your editorial policy is that it is another fine fruit of the Scottish Enlightenment.

Best wishes, as ever,

Graham

Letter from Graham Martin to Karl Miller,
18 October 1989

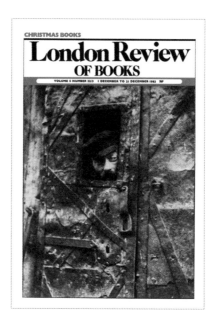

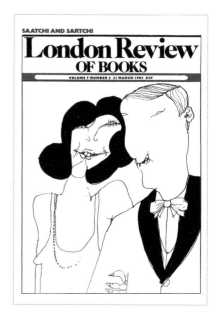

93

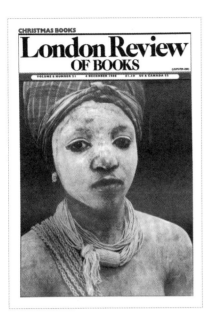

1990-99
Hallelujah! It Works

Women beware men!

London Review
OF BOOKS

(USPS 709–250)

VOLUME 14 NUMBER 14   23 JULY 1992   £1.95   US & CANADA $2.95

London Review of Current Affairs

ARTS COUNCIL

14 GREAT PETER STREET
LONDON SW1P 3NQ

071-333 0100
FACSIMILE 071-973 6590

Chairman
Peter Palumbo
Secretary-General
Anthony Everitt

Tuesday 6 November 1990

Professor Karl Miller
Editor
London Review of Books
Tavistock House South
Tavistock Square
London WC1H 9JZ

Dear Karl

We had a very useful meeting with Nicky Spice recently where we looked at the current figures and expectations. There have been some encouraging trends as well as a slower progression towards self-sufficiency than perhaps we all anticipated two years ago before the current recession set in.

Antonia and I made our comments as helpfully as possible and we are happy for the moment to slow down on the anticipated phased reduction of ACGB support to LRB until we see how a revised three-year financial plan emerges, but we are regularly in touch with Nicky and I have no worries about efficient management.

I did mention to Nicky, however, and he suggested that I should pass it on to you that one or two Panel members, including our Chairperson, P.D. James, have expressed mild concern about the weighting of LRB these days towards political and current affairs articles rather than strictly literary contributions. I must make it absolutely clear that they have no comments to make about the political direction of these pieces and they are not making the point in any kind of party way. There is merely a slight apprenhension about the appropriateness of the literature department here putting quite a considerable sum into what some people may consider to be more of a current affairs paper than a literary one. I think that many of the current affairs contributions are so well written and have a cultural leaning that they are defensible in their own right as worthy of support from us, but I do recognise that with a limited literature budget we must be seen primarily to be supporting work that is creative and imaginative in a conventional sense. I am not attempting to set any alarm bells ringing but merely passing on to you a slight worry which from time to time has been expressed by members of the Panel. I wonder if you have any comments?

I expect that you are approaching your retirement from University College with mixed feelings or are they undiluted in the light of

Telemessage Amec London SW1 · Telecom Gold 75: MUS 180 (Artslink) · Telex 9312102069 AC G
The Arts Council of Great Britain Registered Charity number 313039

Letter from Alastair Niven to Karl Miller,
6 November 1990

Page 2

current government attitudes to the universities?   I saw the
advertisement for your Chair and I hope that there has been a
good field.

It would be nice to get together for lunch some time. Perhaps we
could arrange this towards the end of the year or in January?

With best wishes,

Yours ever

Alastair

DR ALASTAIR NIVEN
Literature Director

Nicholas Spice writes: The LRB received its first Arts Council grant in 1981 – around £20,000, as an offset against writers' fees. The total Arts Council provision for literature has always been meagre, a fraction of the money available for music, theatre, dance and the visual arts, the argument being that magazine and book publishers can, in theory, make money. The LRB was one of the Arts Council's flagship literature clients and continued to receive funding until 2012. Some Tory politicians and some members of the literature panel didn't like the use of taxpayers' money to fund a magazine perceived to be left-wing, a symbol of the liberal intellectual elite, and there were intermittent attempts to remove the grant. To their credit, the Arts Council's literature directors always refused to be drawn.

Spindly Men and Women

When Peter Campbell was asked for an illustration for a subscriptions advert, he tended to reach for a pen instead of a paintbrush. He worked with Quentin Blake for many years, designing a series of Roald Dahl books in the 1990s, and Blake's spindly men and women share a family resemblance with some of the figures Campbell drew. His line-drawings were rarely used on the cover of the paper, with the exception of the one shown at the start of this chapter. 'Why is it always men painting naked women? Why is it never women painting naked men?' Mary-Kay Wilmers had asked him. This cover, a portrait of her, was his response. In his introduction to *Human Relations and Other Difficulties*, a collection of Wilmers's essays published in 2018, John Lanchester describes it as 'a picture which captures not just Mary-Kay's remark about art but also Peter's vision of Mary-Kay as an artist with her back turned, watching, judging, and covertly telling her side of the story'. In need of a logo for the paper's fortieth anniversary celebrations, it was one of Peter's drawings we chose.

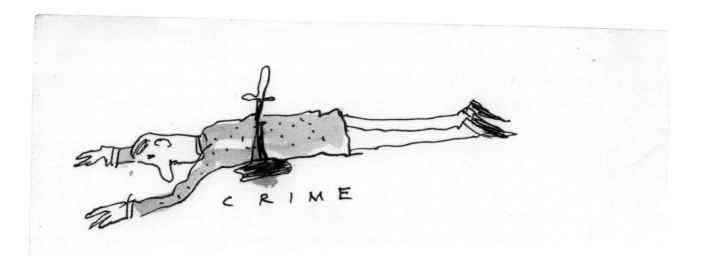

CRIME

Natural History

FILM

DRAMA

BIOGRAPHY

The Street's Intellectual

to the hilt and compel disclosure of documents on a massive scale ... issue a questionnaire ... demand full particulars ... compel discovery of documents . . . demand to see documents made in confidence'. He concluded: 'You might think that we were back in the days of the Inquisition . . . You might think we were back in the days of the General Warrants.' In another case (*Mandla*) Denning castigated the CRE for supporting a Sikh boy who had been required by a private school to have his hair cut, saying that the CRE 'pursued the headmaster relentlessly'. But he was overruled by the Law Lords who called the attack 'entirely unjustified'. As the CRE said in 1983, 'it may be that judges will never be able to accept the fact that Parliament has entrusted the CRE with sweeping investigative powers to work towards the eradication of a great social evil being carried out covertly.' Certainly Denning did not accept it. It is doubtful whether he had much sympathy with these aims.

Similarly, on immigration and deportation, Denning's nose for justice led him in various and variable directions. In 1967, Mauritian citizens of the UK and Colonies were issued with UK passports apparently giving them the right to come to the UK without restriction. Denning's fear that this would also entitle those from 'Hong Kong, Fiji, Gibraltar and St Helena' to enter led him to interpret the legislation perversely (*Shadeo Bhurosah*) and he applied this policy of excluding non-patrials in other cases by reading words into the statute (*Abdul Manan, Azam* and *Margueritte*). He interpreted immigration rules strictly – for example, in *Alexander*, which the Law Lords overruled, and *Marek*. This last was a particularly harsh decision denying an infant admission because the mother was abroad on a business visit at the time of application. She died on the visit, so the application could not be renewed.

The rules of natural justice were ignored when, with Denning's approval, US students who were Scientologists were deported without a hearing. 'I think,' Denning said, 'the minister can exercise his power for any purpose which he considers to be for the public good or to be in the interests of the people of this country' (*Schmidt*). In *Ex parte Soblen*, an infamous decision, a citizen of the USA, who was being flown from Israel in the custody of a US marshal, inflicted wounds on himself. The plane landed in London and Soblen was taken to hospital. He applied for habeas corpus. This was denied on the ground that he had been refused leave to land, and, 'in order to do what the United States wanted', as Denning said, he was served with a deportation notice by the Home Secretary. Shortly before he was due to be flown out of the UK en route for New York he took an overdose and died. With this may be compared the case of Mark Hosenball, the American journalist whom the Home Office decided should be deported as a security risk. Hosenball challenged the decision on the ground that there had been a breach of the rules of natural justice, in that he had been given no details and so could not seek to defend himself. Denning said bluntly that a conflict between the interests of national security and the freedom of the individual was 'not for a court of law', adding for good measure that ministers had 'never interfered with the liberty or the freedom of movement of any individual except when it was absolutely necessary for the safety of the state'. This is not a view that is universally shared. In *The Due Process of Law* Denning wrote:

In recent times England has been invaded – not by enemies – nor by friends – but by those who seek England as a haven. In England there is social security – a national health service and guaranteed housing – all to be had for the asking without payment and without working for it. Once here, each seeks to bring his relatives to join him. So they multiply exceedingly.

Like rabbits?

Denning's attitude to the press shows his quest for justice at its most idiosyncratic. When the British Steel Corporation sought an order of the court to require Granada TV to disclose the source of the information used in a programme critical of BSC, Denning began by saying that 'in general' sources should be protected. But on second thoughts, he has told us, he decided that Granada had not 'behaved with due respect' or 'with a due sense of responsibility'. So he supported the making of the order. Two years later, in *What Next in the Law*, he recanted and said he had made a mistake. The path of the seat-of-the-pants moralist

We were pleased to notice that a recent episode of 'Coronation Street' featured the 'London Review' as the subject of a sparring match between the Street's wide boy, Mike Baldwin, and its intellectual, Ken Barlow, pictured above. At the bar of the Rover's Return the following exchange took place:

    Mike Baldwin: No page three, eh? You know it's clever because it's printed all close together.
    Ken Barlow: That's because they don't have to leave room for my finger.

The paper has also appeared in the Tottenham Hotspur match programme, which recently reprinted – with a sardonic 'sounds great' from its editor – a passage from Karl Miller's Diary in praise of Paul Gascoigne.

is naturally bumpy. In another of his notorious decisions, he supported the expulsion of a student from a teacher-training college despite the most flagrant breaches of natural justice (*Ward v. Bradford*); and on this occasion too, he admitted that he might have been wrong.

When Harriet Harman of the NCCL allowed a reporter to see documents which had been read out in open court, Denning held that she was guilty of contempt of court. Subsequently the European Commission of Human Rights forced the Government into a retraction. Denning said that he regarded the use made by the journalist of the documents to

be 'highly detrimental to the good ordering' of society, with the consequence that 'the machinery of government will be hampered or even thwarted.' Time and again throughout his career, Denning has upheld the executive arm of government against challenges to its authority. This, no doubt, is the natural stance of the judiciary, which is more concerned with the preservation of 'law and order' than with individual rights. Once again, 'justice' is a slippery ground on which to make definitive decisions.

A third area of public law in which Denning became involved was that relating to trade unions. The material here is extensive and I will confine myself to one group of cases. For much of the 19th century, combinations of work people were regarded by the law as illegal. Strike action ceased to be criminal only in 1875, when statute protected those acting 'in contemplation or furtherance of a trade dispute'. This was restated by the Labour Government of the mid-1970s.

In 1978 a union blacked a ship in an attempt to force its owners to pay union wages, but the Court of Appeal held that this 'extraneous' action was not part of a trade dispute, and Denning said that the statutory words must be

limited and 'the court can look at the motive for which the action was taken.' The House of Lords disagreed (*Star Sea*). Undeterred, the next year, in a pay dispute in the newspaper business, Denning and the Court of Appeal held that a strike called by the NUJ was not in furtherance of a trade dispute, whatever the intentions of the union might have been. Again the Law Lords overruled (*McShane*). Six weeks later, the steelworkers' union was in dispute with the British Steel Corporation and decided to extend their strike to the private sector of the industry. Again Denning denied that this was a trade dispute and again the Law Lords reversed the decision (*Duport Steels*). 'My basic criticism of all three judgments in the Court of Appeal is that in their desire to do justice the court failed to do justice according to law,' Lord Scarman said. 'Legal systems differ in the width of the discretionary power granted to judges but in developed societies limits are invariably set, beyond which the judges may not go. Justice in such societies is not left to the unguided, even if experienced, sage sitting under the spreading oak tree.' The matter of the disagreement lay at the heart of party politics and the Law Lords were trying to ensure that the judiciary did not become too obviously involved in the run-up to the General Election of 1979. Denning had no hesitation in taking sides and in describing trade unions as 'the greatest threat to the rule of law'.

The author of this biography does not claim to have provided more than a personal sketch. He acknowledges his 'greatest debt' to Lord and Lady Denning for their patience and kindness in helping him, and the 'sketch' is on the whole adulatory. Heward does, however, put the other side, saying of Denning: 'A serious criticism of him is that he lacked intellectual honesty; this certainly took second place to justice.' He quotes Lady Denning: 'Once he did show me a judgment he was going to give. I told him that I thought he was coming out the wrong way. He said "Oh, do you?" and wrote the judgment the other way.'

The events that led to Denning's retirement are set out in a chapter headed 'Disaster'. Counsel for the accused in the trial after the St Paul's riot in Bristol made 35 challenges to the jurors' panel. This was done, said Denning in *What Next in the Law* in 1982, 'so as to secure as many coloured people on the jury as possible – by objecting to whites. The evidence against two of the accused was so strong that you would think they would be found guilty. But there was disagreement.' Two of the black jurors threatened to sue Denning. The book was withdrawn, Denning apologised publicly and privately, and announced his retirement, which had previously been called for in 1980 after his infamous remarks in dismissing an application to appeal on the part of the Birmingham Six, on the ground that to allow it would mean convicting the Police of perjury and violence.

Earlier this year, Denning joined the then Secretary of State for Northern Ireland in publicly opposing the right to silence during the trial of the Winchester Three, with the result that their conviction was quashed. This was followed by the *Spectator* interview, with the suggestion that the Guildford Four might be guilty and the description of Leon Brittan as 'a German Jew telling us what to do with our English law'. In 1955 Lord Chancellor Kilmuir said that judges should be kept insulated from the controversies of the day: 'So long as the judge keeps silent, his reputation for wisdom and impartiality remains unassailable.'

Heward records that American students embroidered 'Root for Denning' on their T-shirts. I am no more impartial than Lord Denning, but my proudest possession is a T-shirt given me by a student in Toronto with 'That man Griffith' embroidered on it. So there. ☐

London Review of Books

Tavistock House South, Tavistock Square,
London WC1H 9JZ
Telephone: 01-388 6751
Advertising and Distribution: 01-388 7487
Fax: 01-383 4792

Graham King
Coronation Street
Granada Television
Quay Street
Manchester M60 9EA   2 October 1990

Dear Mr King,

We are very grateful indeed to you and to every one else at
<u>Coronation Street</u> . The picture is terrific and we shall be making
use of it in the <u>London Review of Books</u> shortly.

We will, of course, send you some copies of the issue that carries
the picture.

With best wishes,

Inigo Thomas

EDITORS: Karl Miller, Mary-Kay Wilmers DEPUTY EDITOR: Susannah Clapp ASSISTANT EDITOR: John Lanchester
PUBLISHER: Nicholas Spice ADVERTISEMENTS: Andrew Patterson SUBSCRIPTIONS: Michael Coates
EDITORIAL BOARD: Ian Hamilton, Frank Kermode, Michael Neve, V.S. Pritchett

Published by LRB Limited, registered in England at the above address No. 1485413

Inigo Thomas writes: Ken Barlow was seen with an issue of the *LRB* in a 1990 episode of *Coronation Street*. A few weeks later, the paper published a photograph of the actor William Roache holding up a copy of the *LRB* with its cover facing the camera. We'd asked for a still from the episode, what we got instead was a slightly embarrassing publicity image, which we slightly embarrassingly still carried in the paper. The caption read: 'We were pleased to notice that a recent episode of *Coronation Street* featured the *London Review* as the subject of a sparring match between the *Street*'s wide boy, Mike Baldwin, and its intellectual, Ken Barlow. At the bar of the Rover's Return the following exchange took place. Mike Baldwin: "No page three, eh? You know it's clever because it's printed all close together." Ken Barlow: "That's because they don't have to leave room for my fingers."'

Letter from Inigo Thomas to Graham King,
2 October 1990

His Trademark Double Emphasis

'just a careerist with an alliteration complex

the stage is filling w. the inauthentic. Ev. where you look there's a bigger fake advancing towards you.

she's a tremendous pedant & aesthete of the knicker

mustn't grumble [why not ? I was going to if out in the ashtray

I don't demand that he experience having his arse shot off. I just note that he didn't.

Fussell re: Galbraith's gravitie. to spk re: you H o Nagasaki

I want to be famous so as it inconveniences me

There's a terrible shortage of charlatans in this country

When you compare Graves with Rilke & Wordsworth or Rilke you are comparing a re-arrangement of the room w. a subsidence of continents

I walked to work this morning through squares in wh. every second tree was on its knees.

John Lanchester writes: Karl said so many funny and vivid things that we started writing them down – Mary-Kay on post-it notes, then I joined in by starting a file in the office computer system, then Andrew O'Hagan made entries in that same file. I still find myself remembering things Karl said. He was one of those people who could make you laugh not just months but years, decades later. They still come back to me at unexpected moments. He once spoke of his admiration for the last communist leader of Poland, General Jaruzelski, for not resorting to violence during the last days of the old regime. Then Jaruzelski did something bad (I forget the details) and we bearded Karl with this when he came into the office. His response: 'I'm not wedded to his every neural impulse.'

On Karl Miller

John Lanchester

KARL'S SPEECH was even more emphatic than his appearance. The impact of his talk was to do with the content, of course – he was a trenchant, vivid, wild, unpredictable talker, not just funny but the funniest person I have ever known, by a distance. There was also the question of his delivery. He had kept his Edinburgh accent, and it gave his speech an unusual quality: it was as if everything Karl said was in italics. In addition, the things he said would often build to a point involving a yet further degree of emphasis, so it was as if you had both his normal italicised delivery and then yet another level of italics on top. In the early days, when I was learning the ropes at the LRB and would often not know who somebody under discussion was, the italics and double italics would be wielded in giving a description and character summary. For example, the first time Anne Hollander was mentioned, I asked who she was. Karl didn't say: 'She's a distinguished historian of fashion.' He said: 'She's a tremendous pedant and aesthete of the knicker.' This was delivered as: 'She's a [level-one italics] *tremendous pedant and aesthete* [level-two italics] *of the knicker*'. When I quote Karl from now on, I ask you to imagine that no italics means italics, and italics means his trademark double emphasis.

Karl's verbal snapshots, I soon and lastingly learned, were a wonder of the world. R.W. Johnson was in those days writing a series of super-forthright, abrasive pieces that often featured glancing dismissals of all sorts of senior Labour Party figures. One of these pieces had come in and been edited by Mary-Kay, and Karl was reading it in proof. 'Johnson is like some *beast from the pampas*,' Karl said, admiringly and amusedly, 'who's brought in, and immediately *rushes around butting everybody*.' No such animal is known to zoology, and Bill Johnson has no known connection with Argentina, but more than a quarter of a century later, whenever I read a piece in that combative vein, I still think of the beast from the pampas. Another image that has stayed with me came when I opened a book package, took out the review copy and handed it to Karl at his desk. The book, by a 'French deepo' called René Girard, was an ambitious work of theory and history called *Things Hidden since the Foundation of the World*. Karl took a quick look at it and shook his head. 'The stage is filling with the inauthentic,' he said. 'Everywhere you look there's *some bigger fake* advancing to greet you.' Again, 25 years later, I often think of those fakes: larger-than-human beings resembling zombies, arms outstretched, lumbering slowly and inexorably closer. To the left: an enormous fake is advancing. To the right: an even bigger fake. And as for the fake directly in front . . .

Sometimes Karl's talk would be about events of the day, from high politics to gossip. (I once passed on a piece of gossip which caused Karl to look up from his desk and say: 'John, your ear is so close to the ground, it's *coming out in Australia*.' I didn't mind the zinger, but thought Mary-Kay and Susannah had no need to laugh quite as much as they did.) He was particularly interested in the Spanner trial, in which a group of gay men involved in consensual sado-masochistic activity were sent to prison. Karl had no doubt that what the men were doing was none of the state's business, but he was nonetheless riveted by the detail of the trial. 'What about love?' he asked. 'Where's love in all this?' He thought that we his colleagues, in our reflexive liberalism, were missing some of the interest: 'I suppose you lot are in favour of people nailing each other's willies to boards *until the end of time*.' One of the men, it emerged, was married, and he was struck by that too, and by the fact that the man's wife apparently hadn't known about his hobby. 'Amazing,' Karl said. 'He comes home, covered in blood and minus one of his goolies, and *she still doesn't twig*.'

PAUL FARMER: EBOLA

London Review
OF BOOKS

VOLUME 36 NUMBER 20   23 OCTOBER 2014   £3.75 US & CANADA $5.95

Michael Hofmann: Amis in Auschwitz
Owen Hatherley: The Neo-Elite
Colm Tóibín: Marilynne Robinson
Neal Ascherson, John Lanchester and
Andrew O'Hagan on Karl Miller

Dancing with Dogma

The *LRB* is still usually seen as 'broadly leftish', and that characterisation is accurate enough, but it has always been wary of having too close an affiliation with any political party and has tried not to restrict its contributors to those holding political positions with which it might be expected to agree. In the early 1980s the paper supported the SDP surprisingly wholeheartedly (Karl Miller in 1981 talks of its 'deserved initial success'); it has never been similarly enthusiastic about any iteration of any other political party. Despite the flirtation with the SDP, neither of the *LRB*'s editors has been a joiner of parties or movements, and their scepticism (Perry Anderson called it 'contrariness') has inflected the paper's treatment of politics and its choice of writers. In 2002 the paper was accused of censoring its writers after Mary-Kay Wilmers turned down a piece by David Marquand that said Blair's 'handling of the post-11 September crisis was impeccable'. 'I can't square it with my conscience to praise so whole-heartedly Blair's conduct,' she wrote to Marquand.

Ian Gilmour, seen on the cover opposite 'dancing with dogma', as he put it in the title of his memoir, was an early member of Thatcher's cabinet (she sacked him a month before this dance). He wasn't a Thatcherite, favouring what he calls, in the piece on Oakeshott that Wilmers mentions in her letter here, 'middle government'. He wrote in the *LRB* on his own party and its mistaken embrace of 'ideology'; he also prophesied (in 1984) that Michael Foot had killed the Labour Party.

London Review of Books

Tavistock House South, Tavistock Square,
London WC1H 9JZ
Telephone: 01-388 6751
Advertising and Distribution: 01-388 7487
Fax: 01-383 4792

The Editor
Sunday Telegraph
Peterborough Court
South Quay
181 Marsh Wall
London E14 9SR

April 25, 1990

Dear Sir,

Mandrake takes the London Review of Books to task for having carried an Arts Council advertisement for a prize in memory of Raymond Williams. But the advertisement seems to have been the only thing in the journal that Mandrake has ever read. He implies that as 'a broadly leftish monthly' we blindly worship Williams; but the last article we published about him shows that we are quite capable of criticism of eminent left-wingers. In fact, the piece occasioned an editorial of protest in the THES. He says that we wouldn't 'recognise' the 'concept of a Conservative thinker'; a selection of the Conservative thinkers discussed in our pages in last twelve months would include Thomas Macaulay, Harold Acton, Mrs Thatcher, Wyndham Lewis, William Whitelaw, Martin Heidegger, Michael Heseltine, Enoch Powell, Harold Macmillan, Paul Johnson, Winston Churchill, Keith Joseph, Adolf Hitler, Lord Chalfont, Edmund Burke, Larry Lamb and Nancy Reagan. Mandrake cites Michael Oakeshott as an example of the kind of figure we ignore: in fact, we had already invited Sir Ian Gilmour to write about him. We are also, incidentally, a fortnightly, not a monthly paper.

Yours etc,

Mary-Kay Wilmers

Mary-Kay Wilmers
Editor

EDITORS: Karl Miller, Mary-Kay Wilmers DEPUTY EDITOR: Susannah Clapp ASSISTANT EDITOR: John Lanchester
PUBLISHER: Nicholas Spice ADVERTISEMENTS: Andrew Patterson SUBSCRIPTIONS: Michael Coates
EDITORIAL BOARD: Ian Hamilton, Frank Kermode, Michael Neve, V.S. Pritchett

Published by LRB Limited, registered in England at the above address No. 1485413

*Letter from Mary-Kay Wilmers to the
'Sunday Telegraph', 25 April 1990*

English Tunes, Royal Occasions, City Scandals

London Review
OF BOOKS

(USPS 709–250)

VOLUME 14 NUMBER 13   9 JULY 1992   £1.95   US & CANADA $2.95

*Ian Gilmour and Margaret Thatcher dance on the
cover of the issue of 9 July 1992, photograph by
Srdja Djukanovic*

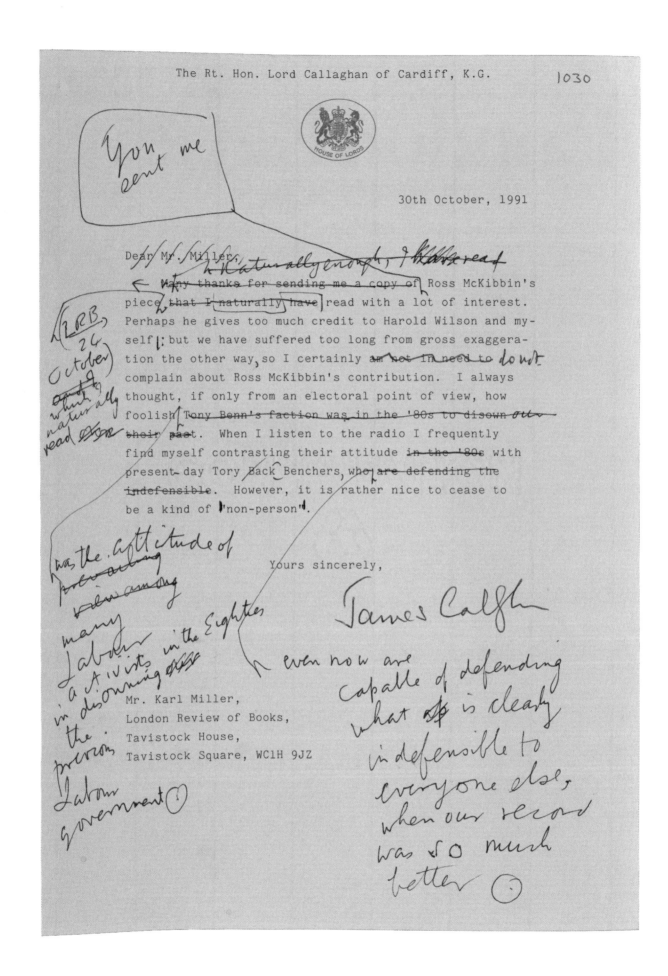

The Rt. Hon. Lord Callaghan of Cardiff, K.G.

1030

You sent me

30th October, 1991

Dear Mr. Miller,

Many thanks for sending me a copy of Ross McKibbin's
piece that I naturally have read with a lot of interest.
Perhaps he gives too much credit to Harold Wilson and myself; but we have suffered too long from gross exaggera-
tion the other way, so I certainly am not in need to
complain about Ross McKibbin's contribution. I always
thought, if only from an electoral point of view, how
foolish Tony Benn's faction was in the '80s to disown
their past. When I listen to the radio I frequently
find myself contrasting their attitude in the '80s with
present-day Tory Back Benchers, who are defending the
indefensible. However, it is rather nice to cease to
be a kind of "non-person".

Yours sincerely,

James Callaghan

Mr. Karl Miller,
London Review of Books,
Tavistock House,
Tavistock Square, WC1H 9JZ

Naturally enough, I have read

(LRB) 26 October) and which naturally read

was the attitude of many Labour activists in the Eighties in disowning the previous Labour Government

even now are capable of defending what is clearly indefensible to everyone else, when our record was so much better

Letter from James Callaghan to Karl Miller,
30 October 1991

When is an ism a wasm?

'I have read with some concern in *Tribune* that Tony Blair wrote in the LRB in October 1987. Can we have an assurance now, for reasons of the continuing intellectual credibility of the journal, that every effort has been made to track down any copies still in circulation and have the offending pages removed?' A worried subscriber wrote this in March 1997, barely two months before the landslide victory that ushered in 13 years of New Labour government. The report was true, and a few copies even now survive – though the existence of a contribution by Blair still seems quite surprising another 22 years later.

The LRB – historically a critical friend to the Labour Party, but sometimes just critical – had been sympathetic to the SDP during the breakaway party's brief heyday. The SDP's effective dissolution in 1987 (Blair's piece has a good line about its last leader, Robert MacLennan, 'a year ago unknown in Britain and today unknown throughout the world') may have encouraged Karl Miller to commission something from a coming man in Labour, itself in a reflective mood after being thumped by the Conservatives in the general election earlier that year. His choice was prescient: Blair had recently been promoted by Neil Kinnock but was yet to reach the shadow cabinet, and the piece, published in October, finds him at a crossroads. He is still comfortable with the language of socialism, and disputes the idea that Thatcherism 'has established a new consensus'. The free market, he says, produces 'inequality and monopoly'. But he frets about Labour's 'extremist image', notes the reduced political salience of the 'working class', and senses a disenchantment with the 'paternalistic state'. His conclusion, that Labour must 'go back to our founding principles . . . and apply them afresh to the world as it is today', is typically (as it would come to seem) vague. As Seumas Milne (heard of him?) pointed out in the LRB in 1996, 'the notion of social and political modernisation is shot through with ambiguities . . . Should the politically driven social changes of the past two decades be regarded as modern simply because they have just taken place?'

This is the question that quivers between the lines in much of the LRB's coverage of the Thatcher and Blair years. Gordon Brown, writing in the paper in 1989, looked forward to the day when Thatcherism would be a 'wasm'. The decade hadn't witnessed an economic miracle, only a 'great missed opportunity'. It's a good essay – much of it holds up. And yet, and yet. In 1991, Ross McKibbin, an exceptionally shrewd observer of British politics in the LRB, defended the record of what was then the last Labour government, headed by Harold Wilson and, after his resignation, by James Callaghan. That record had been disowned by Labour under Kinnock. If Labour was prepared to reclaim it, McKibbin thought, it 'might then be able to argue that the rather rough-hewn social democracy with which [it] is historically associated has worked very much more in the national interest than anything else we are likely to have.' 'It is rather nice to cease to be a kind of non-person,' Callaghan wrote to the paper afterwards, though he didn't cease to be one for very long. In 1994, after John Smith's sudden death, McKibbin assessed his possible successors as Labour leader, hesitating over Blair – 'an impressive performer . . . Quite what he believes, I am less certain' – before concluding: 'I suppose Labour should choose [him] and keep its fingers crossed.' (Brown was dismissed on the grounds that he seemed 'neither likely to win an election nor to be an adventurous prime minister'.) It soon became apparent that, as Milne noted a month after Labour finally returned to power, Blair's would be the 'first explicitly post-social-democratic government in a major Western state'. Thatcherism wasn't a wasm after all.

Tom Crewe

London Review of Books

Tavistock House South, Tavistock Square,
London WC1H 9JZ
Telephone: 01-388 6751
Advertising and Distribution: 01-388 7487

22 July 1987

Dear Mr Blair,

      I wonder if, now that the election is over, you might have time to write something for this paper? What we had in mind is a discussion of the state and future direction of the Labour Party, perhaps in the light of recent statements by Bryan Gould and Roy Hattersley. I hope the idea appeals to you and look forward to hearing from you.

Yours sincerely

Karl Miller

Karl Miller

Letter from Karl Miller to Tony Blair, 22 July 1987

Diary

As the Conference season ends and Parliament resumes, the Tories are in triumphant mood. The Alliance – even the name now seems to mock them – have disintegrated, no longer preparing for government, but for oblivion. Part of the SDP is to go with Robert MacLennan, a year ago unknown in Britian and today unknown throughout the world. The other part, under David Owen, is being re-launched as the political wing of Sainsbury's. At the Labour Conference there was little rejoicing over the demise of the Alliance: instead, the Party engaged in a self-critical assessment of its own part in bringing about a decade of Mrs Thatcher. What makes things even worse for radical, progressive spirits is that the Ultra-Right appears to be even more in control of the Conservative Party this year than it has been previously. Mrs Thatcher clearly regards herself as a *dea ex machina*, sent down from on high to 'knock Britain into shape'. She will wield her power over the next few years dictatorially and without compunction. On the other hand, there is a tremendous danger – to which Dr Owen has succumbed – in believing that 'Thatcherism' is somehow now invincible, that it has established a new consensus and that all the rest of us can do is debate alternatives within its framework. It is essential to de-mythologise 'Thatcherism'.

Mrs Thatcher has enjoyed two advantages over any other post-war premier. First, her arrival in Downing Street coincided with North Sea oil. The importance of this windfall to the Government's political survival is incalculable. It has brought almost 70 billion pounds into the Treasury coffers since 1979, which is roughly equivalent to sevenpence on the standard rate of income tax for every year of Tory government. Without oil and asset sales, which themselves have totalled over £30 billion, Britain under the Tories could not have enjoyed tax cuts, nor could the Government have funded its commitments on public spending. More critical has been the balance-of-payments effect of oil. The economy has been growing under the impetus of a consumer boom that would have made Lord Barber blush. Bank lending has been growing at an annual rate of around 20 per cent (excluding borrowing to fund house purchases); credit-card debt has been increasing at a phenomenal rate; and these have combined to bring a retail-sales boom – which shows up dramatically in an increase in imported consumer goods. Previously such a boom and growth in imports would have produced a balance-of-payments deficit, a plunging currency and an immediate reining-back on spending, with lower rates of growth.

Instead, oil has earned foreign exchange and also produces remittance payments from overseas investments bought with oil money. The situation is neither stable nor healthy in the long term: but in the short term it allows the living standards of the majority to rise rapidly, even though the industrial base, the ultimate foundation of a successful economy, is still only achieving the levels of output of 1979. The fact that we have failed to use oil to build a productive and modern industry for the future is something historians will deplore. Nevertheless, oil has been utterly essential to Mrs Thatcher's electoral success. Academics and commentators may ruminate on the Thatcher ethos and its effect on social attitudes, but the voters are looking in their pockets.

The second undeserved bonus which Mrs Thatcher has been granted is a divided opposition. It is an obvious point but one which cannot be overstated. In 1979 the Tories obtained 43 per cent of the popular vote, in 1983 42 per cent and in 1987 41 per cent. Forty-one per cent is less than Labour obtained in 1959, the year when the question whether Labour could ever win again was first raised. Moreover, in some constituencies Tories were elected with 37 or 38 per cent, or less, of the vote. It would be foolish not to acknowledge that the contours of Tory support have changed: that the Party has more voters in the suburbs and fewer in rural areas. But there have always been changes in the pattern of electoral support. What is new, in post-war politics, is the massive majority of MPs achieved for one party with a relatively low percentage of the vote. Naturally proponents of Proportional Representation see this as a powerful argument for their cause. But the point I want to make is that, although an anti-Tory vote cannot be confused with a pro-Labour one, many more voters, indeed a growing number, voted against Mrs Thatcher rather than for her: and this despite the fact that the opposition parties were divided within themselves. Mrs Thatcher has not just been blessed with a split opposition vote, with Labour and the Alliance often competing for exactly the same political territory, but has been given additional help by the parties' internal squabbling.

Labour faces two sets of problems: those which are the culmination of a process of change and those arising from the Party's more immediate past. The latter tend to be ignored, while the former generate volumes of discussion. The effect of three-party politics has been to make every extra percentage point of support at the margins of crucial importance. So matters that affect the parties' day-to-day fortunes can make a dramatic difference. Anyone in any doubt about this proposition should examine the Labour Party's standing before and after the Greenwich by-election. A victory for Labour would have meant starting the election from a position where at least it seemed within striking distance of the Tories. Defeat meant that it wasn't even in frame when the election was called. Suppose Labour had been three or four points up in 1987: that might have meant thirty or forty extra seats – not a Labour victory, but a very much smaller Tory majority. The whole debate in British politics, which at the moment is taking place along the lines of 'socialism is dead, Thatcherism has won,' would have been set in a totally different context. The pundits would probably now be talking of Thatcher's imminent departure and Labour's springboard for the next election.

It is essential therefore to examine the lessons of the immediate past. There is really no serious doubt that, quite apart from the problems of history, Labour's 'extremist' image has been a crippling liability. This image has been carefully cultivated by a deeply hostile press: but if we are to be honest about our mistakes, the media alone cannot be blamed. In retrospect, the seeds were sown in the Sixties and Seventies, when the leadership of the Labour Party was content to concentrate on stitching up the block votes, manipulating Party Conference – and, to be fair, was preoccupied with governing the country. But at the grass roots the Party was withering. Party members were not being recruited, many local organisations were moribund and participation in key decisions was limited. Once the 1979 defeat occurred, and the pragmatism of the Party's senior figures seemed not just tired but failed, a wave of constitutional reform swept over the Party. Mandatory re-selection of MPs, and the election of the Leader and Deputy Leader by a caucus wider than MPs, were introduced. These reforms were then put to the test in the famous (or infamous) Benn-Healey contest for the Deputy Leadership.

The difficulty was that though the theory of greater democracy and increased accountability of MPs was fine, the practical context in which the theory was operating was fraught with danger. What was missing from the theory was any appreciation of the vital necessity of ensuring that, as well as MPs or leaders being accountable to the Party, the Party was accountable to the electorate. The one without the other was a recipe for disaster. Because the Party was small and did not encourage participation, it became prey to sectarian groups from the Ultra-Left. Moreover, the new situation allowed the Party to engage in the worst delusion of resolutionary socialism – the notion that resolutions passed at Conference have meaning or effect without real support in the wider community. The result was the birth of the SDP and several years of bitter in-fighting at a cost which the Party is still counting.

Enormous strides have been made in the last few years. But by comparison with its sister socialist parties in Europe, the Labour Party still has a very small number of members. The socialist party in Sweden has a million members, in West Germany 900,000, in Austria 700,000. Indeed, the Tory Party in Britain has four times the number of members that Labour has. Given that the Tories can count on the media and capital to support them, Labour has an overriding need for a large active band of supporters to put its case. Ironically, along with its small membership, Labour has a huge untapped source of potential members. Almost six million trade-unionists pay the political levy. Many did not vote Labour in 1983 and 1987, but many still do support Labour and many more might do so if they thought Labour was throwing its doors open to them.

In September, the Tribune Group of MPs published a pamphlet suggesting the steps to be taken in order to produce a 'mass membership' Labour Party. The first stage would be an offer of membership on attractive terms to all trade-union levy-payers. If the experiment, called Levy-Plus, works, the benefits can be extended to other sections of the community. A resolution instructing the Party Executive to implement proposals for a mass party was moved by the shopworkers' union, seconded by my own constituency Sedgefield, and passed overwhelmingly. Time will tell, but, allied to the changes in ordinary members' voting rights on the selection of candidates, the new proposals offer the opportunity for the first time this century of creating a large, participatory, active party. That is the surest possible way to keep the Party in touch with the voters and to ensure that the errors of the past are not repeated. Of course, Labour must meet the challenge of history, adapt to the times, and plan new policy initiatives: but if its deliberations don't reflect the views and aspirations of ordinary men and women, it will never open people's minds sufficiently to convince them of Labour's wider vision for society. People only listen to those they trust.

The problems which are posed by social change will take longer to solve. But there is nothing more ridiculous than the notion that socialism is inexorably dying, or has been compulsorily retired on grounds of redundancy. Socialism, as its name suggests, is based on a belief in the notion of action through the community, in the idea that individuals do not stand alone, and that it is not merely morally right that we should think of ourselves in this way but that it is the most rational way to organise our lives. The world we face today makes a socialist approach all the more relevant: from new technology to the arms race, co-operation surely makes more sense than competition.

There is no need for Labour to be ashamed of its principles or values. The task is to formulate policies that advance those values in a modern world. Post-war Britain has seen two big changes. First, and partly as a result of reforming Labour governments, there are many more healthy, wealthy and well-educated people than before. In addition, employment has switched from traditional manufacturing industries to a more white-collar, service-based economy. The inevitable result has been that class identity has fragmented. Only about a third of the population now regard themselves as 'working-class'. Of course it is possible still to analyse Britain in terms of a strict Marxist definition of class: but it is not very helpful to our understanding of how the country thinks and votes. In fact, of that third, many are likely not to be 'working' at all: these are the unemployed, pensioners, single parents – in other words, the poor. A party that restricts its appeal to the traditional working class will not win an election. That doesn't entail a rejection of socialism's traditional values: but it does mean that its appeal, and hence its policies, must address a much wider range of interests. In doing so, the direction of policy will be governed by another major change closely connected to the first. As people have become better-off and better-educated, so they have become less enchanted with a paternalistic state which says: 'the gentleman in Whitehall knows best.'

By 1979, a conjunction of the change in people's life-styles and dissatisfaction at a corporatist state which people felt had become unaccountable and inefficient was bound to evoke a reaction. Mrs Thatcher didn't create these circumstances: she was a product of them and her policies are a response to them. But the measures most closely associated with her – council-house sales, trade-union ballots, wider share ownership – reflect, at least rhetorically, the notion of devolving power. Her slogan in 1987 was 'power to the people'; her Conference speech borrowed a phrase – 'an irreversible shift in power in favour of working people' – from Labour's 1974 Manifesto. In other words, even Mrs Thatcher has had to pretend that she is extending opportunity and power. The weakness of Thatcherism is that, whatever the rhetoric, the policies don't work. They end up concentrating power in the hands of élites, in restricting freedom and in centralising control. The 'free' market does not distribute fairly or efficiently: it produces inequality and monopoly.

The Tories fail in part because they naturally favour wealth and privilege; and in part because their extreme view of the individual means that they cannot undertake effective government intervention. For them, good government is no government and the only method of exercising choice is through the market. The trick for Labour is not to follow them and abandon the notion of government and collective provision: but to re-fashion it so that real power is exercised by people and not by institutions or bureaucracies. The fundamental error of Dr Owen (and, oddly, of David Steel since the election, though not before it) has been to surrender to Mrs Thatcher's philosophy and say that power can only be devolved through the market. The 1990s will not see the continuing triumph of the market, but its failure. If in 1974 a soothsayer had predicted that by 1984 Birmingham Northfield, with its 10,000 Labour majority, or Sherwood, with perhaps more pits than any other constituency, would be Tory, he would have been considered deranged. It has come to pass, but for reasons that can be analysed and understood and thus overcome. Labour can start its journey on the road to recovery with confidence in its beliefs and values. But it must keep an open mind and face difficult thoughts. The alternatives are not to embrace Thatcherism or escape from reality in some comforting romantic atavism. There is another way: to go back to our founding principles of a hundred years ago and apply them afresh to the world as it is today.

Tony Blair

American Football

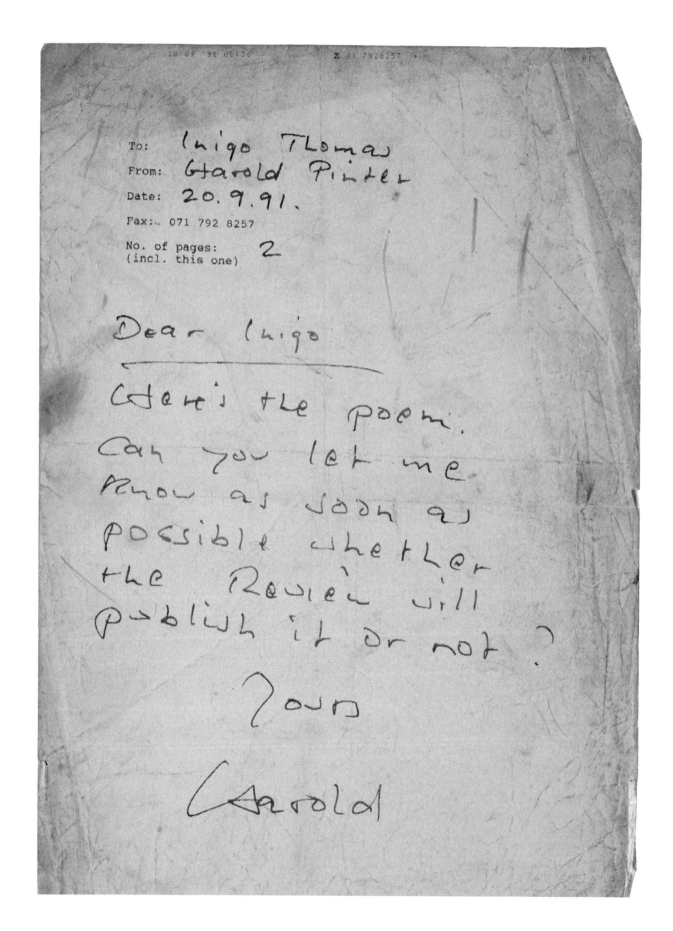

To: Inigo Thomas
From: Harold Pinter
Date: 20.9.91.

Fax: 071 792 8257

No. of pages: 2
(incl. this one)

Dear Inigo

Here's the poem.
Can you let me
know as soon as
possible whether
the Review will
publish it or not?

Yours

Harold

Fax from Harold Pinter to Inigo Thomas,
20 September 1991

After the US army's A-10 tank-buster bombers, known as Warthogs, had finished off the Iraqi armoured brigades on the Basra Road in 1991, Harold Pinter, disgusted by the carnage, wrote a poem called 'American Football'. He sent it to several publications, including the *London Review of Books*. None of the editors much liked it, but because it was by Pinter there was some further deliberation, and we thought we'd defer the decision to the following morning.

Soon after I arrived at the office the next day the phone rang. It was Harold's secretary, Angela. Harold wanted to know there and then whether the paper would publish the poem: he was heading out to Heathrow to fly to New York. I stalled: I said I'd let her know once I'd talked to my colleagues, only no colleagues had yet arrived. The situation was made more complex because I'd known Harold since I was a boy; I played for his cricket team, the Gaieties. I rang Karl Miller's office at the UCL English Department. He said I should write a careful letter explaining why the paper would not be publishing 'American Football'. My letter wasn't careful enough: after I faxed it to Harold, I got an explosive reply.

I didn't hear from him for a while, but then, with the cricket season about to begin, I got a call from Angela: he wanted to know if I could play in the first match, the Gaieties v. the Honourable Artillery Company. Harold arrived at the ground in his black Mercedes coupé. The car and Harold, black on black; the cricketers all in white. I was bowling to one of the Gaieties' opening batsmen on the outfield close to the car park – a bit of practice. I bowled another ball, it hit something on the ground, shot over the batsman's head and crashed into the chrome radiator of Harold's car. He exploded again, but then gave me a wink: he was having me on. We never talked about 'American Football'.

Inigo Thomas

American Football
Harold Pinter

Hallelujah!
It works.
We blew the shit out of them.

We blew the shit right back up their own ass
And out their fucking ears.

It works.
We blew the shit out of them.
They suffocated in their own shit!

Hallelujah.
Praise the Lord for all good things.

We blew them into fucking shit.
They are eating it.

Praise the Lord for all good things.

We blew their balls into shards of dust,
Into shards of fucking dust.

We did it.

Now I want you to come over here and kiss me
            on the mouth

Talentspotting

```
                                               ███████████████
                                               Edinburgh EH6 7EQ


        Karl Miller/Mary-Kay Wilmers
        Editor
        London Review of Books
        Tavistock House South
        Tavistock Square
        London WC1H 9LZ


        Dear Karl/Mary-Kay,

        I enclose an unpublished short story I have just completed. I would be
        delighted if you could consider publishing it in your excellent magazine. I
        am a London Scot who has recently left Hackney to live back in the old
        country. I started writing semi-seriously a few months ago and I have a
        short story which will be published in New Writing Scotland No.9 in
        October.

        I appreciate that the type of writing I veer towards is not every editors
        (or magazines) cup of tea, but if the story is not suitable, I would
        appreciate any feedback you could find time to give.



        Yours sincerely,




        Irvine Welsh.
```

Letter from Irvine Welsh to Karl Miller and
Mary-Kay Wilmers, 1991

Andrew O'Hagan writes: Needless to say, about ten minutes after I wrote to Irvine Welsh, *Trainspotting* became the novel of the decade. I'm glad to say he's still speaking to me, or, at least, he was.

London Review of Books

Tavistock House South, Tavistock Square,
London WC1H 9JZ
Editorial: 071-388 6751   Advertising: 0359 42375
Distribution: 071-388 7487   Fax: 071-383 4792

Irvine Welsh,
██████████████
Edinburgh.

19 July 1991

Dear Mr Welsh,

Thank you for giving us the chance to read your story
'The Cost of Having a Baby'. I regret that we are
unable to make an offer of publication.

Yours sincerely

Andrew O'Hagan

EDITORS: Karl Miller, Mary-Kay Wilmers DEPUTY EDITOR: Susannah Clapp ASSISTANT EDITOR: John Lanchester
PUBLISHER: Nicholas Spice ADVERTISEMENTS: Andrew Patterson SUBSCRIPTIONS: Michael Coates
EDITORIAL BOARD: Ian Hamilton, Frank Kermode, Michael Neve, V.S. Pritchett

Letter from Andrew O'Hagan to Irvine Welsh,
19 July 1991

Aut-o-cracy

Jean McNicol writes: LRB policy on word-splits remains pretty much as recorded on Karl Miller's handwritten list. We try to follow etymology, and so 'interest' is split at 'inter-', not 'in-' or 'int-', and 'psychoanalysis' at 'psych-' or 'psycho-', not 'psy-'. Despite Samuel Reifler's suspicions, we don't use a hyphenation programme, we just split words with the suffix '-ion' after the consonant. There's an example of this on Karl's list: 'nationalisat-ion' (though the word would be better split earlier on). I was about to write that Reifler was wrong to accuse us of splitting words of one syllable, but then I remembered that we do split past tenses ('work-ed'). I'm not sure I can offer a justification for this. We also split 'people' after 'peo-' and words that include 'qu' between the two letters: 'conseq-uence', in Karl's example. I can't justify these either. We don't always agree about where words should be split: etymologically, 'problem' should be split after 'pro-', but this made some of the editors unhappy because it was felt to break a secondary rule that splits shouldn't lead the reader to mispronounce a word, so we continue to split it at 'prob-'.

Reifler thinks it wouldn't take someone long to search through the hyphens in each issue, but as Mary-Kay Wilmers told him, it's actually 'very time-consuming', as is sorting out the 'spacing' (that is, not leaving huge gaps between the words in one line and squashing them up in the next) and capitalisation (the prime minister and the queen are indications of rank and so 'down'; the Master of the Rolls is 'up', on the grounds that it looks too peculiar without caps). The justification for spending so much time on all this is that we're trying to make the paper easier and more pleasurable to read: bad splits and horrible spacing are distractions. The danger, as Mary-Kay was indicating when she told Reifler our policy was 'crazy', is that you can waste hours arguing happily, or indeed bad-temperedly, with your colleagues about whether the duke of Buckingham is merely a title denoting rank or serves as a name (which would mean that 'Duke' has a capital letter).

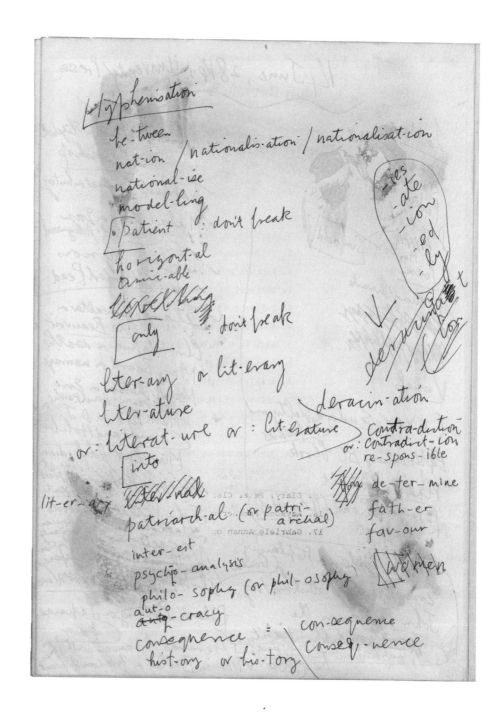

Page from one of Karl Miller's notebooks

From:	Samuel Reifler
Sent:	28 October 2015 15:48
To:	LRB (Editorial)
Subject:	Mash note

A mash note. Not for publication.

Dear LRB,

I always look forward to getting my next issues of both the NYRB and the LRB. Each has its strengths, but the NYRB is a little stodgy compared with the LRB. You seem to welcome irony, humor, sarcasm, as long as it's clever – a great pleasure for your readers. You wouldn't find "The Irish were put on this earth for other people to feel romantic about" in the NYRB.

And congratulations on not having caught LPS (lazy preposition syndrome), which seems to have become endemic among English speakers and writers your side of the pond. Its symptom is the inordinate use of the preposition "to" – especially prevalent, and jarring (to American ears, anyway), with the adjective "different" (which requires "from"). I've never seen "x is different to y" in the LRB. I hear it daily on the BBC and am aghast that it now trips blithely off the lips of my Oxbridge acquaintances.

I do wish you'd do something about your hyphenating program, though. It's disconcerting, in such a literate journal, to find one syllable words hyphenated, and multi-syllable words robotically mis-hyphenated – such as "tradit-ion" in the Eagleton article. Surely, it wouldn't take someone long to search through the hyphens and correct the mistakes in each issue.

Cheers,

Samuel Reifler

'Different to' is bad; so is 'on behalf of' when what's meant is 'on the part of'. As for our hyphenation policy – it's crazy, I agree, and very time-consuming.
Best wishes

Email from Samuel Reifler to Mary-Kay Wilmers, with a draft of her response, 28 October 2015

EXTRACT FROM VOL. 14 NO. 6 · 26 MARCH 1992

Another Subject Responds

Andrew O'Hagan writes: Nobody craves being taken seriously as much as a comic novelist. In 1980 Michael Mason wrote in the *LRB* that 'Vonnegut is a novelist to be taken seriously'; in 1992 he praised him again and was duly described as 'saintly' by the man himself.

Oedipal Wrecks

Michael Mason

REMARKS by Vonnegut in *Fates Worse than Death*, and elsewhere, make it clear that this dedicated novelist has been distressed by the bad reception of *Slapstick* and its successors. He has joked rather brutally that he considered putting a 'contract out' on Salman Rushdie for a bad review of *Hocus Pocus* (1990). Some of the harsh judgments have come from writers personally closer to him than Rushdie, and inflicted correspondingly deeper wounds.

But what is Vonnegut's own assessment of his last twenty years' output? He is not, it seems, completely at odds with his critics in part of their account. In *Palm Sunday* he awarded 'grades' for his novels down to *Jailbird* (1979): *Cat's Cradle* and *Slaughterhouse 5* got A+; *The Sirens of Titan*, *Mother Night*, *God Bless You, Mr Rosewater* and *Jailbird* A; *Player Piano* B; *Breakfast of Champions* C; *Slapstick* D. And more recently he has called *Galapagos* (1985) his 'best book'.

So Vonnegut is not apologetic about any major phase of his career, and certainly not about the kind of novel he writes in general (he has spoken rather acutely of how critics tend to mistake the appearance of literary achievement for the reality, and thus prize the unworkmanlike and clumsy: 'If a literary experiment works like a dream, is easy to read and enjoy, the experimenter is a hack'). But he does agree, to judge by his self-awarded grades, with the notion of a serious (if temporary) falling-off after *Slaughterhouse 5*, starting with *Breakfast of Champions* and reaching its nadir with *Slapstick*. D is, it must be said, a very low mark – and nothing short of abject when you give it to yourself.

The first of these two novels actually wore on its sleeve the author's doubt about its strengths, and his sense that he should push his work in some new direction. When I first encountered Vonnegut's C grade for *Breakfast of Champions* I was rather taken aback, for the novel had seemed one of his most beguiling and in places poignant fictions. It is known to have been an outgrowth from *Slaughterhouse 5*; the Dwayne Hoover figure as originally deployed in the earlier book became a study in itself, and this character is a memorable combination of the monstrous and the vulnerable. But the various explicit indications given by Vonnegut in the text of *Breakfast of Champions* that the book was the end of the road, or the end of a certain road, are obviously heartfelt, and therefore a kind of renouncing of powers in the act of displaying them.

Vonnegut called *Breakfast of Champions*, in the preface, 'my 50th birthday present to myself'; he felt 'as though I am crossing the spine of a roof – having ascended one slope'. He has elsewhere said that the book was his 'promise' that he was 'beyond suicide', and it is no secret that Vonnegut went through a severe personal crisis at this period. Even if we take his word for it that *Breakfast of Champions*, despite its black themes, betokened recovery, and a psychic breakfasting, by Vonnegut the man, it is evident that Vonnegut the novelist was not at ease. He puts himself into the story – which is an oddity in his fiction – and has himself saying: 'this is a very bad book you're writing.'

The only way he is able to find good in the badness, ascent in the descent from the roof's spine, is to regard *Breakfast of Champions* as a sort of dustbin, the receptacle for a salutary chucking-out of what is worthless and exploded in his practice as a writer hitherto. He announces that in this 'cleansing and renewing myself for the very different sorts of years to come' he is going to give up 'all the literary characters who have served me so loyally during my writing career'. He has even 'resolved to shun storytelling' – a declaration echoed in several statements by Vonnegut, at this date, that he was giving up fiction. He had already experimented with drama, in the play *Happy Birthday, Wanda Jane*.

Vonnegut did not give up fiction.

TO KARL MILLER
FROM KURT
VONNEGUT: USE
MY NOTE TO
THE SAINTLY
MICHAEL MASON
HOWEVER YOU
PLEASE.

Above, fax from Kurt Vonnegut to Karl Miller,
1992; right, note and drawing by Kurt Vonnegut,
published on the letters page, 20 August 1992

Bitter cold

Only this morning did I read your essay (*LRB*,
26 March) about my work. For this relief
much thanks; 'tis bitter cold etc.

Kurt Vonnegut

Sagaponack, Long Island

Grey Areas

London Review of Books

Tavistock House South, Tavistock Square, London WC1H 9JZ
Editorial: 071-388 6751   Advertising and Distribution: 071-388 7487
Fax: 071-383 4792

The Spectator
56 Doughty Street
London
WC1N 2LL

18 October 1993

Dear Anne Applebaum,

   You caught me rather on the hop last week,
and I'm sorry I wasn't then able to explain in
greater detail what my objections were to your
Russian piece.

   The LRB has always taken the view that to write about
the Soviet Union, past or present, in the simplified
terms of the Cold War, let alone Good and Evil, was
to do its readers a disservice, as if reinforcing
people's ideas were more important than refining
them. This isn't to condone the ghastly things that
were done under Stalin, even if it may mean making
less of them, on the understanding that there can be
no reader of the LRB anywhere who needs reminding
about the Gulag and so on. I would say exactly the
same thing about a book like Remnick's concerning
Nazi Germany : that to write, read or review it as
a moral tract would be an anachronism because we're
all on the same side when it comes to the horrors
and ought long since to have been trying to explain
rather than merely condemn them.

   So I was unhappy with your claim that there have
always been "two distinct types" of visitors to the
Soviet Union, the ones who saw and the ones who were
taken in, and with the theme of "facades" and the
need to see through or round them. I do not believe
that it has taken until David Remnick for the
Russian facade to be penetrated. We have ourselves
in recent years published a number of admirable and
admired pieces from John Lloyd in Moscow which have
demolished several facades, but without always
having to say that that was what they were doing:
that is, they describe people, events, life in
Russia on the same terms as people, events, life
elsewhere, and not as if that country were some
wholly peculiar moral arena labouring terminally
under its history.

   What I was hoping you would write for us was a
more shaded piece, therefore, with more in it about

EDITOR: Mary-Kay Wilmers   DEPUTY EDITOR: John Lanchester
ASSISTANT EDITORS: Jean McNicol, Andrew O'Hagan   CONSULTING EDITOR: John Sturrock
PUBLISHER: Nicholas Spice   ADVERTISEMENTS: Sarah Roth   SUBSCRIPTIONS: Michael Coates, Jessamy Harvey

Published by LRB Limited, registered in England at the above address No. 1485413

Letter from Mary-Kay Wilmers to
Anne Applebaum, 18 October 1993

London Review of Books

Tavistock House South, Tavistock Square, London WC1H 9JZ

Editorial: 071-388 6751   Advertising and Distribution: 071-388 7487

Fax: 071-383 4792

the "grey areas" as they say, and more analysis of
the years Remnick describes and the terms in which
he describes them. It's not ideology that divides
us, but differing views of what sort of journalism
the LRB should publish. Your own piece would seem
to the majority of our readers a departure from a
tradition of writing and reporting, first on the
Soviet Union and now Russia, which takes the element
of "evil" as a given whose sidelining is not a
matter for regret but an opportunity to understand
more clearly what sort of polity and society Russia
actually has been and currently is.

Yours sincerely,

EDITOR: Mary-Kay Wilmers DEPUTY EDITOR: John Lanchester

ASSISTANT EDITORS: Jean McNicol, Andrew O'Hagan CONSULTING EDITOR: John Sturrock

PUBLISHER: Nicholas Spice ADVERTISEMENTS: Sarah Roth SUBSCRIPTIONS: Michael Coates, Jessamy Harvey

Published by LRB Limited, registered in England at the above address No. 1485413

The Cold War. What it meant was that one was supposed to be on one side or the other. Anne Applebaum – having been commissioned to review David Remnick's first book, *Lenin's Tomb: The Last Days of the Soviet Empire*, in 1993 – felt the need, above all, to remind readers that Stalin was bad. In turning the piece down, Mary-Kay pointed out that most people already agreed he wasn't great, so it was hardly a thing you had to insist on at the expense of any other thought. There are many points of intersection between the LRB and the NYRB; the pieces the two papers have carried on Soviet Russia aren't an example.

In its early years, the LRB published barely anything on the Soviet Union because it seemed impossible to find a contributor who wasn't squarely on one side or the other. But then, in the second half of the 1980s, the paper started carrying pieces by John Lloyd, who had been briefly a communist, and went on to become Moscow correspondent for the *Financial Times*. Who could be more suitable? Nearly thirty years later, it is still overwhelmingly the case that Russia is treated in the West as if it were what Mary-Kay calls in her letter 'some wholly peculiar moral arena'. A handful of writers refuse this treatment – among them Miriam Dobson, Tony Wood, Sheila Fitzpatrick. Their work shows that it is possible to 'describe people, events, life in Russia on the same terms as people, events, life elsewhere'.

A Double Agent

A Russian stamp depicting 'Soviet Secret Agent' Kim Philby appeared on the cover of the LRB in July 1991. The cover infuriated Joseph Brodsky, who wrote about it nine months later in a long piece published by the *New Republic*. In it he said that 'no individual' he knew subscribes to both the LRB and the TLS. There were sides to be taken, and Brodsky implied that he knew the right and winning one. Meanwhile, Mary-Kay Wilmers wrote a letter to the editor of the *New Republic*.

London Review of Books

Tavistock House South, Tavistock Square,
London WC1H 9JZ
Editorial: 071-388 6751   Advertising: 0359 42375
Distribution: 071-388 7487   Fax: 071-383 4792

Letter to the Editor,
New Republic,
Fax: 0101 202 331 0275

Dear Editor,

Joseph Brodsky, writing in your issue of 20
April about 'the newer meaning of treason',
says that no one - or, to be fair, no one he
knows - reads both the <u>TLS</u> and the <u>London
Review of Books.</u>   Much of his piece is about
Kim Philby, who subscribed to both papers.
But then he was a double agent.

Yours sincerely

Mary-Kay Wilmers

Mary-Kay Wilmers

EDITORS: Karl Miller, Mary-Kay Wilmers DEPUTY EDITOR: Susannah Clapp ASSISTANT EDITOR: John Lanchester
PUBLISHER: Nicholas Spice ADVERTISEMENTS: Andrew Patterson SUBSCRIPTIONS: Michael Coates
EDITORIAL BOARD: Ian Hamilton, Frank Kermode, Michael Neve, V.S. Pritchett

Published by LRB Limited, registered in England at the above address No. 1485413

Letter to the editor from Mary-Kay Wilmers to the 'New Republic', 1991

HEALERS AND KILLERS

London Review
OF BOOKS

(USPS 709-250)

VOLUME 13 NUMBER 13   11 JULY 1991   £1.75   US & CANADA S2

СОВЕТСКИЙ РАЗВЕДЧИК

КИМ ФИЛБИ
1912—1988
5
к ПОЧТА СССР 1990

Demands for Exclusivity

Mary-Kay Wilmers writes: It's never a good day when one of your writers lands on the cover of the NYRB or the TLS, but it's good news for the culture of literary magazines that several still survive. I just don't want them putting the LRB's best writers on the cover. Writers want to be loved by everybody – why wouldn't they? – and that presents a challenge. I see in the letter here, from Christopher Hitchens, that I was doing my best to keep him from the clutches of the Murdoch press. I might have been doing him a favour, though that's beside the point.

AMN/JAS

Bodleian Library

Please reply to
Department of Printed Books

2 January 1991

Dear Dr. Harrison,

London Review of Books

Thank you for your recent comment in the Lower Reading Room Suggestions Book asking that the London Review of Books be placed with the Times Literary Supplement.

While the Times Literary Supplement was not published the London Review of Books took its place in the Upper Reading Room. Its confinement to the bookstack now is not only because of the limited space available in the Upper Reading Room but chiefly because of the antisocial wholesale removal of issues of the London Review of Books which occurred while it was on open access. I have tried on a number of occasions to put out at least the current issue, but each time copies were removed. While the current issue was on open access in the Upper Camera the same problem was experienced. Even though issues were returned, considerable inconvenience was incurred.

It is therefore to ensure that the London Review of Books is available at all, although with some inconvenience, that it is now confined to the bookstack. I am sorry that this has been necessary. I will consult with my colleague in English Accessions to see whether we might consider purchase of a second copy so that the copyright copy remains intact. The copyright copy could then be unavailable until bound when it would replace the purchase copy. This solution would not, however, compensate for the antisocial behaviour of readers who in the meantime removed issues of the London Review of Books thereby depriving other people of their use.

Yours sincerely,

███████████

███████████

Assistant Librarian

Dr. B.H. Harrison
Corpus Christi College

Bodleian Library
Broad Street, Oxford OX1 3BG
Telephone OXFORD (0865) 277000
Telex 83656 Fax (0865) 277182

Members of staff are not authorized to give valuations
and opinions are given only on the basis that they are offered
without responsibility on the part of the University of
Oxford or the member of staff.

Letter from A.M. Northover to B.H. Harrison,
2 January 1991

FOR: M·KW.
FROM: C.H.

12·V·96

Hi, sweetie,

Here we are - I hope you find it worth having waited for. I had to try and make the unusual balance between a piece for the time and a piece for "all time" - namely the LRB vol. The strain was greater than you might credit

Sorry that you didn't like my gig for Rupert. I say the following with diffidence, but I did once write a column for that shop and I do have some good friends over there still. They don't ask me that often and I don't always say yes. But I'm a touch reluctant to say I'll dump them altogether. For one thing, I'm already harried at this end by demands for exclusivity (a tendency begun by Tina Brown and not a wholesome one altogether). For another...well it's to do with the freelance temperament and practice, which has taken me a time to build up. I can tell you one thing, though. I don't do it for the money.

And if I *did* - well, let's not. Are you sure you aren't being too possessive? Are you sure I deserve it? (I'll be sorry I asked *that*.) If anybody notices my stuff at all, I'm sure they think I belong to you. I do, at any rate. (Think so, that is.)

Fraternally,

Hitch

Fax from Christopher Hitchens to
Mary-Kay Wilmers, 12 May 1996

Fraternally, Hitch

Feb. 13 '92 0:37   0000 E. HITCHENS D.C.   TEL 202-544-1896   P. 5

Christopher Hitchens

Booze and fags/eleven

  surgical spirit,

  kerosene,car diesel,derv...

This touches on a problem which,at a more refined plane,is understood
even by merely social drinkers such as myself,namely - Where's the next
one coming from? In one of its few klutzy decisions,this volume reprints
the whole of Auden's 1 September 1939,presumably for no better reason
than that it's set in a bar,and omits his poem On the Circuit,where he
confronts a problem that's increasingly urgent in today's America,
especially for those of us who fly and drone for a living:

  Then worst of all,the anxious thought,

  Each time my plane begins to sink

  And the No Smoking sign comes on:

  What will there be to drink?

  Is this a milieu where I must

  How grahamgreeneish! How infra dig!

  Snatch from the bottle in my bag

  An analeptic swig?

Or,and updating only slightly from 1963,dash off to the gents for a
smoke? Experiences like this and reflections like these teach one that
only a fool expects smoking and drinking to bring happiness,just as only
a dolt expects money to do so. Like money,booze and fags are happiness.
This distillate of ancient wisdom requires constant reassertion as
the bores and workhouse masters close in.

prohibitionists and

*and people cannot be
expected to pursue
happiness in moderation⊙*

*Eleventh page of the typescript for 'Booze and Fags'
by Christopher Hitchens, published in the issue of
12 March 1992*

Diary

Jeremy Harding

'I'M DYING,' Christopher Hitchens told Jeffrey Goldberg last year. 'Everybody is, but the process has suddenly accelerated on me.' I don't relish a world without Hitchens: along with many people, I like to hear from a man of principle at moments when recourse to principle strikes him as the greater part of valour, and listen in on his boisterous indiscretion when it doesn't. Hitchens's strong, almost gamey opinions produce a whiff of well-hung grouse in the reactions he provokes, and it tends to linger in the house. Stefan Collini, for the opposition, imagines Hitchens 'as twilight gathers and the fields fall silent, lying face down in his own bullshit'. Colin MacCabe, for the friends, tells us that passages of the memoir, Hitch-22, are 'among the most affecting writing that I know in English'. Hitchens, it seems, seldom meets with moderation.

The LRB was one of several papers lucky enough to catch Hitchens before he took to writing so affectingly in English. There is a consistency in his pieces in the LRB (62 in all) and elsewhere, about his voice and his approach. One formula which he liked to set before the LRB: louche for three column inches, bare-chested at the barricades for another four or five, incisive over a spot of lunch, then back to the struggle. That Left Opposition-Balliol dialectic, a tussle between the truth-teller out on a limb and the inveterate cynic, made for gripping journalism and seemed to those who read him – as well as the editors to whom he condescended – to work pretty well. After 2001, the contradictions began to multiply and then in the heat of battle to resolve. He was quite suddenly a sabre-rattling polemicist with the starkest of views, and the reader's jaw fell open. The best remedy for the hanging jaw is generally to walk away with one's hand cupping one's chin, but you could also cure the condition by hearing Hitchens hold forth in person: to this day he is a captivating talker, as his recent recordings with CBS's 60 Minutes attest.

One effect of Hitchens's movement from not quite left to not quite right is that he seems at one time or another to have covered every base. The point you wanted to argue is one he's already dealt with somewhere back down the road (and he'll tell you exactly where). Much to your astonishment, he agrees with you entirely, he's as true to you now, after his fashion, as he was when he first raised that very question. The Balliol boy wobbles off through the woods, while the juggernaut comes thundering on with a red-eyed ghoul at the wheel. And wait, there's Martin Amis in the cab beside him, with a frozen alcopop in one hand and an unread novel by Victor Serge in the other.

Which is another problem: few of Hitchens's friends are as clever, or fastidious, or well read, or hungry for the telling detail, as he is. Few have the same root and branch obsession with the recent past or the avenger's recall. No one nowadays has his divorce attorney's style when it comes to a historic grudge. It's a particular, keenly attentive disposition and it needs people who can keep the conversation going. Thirty years ago, when I called Hitchens to set up an interview from a gloomy radio studio in New York, his answering machine announced that anyone with news of fame or money was welcome to leave their number after the tone. Irony and panache of that kind were rare among the left-wing producers with whom I worked at WBAI radio and brought a little air into the room. But I wonder now about the road to fame and money and how much more bracing it would have been to follow him along it if he hadn't been obliged to break with his friends on the left, particularly the NLR crowd, who have their own juggernauts parked out the back. Hitchens seems to me a tempestuous figure with many devotees and enemies, and a shortage of equals. And when he falls it won't be on his face.

Christopher Hitchens first wrote for the LRB in 1983, having recently been transplanted to the US as a young columnist for the Nation. Over the years he took aim in the LRB's pages at Tom Wolfe, Henry Kissinger, J. Edgar Hoover, John F. Kennedy, Harold Wilson, Conrad Black, Princess Margaret, Isaiah Berlin, the Clintons etc etc. His typescripts rolled out of the fax machine at any time of night, requiring barely an editor's mark, as can be seen on the page shown here from a 1992 piece, 'Booze and Fags'. He wrote at ridiculous speed, often with large amounts of wine and whisky inside him. He was a frequent telephone caller, ringing from wherever he was and usually reversing the charges. Nothing held him back, and he could be light and funny as well as ferocious. His messages were often signed, like the one on the previous spread, 'fraternally, Hitch'; Mary-Kay Wilmers occasionally signed hers 'sororally, MK'.

Then, in or around 2002, things changed. Hitchens was no longer invited to write; had he been asked he would almost certainly have declined. On Bush's war on terror, on the invasion of Afghanistan, on the war in Iraq: the politics of the paper and the politics of the Hitch had diverged. His penultimate contribution to the LRB wasn't a piece for print but an appearance in a debate the paper held in Bloomsbury in 2002 on the war on terror. The enemy of almost all of the nine hundred people in the room, he fought his corner fearlessly – intolerable now, perhaps, but still extraordinary.

Unfair Comment

The LRB has never yet had to defend a libel action in court. The most serious slip was in the early 1990s, when we printed something we couldn't substantiate about an ex-minister of health in Zimbabwe and had to settle out of court. We also had to apologise to Uri Geller, although no one can remember what for.

SIMMONS & SIMMONS

P. RICHARDSON
S. L. JAMES
D. D. de CARLE
R. C. M. SYKES
SIR DAVID WILSON, Bt.
G. T. MARTYN
A. W. PATERSON
I. D. HOOD
J. S. CALVERT
A. M. CARR
J. P. HUMPHERY
C. A. GARNER
A. P. NEIL
J. M. BRADSHAW
G. H. BREWER
A. FISHER
P. A. de CHAZAL
B. N. BUCKLEY
A. C. DOVE

W. J. L. KNIGHT
C. D. SCANLAN
C. C. SIMPSON
R. D. DANIELS
K. M. MOONEY
CATHERINE HILTON
O. J. R. KINSEY
M. A. ELLIS
R. W. GOUGH
W. E. M. GODFREY
N. F. B. HEALD
A. J. BUTLER
J. C. WALTER
JANET GAYMER
S. J. NESBITT
P. E. FABER
P. J. FREEMAN
M. A. BROWN
S. R. ELVIDGE

CONSULTANTS
R. L. VIGARS
A. J. L. SKELTON

14, DOMINION STREET

LONDON, EC2M 2RJ

TELEPHONE: 01-628 2020
TELEGRAMS: "CONTROL LONDON, E.C.2"
FACSIMILE: 01-628 5386
TELEX: LONDON 888562

AND AT

REGENT BUILDING

BOULEVARD du REGENT, 58, Bte I

1000 BRUSSELS

RESIDENT PARTNER
CATHERINE HILTON

TELEPHONE: BRUSSELS 511 72 70
TELEGRAMS: SIMMONSLAW, BRUSSELS
TELEX: BRUSSELS 22087

YOUR REF.

OUR REF. 7/Y.6141/RS   2nd October, 1979

Professor Karl Miller,
Department of English,
University College London,
Gower Street,
London, WC1E 6BT.

Dear Professor Miller,

Jeremy Thorpe - A Secret Life.

Thank you for your letter of the 28th September. Your assistant telephoned me yesterday and I gave her my view that the article was safe to publish. It is carefully written and the only matters which come anywhere near the danger line are expressions of the reviewer's opinion. The law, I am pleased to say, allows considerable latitude to reviews. In any event, the protagonists in the criminal trial are not likely to sue. I have little doubt that they have been advised that it is impossible to win a libel action unless you go into the Box to be cross-examined. That might be interesting. It might indeed provide the answer to the final question in the review.

Yours sincerely,

Letter from Simmons & Simmons to Karl Miller, 2 October 1979. John Vincent's piece about Jeremy Thorpe was published in the issue of 8 November 1979

2

presure
[g] Mr Hitchens quotes two anecdotes from Nicholas
delete   Garland's book designed to show Conrad Black in a bad
     light.   Christopher Hitchens refers to Conrad Black
     as a "tyrannical egotist and sinister eccentric".

Christopher Hitchens clearly does not like Conrad Black.   He has
used the greater part of his book review to attack him in revenge
for what he perceives as Black's harassment and defamation.

It is essential that Christopher Hitchens provides us with
evidence of all the allegations he makes about Black.   We need
copies of:

   [a] copies of the letters Black wrote to the Spectator
        dealing with Hitchens;

   [b] a statement from James Srodes;

   [c] statements from those who overheard Black's
        conversation with Charles Moore at the Spectator
        dinner party;

   [d] statements from the Editor and the Managing Editor,
        (and their secretaries) of the Sunday Correspondent;

   [e] statements from the guests at the Georgetown dinner
        party.

Two of the anti-Black passages are contained in Nicholas
Garland's book.   This has now been published and I assume has
not attracted a Writ for libel, although it would be as well to
check with Mr Garland or his publishers.   However, the fact that
Mr Black has chosen not to sue the book is no guarantee that he
will not sue the London Review of Books and we have to be
satisfied that the anecdotes told in the book are accurate.

cut,
The real problem comes with Christopher Hitchens' opinions about
Mr Black - that he is a mad, tyrannical egotist, a sinister
eccentric, a megalomaniac.   Under normal circumstances, if Mr
Black were to take offence at these comments, we would have a
defence of "fair comment".   Mr Hitchens is entitled to his
honestly held opinion as to Mr Black and his state of health and
conduct.   However, a defence of "fair comment" can be set aside,
if Mr Black can show that Mr Hitchens was motivated by "malice"
when making his attack.   All Mr Black would have to do would be
to show that Christopher Hitchens had an ulterior motive for his
attack.   It is transparently obvious that Mr Hitchens does have
such a motive and I believe that a defence of "fair comment" may
well fail for this reason.

2.   Michael Meacher

cut
descr.
Mr Hitchens describes Mr Meacher as "a prefect with a reputation
for frigid sadism" and he quotes a sadistic remark made by Mr
Meacher to a boy at school.

*A page of legal advice on Christopher Hitchens's
piece on Conrad Black, published in the issue of
28 June 1990*

Into the Gloom

From left to right, covers from the issues of 21 January 1982, 15 November 1984, 19 June 1986,
29 October 1987, 2 June 1988, 2 March 1989, 28 September 1989, 8 October 1992, 23 September 1993

The first issues of the *LRB* didn't really have front covers, since they appeared inside the *New York Review*. The early issues of the independent paper had a cover photograph, sometimes taken for the occasion, sometimes found in a book or a photo library, accompanied by a couple of lines indicating some of the content of the issue. The photograph of Ian McEwan in the snow, the cover for the issue of 21 January 1982, was taken by Peter Campbell, who had designed the paper. By the end of that year the use of text on the covers was petering out, and the images – usually photographs, sometimes drawings or woodcuts – shared the space only with the masthead and a line of text at the top of the page, alternating red and blue from issue to issue and known to the staff as the rubric.

Some of the covers worked well; others, especially the darker ones (all the images were black and white), reproduced badly on newsprint, which drinks up ink. The dead Eskimo baby (a rather eccentric image choice) and the photo of Rodinsky's room in an abandoned synagogue in Spitalfields, written about by Patrick Wright, are examples of the failures. We knew the picture of Rodinsky's room wouldn't reproduce well but, as Bryony Dalefield, who was responsible for the paste-up (as she still is), remembers, Karl 'went ahead as if it would work by the very act of his will'. Sometimes we used poor or over-familiar stock photos: one issue showed a 'harlequin of the acid house scene', waving his arms all alone in what looks like a tunnel, and another a still of Harry Enfield as Loadsamoney. The figures in Chris-

topher Killip's photographs – James Kelman and Harold Hancock, a miner at Grimethorpe Colliery, are shown here – often disappear, perhaps appropriately, into the gloom.

The rubrics sometimes consorted oddly with the images beneath (you could argue this is still the case), or displayed Karl's fondness for phrases like 'Gray's Elegy, and Wynne Godley's' (in the final issue Karl edited, 8 October 1992) or for nouns connected by assonance ('Rumba, Conga, Communism') or some other patterning ('Shakespeare Nods, Thatcher Staggers'; 'Troubles: Heaney's, Wittgenstein's, Palestine's') or pun ('Conor Cruise O'Zion').

The cover of 23 September 1993, showing a horse from the Parthenon now in the British Museum, was again designed by Peter Campbell, who'd been unimpressed by the editors' amateurish attempts to combine image and text as the covers began to change again after Karl's departure from the paper. It comes during a slightly experimental period, before the covers settled down again into a new model employing Peter's own watercolours.

Jean McNicol

UNICEF
PO Box 7429 ADC
Pasay City
Metro Manila
Philippines

September 9, 1991

Dear Sir,

After several aborted subscriptions I have grown
to like the LRB. But I am deeply troubled by the covers.

It is not that I feel I don't appreciate them enough;
I don't appreciate them <u>at all</u>. The royal twins I accepted
as curious nostalgia. But the Derrida cover has me floored.
Am I meant to savour the sharply focussed hair emerging
from the left nostril? Is there some allegorical implication
in the juxtaposition with the rest of his blurred features?

I am taking advice on the matter, but there is
no gainsaying my growing feeling of intellectual
inferiority. I <u>have</u> to be missing something. I may not
mind if I am, but I want to <u>know</u>, I want to be let in
on the secret.

If you do, I'll let you print my Rudyard Kipling
letter. It reads:

Dear Sir,
I have been accustomed to sell a certain amount
of potatoes to an hotel proprietor in London, and
I have some of No. 2 grade ready to go to him now.
I shall be glad if you will send me a licence to
sell him two tons now, and possibly two tons in
another fortnight.

Yours faithfully,

Rudyard Kipling

How about <u>that</u> for literary innuendo/nuance/implication?

Yours faithfully,

David Mason.

Letter from David Mason to the editor,
9 September 1991

Or Philip Roth

Bernard Williams: What's fair?

London Review
OF BOOKS

VOLUME 15 NUMBER 9   13 MAY 1993   £2.10   US & CANADA $2.95

Frank Kermode on E. M. Forster

Jenny Turner on Philip Roth

Philip Roth drawn by R.B. Kitaj on the cover of the
reprinted issue of 13 May 1993

Andrew O'Hagan writes: I was 25. I had
a hangover. I hadn't been in the office
the previous week and didn't know
what was in the paper. Yet I got up very
early on Monday morning and travelled
from Marylebone station to Bicester – it
was my turn – to check the test copies
of the paper before the print run
started. When I was shown the cover
it looked to me like a good enough
drawing by R.B. Kitaj of a horse. In his
younger days, Kitaj had followed a
rather complex line which he called
'agitational usage'. But that's no excuse.
I thought the cover of the *LRB* for the
issue dated 13 May 1993 was of a horse.
The presses rolled and I took a few
copies back to the office. I read the
paper on the train. It contained a piece
by Bernard Williams on John Rawls's
Political Liberalism, and one by Jenny
Turner on Philip Roth. When I reached
the office, after an hour's kip and four
litres of Evian, I was unhappy to find
that my colleagues considered the cover
too dark. 'Too dark?' I said. 'You can see
perfectly well it's a drawing by Kitaj of a
horse.' 'Or Philip Roth, as some people
might say,' Mary-Kay Wilmers
remarked, before ordering the presses
to be halted and the dark copies to be
scrapped.

I wasn't allowed to go again.

The Editorial Chair

Karl Miller left the *London Review* in 1992. Neal Ascherson said a light had gone out and E.P. Thompson thanked Karl for his 'long editorial indulgence' and said he would be 'much missed'. Thompson began a new conversation with Mary-Kay Wilmers, 'the remaining editor'.

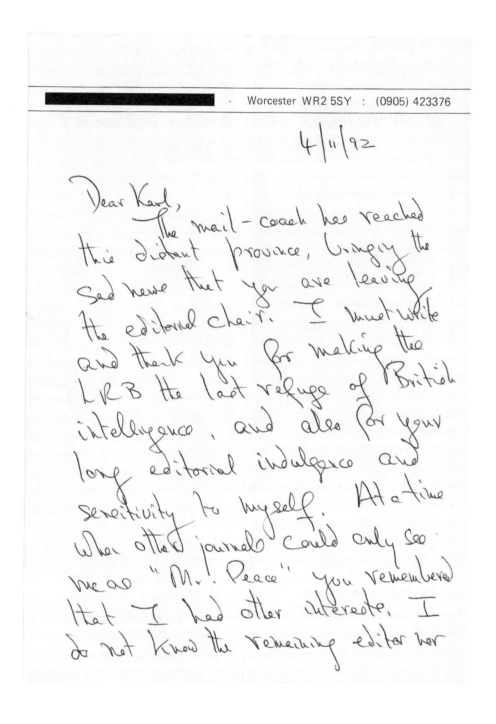

Worcester WR2 5SY : (0905) 423376

4/11/92

Dear Karl,
The mail-coach has reached this distant province, bringing the sad news that you are leaving the editorial chair. I must write and thank you for making the LRB the last refuge of British intelligence, and also for your long editorial indulgence and sensitivity to myself. At a time when other journals could only see me as "Mr. Peace" you remembered that I had other interests. I do not know the remaining editor her

Letter from E.P. Thompson to Karl Miller,
4 November 1992

know whether she will be interested in
my projected piece on Blake or not.

I hope you thrive in your
retirement or whatever your next
stage is. I am sure that
you will keep yourself busy.

My study of my father's
relations with Tagore is coming
out shortly (OUP New Delhi)
and the one on Blake and
antinomianism is with CUP. I
still hope to work up my
material on the Romantic poets
in the 1790s — a theme of my
Northcliffe lectures — into a book.

Your editorial presence will
be much missed —

Thankyou again,
Edward Thompson

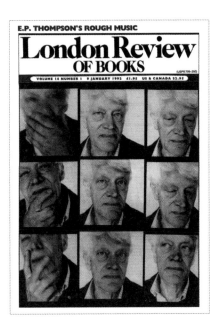

E.P. THOMPSON'S ROUGH MUSIC

London Review
OF BOOKS

VOLUME 14 NUMBER 1 · 9 JANUARY 1992 · £1.95 · US & CANADA $3.95

Transcription:

Dear Karl,

The mail-coach has reached this distant province, bringing the sad news that you are leaving the editorial chair. I must write and thank you for making the *LRB* the last refuge of British intelligence, and also for your long editorial indulgence and sensitivity to myself. At a time when other journals could only see me as 'Mr Peace' you remembered that I had other interests. I do not know the remaining editor nor know whether she will be interested in my projected piece on Blake or not.

I hope you thrive in your retirement or whatever your next stage is. I am sure that you will keep yourself busy.

My study of my father's relations with Tagore is coming out shortly (OUP, New Delhi) and the one on Blake and antinomianism is with CUP. I still hope to work up my material on the Romantic poets in the 1790s – a theme of my Northcliffe lectures – into a book.

Your editorial presence will be much missed.

Thank you again,
Edward Thompson

Witness

Memory
Martha Gellhorn

Jeremy Harding writes: Martha Gellhorn seldom found writing easy – X or Y, she used to say, could 'write like an angel', while others soldiered on as mere mortals. Her report about street children in São Paolo was her last stint in the field as a mortal: she was in her late eighties and reading it over, she felt she'd blown it. Ian Jack, the editor of *Granta*, turned it down. 'The fact that the writer had seen the situation for herself seemed the important thing,' he wrote later. But Gellhorn had always gone about her reporting as a witness – she wasn't much of a researcher, or a layer-peeling investigator – and in that sense the Brazil article was consistent with the rest. The *LRB* ran it, warts and (nearly) all: she was prickly about editing, even on a piece she claimed to think ill of. A few months later she offered us a shorter piece: a series of scenes from memory, centred on the fall of the Spanish Republic. They had come to her out of the blue while she was on holiday in Egypt. It was the better of the two pieces by far, and she was pretty happy with it.

THIS IS how my memory works. I was sitting in the big inner courtyard of the New Tiran Hotel, Naama Bay, south Sinai, drinking duty-free whisky and watching the new moon. The sky was dark blue with light behind it, not yet the real desert blackness. I had the place to myself, silence made the evening faultless. I was not thinking, I was basking in sensations of my skin. I could still feel the cool smooth water of the Red Sea from that late afternoon's snorkelling. The warm air now was soft on my arms and legs, the tiles of the paving hot under my bare feet. It is wonderful to know exactly when you are happy.

Without warning or reason, I was in a room in Gaylords Hotel in Madrid. It was winter, late 1937 at a guess. From Madrid, my memory took me without pause to Prague. It was right after Munich, after Chamberlain waved his piece of paper and said 'peace for our time', and was cheered for his evil stupidity. A long, dark corridor in the Hradčany Palace was lined with wood benches. I suppose anyone could walk there for I had no special pass and I must have been wandering around trying to get the feel of things, smell the atmosphere. I found Koltzov sitting on a bench, the only person in that corridor. He looked shrunken, all his brilliance gone. I sat beside him. He had no energy for talking and I could not stop.

I babbled the nightmare news of Barcelona, a whole city starving to death. In the children's wing of the big general hospital the wards were filled with beautiful small children wounded in the daily air-raids. Languid, silver Italian planes flew very high and casually dumped their bombs anywhere, everywhere. The children were silent, none cried or complained. There were also the children wounded by hunger. Four-year-old tuberculars. An adorable little girl, maybe two years old. She laughed when the nurse picked her up, laughed with joy at the game when the nurse held her up high. Her legs were limp as rope, this pinkish rope dangling below a swollen belly. I tried to talk about their eyes, huge and dark, and how they followed the clanking trolley that brought their food. Twice a day, always the same. Soup that was only hot water with a few green leaves and a few slivers of grey meat floating in it, and a small piece of bread, war bread, made of sawdust or sand.

The roads along the coast from Tarragona had become a sluggish human mire, carts, bicycles, prams, but mainly people trudging with heavy bundles. The smallest child who could walk also carried some family possessions. The old walked, too. The Moors were advancing and the soldiers of the Republic were fighting in retreat. These refugees were a new sight of war. No one had yet seen such a thing, thousands, tens of thousands of peasants, moving away from what they had always known to nowhere. They were exhausted and must have been deeply afraid but they were silent, too. No one talked, wept, screamed, cursed God and man. They were machine-gunned if the Germans felt like it, the Germans had the fighter planes, but this beaten army of refugees was hardly worth the trouble, the bullets. Too much pain, I said, nameless, helpless millions. Who cares about their pain?

Here my memory cut off, closed down, blanked out. I was back watching the brilliant new moon. Memory must be structured on dates. There can be no coherence or sequence to it unless it is anchored in time. But I have no grasp of time and no control over my memory. I cannot order it to deliver. Unexpectedly, it flings up pictures, disconnected with no before or after. It makes me feel a fool. What is the use in having lived so long, travelled so widely, listened and looked so hard, if at the end you don't know what you know?

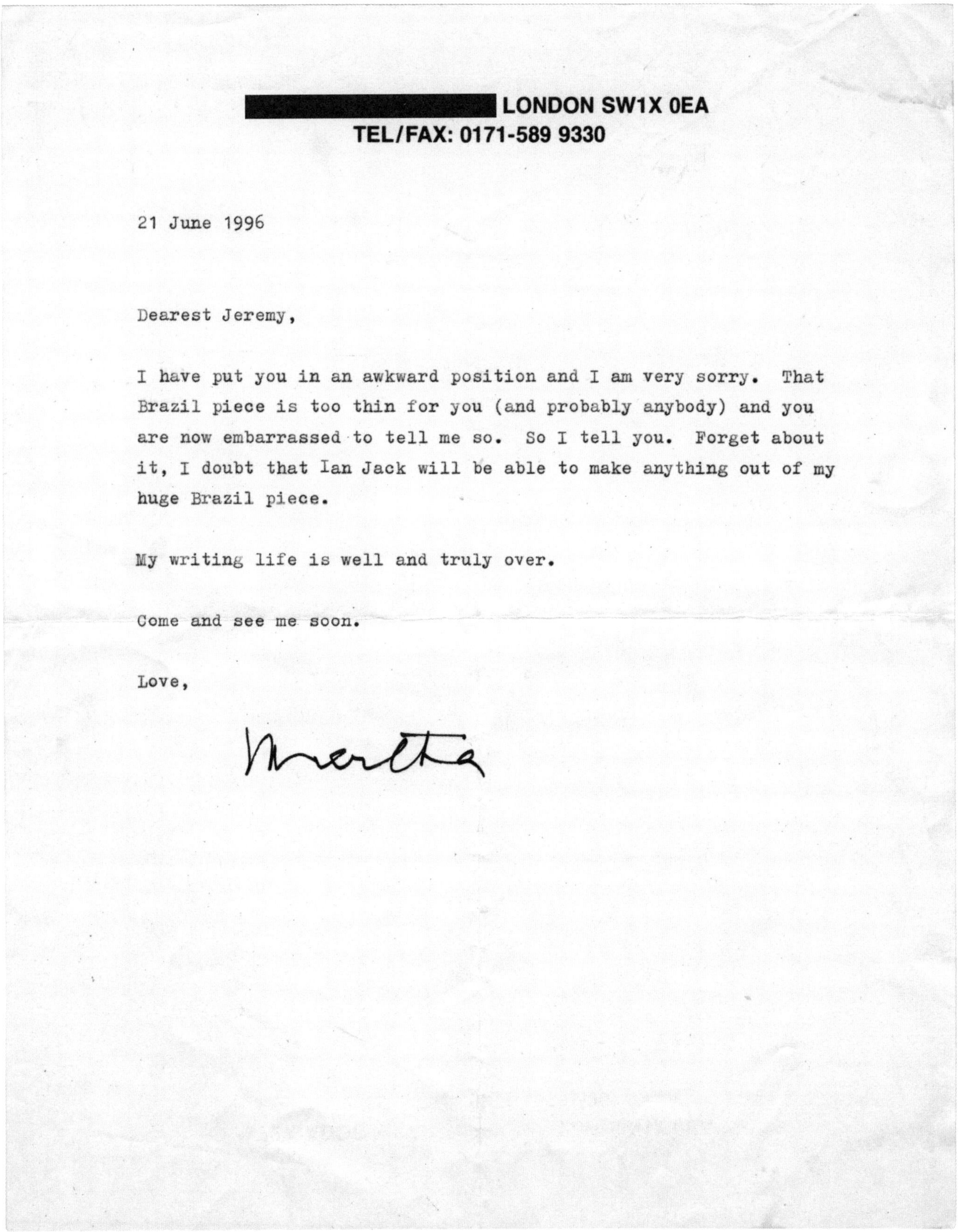

LONDON SW1X 0EA
TEL/FAX: 0171-589 9330

21 June 1996

Dearest Jeremy,

I have put you in an awkward position and I am very sorry. That Brazil piece is too thin for you (and probably anybody) and you are now embarrassed to tell me so. So I tell you. Forget about it, I doubt that Ian Jack will be able to make anything out of my huge Brazil piece.

My writing life is well and truly over.

Come and see me soon.

Love,

Martha

Letter from Martha Gellhorn to Jeremy Harding,
21 June 1996

Marina Warner: Queen Elizabeth's Homework

London Review
OF BOOKS

VOLUME 15 NUMBER 19   7 OCTOBER 1993   £2.10 US & CANADA $2.95

Childhood in the Wars

Lorna Sage

Public School Memories
Michael Hofmann

Ian Hamilton, Jerry Fodor, Richard Wollheim

The Old Devil and his Wife

Lorna Sage

GRANDFATHER'S skirts would flap in the wind along the churchyard path, and I would hang on. He often found things to do in the vestry, excuses for getting out of the vicarage (kicking the swollen door, cursing) and so long as he took me he couldn't get up to much. I was a sort of hobble; he was my minder and I was his. He'd have liked to get further away, but petrol was rationed. The church was at least safe. My grandmother never went near it – except feet first in her coffin, but that was years later, when she was buried in the same grave with him. Rotting together for eternity, one flesh at the last after a lifetime's mutual loathing. In life, though, she never invaded his patch; once inside the churchyard gate he was on his own ground, in his element. He was good at funerals, being gaunt and lined, marked with mortality. He had a scar down his hollow cheek too, which grandma had done with the carving knife one of the many times when he came home pissed and incapable.

That, though, was when they were still 'speaking', before my time. Now they mostly monologued and swore at each other's backs, and he (and I) would slam out of the house and go off between the graves, past the yew tree with a hollow where the cat had her litters, and the various vaults that were supposed to account for the smell in the vicarage cellars in wet weather. On our right was the church; off to our left the graves stretched away, bisected by a grander, gravel path leading down from the church porch to a bit of green with a war memorial, then – across the road – the mere. The church was popular for weddings because of this impressive approach, but he wasn't at all keen on the marriage ceremony, naturally enough. Burials he relished, perhaps because he saw himself as buried alive.

One day we stopped to watch the grave digger, who unearthed a skull – it was an old churchyard, on its second or third time around – and grandfather dusted off the soil, and declaimed: 'Alas, poor Yorick, I knew him well ...' I thought he was making it up as he went along. When I grew up a bit and saw Hamlet, and found him out, I wondered what had been going through his mind as he mystified me and the gravedigger, our jaws doubtless dropped to match Yorick's. I suppose the scene struck him as an image of his condition – exiled to a remote, illiterate rural parish, his talents wasted, and so on. On the other hand, his position afforded him a lot of opportunities for indulging secret, bitter jokes, hamming up the act and cherishing his ironies, so in a way he was enjoying himself. Back then, I thought that was what a vicar was, simply. Someone bony and eloquent and smelly (tobacco, candle grease, sour claret), who talked into space. His disappointments were just part of the act for me, along with his dog collar and cassock. He occupied the whole foreground. I was like a baby goose imprinted by the first mother-figure it sees – he was my black marker.

It was certainly easy to spot him at a distance too. But this was a village where it seemed everybody was their vocation. They didn't just 'know their place', it was as though the place occupied them, so that they all knew what they were going to be from the beginning. People's names conspired to colour in this picture. The gravedigger was actually called Mr Downward. The blacksmith who lived by the mere was called Bywater. Even more decisively, the family who owned the village were called Hanmer, and so was the village. The Hanmers had come over with the Conqueror, got as far as the Welsh border, and stayed ever since in this little rounded isthmus of North Wales sticking out into England, the detached portion of Flintshire (Flintshire Maelor) as it was called then, surrounded by Shropshire, Cheshire and – on the Welsh side – Denbighshire. There was no town in the Maelor district, only villages and hamlets: Flintshire proper was some way off; and (then) industrial, which made it in practice a world away from these pastoral parishes, which had become resigned to being handed a Labour MP at every election.

My Black Marker

It was John Sturrock who suggested to Lorna Sage that she write about her childhood for the London Review. In 1993 she was teaching English at the University of East Anglia, where she was soon to be made a professor. She had published books on Peacock, Doris Lessing and Angela Carter, as well as Women in the House of Fiction, a study of postwar women's writing. Her three pieces of memoir – the first things she wrote for the LRB – were published in consecutive issues of the paper in October and November 1993. 'Grandfather's skirts would flap in the wind along the churchyard path,' the first of them began, 'and I would hang on.' Her first review for the LRB, of a biography of Mary McCarthy, appeared a few months later. She also wrote on Terry Castle's Apparitional Lesbian (it was in part on the strength of that review that we asked Castle to contribute to the paper), Katherine Mansfield, Salman Rushdie and Toril Moi, among others. In 1994 she reviewed Jenny Diski's novel Monkey's Uncle. The piece appeared under the headline 'Bad Blood'. And that was the title Sage gave her memoir when it was published as a book in 2000. The first three chapters weren't much changed from the way they'd appeared in the LRB, but she took the story further, to her pregnancy at 16, 'making a baby the first and only time, and without really going all the way'. She and the baby's father, Vic Sage, went to Durham together, and became 'the first married couple of ordinary student age to graduate in the same subject at the same time, both with Firsts'. They separated in 1974. The LRB published his words at her memorial service in 2001 as a Diary: 'When I was fifteen and a half I received a letter from my new friend Lorna Stockton which announced that she was reading T.S. Eliot, "in a tree".'

This Kind of Work

In the early 1990s the LRB started to encourage writers to produce lengthy reported pieces. The first of them was Ronan Bennett's exposé of the framing of the Guildford Four. Published in June 1993 it was, at almost 24,000 words, by far the longest essay the paper had ever published. The only time the LRB has devoted the whole issue to a single subject, to controversial effect, was when we carried Andrew O'Hagan's piece 'The Tower', about the Grenfell disaster, in June 2018.

Ronan Bennett
London E8 3EP
tel. and fax 071-241 0675

1.iii.92

Dear Andrew,

It was good to meet you the other night. I'll be phoning round the publishers to ask for their catalogues, and will let you know if I find something I think might appeal to both of us.

As to the reportage proposal - it's a great idea, and I am very pleased that I am one of those the LRB has in mind to do this kind of work. I've been thinking about this and would like to suggest a few possibilities.

First, the trial of the three detectives accused of framing the Guildford Four. This is due to open in April. As you may know, I co-wrote Paul Hill's account of the aftermath of the Guildford bombings, and I know a good deal of the background to the case (I also know one of the solicitors involved in the case who has on a number of occasions supplied me with useful information). It could be an important piece. If you cast your mind back to 1989, when the Guildford Four were released, the press were full of demands that those responsible for framing the Four be prosecuted (the then-Lord Chief Justice, Lord Lane, demanded the same thing), yet this prosecution is going ahead only with extreme reluctance on the part of the CPS and the DPP.

Linked to this is the question of the May Inquiry. When the Four were released the Government set up an Inquiry to "get to the bottom of things" - yet all the indications are that the Inquiry is going to run into the ground. Lord May has on several occasions admitted that his Inquiry has been blocked and is going nowhere.

The point really is that someone framed the Guildford Four, someone was responsible for putting them away, but so far no one has paid for doing so - and if the predictions about the trial of the three detectives (the Guildford Three, as the police dub them) prove correct - no one will be paying. Before the whole issue of miscarriages of justice fades into the background for ever, a piece on this might be useful. (Do you remember I told you about a serial I was writing for Channel Four? It's on a - fictional - miscarriage of justice

Ian Gilmour: In Praise of Industry

London Review OF BOOKS

VOLUME 15 NUMBER 12 24 JUNE 1993 £2.10 US & CANADA $3.95

'I was released from my wrongful imprisonment by the Court of Appeal, mercifully after a much shorter time inside. I write, then, as a former prisoner, and I write as an Irishman, as someone who believes that the ramifications of the Guildford case say as much about Britain's unhappy relationship with Ireland as they do about the system of criminal justice in this country.'

Ronan Bennett on the retrial of the Guildford Four

First two pages of a letter from Ronan Bennett to Andrew O'Hagan, 1 March 1992

case.) Something else that might appeal to you in this connection: Daniel Day Lewis will be filming during April - during the trial, that is - the story of Gerry Conlon, one of the Four. Has it been left to Hollywood to "do justice" to the case?

A second suggestion is Zaire. This awful place is of interest to me because Cursed to Eat Bread, the novel I am now writing, is set partly in the old Belgian Congo (in 1960, at the time of Lumumba and independence). I've been researching it for some time, and recently had a long and useful meeting with George Ivan Smith, who was Dag Hammarskjold's press aide during the independence crisis. As you know, Zaire is in a terrible state at the moment as opponents of Mobutu continue to try to oust him. I have to go to Zaire to finish the research. Everyone tells me I'm mad to consider it at this time, but my feeling has always been: if you don't take the risks you don't get the material, so either go or set the novel in Hampstead. Perhaps the research trip and a piece for the LRB could be combined?

Alternatively - though it's pretty well covered in many ways, I have to admit - what about something on the deportations from the occupied territories? Friends of mine who have returned from the Lebanon and/or the occupied territories stress that one reason behind the surge in support for Hamas is the discipline and energy the organization has injected into an otherwise demoralized people. The same phenomenon is visible in Peru with Sendero Luminoso: at a time of grave crisis, an authoritarian, disciplined, committed organization can command significant support. Something on Hamas and the background to the deportations - an attempt to get to the deportees' camp in no-man's-land?

A fourth option is the one I mentioned to you the other night - I'm not sure how it would turn out, but it might be fun to do. I don't know if you know that Stephen Rea is married to Dolores Price. Dolores was sentenced to life imprisonment after the 1973 Old Bailey bombing - the first IRA bomb in London in this round of the "Troubles". In Northern Ireland, the Unionist/Loyalist press hate Rea because of this, and they always try to avoid mentioning him by name: when his Oscar nomination was announced the Unionist press ignored him and instead concentrated on Emma Thompson, "wife of Belfast-born Ken Brannagh". Yet now Rea is a celebrity in the States, feted by actors and producers alike. As I told you, I received a message a week or so ago from Rea asking me to come to New York to discuss a film he wants to do (with me as writer). There may be something here, though we would have to talk about the focus.

The Mercenary Business

In the 1980s and most of the 1990s, the LRB relied for foreign stories on journalists working for other media outlets, and academics based overseas. Travel expenses were rarely on offer. A nervous contributor once asked Karl Miller if the paper could help out with air travel. Karl made the position plain: 'not unless you get on my back and I start flapping my hands.' I was one of the first staffers to have my foreign research trips funded, for a long piece published in February 2000 on refugees and migrants. Flights and overland journeys with minders – in the Balkans, Italy and North Africa – were paid for; dry cleaning and a box of Havana cigars, which one contributor tried to bill us for, were not.

Starting out at the paper, I'd written from southern Africa, Eritrea and Palestine, on the back of commissions from large news organisations, including the BBC. In 1996 I was offered an assignment in Sierra Leone by NHK Japan. I would be semi-embedded with a new and controversial mercenary organisation, Executive Outcomes. Several of EO's officers had soldiered for the apartheid regime in the 1970s and 1980s, fighting in Angola as 'special forces'. The rank and file were drawn from Angolan rebel forces recruited during apartheid's wars against its neighbours. EO was a battle-hardened organisation reconfigured as a slick, top-of-the-range security service, available for a fee to governments of precarious states.

In Sierra Leone (stone broke and ravaged by the Revolutionary United Front, a violent insurgency) the government paid EO by allowing them to access the country's minerals. EO guarded the diamond mines against RUF attacks. Locals, who had been at the mercy of the rebels before the mercenaries pulled in, were grateful. Other civilians, who weren't living in mineral-rich areas, saw fewer benefits. Many underage soldiers had been recruited by the RUF, or pressed into the government's army. A large group of orphaned and injured children were living in a rehabilitation unit on the outskirts of Freetown. I took notes at the unit: not just the names of children but the songs they sang. One was a version of 'Dry Bones', about joints and

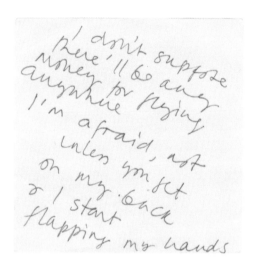

articulations in the unharmed human body ('The toe bone's connected to the foot bone' and so on). The RUF was notorious for summary amputations. I'd missed the significance of the song when I noted down the lyrics. But I get it now. A short passage about the children appeared in the published piece:

Safea Komba, an 11-year-old from the diamond area in Eastern Province, had been running ammunition for the government through RUF positions . . . Komba had been caught in the bush by the rebels; he said he was carrying food to his relatives, but live rounds were discovered in his bags. He was assaulted and cut at the shoulder and head with a machete and left to die. EO picked him up a few months after his recovery. There were many others: a 16-year-old girl called Florence who had gone crazy after seeing a rebel mutilated by her commander; a 15-year-old boy convalescing from a bullet wound in the arm; a private of the same age who went about the centre with a toy revolver tucked into the top of his shorts.

Jeremy Harding

4. Any miracle has started x 4

^   ^   ^   ^
^   ^   ^

[The back bone's connected to the kneebone]
  kneebone connected
[waistbone connected etc
  backbone shoulder neck

1) Kono   SAFEA KOMBA, 11   April —
   (RUP)   something [95
          [reconnaissance | small boys spy]   left him
                                                  to read

2) Kono ALUSINE MANSARAY, 17   St. — papa +
         (92-95)   12, 13   ARMY   auntie
                                         read

3) ABUBA BAKAR JAWARD, 16
   uncle   11 yrs   1991-95   St Army
   behind him   trained army
                                          + SAS

4) Florence Fillie, 16   ] uncle shot dead
   Kono   by soldiers
   District   15 yrs for 1 yr 1995   cook
               saw a mutilation of RUP suspect
                                   + began to want out

5)   (SA FIR JABIA)   15
    Kono   1 yr. 14   1993
    District
             "washington"   mmm + good read]

4th March.

Down of the sorties into ?? town
village, through a series of villages
ravaged + burnt out by rebel activity.
Colonel ___ has called a into of the
paramount chief — the only one or 3
local paramounts, he claims — who did
not flee the war. The chief is a
riot, as far as I can tell from his
speech in ___, + gracious. The
children + ___ nobody the entire population
of the town love EO. Kids cluster
round the men — it's easy here to
mount a hearts + minds campaign. All
you have to do is secure the area
+ refuse to behave in any way that
resembles the conduct of the RUF or
the Sierra Leone army.
It is raining — a gummy drizzle
over everything — + tearing around
on the open jeeps is chilly.
Strange roadblocks in some of the
villages

Pages from Jeremy Harding's field notes for 'The
Mercenary Business', published in the issue of
1 August 1996

Sorry, Ladies

Alice Spawls writes: Elaine Showalter's dissection of Camille Paglia's *Sex, Art and American Culture* provoked a predictable – and predictably amusing – response from Paglia, whose campaign against prominent feminists, and the feminist issues of the previous twenty years, was well underway. Showalter quotes Paglia to great effect but also points out that her 'self-presentation as an academic outcast is somewhat marred by the fact that she received her doctorate at Yale under the direction of the not exactly powerless Harold Bloom, and that *Sexual Personae* was published by Yale University Press.'

The LRB has taken stock of the developments and internal battles within feminism at various points over the last forty years. Questions of agency, performance, patriarchy and power have played out in the pieces and the combative letter exchanges that followed. As Jenny Turner wrote in 2011, 'Long before they were shouting "Ban the Bunny" and dressing up as butchers, feminists were annoying people, not just misogynists and sexists, but the very people you'd think would like them best. It was true in suffragette days, as it was during Women's Liberation in the 1960s and 1970s, and it's very much a problem for what boosters have been calling "the third wave" since the early 1990s.'

The Divine Miss P.

Elaine Showalter

WHO IS HOTTER than Mary McCarthy? Smarter than Susan Sontag? Funnier than Harold Bloom? Well, if you take her word for it, it's Camille Paglia, come to set the world straight on the burning issues of our time: tenured radicals, date rape, the aesthetic evolution of Madonna. The self-styled genius and warrior woman seized public attention with her first book, *Sexual Personae: Art and Decadence from Nefertiti to Emily Dickinson* (1990), a sweeping, Strindbergian analysis of culture as the war of the sexes. But what really made her famous were her attacks on feminism and academia, coupled with her paeans to pop culture. Naming names and kicking butt, Paglia quickly became a media celebrity, who hit the gossip columns when the model Lauren Hutton took her to the National Motorcycle Show in Manhattan, and posed for *Vanity Fair* in full make-up and a bulging décolletage, her arms around the bare biceps of the two black bodyguards she calls 'my centurions'. In the introduction to *Sex, Art and American Culture*, a bizarre grab-bag of book reviews, interviews, transcribed lectures, classroom notes and personal memorabilia, Paglia gleefully provides an annotated bibliography of all the news articles about herself, and attributes her fame to astrological cycles, the zeitgeist, and a new Age of Aquarius: 'At the end of the century and the millennium,' she writes, 'the culture has suddenly changed . . . Anti-establishment mavericks like me are back in fashion.'

Like her first book, *Sex, Art and American Culture* is on the American bestseller lists. But although it purports to have various cultural subjects, this book is really about the divine Miss P., her Catholic girlhood in Syracuse, New York; her intuitive feminism ('Before feminism, Paglia was! Out there punching and kicking and fighting with people!'); her Italian-American identity; her struggles with gender and sexuality; her education; her traumatic rejection by the New Haven Women's Rock Band for admiring the Rolling Stones; her subsequent alienation from the women's movement;

her failure to make it in the academic world; her long exile in Philadelphia; her triumphant return. As she recently announced to a bemused audience at Princeton (the bodyguards discreetly out of sight), 'You are in the presence of one of the great woman scholars in the world.'

To be neglected and forgotten and then lifted to fame is a story with universal appeal, and Paglia presents herself as a scrappy Cinderella fighting against the ugly sisters of American academic feminism. In contrast to her own deep learning, personal daring, appreciation of beauty and refusal to cohabit with men, Paglia asserts, feminist critics are 'poor or narrowly trained scholars', 'conventional married women who never rocked a boat in their lives'. These 'beaming Betty Crockers, hangdog dowdies, and parochial prudes' don't appreciate the rough, sweaty appeal of real men, and are so benighted that they admire their 'nerdy bookworm husbands', those 'eunuchs' from 'elite schools' who lack the 'primordial male sexuality' of the stupid. They don't understand the 'fun element in rape', they 'loathe Madonna', they have no feeling for Beauty and Art. And yet, by dint of toadying and sucking up and being nice, these women have snagged all the best teaching jobs, while Paglia has laboured alone and unheard at the Philadelphia College of Art. Her ethnicity, her integrity, her innocence, her refusal to play the academic game, have kept her back while less talented – much less talented – Ivy League schemers rose through the ranks. Even a trip to the library at the nearby University of Pennsylvania sends her into a rage at 'those prep-school voices'. Nonetheless, the story has a happy ending, for out of her years of exile, solitude and cunning, out of teaching scholarship students and being spared 'all these poisons that have swept over the Ivy League', comes the great work of *Sexual Personae*.

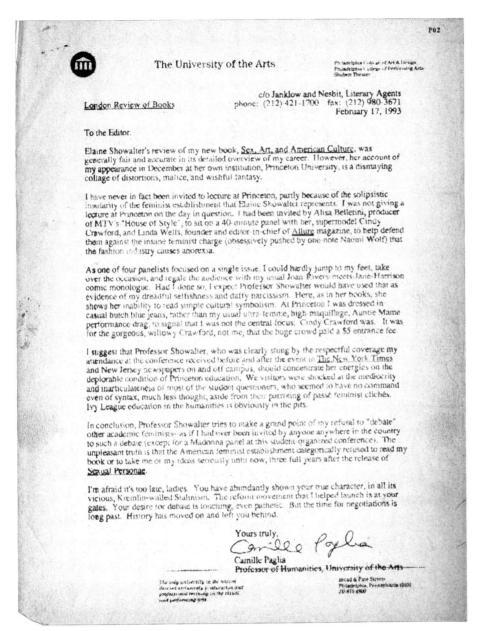

The University of the Arts

Philadelphia College of Art & Design
Philadelphia College of Performing Arts
Student Theater

London Review of Books

c/o Janklow and Nesbit, Literary Agents
phone: (212) 421-1700   fax: (212) 980-3671
February 17, 1993

To the Editor,

Elaine Showalter's review of my new book, Sex, Art, and American Culture, was generally fair and accurate in its detailed overview of my career. However, her account of my appearance in December at her own institution, Princeton University, is a dismaying collage of distortions, malice, and wishful fantasy.

I have never in fact been invited to lecture at Princeton, partly because of the solipsistic insularity of the feminist establishment that Elaine Showalter represents. I was not giving a lecture at Princeton on the day in question. I had been invited by Alisa Bellettini, producer of MTV's "House of Style", to sit on a 40-minute panel with her, supermodel Cindy Crawford, and Linda Wells, founder and editor-in-chief of Allure magazine, to help defend them against the insane feminist charge (obsessively pushed by one-note Naomi Wolf) that the fashion industry causes anorexia.

As one of four panelists focused on a single issue, I could hardly jump to my feet, take over the occasion, and regale the audience with my usual Joan-Rivers-meets-Jane-Harrison comic monologue. Had I done so, I expect Professor Showalter would have used that as evidence of my dreadful selfishness and daffy narcissism. Here, as in her books, she shows her inability to read simple cultural symbolism. At Princeton I was dressed in casual butch blue jeans, rather than my usual ultra-femme, high-maquillage, Auntie Mame performance drag, to signal that I was not the central focus: Cindy Crawford was. It was for the gorgeous, willowy Crawford, not me, that the huge crowd paid a $5 entrance fee.

I suggest that Professor Showalter, who was clearly stung by the respectful coverage my attendance at the conference received before and after the event in The New York Times and New Jersey newspapers on and off campus, should concentrate her energies on the deplorable condition of Princeton education. We visitors were shocked at the mediocrity and inarticulateness of most of the student questioners, who seemed to have no command even of syntax, much less thought, aside from their parroting of passé feminist clichés. Ivy League education in the humanities is obviously in the pits.

In conclusion, Professor Showalter tries to make a grand point of my refusal to "debate" other academic feminists—as if I had ever been invited by anyone anywhere in the country to such a debate (except for a Madonna panel at this student-organized conference). The unpleasant truth is that the American feminist establishment categorically refused to read my book or to take me or my ideas seriously until now, three full years after the release of Sexual Personae.

I'm afraid it's too late, ladies. You have abundantly shown your true character, in all its vicious, Kremlin-walled Stalinism. The reform movement that I helped launch is at your gates. Your desire for debate is touching, even pathetic. But the time for negotiations is long past. History has moved on and left you behind.

Yours truly,

Camille Paglia
Professor of Humanities, University of the Arts

The only university in the nation
devoted exclusively to education and
professional training in the visual
and performing arts.

Broad & Pine Streets
Philadelphia, Pennsylvania 19102
215-875-4800

Transcription:

To the Editor,

Elaine Showalter's review of my new book, *Sex, Art and American Culture*, was generally fair and accurate in its detailed overview of my career. However, her account of my appearance in December at her own institution, Princeton University, is a dismaying collage of distortions, malice and wishful fantasy.

I have never in fact been invited to lecture at Princeton, partly because of the solipsistic insularity of the feminist establishment that Elaine Showalter represents. I was not giving a lecture at Princeton on the day in question. I had been invited by Alisa Bellettini, producer of MTV's *House of Style*, to sit on a 40-minute panel with her, supermodel Cindy Crawford, and Linda Wells, founder and editor-in-chief of *Allure* magazine, to help defend them against the insane feminist charge (obsessively pushed by one-note Naomi Wolf) that the fashion industry causes anorexia.

As one of the four panellists focused on a single issue, I could hardly jump to my feet, take over the occasion, and regale the audience with my usual Joan-Rivers-meets-Jane-Harrison comic monologue. Had I done so, I expect Professor Showalter would have used that as evidence of my dreadful selfishness and daffy narcissism. Here, as in her books, she shows her inability to read simple cultural symbolism. At Princeton I was dressed in casual butch blue jeans, rather than my usual ultra-femme, high-maquillage, Auntie Mame performance drag, to signal that I was not the central focus: Cindy Crawford was. It was for the gorgeous, willowy Crawford, not me, that the huge crowd paid a $5 entrance fee.

I suggest that Professor Showalter, who was clearly stung by the respectful coverage my attendance at the conference received before and after the event in the *New York Times* and New Jersey newspapers on and off campus, should concentrate her energies on the deplorable condition of Princeton education. We visitors were shocked at the mediocrity and inarticulateness of most of the student questioners, who seemed to have no command even of syntax, much less thoughts, aside from their parroting of passé feminist clichés. Ivy League education in the humanities is obviously in the pits.

In conclusion, Professor Showalter tries to make a grand point of my refusal to 'debate' other academic feminists – as if I had ever been invited by anyone anywhere in the country to such a debate (except for a Madonna panel at this student-organised conference). The unpleasant truth is that the American feminist establishment categorically refused to read my book or take me or my ideas seriously until now, three full years after the release of Sexual Personae.

I'm afraid it's too late, ladies. You have abundantly shown your true character, in all its vicious, Kremlin-walled Stalinism. The reform movement that I helped launch is at your gates. Your desire for debate is touching, even pathetic. But the time for negotiations is long past. History has moved on and left you behind.

Yours truly,
Camille Paglia
Professor of the Humanities,
University of the Arts

Letter to the editor from Camille Paglia, 17 February 1993

Homelessness

Edward Said began writing about the politics of the Middle East for the *LRB* in the early 1980s, when the PLO was still an important national liberation movement, along with others struggling against colonialism or military occupation in South Africa, Namibia, East Timor and Western Sahara, with solid support at the UN General Assembly. His last piece on Palestine – in 2003, the year he died – came long after the other movements, with the exception of Western Sahara, had achieved their objectives. Nelson Mandela had said that the freedom of South Africans was 'incomplete' without a just settlement in Palestine, but the Palestinians were still isolated, their society – in Said's words – 'devastated, nearly ruined, desolate in so many ways'. In 1993 he deplored the Oslo Accords and in 2000 mapped the growing fragmentation of Palestinian territory enabled by the agreement. But he remained optimistic that a surge of radical energy would take the Palestinian leadership in the West Bank by surprise and in his last years looked for inspiration to the rise of a civil rights movement in the Occupied Territories and the diaspora.

Said established a rapport with the *LRB* editors from the outset. He was the paper's most distinguished postcolonial scholar and an energetic free-ranger: he wrote on Conrad, Hemingway, Edmund Wilson, Mahfouz, Hobsbawm and Joan Didion; he declared his affection for the Western musical canon in pieces about Bach, Beethoven, Wagner. He was fun to hang out with, witty and inquisitive. The letter here thanks me for the loan of a cab fare after an evening out in London: it was mailed the following day with a cheque. He makes a characteristic joke. Said, an elegant dresser, though not quite a dandy, was never going to be mistaken for a homeless person, even if he was hawking papers on the street.

When the Cold War ended the Palestinians were left stranded, despite the fact that most outstanding business for 'Third World' liberation movements was concluded in short order. Apartheid was finished; Angola and Mozambique were no longer at war with Pretoria; East Timor was an independent state. But sympathy with the Palestinians persisted, and it looked to some readers as though Israel was being singled out as a world-historical demon. And that could only mean one thing to its fiercest defenders – antisemitism, something that no one at the *LRB* was tempted by.

Jeremy Harding

Murray Sayle: Everest and Empire

London Review
OF BOOKS

VOLUME 20 NUMBER 9   7 MAY 1998   £2.50 US & CANADA $2.95

'With an unexceptionally Arab family name connected to an improbably British first name – my mother very much admired the Prince of Wales – I was an uncomfortably anomalous student all through my early years.'
Edward Said

Edward Said

Wednesday
11 July

Dear Jeremy –
Thanks so much for bailing us out the other night! It was a joy to see you. And many thanks also for the ton of LRBs which arrived yesterday most of which I shall have to post home. I tried giving away some on Knightsbridge this morning but, as one passerby said, "You don't _look_ like a homeless person!"
Hope to see you again soon –
Warmly
Edward

check enclosed

MANDARIN ORIENTAL
HYDE PARK
LONDON

In residence at Mandarin Oriental Hyde Park
66 Knightsbridge London SW1X 7LA
Telephone (44 020) 7235 2000 Facsimile (44 020) 7235 4552
A Mandarin Oriental Hotel

Letter from Edward Said to Jeremy Harding,
11 July 1998

Transcription:

Dear Jeremy –

Thanks so much for bailing us out the other night! It was a joy to see you. And many thanks also for the ton of *LRB*s which arrived yesterday most of which I shall have to post home. I tried giving away some on Knightsbridge this morning but, as one passerby said, 'You don't *look* like a homeless person!'
Hope to see you again soon –

Warmly –
Edward

Only Zealots

'Please forward to Said, with note,' Mary-Kay Wilmers wrote in 2000 on an email from a reader thanking the LRB 'for publishing Mr Said's delineation of the other side'. It was, she said, 'a ray of sunshine amid the cancellations'. Every time Edward Said wrote about Palestine in the LRB, it provoked a pile of responses accusing the paper of one-sidedness. Isaiah Berlin's letter is an early but representative example.

David Sylvester: Hanging at the Academy

London Review OF BOOKS

VOLUME 15 NUMBER 20 21 OCTOBER 1993 £3.10 US & CANADA $2.95

'Let us call the agreement by its real name: an instrument of Palestinian surrender, a Palestinian Versailles.'

POLITICS

Edward Said: why the Israeli-PLO pact is a historic capitulation;
Avi Shlaim: why it
is a historic breakthrough.
Peter Clarke: Homage to John Smith
John Lloyd: why everyone's
backing big Boris.

EXTRACT FROM VOL. 15 NO. 20 · 21 OCTOBER 1993

The Morning After

Edward Said

Now that some of the euphoria has lifted, it is possible to re-examine the Israeli-PLO agreement with the required common sense. What emerges from such scrutiny is a deal that is more flawed and, for most of the Palestinian people, more unfavourably weighted than many had first supposed. The fashion-show vulgarities of the White House ceremony, the degrading spectacle of Yasser Arafat thanking everyone for the suspension of most of his people's rights, and the fatuous solemnity of Bill Clinton's performance, like a 20th-century Roman emperor shepherding two vassal kings through rituals of reconciliation and obeisance: all these only temporarily obscure the truly astonishing proportions of the Palestinian capitulation.

So first of all let us call the agreement by its real name: an instrument of Palestinian surrender, a Palestinian Versailles. What makes it worse is that for at least the past fifteen years the PLO could have negotiated a better arrangement than this modified Allon Plan, one not requiring so many unilateral concessions to Israel. For reasons best known to the leadership it refused all previous overtures. To take one example of which I have personal knowledge: in the late 1970s, Secretary of State Cyrus Vance asked me to persuade Arafat to accept Resolution 242 with a reservation (accepted by the US) to be added by the PLO which would insist on the national rights of the Palestinian people as well as Palestinian self-determination. Vance said that the US would immediately recognise the PLO and inaugurate negotiations between it and Israel. Arafat categorically turned the offer down, as he did similar offers. Then the Gulf War occurred, and because of the disastrous positions it took then, the PLO lost even more ground. The gains of the intifada were squandered, and today advocates of the new document say: 'We had no alternative.' The correct way of phrasing that is: 'We had no alternative because we either lost or threw away a lot of others, leaving us only this one.'

In order to advance towards Palestinian self-determination – which has a meaning only if freedom, sovereignly and equality, rather than perpetual subservience to Israel, are its goal – we need an honest acknowledgment of where we are, now that the interim agreement is about to be negotiated. What is particularly mystifying is how so many Palestinian leaders and their intellectuals can persist in speaking of the agreement as a 'victory'. Nabil Shaath has called it one of 'complete parity' between Israelis and Palestinians. The fact is that Israel has conceded nothing, as former Secretary Of State James Baker said in a TV interview, except, blandly, the existence of 'the PLO as the representative of the Palestinian people'. Or as the Israeli 'dove' Amos Oz reportedly put it in the course of a BBC interview, 'this is the second biggest victory in the history of Zionism.'

By contrast Arafat's recognition of Israel's right to exist carries with it a whole series of renunciations: of the PLO Charter; of violence and terrorism; of all relevant UN resolutions, except 242 and 338, which do not have one word in them about the Palestinians, their rights or aspirations. By implication, the PLO set aside numerous other UN resolutions (which, with Israel and the US, it is now apparently undertaking to modify or rescind) that, since 1948, have given Palestinians refugee rights, including either compensation or repatriation. The Palestinians had won numerous international resolutions – passed by, among others, the EC, the non-aligned movement, the Islamic Conference and the Arab League, as well as the UN – which disallowed or censured Israeli settlements, annexations and crimes against the people under occupation.

It would therefore seem that the PLO has ended the intifada, which embodied not terrorism or violence but the Palestinian right to resist, even though Israel remains in occupation of the West Bank and Gaza.

Isaiah Berlin

▄▄▄▄▄▄▄▄▄▄▄▄▄▄▄▄

OXFORD, OX3 9HU

TEL: OXFORD 61005

24 February 1984

Dear Karl,

I <u>have</u> had a bad time with the London Review! first, Aarseff (I did not much like Nigel Hamilton's wholly contemptuous review of 'my' Washington Despatches, but I thought that what he said was quite just); then a nasty piece about the domination of America by the 'Elders of Zion', with their mysterious, unlimited power, by the fanatical Ian Gilmour, who obviously really does think there is a conspiracy and that American Senators are manipulated even in states like Idaho, where there are virtually no Jews - by horrid methods that he only mysteriously hints at; but I know what he means, and it won't do. On the same page there was an even more obsessed piece by Malise Ruthven, who really must be a little crazy, in which he declares that the famous Kahan Report on the massacres in the Lebanon - which had an enormous impact on opinion in Israel - was nothing but a cynical whitewash which could not take in a cat. These are surely the outpourings of pure fanaticism. The present Government of Israel is, in my view, wicked and odious, but that is not the point. Your Middle Eastern experts seem to me possessed - and have been for some time - by a hatred beyond reason of the entire horrid enterprise of Zionism, of the springs and nature of which they show not the slightest knowledge - as if it was something frightful, exploding out of nothing.

Stuart telephoned me the other day and asked me if I had seen the latest copy of the <u>LRB</u>. I said I had not. He begged me not to look at it, since the article by Edward Said would surely cause me to cancel my subscription, and would send me into a sharp decline. I did, of course, read it at once. Stuart's disapproval was concerned not to much with the first part of the article, which, we agreed, was routine PLO stuff, only more repetitive, pretentious, and confused than the shorter and clearer statements by Arafat, but with the encomium to Chomsky. I know Chomsky quite well, and like him - he is a man of brilliant gifts and great personal charm; but his polemical writings are not exactly notable for scruple or unswerving adherence to the truth. This is true about all his writings, including linguistics, but he lost all political credibility after he maintained that the reports of massacres by the Khmer Rouge were largely inventions of the American media, and after a piece by him was published, with his permission, as an introduction to a book by a man called Faurisson, who said that the Nazi holocaust had never

First page of a letter from Isaiah Berlin to
Karl Miller, 24 February 1984 (continued overleaf)

- 2 -

occurred, but was a Zionist invention. The tribute to Chomsky's integrity irritated Stuart because of its patent falsity. (He said that this was intended only to support the right to free speech, but it went too far even for his followers.) One cannot, of course, blame any Palestinian Arab for hating Israel, whatever he writes; but so far as serious students of the subject are concerned, Said was laid out once and for all by the formidable Bernard Lewis, in an article in the NYRB: his Harold-Bloom hypnotised critical essays seem to me, in their own silly way, no better (though I expect Frank K. might defend them on principle).

What I really want to ask you is, must you use only zealots in writing about the Middle East? If you employ members of the Council of the PLO or CAABU, should this not be balanced with pieces by some ghastly ex-member of the Irgun or the Stern Gang? It is clear that nobody can be neutral about either the Soviet Union or Israel. Nevertheless, there are degrees of rabidity - there must be more temperate people who can write. In Israel itself there exists a movement called 'Peace Now', which is entirely decent and very moderate - prepared to talk to the PLO, give up the West Bank, etc. - they organised huge meetings to protest about the invasion of Lebanon, the treatment of Arabs, and everything that goes with it (one of its members, the novelist Amos Oz, who is a genuinely brave protester, is one of the people whom Chomsky - approved by Said - regards as a greater menace than the nationalist fanatics): these people are not favoured by the Government, nor even by sections of the Israel Labour Party, for whom they go too far, but I admire them greatly. Can't there be something by, or at least about, them? (there are no other moderates in the Middle East) – they write calmly and well. I wish I could offer you something – even if you declined it – but I am no expert.

But why am I going on like this? What right have I to write a letter simply to say that I keep having an awful time with your otherwise excellent periodical? – my unfortunate experience is probably unique. It is only that I wanted to get all this off my chest, but that is no reason why you should be subjected to a tirade. Please forgive me. I should have preferred to say this to you, but we see each other, sadly, so seldom, that the only say of dealing with this is in writing. No doubt the Edwards - Said, Mortimer, etc. - would ~~say that my letter is precisely the kind of~~ attempt at censorship that ~~the wicked Zionists are so good at. They~~ are impervious to argument. [The bitterly committed seem to me] Anyway, Stuart encouraged me to write to you, else I don't think I should have. Dixi, et salvavi animam meam.

Yours, in unbroken friendship, (I actually said "affection" but this will do as well)

Isaiah

Through the pieces the paper has carried, the *LRB* has demonstrated a commitment to the principle that Palestinian Arabs have as much right to freedom and self-determination in historical Palestine as the Israeli Jews whose state expelled them and occupied their lands. Upholding this principle has led to accusations of extremism, support for 'terrorism' and of antisemitism, raised not only by right-wing Zionists but by self-styled 'moderate' defenders of the Jewish state such as the late Isaiah Berlin. While Berlin and much of the Western liberal press celebrated writers like Amos Oz as the face of a humane, tolerant Zionism that would ultimately be restored to its mostly imagined glory, the *LRB* has always insisted that Zionism and liberal principle are in irreconcilable tension, and that the former will almost always prevail over the latter in a state defined as belonging to a single religious group. To read Berlin's letter complaining that the *LRB* used 'only zealots' to write about the Middle East against the backdrop of Netanyahu's Israel is to see a man clinging to the mast of a ship that has now sunk. The *LRB*'s zealotry, by comparison, looks like prescience.

Another accusation the paper has faced over the years is that it speaks with one voice about Israel-Palestine (as if other journals were a garden of diversity on this question). It is true, of course, that the paper has never published flattering portraits of Israeli liberals, much less apologias for Israeli policy. A fundamental ethical conviction that a tremendous historical wrong was and is still being perpetrated against the Palestinian people has anchored its perspective. But it's not the case that the paper has a 'line' on Israel-Palestine. The coverage has been a confluence of three intellectual traditions: British Arabism, radical anti-imperialism and Jewish dissidence, or what Isaac Deutscher called the tradition of the 'non-Jewish Jew' who rejects tribalist identification and adheres to cosmopolitan, humanist values. These traditions overlap but also diverge and even clash, and the paper has welcomed their counterpoint, to borrow a word that Edward Said often used. The *LRB* has also tried to avoid pushing for a specific 'solution' – two states, one state etc – precisely because of its awareness that, in the Middle East, today's 'solutions' invariably become tomorrow's problems. This is not cynicism so much as worldliness.

The person who deserves more credit than anyone for the *LRB*'s record on Israel-Palestine is Mary-Kay Wilmers, who has waged a courageous battle to keep the question of Palestine alive in the conscience of the West. Many writers who have felt homeless because of their stance on this issue have found a sanctuary in the *LRB*. I am one of them. Fear and self-censorship were the norm in American journalism when I started to write about the Middle East in the early 2000s. I was instructed not to use the word 'Palestine' by the *New York Times Book Review*, since the state of Palestine did not exist. (Golda Meir, who claimed the Palestinians did not exist, would have been pleased.) Joining the *LRB* marked both the beginning of my exile from American journalism and the end of my intellectual exile, since I was now free to speak my mind and call things by their name. At the paper I was no longer seen as a strange, wandering Jewish critic of Israel, much less a 'self-hating Jew'.

Mary-Kay understood that my writings on Israel did not emerge from hostility to Israeli Jews, or from doctrinaire opposition to Israel's existence, but from the universalist principles that motivated her and the other 'non-Jewish Jews' who published in the paper, such as the Israeli activist Uri Avnery, the historians Avi Shlaim and Ilan Pappé, and the literary critic Jacqueline Rose. I think it's important to mention this because the paper's position on Palestine has so often been misconstrued as a lack of concern for Jewish sensitivities, rather than as the continuation of a heretical, cosmopolitan, prophetic strain of secular Judaism, grounded in the memory of the Judeocide. For this tradition, 'never again' does not mean that it should never again happen to 'us', but that it should never again happen to anyone.

Under her editorship, the paper has taken the lead in confronting two of the great taboos that have prevented an honest reckoning with the question of Palestine. The first is the influence of the Israel lobby in shaping American policy and public opinion. Stephen Walt and John Mearsheimer's article offered a powerful challenge to the lobby that few other magazines – certainly no American magazine – would have dared publish. The second taboo – harder to question, because of the halo of good intentions that surrounds it – is the inherent virtue of the 'peace process'. Just after the Oslo Accords were signed in October 1993, Edward Said wrote in the *LRB*: 'So first of all let us call the agreement by its real name: an instrument of Palestinian surrender, a Palestinian Versailles.' Said and the *LRB* were dismissed as naysayers and 'rejectionists', but this judgment – like much of the paper's writing on Israel-Palestine – has stood the test of time.

Adam Shatz

The Dame

Mary-Kay Wilmers writes: 'I'm very good at getting what I want,' Jenny Diski said of herself, and she was. She also said: 'I'm not entirely ill at ease with boundaries.' She meant the kind of boundary you have to observe on your tricycle ('I was a city-bred child'). But she was equally at home with the boundaries that journalists observe – deadlines, number of words. In every aspect of her life I came across she was neat, practical, organised, exact. What she couldn't control she kept out of sight. She wrote about herself a lot – almost never didn't one way or another. That in a sense was the point – 'everything I write is personal,' she once wrote – but she wasn't self-obsessed. She didn't hijack the subject or intrude herself in the middle of it. At the same time whatever she was writing about – cannibalism or Martha Freud ('housekeeper of a world-shattering theory') – the accounts she gave were ones only she could have given.

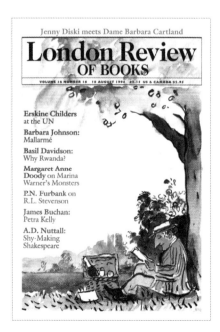

Homage to Barbara Cartland

Jenny Diski

ICOULD have left well alone; read the new autobiography and a novel or two and got stuck in. I'm not a great believer in the principle that talking to people is the best way of finding out who they really are. I'm not sure I'm even a great believer in the notion that there is a who-they-really-are to be found out. So why I petitioned for an interview with Barbara Cartland still baffles me, except perhaps that I enjoy improbability and (occasionally) being in situations that are entirely beyond my ken.

We spoke on the phone, and she explained why I had to sign an indemnity form before meeting her. 'You see, my dear, people come and see me and then they go away and write that I wear too much mascara and that I am ugly.' My heartstrings twanged, as they would faced with any 93-year-old who has been ill-used by the grown-ups. People can be so unkind. We negotiated and came to a compromise about the indemnity form: she could not have a veto over anything I wrote, but she could reject anything I quoted directly from our meeting. After reading the typescript Dame Barbara did, in fact, delete several passages and expanded all spoken contractions.

Camfield Place is a large gloomy house which was Elizabethan until Beatrix Potter's grandfather ('rich and without much taste') demolished it to build himself a proper mansion. It's dark and shadowy inside, so far removed from the world outside that you feel alarmed at stepping across the threshold and leaving the light behind. The dimness is relieved only by a scattering of gleaming rococo occasional tables, all cherubs and curlicues, but which look at first glance as if Jackson Pollock has been let loose with someone's upchucked lunch and pots of gold paint. The room in which she received me was the green the Nile is supposed to be, but almost certainly isn't. Not, alas, pink, though the dozen or so urns of flowers – two held spiritedly aloft by a pair of life-sized gilded satyrs – were symphonies of pink carnations, lilies and the like. But in common with the threadbare, taped-up carpets, the blooms had seen better days, and sagged with the effort of living up to the complexity of their arrangement.

Dame Barbara, on the other hand, was remarkably fresh and vigorous, in a multi-coloured silk tea-frock, tripping along on her sandals and smiling quite a lot. She has a very nice smile, and hair like cumulus clouds, billowing white, tending upwards, and, being rather sparse, transparent enough to see the light from the window behind her scintillate through the wisps. The false eyelashes are a mistake because, being heavy, they tend to make her lids droop, concealing a pair of vivid green eyes, alert and interested, which you'd like to see more of. Still, we all need protection from the stranger's glance. Me, I leave my spectacles on when I'm not sure of the company I'm keeping.

There is very little difference between the way Barbara Cartland writes about herself and the way she talks. In either mode what occurs is stream of consciousness, the like of which I haven't encountered since Molly Bloom had her final say. One thought follows another, though rarely consequentially. Occasionally, it's possible to glimpse an underlying connection, if not logic, as ideas hurtle along bumping into one another and doffing their hats.

When she speaks there is a problem about the ends of her sentences. The words come very fast, bubbling over to be released, but by the end of the sentence something goes – energy, the original intention, perhaps – and the last words dribble away, seeming to drop off and plummet into some deep underground cavern where all the words of all the ends of sentences lie tumbled and tangled together. It's likely that the speed with which the words are delivered is an attempt to get as many as possible out before coming to the edge of the word precipice.

First page of Jenny Diski's transcription of her interview with Barbara Cartland, for a piece published in the issue of 18 August 1994

Transcription:

Doctors: It's all got out of hand, you see. Half the doctors are black . . . they come into those countries, and you and I know you can buy the whole thing in any bazaar in the east, and they come into the country and say I'm a doctor. That's why they took a woman's leg off the other day. She wasn't meant to have her leg off at all. The whole thing is simply not what it used to be, simply and solely because half the people don't know what they're doing.

Sex and Books: I've just been talking to a man in America. In America, the only thing that sells is dirty sex, as dirty as possible, and something really nasty about you, they can't sell any other thing at all. And the same here. If you have a nice book they don't want to do it. Just had a contract for eight million in Russia. I've just told the prime minister, we're moving.

Gradually, we're just getting back to romance, and that's what the prime minister calls getting back to the beginning. What we're trying to do is get rid of this sex business. Sex, sex, sex. What's the matter with people, why do they want to read that? I think it's very vulgar and it doesn't make people happy. People write saying I've made them much happier.

'In your novels there's a great deal of suppressed passion.'

No no no, men are allowed to have affairs before marriage, but not the woman.

'But the woman feels passionately, doesn't she?'

Feels what? *Passionately*. When you're four they tell them about sex, and then they try it. Children are mimics. And they give them all these condoms at schools. They're ruining the children, because they're neglected and nobody loves them, and the mothers are so busy having careers they haven't got time for the children, now of course we've got these children absolutely miserable because they're never quite the same from a broken marriage. Princess Di was a broken marriage. She cuddles children psychologically.

Prayer: What I'm so terribly upset about is the children. Now they say that a child must learn about four gods. I can't remember, the other people, the people who are . . . oh dear . . . with the . . . the Methodists. A child wants to know that God's in the heaven and if you pray to God he'll help you. *But I think people are no longer sure that God does help if you pray*. When I want a plot, I say to God, please give me a plot. And it works. I just have to put it down. The other day, he was a bit slow, I thought perhaps he's bored with me. I said, bring me up all my stuff on the Restoration . . . you know, George V . . . and as it was coming a voice said, absolutely clearly, 'Panama Canal'. I know absolutely nothing about the Panama Canal, but as I read about it, it was riveting. Because Disraeli wouldn't let le [???] because we have slave labour, of course slave labour stopped it. And in the end of course if you remember the Jew, what's he called, Lord um . . . what's the name of the Jewish people, he gave a million pounds or something, and then Disraeli went to the queen and I said I bought you the Suez Canal, ma'am. It wasn't quite all of it. The French had got in in front of us, and then of course it was a wonderful way to India. I get these wonderful plots . . .

Graveyard Style

Diana...

On hearing the sound of the bell, a million and one tears fell
a lady who tried to do right, showered many with her radiant light
she projected humanity and care, that in this day and age is so rare
loved throughout the world, now many are touched by the cold
the void that is left behind, is vast for her that was so kind....

Little of what happened makes sense, how can mankind be so dense
the price of a tabloid cover, cost three lives - one being a mother
it's all down to human greed, that comes from this modern day breed
money is some people's aim, they should hang their heads in shame
for the sake of a world exclusive, the results being so conclusive
a light that shone so bright, has now gone out and taken flight.....

B.J.Allen

Tribute to Diana, Princess of Wales

Honoured that this poem was broadcast by the BBC & ITV Networks,

along with other Media outlets throughout the UK and Abroad

Unpublished poem by Bryan J. Allen, 1998

About as Useful as a String Condom

Glen Newey

TIME'S WHIRLIGIG, as one surly underling told another, brings in its revenges. For the royal family, 2002 went bad faster than an overhung widgeon. In September the Prince of Wales emerged as a nuisance letter-writer, badgering government ministers with green-ink missives about the Human Rights Act and the hunting ban, and moans that Cumbrian farmers got a worse deal than blacks and homosexuals. In November the Princess Royal got a criminal record after her pet pit bull gored a child (the dog escaped the chop thanks to the princess's top-dollar brief). Even Prince William, once the press's golden boy, was reported to have dispatched flunkeys to buy him porno mags from the local newsagent. Then came bruits of rape within the precincts of Buckingham Palace, and reports that the royals' London flophouses doubled as totters' yards for laundering swag ('Del Boy Royals' was the *Sun*'s unimprovable headline). All this knocked the gilt off the 'Golden' Jubilee.

The last ten years have been a bum decade for the Royals. Phone taps revealed that the heir apparent, previously thought to be interested in nothing more risqué than the *Goon Show* and chats with root vegetables, aspired to be his mistress's jam-rag. His younger son, third-in-line Prince Harry, was busted after splitting a splifferooney or three with low-life cronies, and packed off to a suitably downmarket rehab bin. Although public indignation at the burgeoning Civil List led to some drastic pruning, the royal supernumeraries continued to live high on the hog. When the public purse snapped shut, they resorted to ever more mercenary ways of earning a crust. Whereas the royals' rent-a-nob biz had previously been confined to minor scions of the dynasty, the clampdown on the Saxe-Coburg benefit scam brought it much closer to home. In an effort to drum up business for her PR firm, Sophie, 'Countess of Wessex' sounded off about the prime minister's wife to a couple of *News of the Booze* hacks posing as Middle Eastern sheikhs. Then, following the brouhaha about 'media intrusion' on Prince William's arrival as a student at St Andrews University, it turned out that the prince had indeed been stalked – by his uncle's TV crew.

Until the June roisterings, 2002 had, by general consent, been another annus horribilis. Nothing as bad as the Windsor Castle fire, let alone the nasty arrival of a tax demand from the Inland Revenue on the queen's doormat a few years back; but it had nonetheless seen the deaths, within a few weeks of each other, of the queen's 'much loved' sister and of her mother. Of course everybody had been expecting Mustique Meg and 'the Problem' (the queen's affectionate soubriquet for her mother) to peg it for any number of years, and the QM's one benefaction to the nation – which got nothing in inheritance tax – was to croak over Easter, elbowing Jesus out of the TV schedules. Meanwhile the Prince Consort's capacity to goof remains undimmed by age. On the Jubilee tour of the UK the duke picked out a blind woman from a crowd of 'well-wishers' and asked her if she knew that there are now 'eating dogs for the anorexic'.

In the background to the Jubilee lay the fluff-ball Jacobinism of September 1997 which surfaced in the media after Diana's tryst with the underpass. It was rightly observed that the blood royals inhabited an emotional tundra, where feeling was subjugated to 'duty' and 'the Firm'. By contrast, Diana had 'soul'. She bared all about self-harm and her frequent calls, during her bulimic phase, on the great white telephone. She fondled children and animals, dabbled in New Age pursuits, kibitzed in operating theatres and had been stiffed on a pedalo by the thick-set offspring of a Levantine grocer. In op-ed fable she presented the Windsor family's lone human face, Avon Lady to the House of Atreus.

This wasn't so long ago, and the royals' supposed bounce back to public favour came as a shock to many in the commentariat. Before the day few thought that on 3 June a million or two groupies would throng the Mall to watch a bunch of clapped-out old-stagers presuming on the public's indulgence for one last hurrah. But so it proved.

Among the 'great banks of flowers' that lined the Mall before the funeral of Diana, Princess of Wales, Ross McKibbin wrote, 'almost every bouquet was accompanied by a card, letter or poem . . . What was characteristic of the letters and poems as a whole is how highly charged and emotionally uninhibited they were . . . written in an instantly recognisable, though very heightened graveyard style which is, if anything, mid-19th century.' The LRB received a number of poems in a similar vein. We didn't publish any of them, until now. Glen Newey's 2003 piece about the royal family could also be thought to exhibit a 'heightened graveyard style'. A subscriber came to the office to express in person his displeasure at our having published it, almost speechless with rage at the coarseness of the piece. Did we realise that his wife read the paper? (He didn't mention his servants.)

PENELOPE FITZGERALD

████████████ Highgate, London. N6 4HP

Telephone
0181 340 0805

Oct 3rd

Dear Sir Frank, I hope you won't
mind my writing to thank you
for your review of *The Blue Flower*,
I started from DHLawrence's 'fatal
flower of happiness' at the end of
The Fox, having always wondered
how DHL knew it was blue, & never
quite managed to find out all I
wanted to, partly because Novalis'
letters to Sophie have disappeared,

buried in her grave I daresay.
    I was so glad you defended
N. against Carlyle. The person who
really understood him, it seems to
me, was George Macdonald, but nobody reads *Phantastes* now.

    I don't know whether you'd
agree that writing, like teaching,
produces considerable spells of
depression & moments of great
happiness, which seem to justify
everything, – that's what I felt,
anyway, when I read the LRB
this week – with thanks & best wishes

Penelope Fitzgerald

Note from Penelope Fitzgerald to Frank Kermode,
3 October 1995. 'N.' is Novalis, the German
Romantic poet, and Fitzgerald's protagonist.

'Sly Sir Frank'

Frank Kermode, without whose encouragement the *LRB* would never have existed, died on 17 August 2010 at the age of ninety. He had written more than two hundred pieces for the paper – more than anyone else, if you consider only full-length essays and reviews. Kermode's first piece, in the very first issue, was on millenarianism, the 'myth concerning the End'; his last was on Philip Pullman and the parable of the Prodigal Son. In between he wrote on everything: Tennyson, Eliot, Auden, Pound; Updike, Roth, Pynchon, DeLillo; McEwan, Amis, Rushdie, Barnes; Saussure, Empson, Genette, de Man; Golding, Spark and Penelope Fitzgerald (three times, each time prompting her to respond with a grateful note, one of which is shown opposite). Also Shakespeare, from many angles, and – in a piece first delivered as a *LRB* lecture a few months before his death – 'Eliot and the Shudder'. It didn't matter whether it was old or new, of the canon or hot off the presses, conforming or radical: on subjects from Jane Austen to Zadie Smith, Beryl Bainbridge to Christine Brooke-Rose, Kermode applied the same critical care. He was always curious about what was just coming out, and he always knew how it spoke to and responded to what had always been. Serial holder of the most prestigious chairs in English universities, former co-editor of *Encounter* and mastermind of the Fontana Modern Masters, author or editor of nearly sixty books, he provided the perfect model of how to hover as a writer between academia and journalism. It's important that you know your stuff; it's important that you make a statement. But it was the writing that did it – and the thought that lay behind the writing. He was jokily called 'Sly Sir Frank' in the office: in his reviews he could give with one hand and take with the other, as when in his review of Zadie Smith's *On Beauty* he praised her to the skies and then noted that she didn't know the difference between Latin and Greek.

Kermode's influence helped form all those who were taught by him or who read his pieces or his books, especially *The Sense of an Ending*. Just look at the tributes the *LRB* presented after his death by Jacqueline Rose, Stefan Collini, Adam Phillips, James Wood and Michael Wood: as critics, they were who they were in part because of him. (The young Phillips – whom Kermode commissioned to write something about Winnicott for Fontana, on the basis of a two-page essay he had submitted on the subject of tickling – asked him how one actually gets a book written. 'Immerse yourself in the material,' Kermode replied, 'and the book will write itself.') The paper has published plenty of great critics, writers in and out of the academy, on subjects from Homer and Sappho to Knausgaard and Cusk: in the early years, William Empson, V.S. Pritchett, Christopher Ricks; still continuing, Barbara Everett, Fredric Jameson, Michael Wood; from a younger generation, James Wood, Michael Hofmann, Colin Burrow and Jenny Turner; from a younger generation still, Rivka Galchen, Patricia Lockwood. But Kermode, more than anyone else, gave the paper its style and its sensibility.

Daniel Soar

A Whole Lot to Say

Andrew O'Hagan writes: On my bookshelves at home, only one book has its cover facing out: *A History of Courting* by E.S. Turner. It has a very amusing cover, and, obviously, it's the kind of book you want to be able to grab in a hurry, but my real reason for wanting to see it regularly is my undimmed affection for the author. Turner wrote his first piece for the *Dundee Courier* in 1927 and was a star writer for the LRB until his death at the age of 96 in 2006. In 1998 I went to talk to him at his home in Richmond. He said to me that when he told his headmaster he wanted to work on a newspaper he was warned that it was 'a filthy trade'. But all those years later, as can be seen from the letter opposite, he still looked forward to writing reviews. He was far more interested in his subjects than he was in himself. 'I don't know how you'll get a whole article out of me,' he said as I packed up my things. 'I haven't a whole lot to say.' It wasn't true, but it showed the newspaper man still at work, after seventy years in the filthy trade, wondering if we had enough to fill the page.

Seventy Years in a Filthy Trade

Andrew O'Hagan

ERNEST Turner was a good pupil. He won a few prizes and enjoyed himself memorising passages of Macaulay's *Lays*. By the time he was at Orme Boys' School (Arnold Bennett's alma mater) young Turner was inclining towards journalism.

Ernest Turner went to Glasgow. He became a sharp eye on the *Evening Times*, and in time a sharp voice, with columns and leaders and bits for a giggle. He describes those days in his *ABC of Nostalgia*: 'How backward, how mealy-mouthed, how cliché-ridden and yet how endearing were the newspapers of between the world wars. The secret of the identity of Santa Claus was never wantonly disclosed in their pages . . . It was no job for a university man, whose only job on a newspaper was to write leaders urging the Dictators to look before they leaped.' Certain things surprised Mr Turner about Glasgow. The tram went all the way to Loch Lomond. Some areas had pubs on every corner, others had sweet shops. He also remembers the staggering number of cinemas and the staggered newspapers, four mornings and three evenings, all receptive to freelance contributions. 'The subs on the Glasgow *Evening Times* were a profane lot,' he says, 'but they knew their jobs. I could never master the business of getting the racing results into the Stop Press. One of them wrote well-esteemed poetry; one wrote a Life of Keir Hardie, the cloth-capped Old Labour MP.' Later, on the Scottish *Daily Express*, he shared the subs table with James Cameron, 'a good friend, a brilliant reporter. In my lifetime the coarsening of the press has been astonishing. Papers are bigger, but there's less and less news.'

He went to America on the maiden voyage of the *Queen Mary*. 'About a hundred reporters,' he says, 'each of us desperate to find a stowaway.' At one brief period, while going back and forth, he owned a £10 Chrysler on each side of the Atlantic. ('There's glory for you.') Between the wars he travelled on Hitler's *Bremen* and *Europa*, also on Mussolini's *Conte di Savoia*, and the ships of the Anchor Line, out of Glasgow. In 1934 he motored through a swastika-hung Rhineland in a Morgan sports three-wheeler. 'This fascinated the Brownshirts everywhere,' he says, 'but failed to promote an entente cordiale.'

He joined the army in 1941 and served in the Royal Artillery (anti-aircraft). His battery engaged night raiders over Clapham Common and Raynes Park, and later shot down many V1s at Dungeness. He was posted to Brussels to help launch the army magazine *Soldier*. 'It's still going,' he says, 'and if you'd asked me then which magazine would die first, *Soldier* or *Punch*, I should certainly have said *Soldier*.' He moved the magazine to a devastated Hamburg in 1945, where it was printed on the presses that had turned out Goebbels's famous magazine *Signal*. 'A very good magazine,' says Major Turner.

He came back to London as *Soldier*'s editor after the war. He wrote a book about blood-and-thunder literature, intending it to be called *The Penny Blood*, but the creator of Billy Bunter was appalled at the idea of his work being corralled under such a heading, and so the book became *Boys Will Be Boys*, and a bestseller. Some people felt that E.S. Turner may have invented a new kind of book – the popular social history, very British, very funny, but written with a glistening elegance.

Mr Turner wrote books about courting and courtiers, about doctors and servants, army officers and beaks. Who but E.S. Turner could be the author of a book such as *Taking the Cure*, a history of spa-going? Or *Amazing Grace*, a cool look at dukes? Before there was Dava Sobel, or Nick Hornby, or *Fermat's Last Theorem* or Andy McNab, there was Mr Turner, and his series of second-hand typewriters. 'I remember a van arriving out of the blue with a fine stock of near prehistoric machines,' he says. 'My father very decently bought one of these for £5 and I used it for many years.'

██████   ██████

Richmond, Surrey TW9 2DD

September 28,1992

Dear Karl,

Back from foreign parts I got down to the Jules Verne book,
Backwards to Britain. It presents a bit of a problem. Though never published
before, it has already been milked of its minor interest by previous writers
on Verne (eg. Peter Costello and Jean Jules-Verne). The Introduction, by
William Butcher, Vocational Training Council, Hong Kong, oversells quite
ludicrously what is essentially a juvenile what-we-did-in-the-hols record,
full of howlers, awful jokes and padding. The book is a fictionised account
of a tour to central Scotland in 1859 by Verne and a companion, who took 21
days to get there because they took a 'freebie' on a coaster. The travellers
had read up on Walter Scott and were keen to follow in his footsteps. Throughout the editor mentions incidents and sights in the tour which were worked into
Verne's later writings, but none of them are of much interest.

Butcher calls the book both a time-bomb and a time-capsule. "It
proves," he says, "that Verne is not a science-fiction author" (meaning that
he is a real novelist). Butcher also claims that "The ultimate mechanical
metaphor, sex, throbs everywhere in the text." It does nothing of the sort. As
an example
[He tells us that a tart has "creamy plums hidden in its moist golden sides"
(the word tart has carried him away). Ships couple in mid-stream; but at
least we are spared the symbolism of trains entering tunnels. For some reason
sandwich-men are thought to have sexual symbolism.

Every now and then there is a wild piece of invention. In a
Glasgow shop the travellers see a machine in which a pig goes in one end and
comes out of the other as sausages. Dumbarton Rock on the Clyde, near
Glasgow, is pointed out as a place where the British Government proposed
to exile Napoleon after Elba. The show-off narrator tells us that during the
Crimean War a British company offered to take over the siege of Sebastopol
on a commercial basis, which I suppose is unlikely enough to be true. He also
confidently assures us that Roman Catholics will soon expel Protestantism from
Britain by force of numbers. He gives the usual traveller's account of
horribly exploited workers in Liverpool and Edinburgh (nothing like that,
of course, in Paris)

I could make a short comic piece out of all this, but I would
blush to stretch it to the usual length. But Perhaps you have some other
book (s) which could go along with it?

Yours
Ernest Turner

Sexually, I'm More of a Switzerland

Nicholas Spice writes: The easiest magazines to sell are those that don't require to be read: pictures, cartoons, puzzles are enough to give purchasers a sense that they're getting their money's worth. For a while, in the 1970s and early 1980s, a reader of the *New York Review of Books* could always turn to the personal ads for light relief: pages of classifieds mapped in eye-opening detail the remoter regions of the American sexual habitat. Aids dampened this exuberance just around the time the *LRB* was getting into its stride as an independent magazine. For years it was touch and go for the *LRB* classified section. And then, after two decades scratching about with ads for bookshelves and writers' retreats in Gascony or the Marche, things began to look up: in 1998, David Rose, the paper's advertising manager, conceived the idea of the *LRB* personal ads. Their success was extraordinary (Profile Books published two anthologies: *They Call Me Naughty Lola* and *Sexually, I'm More of a Switzerland*) and for a while the *LRB* was as famous, among those who did not read it, for its ads as for its essays. When David Rose left the paper, the personal ads dwindled away.

Detail from page 42, 15 October 1998, the first issue to include personal ads

MICHAEL MONK ASSOCIATES

70 Lower Park Road, Hastings, East Sussex TN34 2LD

Telephone 0424 426906
direct: 427963

PUBLICITY — ADVERTISING — PUBLIC RELATIONS

MEDIA BOOKING ORDER

No: T/C 598

Media	THE LONDON REVIEW OF BOOKS...6A Bedford Square, London WC1B 3RA
Date sought	see below
Requirement	classified/personal column rate wordage 20p discount agy 15%
Contact (any query)	Michael Monk Hastings (0424) 427963

attention Mr Michael Richards......my client a literary lady one Mary
Valentine principal of Together & Company wishes to try a modest series
of classified advertisements in your columns. Hopefully you will find
the copy 'lively' and of the nature to generate readership interest.

Your rate card is the most fetching I have ever seen!

'Off the record' one notices a classified ad for Concorde with a
box number. Supposedly this is a venture associated with the reputable
Datline operation who are said to have given assurances to the
advertising authorities that they would have no further advertisements
of this nature. Please do not interpret this comment as any form of
complaint, it is purely an observation.

Michael J Monk

publication date.....20th August

Smiley

Aug 20

TINKER, tailor, soldier, sailor: 'forget' ~~Ian Le Carré~~ remember
Mary Valentine matchmaking since 1968 at Together & Company, 2
Claremont, Hastings: weekdays until 6.30pm 0424/422756.

(22 words)

publication date....3rd September

kindly set as 'poem' charge extra £4 for semi-display but NOT boxed
just straighforward linage please

Sept 1

DEAR men of Kent*, of forty and above,
where are you hiding from the realms of love?
We need you badly, ladies here agree,
won't you come and join our company?
Mary Valentine matchmaking since 1968 at
TOGETHER & COMPANY 2 Claremont, Hastings
ring weekdays until 6.30pm 0424/422756

words underlined in capitlas

* anywhere wouldn't rhyme!

A Partnership of Michael and Mary Monk: Registered in England. No. 2405666

Media booking order for the classified column, 1981

A Genuine Hatred of Eng. Lit.

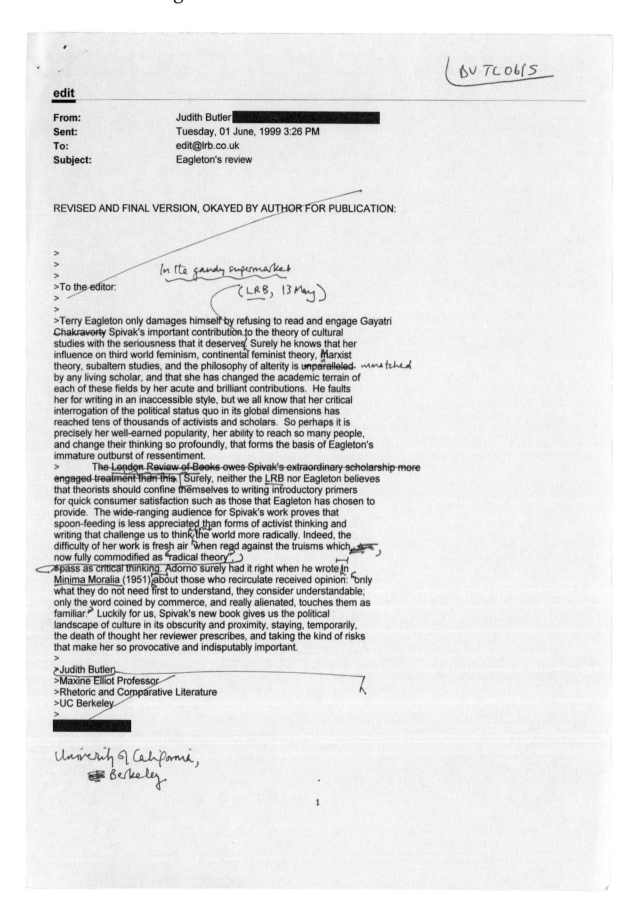

edit

From:	Judith Butler
Sent:	Tuesday, 01 June, 1999 3:26 PM
To:	edit@lrb.co.uk
Subject:	Eagleton's review

REVISED AND FINAL VERSION, OKAYED BY AUTHOR FOR PUBLICATION:

>
>
>
>To the editor:
>
>
>Terry Eagleton only damages himself by refusing to read and engage Gayatri Chakravorty Spivak's important contribution to the theory of cultural studies with the seriousness that it deserves. Surely he knows that her influence on third world feminism, continental feminist theory, Marxist theory, subaltern studies, and the philosophy of alterity is unparalleled by any living scholar, and that she has changed the academic terrain of each of these fields by her acute and brilliant contributions. He faults her for writing in an inaccessible style, but we all know that her critical interrogation of the political status quo in its global dimensions has reached tens of thousands of activists and scholars. So perhaps it is precisely her well-earned popularity, her ability to reach so many people, and change their thinking so profoundly, that forms the basis of Eagleton's immature outburst of ressentiment.
> The London Review of Books owes Spivak's extraordinary scholarship more engaged treatment than this. Surely, neither the LRB nor Eagleton believes that theorists should confine themselves to writing introductory primers for quick consumer satisfaction such as those that Eagleton has chosen to provide. The wide-ranging audience for Spivak's work proves that spoon-feeding is less appreciated than forms of activist thinking and writing that challenge us to think the world more radically. Indeed, the difficulty of her work is fresh air when read against the truisms which now fully commodified as "radical theory", pass as critical thinking. Adorno surely had it right when he wrote in Minima Moralia (1951) about those who recirculate received opinion: "only what they do not need first to understand, they consider understandable; only the word coined by commerce, and really alienated, touches them as familiar." Luckily for us, Spivak's new book gives us the political landscape of culture in its obscurity and proximity, staying, temporarily, the death of thought her reviewer prescribes, and taking the kind of risks that make her so provocative and indisputably important.
>
>Judith Butler
>Maxine Elliot Professor
>Rhetoric and Comparative Literature
>UC Berkeley
>

Letter to the editor from Judith Butler, 1 June 1999

Terry Eagleton's spiky 1999 review of Gayatri Chakravorty Spivak's *Critique of Post-Colonial Reason* was a late reverberation from the 'theory wars', which by this time had all but died down – in the pages of the *LRB*, at least. Here the theorists turn on one another. Judith Butler was among those who took issue with Eagleton's account. Butler would later write pieces for the paper on Kafka, Arendt and Derrida, as well as defending the right to criticise Israel without being accused of antisemitism. Eagleton, long used to being assailed from all sides (in 1991, John Bayley wrote to Karl Miller to complain of Eagleton's 'genuine hatred of Eng. Lit.'), turned his sights on other targets: 'Imagine someone holding forth on biology whose only knowledge of the subject is the *Book of British Birds*,' he wrote in 2006, 'and you have a rough idea of what it feels like to read Richard Dawkins on theology.'

Note from John Bayley to Karl Miller, 1991

Transcription:

Dear Karl,

Thanks so much for Conrad(s). Meyers is crude but not uninteresting, as you might suppose. Perhaps I could do a general piece with them all, taking a bit of time.

I enclose a rather touching letter since it expresses real pleasure in the *LRB* generally and I thought you and MK might like to see that *old* people find the paper stimulating – never mind the young!

Sombre thoughts is what I think too (much amused by your PS!) tho' I also feel a bit Louis XV about it. The thing about Terry E. and his pals is their genuine hatred of Eng. Lit. and their wish to get rid of it or show it doesn't exist. I fear many of the young rather go for that, and for being told their theory is as good as anybody else's, e.g. Shakespeare's . . .

Best, John

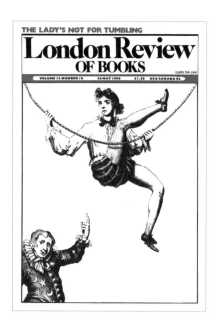

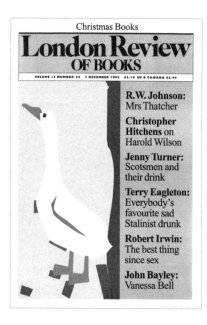

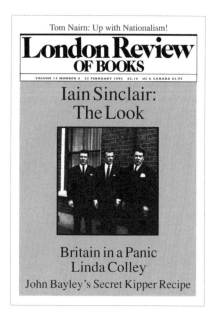

Hilary Mantel: Aux Armes, Citoyennes

London Review OF BOOKS

'A hoax barely worth the perpetration'
John Sturrock takes on Alan Sokal

BIG JUNE ISSUE!

London Review OF BOOKS

Stephen Sedley in His Lodgings

London Review OF BOOKS

James Buchan: The Dark Side of the Euro

London Review OF BOOKS

Christopher Hitchens: The Case of Whittaker Chambers
James Davidson: On First Hearing Homer
Charles Simic: Oh Those Awful Serbs!
Anita Brookner on Colette
Gaby Wood: A Scary Kook
Emma Tennant: My Uncle Stephen
Penelope Fitzgerald:
The Philandering
Philologist

Jacqueline Rose on Virginia Woolf

London Review OF BOOKS

R.W. Johnson: The True Importance of Enoch Powell
Ruth Padel: Piangi, piangi, o misera
Donald MacKenzie: Disinventing Nuclear Weapons
James Davidson: Indigestion in Ancient Times

Iain Sinclair:
Transporting Beneficial Herbs

Ronan Bennett: A Lifer's Life

London Review OF BOOKS

Stanley Cavell raises his glass to Adam Phillips

Zoë Heller on Claire Bloom

Donald Rayfield: Chekhov and the Women

Christopher Hitchens: Small is Ugly

Michael Wood: The Remains of Eva Peron

Fred Halliday: Vietnam before the War

Neal Ascherson: Redoing Europe's Past

John Sturrock pops a cork for Nathalie Sarraute

Marina Warner: The Curse of Myra Hindley

London Review OF BOOKS

Alan Bennett:
Me Looking like a Flustered Turkey

20TH ANNIVERSARY ISSUE

London Review OF BOOKS

John Ashbery
Alan Bennett
Terry Castle
Amit Chaudhuri
James Davidson
Jenny Diski
William Empson
Jerry Fodor
Ian Hamilton
Christopher Hitchens
Frank Kermode
August Kleinzahler
John Lanchester
Ross McKibbin
Hilary Mantel
Andrew O'Hagan
Tom Paulin
Adam Phillips
Jacqueline Rose
Lorna Sage
Edward Said
Colm Tóibín
Jenny Turner
James Wood
Michael Wood

Slavoj Zizek: The World Turned Back to Front

London Review OF BOOKS

The superego inverts the Kantian 'You can because you must,' turning it into 'You must because you can.' This is the meaning of Viagra.

2000-09

Your Loony Leftist Faces

Iain Sinclair: The Razing of East London

London Review
OF BOOKS

VOLUME 30 NUMBER 12   19 JUNE 2008   £3.20 US & CANADA $4.95

Thomas Jones: The Last Days of eBay

James Davidson: Atlantis at Last!

Patrick Cockburn: A New Deal for Iraq

Keith Gessen: A Sad Old Literary Man

A Grid of Nine

From the beginning of 1994 until his death late in 2011, Peter Campbell's watercolours were on the cover of every issue of the LRB. When he was thinking up ideas for them, he would sit on a sofa in the room at the top of his house, and close his eyes for a long time. Then he'd draw a grid of nine rectangles with a pencil in his sketchbook, and quickly fill in each rectangle with a postage-stamp-sized sketch of an idea. Details would be highlighted and colour schemes specified. Usually at least one of these sketches, sometimes as many as three, would be worked up into a watercolour that he'd take into the LRB office.

Pages from Peter Campbell's sketchbooks, and the designs that became the covers of the issues of 25 June 2009 and 3 January 2002

Record of a Nightmare

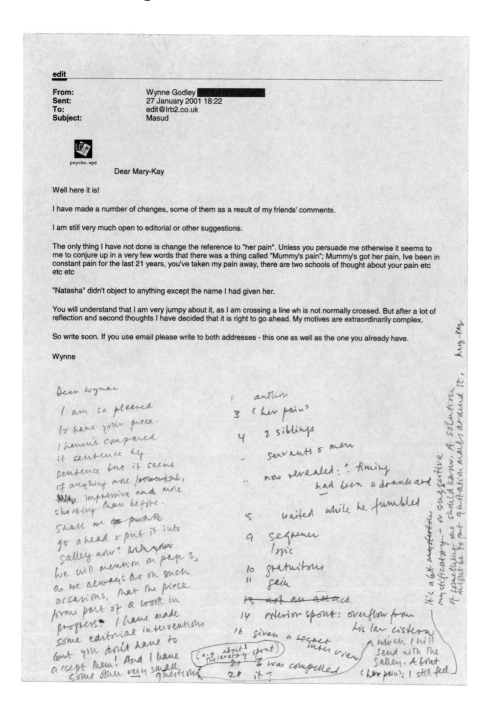

edit

From: Wynne Godley █████████████
Sent: 27 January 2001 18:22
To: edit@lrb2.co.uk
Subject: Masud

psycho.wpd

        Dear Mary-Kay

Well here it is!

I have made a number of changes, some of them as a result of my friends' comments.

I am still very much open to editorial or other suggestions.

The only thing I have not done is change the reference to "her pain". Unless you persuade me otherwise it seems to
me to conjure up in a very few words that there was a thing called "Mummy's pain"; Mummy's got her pain, Ive been in
constant pain for the last 21 years, you've taken my pain away, there are two schools of thought about your pain etc
etc etc

"Natasha" didn't object to anything except the name I had given her.

You will understand that I am very jumpy about it, as I am crossing a line wh is not normally crossed. But after a lot of
reflection and second thoughts I have decided that it is right to go ahead. My motives are extraordinarily complex.

So write soon. If you use email please write to both addresses - this one as well as the one you already have.

Wynne

*Email from Wynne Godley to Mary-Kay Wilmers,
with her response, 27 January 2001*

Transcription:

Dear Wynne,

I am so pleased to have your piece. I haven't compared it sentence by sentence but it seems if anything more impressive and more shocking than before. Shall we go ahead and put it into galley now? We will mention on page 2, as we always do on such occasions, that the piece forms part of a work in progress. I have made some editorial interventions but you don't have to accept them! And I have some other *very* small questions (e.g. about the lavatory spout) which I will send with the galley. About 'her pain': I still feel it's a bit mystificatory – or suggestive of something one should know. A solution might be to put quotation marks around it.

Mary-Kay

Saving Masud Khan

Wynne Godley

WE HARDLY ever spoke of my childhood. Khan preferred, he said, to 'work out of' the material which was thrown up by contemporary experiences. Everything of significance that had happened in the past could be reinterpreted in terms of what was happening now. This gave him a licence to interfere actively, judgmentally and with extraordinary cruelty in every aspect of my daily life.

We entered a long period of painful stasis. 'When is something going to happen?' I would ask and he would reply: 'I wonder too when something is going to happen. I have exhausted' – these were his exact words – '*every manoeuvre that I know*. You are a tiresome and disappointing man.'

How did I account to myself for what was happening? I thought that everything unkind Khan said to me was justified and that I was learning to accept home truths; that this was extraordinarily painful but the essence of what a good and true analysis should be. We weren't having one of those soppy analyses that the ignorant public imagines, where a pathetic neurotic talks about himself and is passively listened to, and endlessly comforted. The characteristic sensation I experienced was a smouldering rage which carried me from session to session. I felt like a kettle that had been left on the flame long after the water had boiled away.

Khan liked it when I moved up through the Treasury ranks, greatly overestimating the importance and significance of the positions which I held. Meanwhile he began increasingly to fill the sessions with tales about his own social life in London or, occasionally, New York. The stories were not good ones. Many were obscene and many were flat, but there was one feature common to every one of them: Khan had got the better of someone. He had rescued Mike Nichols from a man with a fierce dog in New York. He had fought physically with Peter O'Toole, using a broken bottle. He had got the overflow from his lavatory to pour a jet of water onto the head of a woman who was making her car hoot in the street below. Often it would be nothing more than an ugly exchange at a drinking party for which he needed my approval and endorsement. The following characteristic tale, being brief, must stand in for a limitless number of other stories that I can immediately recall

A man comes up to Khan at a party and says: 'Every night I go to bed with two beautiful women. I make love to one of them and then, if I feel like it, I turn over and make love to the other. Sometimes I make love to both of them at once.' 'Yes,' Khan says, 'but by the laws of topology there must always be one orifice which remains vacant.'

Very occasionally he appealed to me for sympathy. Princess Margaret had tripped him up over the way he had pronounced something. Lord Denning (it was Profumo time) had not replied to his invitation to come to dinner. Khan always answered telephone calls during sessions. When Winnicott rang up I could clearly hear both sides of the conversation, so presumably he angled the phone towards me. Winnicott spoke respectfully to Khan, for instance about a paper which he had recently published. 'I learned a great deal from it,' Winnicott said deferentially. This particular conversation ended with a giggly joke about homosexual fellatio – the final two words of the conversation – accompanied by loud laughter.

A gynaecologist rang up during one of my sessions to enquire about a patient of Khan's, Marian, who was expecting a baby. Khan spoke harshly about her to the gynaecologist, closing the conversation with the advice: 'And charge her a good fee.' Khan kept me in touch with the progress of Marian's pregnancy. She was not married, and as her confinement approached he referred to it bitingly as 'the virgin birth'.

After the child was born, Khan started speaking of Marian as a suitable partner for me – although I was happily married and although, as I much later discovered, he had secretly invited my wife Kitty to an interview with him.

Mary-Kay Wilmers writes: It isn't strange that psychoanalysts are seldom written about. The risk of exposure is too great – for the analyst as well as the patient. Suppose you are the analyst who has to face the fact that you shouted 'They're coming to get me' when the lights suddenly went dark over New York City (a friend of mine was his patient and on the couch at that very moment). 'No decent analyst would let his picture appear in the *Times*,' another New York analyst snapped at a colleague. I once wrote a piece in the *LRB* about this sort of preciousness; a lot of it was about Janet Malcolm, who speaks of the 'chilly castle of psychoanalysis' while admiring its austerities. One might less admiringly think of it as 'Fortress Freud' and question whether, or why, it needs to be so insistently defended. One answer to that question came unexpectedly from the Cambridge economist Wynne Godley, whose piece about his own encounter with psychoanalysis created a considerable stir. 'I am getting indirect reports which make it sound as though I had dropped an atom bomb somewhere up the Finchley Road,' he said to me in an email. Interesting that the analysts – there were two, both very eminent – were thought to be the victims.

I once – i.e. for many years – saw an analyst five times a week. The days and the times varied – for example, eight in the morning on Tuesdays but seven in the evening on Thursdays – and so did his behaviour: calm in the morning, over-excited at night. For the first few years I assumed, as he seemed to, that it was my fault, which he confirmed by repeatedly asking me what it was in my family history that caused me to find reasons for alarm in other people's behaviour. Eventually I talked to other analysts in the hope of understanding mine but they too blamed my family history. Fifteen years later, a former analyst who'd left psychoanalysis behind told me what should have been clear all along: he – my man – was an alcoholic. Analysts, it turns out, are no saner than anyone else – just more unfair.

EXTRACT FROM VOL. 41 NO. 8 · 18 APRIL 2019

Publicity and Sales

I want to love it

Susan Pedersen

Eric Hobsbawm's many books include a three-part study of the 'long 19th century' and *Age of Extremes: The Short 20th Century*. He was unwilling to be interviewed in 2000 because of his shrewd sense of the value of what Susan Pedersen calls his 'brand': 'such,' he writes, 'is the logic of publicity and sales.' Compensations arrived over the next decade in the form of occasional memoir pieces: on Gorbachev; on his days as the *New Statesman's* jazz critic under the name 'Francis Newton' (a communist trumpeter who played on Billie Holiday's 'Strange Fruit'); and on his memories of Weimar. In his review of *Interesting Times*, the autobiography to which Hobsbawm refers in the letter opposite, Perry Anderson described it as 'a kind of fifth volume, in more personal register, of a continuous project. This one could be called simply "The Age of EJH".' Two years after his death in 2012, MI5 released a thousand pages of its file on Hobsbawm, whom it classed as a 'hardliner' or 'Category A' communist. Francis Stonor Saunders wrote about it for the LRB in 2015. Hobsbawm had long wished to see it for himself.

H OBSBAWM did what he loved best: he read, travelled, talked and wrote. His Birkbeck teaching proved a perfect foundation for that writing. *Industry and Empire*, delivered five years late and published in 1968, was based – as *The Age of Revolution* had been – on his lectures. Always intellectually promiscuous and alert to opportunities, he brought out other books – *The Jazz Scene*, *Captain Swing* with George Rudé (who mostly did the research) – but he had begun to write to formula. *The Age of Capital*, which appeared in 1975, mirrored the two-part structure ('developments' and 'results') of *The Age of Revolution*; so did *The Age of Empire*, which appeared in 1987, just before he turned seventy. The books were uniformly lauded as major achievements, especially as it became clear they had become a series. They evoked predictable criticisms: David Landes complained of his pessimism about industrialisation, Edward Said of his Eurocentrism, Catherine Hall of his neglect of women and gender, Tony Judt, after *Age of Extremes* appeared in 1994, of his disdain for the protean force of nationalism and his gingerly treatment of the Soviet Union's crimes. Controversy just helped sales, and Hobsbawm never paid much attention to criticism.

Academics will find Richard Evans's account of how Hobsbawm turned his books into a 'brand' very revealing. University expansion in the 1960s meant there were ever larger numbers of student readers for books that could synthesise the multinational mess of 19th-century European history and (better still) could do it in a thematic, engaging, but quite obviously left-wing way. The uniform format and age-of-this-or-that titles added to the books' marketability: people buying 'a Hobsbawm' knew what they were getting – a well-paced, sharply argued, not-too-short-and-not-too-long account of a defined historical period, Western-centric but set in a global context, Marxisant but not mindlessly deterministic. It was a winning formula, and Hobsbawm made it pay. In 1978, just after he turned sixty, his earnings from his books surpassed his income from

teaching, and that disparity continued to grow. Hobsbawm often delivered late, but Bruce Hunter, his agent for most of this later period, negotiated hard over translations, world rights and advances. In 1987, when Weidenfeld offered an advance of £100,000 (about six or seven times a new lecturer's salary) for what became *Age of Extremes*, his agents turned it down and put the proposal out to bid instead.

His readership was from the outset a global one, and it expanded steadily. Hobsbawm knew the United States was an important market, telling his agent in 1978 that he needed a paperback American publisher for *The Age of Capital* with 'links with the many radical dons aged 30-35 who would prescribe a Hobsbawm'. But virtually all his books appeared in dozens of languages: indeed, the translations were so numerous, and so expected, that he was able to paint Gallimard's unwillingness to bring out a French edition of *Age of Extremes* almost as censorship, an elitist plot to deprive the French people of a chance to read the works of historians, as he put it in a combative lecture, 'who did not enjoy the favour of the fashionable orthodoxies of the 1990s'. (Brought out by a Belgian publisher, the French-language edition sold forty thousand copies.) Hobsbawm's multilingualism, his readiness to travel and promote his books, helped sales too. Latin America, where he became a left icon, provided an especially receptive audience. Hobsbawm had sold 600,000 copies of earlier works in Brazil before *Age of Extremes* was published; it sold another 265,000 copies. In 1987, thirty years after a friend had caught sight of Hobsbawm interviewing a peasant in an Italian field, another friend caught sight of a shambling figure who 'walked like Eric Hobsbawm' in the street outside a tea-room in Seoul. The friend rushed out to find 'it was indeed Eric.' He was there to see his publisher.

Colm Tóibín: 'It's curable,' he said

London Review
OF BOOKS

VOLUME 41 NUMBER 8 18 APRIL 2019 £4.25 US $ CANADA $5.95

Jonathan Parry: Parliament's Hour
Susan Pedersen writes about Eric Hobsbawm
Robert Crawford: Was Eliot a Swell?

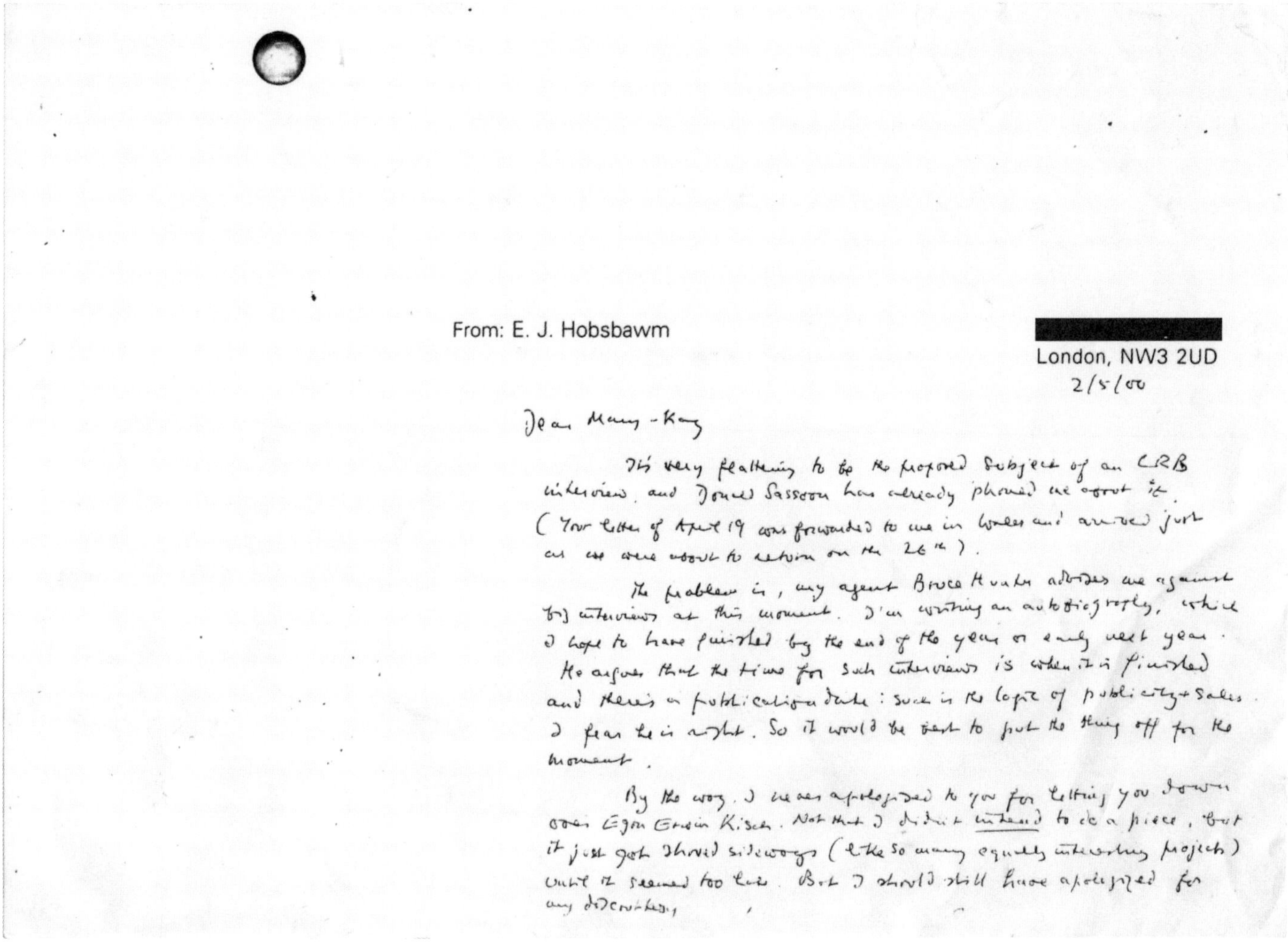

From: E. J. Hobsbawm

London, NW3 2UD

2/5/00

[handwritten letter]

Fax from Eric Hobsbawm to Mary-Kay Wilmers,
2 May 2000

Transcription:

Dear Mary-Kay

It's very flattering to be the proposed subject of an *LRB* interview, and Donald Sassoon has already phoned me about it. (Your letter of April 19 was forwarded to me in Wales and arrived just as we were about to return on the 26th.)

The problem is, my agent Bruce Hunter advises me against any interviews at this moment. I'm writing an autobiography, which I hope to have finished by the end of the year or early next year.

He argues that the time for such interviews is when it is finished and there's a publication date: such is the logic of publicity and sales. I fear he is right. So it would be best to put the thing off for the moment.

By the way, I never apologised to you for letting you down over Egon Erwin Kisch. Not that I didn't *intend* to do a piece, but it just got shoved sideways (like so many equally interesting projects) until it seemed too late. But I should still have apologised for my discourtesy.

Reflections on the Present Crisis

MUCH has been said in recent days about the instability of Pakistan. But the danger lies not so much within the population as a whole, where religious extremists are a small minority (more confessional votes are cast in Israel than Pakistan), as within the Army. Officers and other ranks who have worked with the Taliban in Afghanistan and the Lashkar-i-Tayyaba in Kashmir have become infected with zealotry. At the same time native Islamists, aware of their weakness in the country, have focused their efforts on the Army. Estimates vary between 15 and 30 per cent: whatever the exact figure, these men will not look on in silence while their colleagues in Afghanistan are attacked from bases inside Pakistan. In Kashmir there has already been open opposition to the last ceasefire. An Islamist Pakistani captain refused to vacate Indian-held territory. A colonel despatched by the Pakistani High Command to order an immediate withdrawal was shot dead as a traitor to Islam. Already a partial wreck, Pakistan could be destroyed by a civil war.

The terrorists who carried out the killings in the US were not bearded illiterates from the mountain villages of Afghanistan. They were educated, middle-class professionals from Egypt and the Hijaz province of Saudi Arabia, two key US allies in the region. What made them propagandists of the deed? The bombing of Iraq, economic sanctions, the presence of American Forces on Saudi soil. Politicians in the West have turned a blind eye to this, as they have to the occupation of Palestine and the crimes of Israel. Without profound change in the Middle East, Osama bin Laden, dead or alive, is of little significance.

In the West, Saudi Arabia is simply a source of oil. We prefer not to notice the scale of social and religious oppression, the widespread dejection and anxiety, the growing discontent among Saudis. The Wahabbi Islam practised there has been the inspiration of the Taliban. It was the Saudi monarchy that funded fanaticism in South Asia; it was they (and the CIA) who sent bin Laden to fight the Russians in Afghanistan. Islam was seen by all the experts as the main bulwark against Communism. Denied any secular openings, dissenting graduates have turned to radical Islam, accusing the Saudi royal family of hypocrisy, corruption and subservience to America. These are clever tacticians, open in their admiration of bin Laden and the regime headed by his father-in-law, Mullah Omar, in Kabul. When they blow up bases or foreigners in the Kingdom, the security forces round up a few Pakistani or Filipino immigrants and execute them to show the US that justice has been done, but the real organisers are untouchable. Their tentacles reach into the heart of Saudi society, and it's debatable whether they can now cut them off, even at the request of the United States.

Tariq Ali
London

MANHATTAN that morning was a diagram, a blue bar-chart with columns which were tall or not so tall. A silver cursor passed across the screen and clicked silently on the tallest column, which turned red and black and presently vanished. This is how we delete you. The cursor returned and

11 September
Some LRB writers reflect on the reasons and consequences

clicked on the second column. Presently a thing like a solid grey-white cauliflower rose until it was a mountain covering all south Manhattan. This is how we bury you.

It was the most open atrocity of all time, a simple demonstration written on the sky which everyone in the world was invited to watch. This is how much we hate you.

Six thousand lives: men and women and some children, Americans and foreigners, Christians and Jews and Taoists and Muslims and all those who asked a god to save them in the last minutes. Five thousand was a heavy task for the SS backshift at Auschwitz-Birkenau, in the summer of 1944. Two or possibly three trainloads. But they could process that in an afternoon and evening, if they tried. The difference was that their killing was a secret. People living a few miles away could see tall towers which every few hours gushed flame-red and black. But they were not meant to know why. Once there was a time when the most evil people on earth were ashamed to write their crime across the heavens.

Now, too late, leaders are writing 'Retribution' on the clouds. Nothing good will come of that, and a choking fog of speeches and bulletins will fall between the dead and those who swear they will remember them. Auden wrote once of powers that direct us. He meant blind chance, but the poem also works for powers who wear suits and mount platforms:

It is their tomorrow hangs over the earth of
the living
And all that we wish for our friends; but
existence is believing
We know for whom we mourn and who is
grieving.

Neal Ascherson
London

IN a telephone poll last week, readers of the *Cambridge Evening News* voted decisively against any military action aimed at those responsible for the attacks on the USA. A readership better known for its implacable hatred of joyriders on the A14 ('flogging would be too good for them') was having no truck with the cowboy President's plans for battle; still less with Prime Minister Blair's idea of dispatching our few remaining gunboats and jump-jets to cheer him on. This was just one of the domestic surprises that came in the wake of 11 September. Another was Peter Mandelson's strangely off-key suggestion that the secret services should be recruiting in Bradford rather than St James's (apparently on the grounds that immigrants would find it easier than Old Etonians to disguise themselves as Islamic extremists). But almost the oddest response has been our terrified certainty that there remains a plentiful supply of suicide pilots and bombers. Anyone who has scratched the surface of early Christianity will realise that full-blown martyrs are a rare commodity, much more numerous in the imagination than on the ground.

The horror of the tragedy was enormously intensified by the ringside seats we were offered through telephone answering machines and text-messages. But when the shock had faded, more hard-headed reaction set in. This wasn't just the feeling that, however tactfully you dress it up, the United States had it coming. That is, of course, what many people openly or privately think. World bullies, even if their heart is in the right place, will in the end pay the price.

But there is also the feeling that all the 'civilised world' (a phrase which Western leaders seem able to use without a trace of irony) is paying the price for its glib definitions of 'terrorism' and its refusal to listen to what the 'terrorists' have to say. There are very few people on the planet who devise carnage for the sheer hell of it. They do what they do for a cause; because they are at war. We might not like their cause; but using the word 'terrorism' as an alibi for thinking what drives it will get us nowhere in stopping the violence. Similarly, 'fanaticism', a term regularly applied to extraordinary acts of bravery when we abhor their ends and means. The silliest description of the onslaught on the World Trade Center was the often repeated slogan that it was a 'cowardly' attack.

Mary Beard
Cambridge

IT has been hard in the past twenty years for Americans to think about the United States and the world; and it is going to be harder now. Yet the terrible events of 11 September have alarmed us into reflection. Terrorism, religious orthodoxy, and nationalism of all kinds (insurgent as well as established) have become in our time inseparable companions: those who apologise for one thereby take on their conscience the crimes of the rest. If the US should seek to avenge these thousands with new thousands of innocent dead, it will be the response of a nation merely. I fear that we may do that, but hope that we will not. By what we do now, and what we refrain from doing, we ought to wish to be seen to act on behalf of the human nature from which the agents of terror have cut themselves off. In the days after the planes hit, the US appeared to be governed from New York, where the leaders of the city and the state all spoke in voices of dignity, compassion and deliberation. Those should be the examples our lawmakers bear in mind when they frame a policy of response in the days to come.

David Bromwich
New Haven

THE news from the Middle East is not all bad. The savagery of the attacks on 11 September has, in at least one country, brought Muslim militancy into disrepute and swelled the ranks of the moderates. At the main public prayers in Tehran on 14 September, for the first time since the revolution in 1979, the cry of *Marg bar Amrika*, 'Death to America', was not to be heard. There have been candle-lit vigils for the American dead in Tehran squares and messages of sympathy from the Mayor of the city to the Mayor of New York. While Iran is not suddenly going to allow the US the use of airfields and harbours for missions against the suspects in Afghanistan, it is doing surprisingly little to hinder them. In the 22 years since the US diplomats were taken hostage in Tehran the Iranians have had ample time to consider the virtues of Islamic government and international isolation. Looking beyond their borders, they contemplate 'emirates of rubble' in Iraq and Afghanistan and count themselves lucky.

Since the death of Ayatollah Khomeini in 1989, the 'Terrorists' (in the French-Revolutionary rather than the George-Bushian sense) have been losing ground in Iran. The Presidencies of Hashemi Rafsanjani were a slow-motion Thermidor. Since Muhammad Khatami was elected President in a landslide in 1997, Iran has stumbled towards accommodation, first with the Arab countries, then with Western Europe and even its old bugbear, Britain. Out on the horizon is the US.

The vast majority of Iranians have forgotten their grievance against the US, have shed many of their complexes about Western intrigue and want nothing more than to join the mainstream of world affairs. While Khatami's 'dialogue between the civilisations' sounds pale in the light of exploding buildings, it is the only thing on offer for those who don't want 'the war between the civilisations' that Osama bin Laden and others are seeking to inaugurate.

Rarely have both wings of what is known as The System in Iran moved in the same direction. Religious conservatives have doctrinal differences with Sheikh Osama and dislike the Taliban as a thorough regional nuisance. (Iran's Afghan policy has been as disastrous as everybody else's.) The chastened revolutionaries around Khatami see a 'historic opportunity' – that is the phrase that keeps recurring – to break out of their corner and restore relations with the United States. Women and young people, with their vigils for the American dead, express both an ardent sympathy for a loss they comprehend and an intense frustration with the stale taboos of a superannuated revolutionary culture. A raw and rattled US has responded with warmth. Iran, the first country into Islamic millenarian government in modern times, looks set to be the first out.

James Buchan
Norfolk

LAST Tuesday morning, 11 September, I was planning on finishing up an LRB review I was writing – of a book called *The Devil's Cloth: A History of Stripes and Striped Fabric*, by the medievalist Michel Pastoureau. Now, as I stagger numbly round my house in San Francisco, hardly able to read or eat or think, I don't know when I'll get back to it. Too bad, because, in any normal time, the book would be one worth mulling over. Pastoureau argues that over the centuries stripes (and striped clothing) have gone from being 'bad' to 'good'. In the Middle

Letters

11 September

With a few exceptions, your 11 September roundtable (LRB, 4 October) is agreed on one central point: what happened in New York and Washington can be directly blamed on US policies and actions from the 1960s to the present, with Israel's treatment of the Palestinians as the last straw. Fredric Jameson reminds us that the recent 'events', as he calls the horrific attacks that killed thousands, provide us with 'a textbook example of dialectical reversal'. Others – Tariq Ali, for instance – warn us not to incense Arab nations even further, as if a mea culpa on our part could now end the threat of further attacks, this time quite possibly ones of biological warfare.

But what I wish principally to address here is part of Mary Beard's contribution. 'When the shock had faded,' she writes, 'more hardheaded reaction set in. This wasn't just the feeling that, however tactfully you dress it up, the United States had it coming. That is, of course, what many people openly or privately think. World bullies, even if their heart is in the right place, will in the end pay the price.'

On 11 September, according to the latest figures as I write, 6333 Americans and 2593 foreign citizens died in New York. That's approximately 9000 people. (I am not counting those who died at the Pentagon.) Most of us know someone or know of someone who has died in the WTC debacle. And most of the people who died had relatives, including thousands of now orphaned children. If you multiply 9000 by, say, four you have 36,000 innocent people whose lives have been destroyed in one way or another. The victims, incidentally, included a high proportion of Latinos and blacks as well as a good number of Muslims. And, contrary to the cliché about the WTC and the Pentagon being emblems of US imperial power, the victims held a great variety of jobs: they worked for travel agencies, restaurants, public relations firms, TV networks, insurance companies, law firms, art supply manufacturers. In short, they were a cross-section of America.

But Mary Beard, writing from Cambridge, surely one of the most idyllic safe havens in the world, tells us that 'the United States had it coming' and that this is 'of course' what many people 'openly or privately think'. In the circles in which Beard travels, perhaps many people do think this. Certainly most of the LRB's contributors seem to. Perhaps this is why academics are now so poorly regarded by the rest of the population and why there are so few academic jobs for recent Humanities PhDs,

either in the US or the UK. Outside the ivory gates, 95 per cent of the US population evidently disagree with Beard's assessment.

But of course we know how spurious this 'fact' is. As Jameson tells us, the people 'are united by the fear of saying anything that contradicts this completely spurious media consensus'. Fear, one wonders, of what? Has Jameson ever been silenced for his views? Beard, in any case, goes on to complain about our 'glib definitions of "terrorism"' and our 'refusal to listen to what the "terrorists" have to say'. 'There are,' she continues, 'very few people on the planet who devise carnage for the sheer hell of it.'

Well, I suppose it depends on what one means by 'the sheer hell of it'. By analogy to terrorism, perhaps we should not have bothered with definitions of Nazism or Fascism, but should have listened to what Hitler and his friends had to say. I seem to recall that Neville Chamberlain tried just that; he even had 'a piece of paper from Herr Hitler'. But as Churchill knew, 'an appeaser is one who feeds the crocodile thinking it will eat him last.' As it turned out, after all that 'listening' at Berchtesgaden, there were quite a few people on the planet who were quite happy to devise carnage 'for the sheer hell of it', taking that phrase quite literally. Hell is, in any case, what transpired.

It is true that the US has committed some atrocities in the Middle East and that, say, Clinton's bombing of the wrong target – a beautiful new hospital – in the Sudan was a major crime. Does it therefore follow that 'the US had it coming'? And which of us in the US are included?

I have been a subscriber to LRB since the journal's inception some twenty-five years ago. But I hereby cancel my subscription and shall urge my Stanford students and colleagues to boycott the journal. Let me end, however, on an upbeat note that speaks to Beard's 'of course'. The man who takes care of our garden in Pacific Palisades, Ruben Vargas, was here the other day. A Latino who came to California from Mexico not all that long ago, Vargas has a daughter who is a freshman at UCLA. Some of us like to think that such upward mobility is what makes the US unique. I asked Ruben what he thought of the attack. 'Well,' he said, 'at least now we're all in it together.' I responded: 'But Ruben, many of my friends think it's all America's fault.' He smiled and said: 'Excuse me, Marjorie' – yes, in California, one has only a first name – 'but isn't that a minuscule part of the population?' Of course!

Marjorie Perloff

Los Angeles

Mary-Kay Wilmers writes: Towards the end of the week of 10 September 2001, we sent an email to around thirty of the paper's contributors: 'For the last few days we've followed the coverage of events in New York, and their international repercussions, with a sense that the intensity of the shock and the extent of journalistic spectacle have left little scope for reflection of the kind we try to muster in this paper. We were wondering what our contributors thought and if they'd like to say something about what had happened and why. The brief is very limited – 500 words – but, within those limits, we'd be really interested to have (and to publish) your views.' The deadline given was the following Tuesday afternoon, UK time – a week after the events of 9/11. Print schedules being what they were, a warning was added to the effect that subscribers wouldn't be reading the entries until at least 26 or 27 September. 'So if it's a case of looking forward, it would do to bear those dates in mind. And if you're inclined to look back, please look back well before 11 September.'

In the next issue we published four letters in response to what our contributors had said. One of the letter-writers threatened to 'shove your loony leftist faces into some dog shit' (he later apologised), but a letter from the Stanford poetry professor Marjorie Perloff elicited a much larger response in the issue after that. What riled Perloff most was the implication in Mary Beard's letter that 'the United States had it coming.' Beard didn't quite say that, though she didn't wholly not.

'I'm no expert'

Mary-Kay Wilmers writes: After the issue with Marjorie Perloff's letter in it was published I was invited to speak on the radio. Perloff would speak too but we wouldn't speak to each other. I had never spoken on the radio and prepared myself with the help of my colleagues. Some of my notes are shown on these pages. The post-it notes here refer to the number of pro and anti-Perloff letters we received.

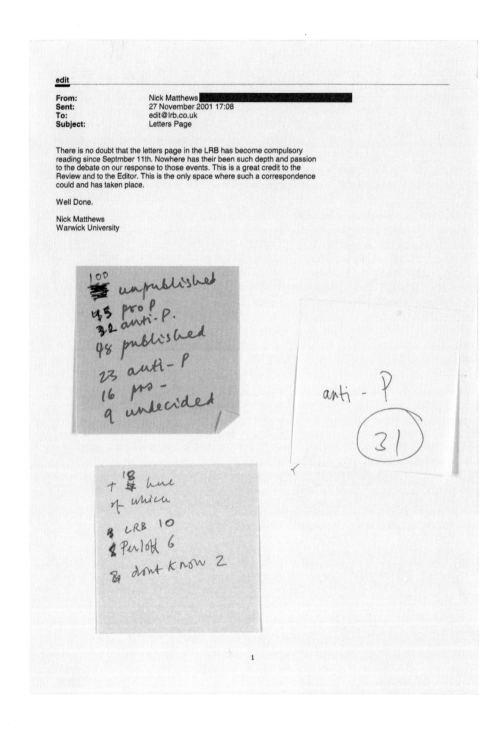

Email from Nick Matthews to the editors, with post-it notes written by Mary-Kay Wilmers (except the yellow one)

LIFE BASED ON
CLOSE READING
NOW WON'T ALLOW
STUDENTS TO READ

THINGS SHE DOESN'T
AGREE WITH.

diversity of views
acknowledgment
of atrocity.

(Gore Vidal)

for citing
occasions
when US
has invaded
or bombed
other countries.

en absolute-
ich some of
of fear."
yranny of a
gin with the
the Nation,
ng—they all
k the same
e same con-
ing, a con-
bia Journal-
limate that's
ads journal-
their necks
us that has
on tends to
icularly af-

confined to

their window (which so outraged the conservative *Weekly Standard* and the *New
York Post* that they printed Pollitt's address,
inviting readers to inundate her daughter
with flags). "Anyone who asks, 'Why do
they hate us so much?' and gives an answer
other than 'They hate us because we're so
great'—that's considered to be a subversive
answer," Pollitt adds.

Sontag herself was "astonished by the
virulence of the response to what I said,"
she admits. "Of course I was suggesting
that American foreign-policy engage-
ments need to be rethought. Is that such
an odd thing to say? There has to be a
political opposition in this country; that's
part of the process. I'm a liberal Democrat. Is that off the map? I thought we
were a rowdy, rambunctious, quarrelsome

"The test of democracy is during
times of adversity," says
Representative Barbara Lee.

democracy, but it turns out we
have increasingly become incredibly conformist, and very afraid of
debate and criticism."

Many observers worry that the
result will be an isolated and ill-

APPEASEMENT: HER
COMPARISONS AREN'T USEFUL.

US power hasn't been
seriously challenged

Appeasing German empire

Stalinism / McCarthyism
Arab countries /
Israel allow
after freedom
of speech

EMPTY INSULT. I'M
NO EXPERT.

(Appeasement to be w
being in w. the victors;
tea in Berchtesgaden

21st Century's Dominant Metaphor

Art Spiegelman – cartoonist, illustrator and author of *Maus*, a graphic novel based on his father's recollections of the Holocaust – spent the decade before mid-September 2001 producing cover artwork for the *New Yorker*, though he felt increasingly restless, alienated, he later said, by 'the magazine's complacent tone'. One of his final *New Yorker* covers, published six days after the 9/11 attacks, was a ghostly image of the Twin Towers, paler black on blacker black, the silhouettes barely visible.

In the aftermath of those events – as hysteria and panic gripped America and the world, as a terrifying 'new normal' set in, as Bush and his cabal moved into 'full dystopian Big Brother mode' – Spiegelman decided that he had to retrieve 'the fragments of what I'd experienced from the media images that threatened to engulf what I actually saw'. Which meant going back to making comics. So in late 2002 he began the series that became *In the Shadow of No Towers*, with each strip appearing initially in *Die Zeit*. With the exception of the small-circulation weekly *Forward*, US publications including the *New Yorker* and *New York Review of Books* ran a mile when invited to serialise it, but Spiegelman found 'a coalition of the willing' in Europe – and his home in the UK was the LRB.

Over the course of a few months in 2003, as the Iraq War rumbled on, the paper printed each instalment in Spiegelman's extraordinary series, one or two a fortnight. It was a production challenge of a kind the LRB hadn't faced before. The strips appeared on each issue's centre spread, on high white glossy stock. The office computers were old and slow, not well equipped to handle Spiegelman's large and complex multi-layered digital files, but Ben Campbell – Peter Campbell's son and the LRB's production guru – juggled images and words to reassemble them on the page exactly as Spiegelman intended, making trips to the printer to make sure they came out just right. There was one grievous error, when Crazy Bag Lady's words popped out of their speech bubble. But all the best contributors are forgiving, and Spiegelman was one of them.

Daniel Soar

*Episode 1 from 'In the Shadow of No Towers' by
Art Spiegelman, published in the issue of*
6 March 2003

Bitter Fame

'The year 2040,' Anthony Thwaite wrote in the tenth anniversary issue of the LRB in 1989, 'doesn't look too far off for the definitive Life of Sylvia Plath.' The writing about Plath in the LRB's archive shows that we are not even close. The problem is clear in Olwyn Hughes's response – she was a representative of the Plath Estate, and Ted Hughes's sister – to Thwaite's review of *Bitter Fame* by Anne Stevenson, the first authorised biography. 'People with Sylvia's type of mental problem,' Olwyn Hughes writes in this letter, 'can and do rouse pretty negative emotions.'

While Karl Miller was literary editor of the *New Statesman*, he rejected the tranche of *Ariel* poems Plath sent him in 1962, perhaps out of loyalty to Ted. (He maintained in a 1991 answer to a letter in the LRB that his 'first response was to consider her state of mind and make enquiries. I was afraid she might take her life.') Miller gave her some books to review instead, and she took on a biography of Byron's wife. 'Incredibly, the portrait of Augusta, Byron's sister, is the dead spit of Olwyn!' she wrote to her mother in November 1962. 'Only she sounds immensely nicer & had lots of children.' Sides were already being taken.

The *New York Review of Books*, which first appeared in February 1963, the month Plath died, carried pieces by Robert Lowell, Elizabeth Hardwick and Al Alvarez that helped establish her as one of the greatest poets of the century; by the time the LRB arrived in 1979 her poetic reputation was sure, but the battles over her first authorised biography were just beginning. She died intestate, and control of her writing passed to Hughes, who destroyed the journal she kept of her last months because, as he wrote later, it seemed to him then that 'forgetfulness' was 'an essential part of survival'. The draft of her second novel, *Doubletake*, which she described as the story of 'a wife whose husband turns out to be a deserter & philanderer although she had thought he was wonderful and perfect', disappeared too. (That one I hope will yet turn up.) There were versions of Plath in circulation that were absolutely intolerable to the estate. In *The Haunting of Sylvia Plath* (1991), Jacqueline Rose documented Olwyn and Ted's resistance to her psychoanalytic literary-critical readings of poems such as 'The Rabbit Catcher' in endnotes as fascinating as the text itself. Biography had been forced on criticism: Rose's book showed us the complexity and beauty of the poetry, while documenting the very many ways a woman's life, particularly a dead woman's life, is barely her own.

Too extreme

Elaine Showalter (*LRB*, 11 July) refers to occasions when Sylvia Plath's best-known poems ('perhaps the greatest of her generation') were 'rejected by literary editors as "too extreme"'. Is it possible that one of those editors now has something to do with the *LRB*?

Richard Jacobs

London SE14

Karl Miller writes: When I was literary editor of the *New Statesman*, I was in the habit of publishing verse and prose by Sylvia Plath, and I came to know her a bit. When a selection of her last poems was sent, my first response was to consider her state of mind and to make enquiries. I was afraid she might take her life. Such is the tormented state of Plath studies that it is only to be expected that this response, and the delays and uncertainties to which it may have led, should sometimes appear to be spoken of as part of a process of flat rejection.

In her LRB review of *The Haunting* Elaine Showalter mentioned that Rose called Plath 'the Marilyn Monroe of the literati'. (In 2012, Rose would write in the LRB about Monroe.) Looking back on her book's publication in a piece in the LRB 11 years later, Rose psychoanalyses us too, the peanut-crunching crowd who love to see Plath die again and again. Sylvia, like Cordelia, like Marilyn, is never so 'deadly than when so perfect'; if you can't tolerate these women's rage and desire, if you can't let them be anything other than a saint to venerate or a sinner to be punished, 'to what forms of uncertainty – of language, sexuality and knowing – do you have the right?'

Joanna Biggs

Olwyn Hughes

London NW1 9SG Telephone 01-485 8437

Literary Agency

10 May 90

Dear Susannah Clapp,

Thankyou for Thwaite on BITTER FAME. A pity Stevenson insisted on the
innane note re my help which seems to have put everybody in a state (my
role was to make up by hard graft for her almost total unsuitability for
biographical work). Its depressing for me to see people like Thwaite
trailing out anti-Olwyn Hughes stuff that I thought the reserve of cultists
and bandwaggon half wits. Please tell Thwaite from me that the only things
in such writings Ive objected to, have been pure inventions and/or wild
misconceptions, usually highly damaging to living people and farcical about
Sylvia herself. Earlier biographers had such thin, doubtful sources on
Plath's adult life, so little understanding of her work and difficulties,
that they (first Butscher, then - copy-cat - dreary Wagner-Martin) hit on a
way to make their books seem hot stuff - claims of censorship, and my
opposition to their (non existent) revelations. (Holbrook, a special case,
wants Sylvia 100% mad, which she wasn't.) Its been a miserable business.
To see such as Hamilton, Alvarez and (to his modest degree) Thwaite lining
up with this unholy rubbish has been distressing.

Whatever does he mean by his sentence re. the appendices: 'all of them
emphasising the role of Sylvia Plath as agressor and catalyst, and of Ted
and Olwyn Hughes as victims and largely passive agents.'?? As at the time
I lived abroad, never got beyond a fairly distant cordiality (albeit with a
few alarming moments) in my occasional meetings with Sylvia, and of the
three writers of appendices knew only Myers (a Paris friend and the only
one to mention my existence), how do these accounts show me as 'victim and
passive agent'. (And what are we to do if. as regards Ted, that is how he
seemed, to some degree, to be?) Further, though Dido's piece shows Sylvia
mostly on the rampage, I would have thought the others lack emphasis of
that kind (I know Myers account to be positively gentlemanly). The reason
for my vote for the inclusion of these pieces - apart from the fact that
they are fascinating & - in the cases of Myers and Merwin - the records of
people who knew the adult Plath more closely and over a longer period than
anyone outside her husband and mother - is that I wished it to be seen that
for once this biography actually took its material from authentic and
informed reportage - a VERY new step in Plath biography.
                                                    and disgust

Is Dido's tone 'bitter'? It was written, rather, in outrage/at the seas of
rubbish on both Sylvia and Ted. Would that a few more of Ted's countrymen
and fellow poets shared her outrage. (Most inteligent people were simply
baffled by Sylvia and her contradictory signals, and occasionally
appalled. Dido received more negative stuff than most). . She has both
total recall of facts and of how it felt at the time. People with
Sylvia's type of mental problems can and do rouse pretty negative
emotions. After 25 years these emotions can grow dim - or with someone as
tragic as Sylvia, be discreetly forgotten.   Its surely a plucky &
remarkably honest piece. It appears, though, it is 'partisan' to be honest
where Sylvia is concerned.

I enclose an extra copy of this page. Could you be a dear and forward it
to Antony Thwaite with my regards and regrets.

V.A.T. Registration No. 230 3665 90

*Left, letters, 15 August 1991; above, letter from
Olwyn Hughes to Susannah Clapp,
10 May 1990 (continued overleaf)*

I enclose Nini Herman's piece. This seems to embody at least a line on the
sort of professional understanding BITTER FAME everywhere hints at but
never gets to grips with. Nini is at home with both psychiatry and
literature - essential I think if one is to properly grasp Plath. The
continued separation of the 'two cultures' has certainly meant that she
has remained more or less misunderstood - a reason possibly for all the
third rate rubbish about her - an attempt to fill the incomprehensible
gap. If you like it you could perhaps pin it to the paperback ed of
BITTER FAME (July, I think). Or just present it as a general musing on
Plath, rather than as a review per se. Nini's phone No. is 603 5091.

Nini wrote this as a review for the JOURNAL OF FREE ASSOCIATION. If you
would like it first (I dont imagine they would mind) let me know fairly
quickly.

Good luck with Dido.

Yours,

Olwyn Hughes

Susannah Clapp,
The London Review of Books,

EXTRACT FROM VOL. 24 NO. 16 · 22 AUGUST 2002

This is not a Biography

Jacqueline Rose

BIOGRAPHY loves Sylvia Plath. When I ask students what they know of Plath, they almost invariably reply that she killed herself and was married to Ted Hughes. Occasionally they run these two snippets together as if the second were, in some mysterious and not wholly formulated way, related to the first; as if together they add up to something that leaves nothing more to be said. I watch this story shut down around her, clamping her writing into its hollow wooden frame. Death and marriage may have fed and fuelled her writing, but – posthumously at least – they cramp her style.

According to Freud, the act of suicide always involves more than one person. Maybe that is one reason why suicide is classified as a crime. Maybe, too, that is why biographies of Plath always take on the aura of hunt the culprit: not because, as is most often assumed, someone – usually Hughes – must be held accountable for her death, but because there is an unacknowledged crime calling out to be uncovered, another body to be found. Suicide, as everyone knows, casts a shadow over those it leaves behind. In my conflict with the Estate of Sylvia Plath (more below), I often felt that I was not the real quarry, but more like a diversion; that I was duelling, hit and miss, in the dark. Although they have often denied it, the defensiveness of the Plath legatees is notorious. But perhaps the fervour with which they have warded off incursions from the world outside has been part of a deeper struggle. To kill the killer. Even though she is already dead. It is a paradox of suicide that the murderer, who lives on for ever, is the one who didn't survive.

It has become a commonplace to say of biographies of Plath that they take sides. In *The Silent Woman* (1994), her openly partisan study of Plath biography, Janet Malcolm insists that this is unavoidable: 'As the reader knows, I, too, have taken a side.' One flier for her book stated: 'A writer finds Ted Hughes innocent but biographies as a group guilty,' which suggests the process is interminable and that, as a form of writing, bio-graphy has the capacity to indict itself. No biography, no act of writing can be neutral, but something far more serious, indeed deadly, seems to hang in the balance when biographers of Plath dispute whether or not she was bearable, whether she was disliked or liked by her friends. Out of the mire, a banal but chilling proposition starts to emerge – that we decide on the innocence or guilt of a plaintiff according to whether we like them or not. Legality, our conviction in the rights and wrongs of the matter, trails our desires (whether the reverse would be preferable is not clear). Whenever I read biographies of Plath, I always have the suspicion that someone or other is being criminalised simply for being who they were.

In the case of Plath, the subjective component of all biography takes on a special edge. Someone has to be guilty. Someone is to blame. And if someone is going to be proclaimed guilty, then someone else – the person telling the story – has to be certain. Plath biographies are remarkable for their rhetoric of conviction. We are in a court of law, the biographer is mounting her case. Beyond the normal demands of biographical discovery – the search for the crucial detail, the painstaking reconstruction of every facet of a world (biographies, as we know, are getting longer and longer) – incriminating evidence is being gathered. Plath biographies tend to answer each other, shouting like opponents across a legal gulf, each one insisting that it has a greater claim to the truth than the one that went before (why otherwise write a biography at all?). The greater the fervour, the fiercer the claim. In the case of Plath, truth is not just subjective, it is mortal. To die for.

Bloody Sunday

Murray Sayle came to the paper late in his journalistic career. He had covered the war in Vietnam, the Soviet invasion of Czechoslovakia and the conflict between India and Pakistan; he had tracked down Che Guevara in the Andes and interviewed Kim Philby in Moscow. Now, in quasi-retirement in Japan, he wrote reviews for the LRB. In 2002, a document resurfaced in Hull University Library: the original copy of the report he and Derek Humphry – then members of the *Sunday Times*'s Insight team – had filed on the events in Derry on Bloody Sunday, 30 January 1972, when British soldiers killed 14 unarmed Irish civilians.

Harold Evans, the *Sunday Times*'s editor, had killed Sayle and Humphry's piece – under some pressure from the government – and commissioned another. Sayle resigned and the original copy was lost. Thirty years later, with Sayle called to give evidence to the Saville Inquiry, set up in 1998, the LRB published the full version of his report. Through rigorous research and extensive interviews Sayle and Humphry had established as best they could where everyone had been that day, and what shots were fired by whom. The map shown here had been meant to accompany their original story. The appearance of the piece in the LRB provoked a memorable letter from Richard Eyre (opposite).

Top, photocopy of a map of 'the scene of Bloody Sunday', published in the 'LRB' of 11 July 2002; right, part of an email from Murray Sayle to the editors, 20 May 2002, with post-it notes written by different editors

eyre 0808

Bloody Sunday

~~in his piece about Bloody Sunday (LRB, 11 July)~~

Dear Mary-Kay

~~A meeting I had in 1979 with a senior Army public relations officer~~ provide

~~I've been meaning to write for several weeks, or at least after reading Murray Sayles'~~

~~excellent piece on Bloody Sunday, and seeing Stephen the other day reminded me.~~ As

anecdotal support for Sayles' argument that the army had a plan to 'bring the enemy to

battle' ~~I can cite my meeting in 1979 with the a man responsible for the army's public~~

~~relations.~~ I was producing a series of TV plays for the BBC, ~~called Play for Today.~~ One

of them was a film written by Robert Holman about a 16-year-old boy in the North-East

who joined the army, served in Northern Ireland and was shot. Naively I imagined that

we might get help from the army — filming in a Recruitment Office, use of equipment etc.

I fixed a meeting with a Colonel ███████████ 'What,' I asked him, 'is the army's

policy in Northern Ireland?' 'Well, if I had my way,' he said, 'we'd line all the Catholics

up against a wall and shoot the fucking lot of them.' ~~And this was the Head of Public~~

~~Relations.~~

~~very best wishes~~

Richard (Eyre)

London

put this first

Letter from Richard Eyre to Mary-Kay Wilmers,
published in the issue of 25 July 2002

File under T for tosser

Three Poems by John Ashbery   ⌐0503

I Asked Mr Dithers Whether It Was Time Yet He Said No to Wait

use

[brontosauruses]

Time, you old miscreant! Slain any brontosaurs lately? You~
Sixty wondering days I watched him navigate the alkali lick,
always a little power ebbing, streaming from high windowsills.
Down here the tetched are lonely. There's nothing they can do
except spit.

We felt better about answering the business letter
once the resulting hubris had been grandfathered in,
slowly, by a withered sage in clogs
and a poncho vast as a delta, made of some rubbery satinlike
material. It was New Year's Eve
again. Time to get out the punchbowl,
make some resolutions,
I don't think.

—John Ashbery

Poem by John Ashbery, with a correction by
David Kermani, published in the issue of
22 August 2002

London Review of Books
28 Little Russell Street
London   WC1A 2HN

*File under T
for tosser*

27th April 2001

For Attention :   Editorial Department

Dear Sirs,

        It would be very helpful to many ordinary readers
of english poetry, including myself, if you could invite
some one from Carcanet Press to explain to us what the
reasons are for why some critics value the work of
John Ashbery above that of most other contemporary poets.
It would be especially instructive to have pointed out
those things in a specific poem which are particularly good
and what it is that makes them good.

Yours sincerely,

M J Gerrard

Tadworth Surrey
KT 20 7LP

Jeremy Harding writes: John Bayley was the first LRB contributor to engage in earnest with John Ashbery. In his review of *Shadow Train* he lured the poetry away from its prestigious East Coast chaperones to a quiet corner of the room and confessed his admiration. Ashbery's 'vision' was 'homeless', Bayley felt, even if it had rented rooms in the canon: Bayley thought first of Keats and Shelley before mentioning Ashbery's go-to precursor, Wallace Stevens. Ashbery could make English hackles rise. His poems occasioned grumpy letters to the editors: the poet Michael Horovitz denounced him as a 'mandarin individualist' and M.J. Gerrard, whose letter is shown here, wanted to know 'what it is that makes them good?' ('File under T for tosser' is in my handwriting). It wasn't until 1995 that the LRB asked Ashbery for a poem. He sent in five, and went on to contribute another fifty before his death in 2017. 'I asked Mr Dithers Whether It Was Time Yet He Said No to Wait' seems to recoil as the world spins by in a self-important hurry ('It was New Year's Eve/again'): poems can age quickly, it suggests, if they make too many resolutions. Ashbery's didn't.

Letter from M.J. Gerrard to the editor, 27 April 2001

Mechanical Things

Peter Campbell designed the first issue of the LRB in October 1979 and redesigned it six months later after the papers' divorce; in 1997 he re-redesigned it. But saying that gives no sense of his importance to the paper. As much as the original editors, Peter shaped the LRB. Unlike us, he never lost his temper. More adjusted than most to his own wants and necessities, and so better able to accommodate other people's, he was an exemplary person to work with.

He was born in New Zealand in 1937 (in a taxi in a tunnel: he never told us that). At university in Wellington, he did 'the kind of degree in which you are allowed to mix subjects' and spent his first year reading philosophy, geology and English: 'I never quite got a grip on these subjects,' he said in a review of George Landow's Hypertext in 1992, 'but the memory of what it is like to do philosophy or geology remains; and when I read about debates that are going on in these areas I believe I know, even if I cannot follow it all, what kind of row or celebration is taking place.' There are people whom getting a grip doesn't suit, who don't want to be confined. One can honour the world in depth or across a wide range and there were few aspects of the world that Peter didn't wish to honour.

He paid for the month-long sea voyage from Wellington with money he'd earned as a typographer and illustrator, and arrived in London in 1960. He found work at BBC Publications designing schools pamphlets. Karl Miller and I got to know him a few years later when he'd begun to design the BBC books that accompanied the famous television series of the late 1960s and we were working on the Listener. Peter had no great liking for corporate life; he preferred to get around, talk to people, find out what they did and how they did it.

A comprehensive show of 1930s art was the first exhibition he wrote about in the LRB; it was, he felt, misconceived: 'an attempt at total recall' that reduced the works on display 'to the status of evidence'. But once the point had been made there was no further reason to mope. Peter didn't like everything he saw, but mostly he avoided writing about work that didn't accord with his taste or his sense of things; if he couldn't find a reason to be interested he wrote about something else – another exhibition or the trees on the street. He tells you things about painting and how it's done that no one else thinks to tell you – of an Alice Neel nude self-portrait, for example: 'Her face is rather tight around the mouth, as a painter's face can be when reaching a decision about just how a detail seen in the mirror can be put down with the next stroke' – or maybe hasn't noticed: 'It comes to you that when you can see a sitter's feet . . . the view is wide enough to let you in.'

He was unusual in getting equal pleasure from the world and from its representation; from understanding Ingres-flesh and the anatomy of the stifftail duck. In the same way I imagine that he got equal pleasure from writing about pictures and from looking at them.

Mary-Kay Wilmers, writing in 2011

EXTRACT FROM VOL. 24 NO. 5 · 7 MARCH 2002

Why does it take so long to mend an escalator?

Peter Campbell

STEPPING onto an escalator is an act of faith. From time to time you see people poised at the top, advised by instinct not to launch themselves onto the river of treads. Riding the moving stairs is an adventure for the toddling young and a challenge to the tottering old. Natural hesitancy puts a limit on throughput. London Underground escalators carry passengers at a top speed of 145 feet per minute – close to the maximum allowed under the British Standard specification. There is little temptation to run the machines faster, as trials show that above 160 feet per minute so many people pause timidly that fewer are carried. In the early days they had to be persuaded to get on at all. A one-legged man, 'Bumper' Harris, was hired to ride for a whole day on the first installation – it was at Earls Court – to show how easy it was. Some people were sceptical (how had he lost his leg?) but others broke their journey there just to ride up and down.

Competence, once achieved, breeds contemptuous agility: young men run down, two steps at a time, and stop aggressively behind anyone who has ignored the notices telling them to stand on the right. London Underground began promoting a walk-or-stand culture in 1944 – 'Here's another bright suggestion, standing right avoids congestion.' Silly boys run up the down escalator and arrive panting at the top – sometimes having overtaken the line of passengers on the parallel, upward-moving flight. In 1954 a man was fined for sliding down the moving handrail. He said he was in high spirits after getting married.

Most of those who use escalators regularly become calmly capable. They even begin to notice differences between one kind and another: to realise, for example, that those on the Underground are exceptional – longer and wider, generally speaking, than the compact shop and office variety. This is because more is demanded of them. They must run 20 hours a day, 364 days a year; they must cope with heavier loads – bags, trolleys and pushchairs, as well as up to 13,000 people an hour. Even the weight of those who dutifully stand on the right must be taken into account, because it means that the steps are stressed unequally. There are 409 escalators on the London Underground. At present about 95 per cent of them are operational at any one time. Statistics come with a whiff of smoke and a flash of mirrors. Numbers are a distraction when the grind of a necessary escalator is silenced. They do, however, tell you that one dead escalator in twenty is more of a nuisance than you would have guessed, and they put what is demanded of public-service escalators into focus. For a store escalator 85 per cent planned availability is acceptable. Those in airports or the Underground are typically installed under contracts specifying 98 per cent availability and usually achieve 99.5 per cent. As machines age, unplanned outages increase, so a proportion – perhaps half – of the out-of-service escalators on the Underground are machines which age, wear and tear have made less reliable than originally specified.

London Transport is used to explaining the difficulty of making repairs in cramped conditions on a complicated, sometimes old system which had, in many cases, to be shoehorned into a tight space in a station designed for lifts. The mysterious inactivity is not really that mysterious. Most escalators can only be worked on during the four or so hours when the station is closed. Then, mechanics are not put in danger by the moving parts of the machine next door, and there are no passengers to get in the way when machinery is brought in through the ticket hall, or to be panicked by the smell of burning when a welding torch is used.

Such explanations lead to more questions. Have escalators always been so fragile? Can broken ones be read as a symptom of a deeper malaise? Are broken-down escalators evidence that we ask for the impossible: that to get the Tube to run smoothly is politically unfeasible because it would involve so many resources being taken away from the other good things we demand – public and private.

Peter Campbell had contributed to the LRB from the beginning, but in October 2000 he began writing an exhibition review for each issue, slightly shorter than a normal piece and enclosed in a box. His first 'At the . . .' was about a Gerrit Dou show at Dulwich Picture Gallery. During the next 11 years he often went beyond the gallery walls, casting his eye over gardens, street signs, catwalks, horse races, beach clothes, Brighton stucco, New Zealand timber houses, the Tour de France and St George's Church, Bloomsbury, as seen from the LRB windows. He was the sort of writer that you could put a question to – 'Why does it take so long to mend an escalator?', for example – and know that he would come back with something surprising and far more interesting than you'd imagined. Short Cuts became a fortnightly fixture the same year and six years later a semi-regular movie column was inaugurated, written by Michael Wood. Occasional boxes about poetry pamphlets, TV shows and unclassifiable subjects have followed.

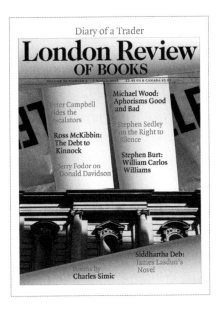

Lovely, lovely, lovely

We usually say that we don't go in for
anniversaries (it's unlikely, for instance,
that we'd publish something just in time
for so-and-so's centenary), but we quite
like celebrating our own, if only because
inclusion in a special anniversary issue is
a useful carrot to dangle in front of a
favourite writer. The 25th anniversary
issues featured Colm Tóibín, Hilary
Mantel, Terry Castle, Jacqueline Rose,
Alan Bennett, Judith Butler and Ian
Sansom, who was very sweet about it,
thus ensuring himself further honour:
'Let's file this on paper . . . cos it's so
nice,' someone scribbled on his email.

Covers from the issues of 21 October 2004 and
4 November 2004

Let's file this as paper, too, 'cos it's so nice.

LRB (editorial)

From: ian sansom ████████████████

Sent: 18 October 2004 11:07

To: LRB (editorial)

Subject: Lovely, Lovely, Lovely

Dear Everyone,

I'm just writing to say that both the 25 Year Anniversary edition and the cheque have arrived here safely. For which, many thanks: I greatly enjoyed the paper, particularly Colm Toibin and the Security Guard, and my children shall doubtless enjoy the proceeds of the cheque.

You are doubtless having to put up with lots of slightly-fat and short-sighted people offering dewy-eyed reminiscence and shameless praise to you at the moment, but I thought I would add my own sniffle to the sob-fest and say that the *LRB* - which I first came across, I think, among the periodicals in Romford Public Library many years ago, whilst waiting for my grandad to finish shopping for broken biscuits in the market - has been an example and encouragement to me for my entire adult life, which puts it right up there with John Coltrane's *A Love Supreme*, Chekhov, E.B. White, Chomsky, Bushmill's, and *The New Yorker*. The magazine has remained one of the great and few constants in my life and I count it as a privilege to have been a contributor. Anything else I might say would only be an embarrassment to me and have you all blubbling uncontrollably, and although I am tempted! to quote Auden - from the end of 'September 1, 1939' - I shall refrain, since that would clearly be both unnecessary and egregious (in both senses). So.

Paul mentioned that you might be having a party to celebrate, which I may already have missed and to which I may not anyway have been invited, but if there is still such being planned and in the pipeline do let me know and I may cast my customary caution to the wind, leave my hermit's cave, sell the children into white slavery, trim my matted beard and hair to a socially-acceptable length, and work my passage on a steamer to make it over. Or not, depending: I find that these days I can only drink if there's food as well, so I shall be interested to know the situation re: canapes.

With many thanks to all of you,

I remain, etc.

Ian Sansom

Fed up of receiving junk e-mail? Find out how to deal with spam here.

18/10/2004

Email from Ian Sansom to the editors,
18 October 2004

Retail Wing

*Above, watercolour of the London Review Bookshop
by Simone Menken, 2015; right, cartoon of the London Review
Bookshop's first birthday party, by Martin Rowson, first
published in the 'Times', 2004*

It's not unprecedented, but it is unusual, for a magazine to own a bookshop and a café. The idea for the London Review Bookshop was Mary-Kay's – it came to her one spring morning in 2002 and, there happening to be an attractive retail space vacant at 14 Bury Place, just around the corner from the magazine's offices and within a stone's throw of the British Museum, the idea quickly acquired an irresistible momentum.

It was not the most propitious moment to open an independent bookshop: Amazon's relentless progress towards online monopoly was sucking trade out of the retail sector and the advent of ebooks looked ominous for the printed word. Despite all this, the London Review Bookshop, beautifully designed by Peter Campbell, opened in 2003, in a blaze of enthusiastic press coverage. In 2007, we put a door in the middle of the history section and opened a café in the adjacent unit.

News of the death of the book turned out to be premature and the London Review Bookshop and Cake Shop have thrived. Despite the ease and attractions of online book-buying, people still seem to like browsing in a small shop where the booksellers know and understand their stock, and where you can meet your friends for lunch or tea. Moreover, the internet has made possible a renaissance in the culture of bookshop events: the London Review Bookshop puts on around a hundred readings and discussions a year.

Nicholas Spice

Squeamish about Sentiment

LRB (editorial)

From:	Terry Castle ▓▓▓▓▓▓▓▓
Sent:	28 January 2005 17:38
To:	LRB (editorial)
Subject:	RE: to Mary-Kay W.

Dear Jean--thanks for the quick reply. I will try to rough something up this weekend.
I don't believe sentimentality will be an issue:
I'm like one of those orphaned baby monkeys who in the famous experiment got the
'barbed wire monkey-mother' instead of one of the stuffed toy ones.... And in many
ways SS lived up to her initials...

Kindest regards, Terry

>L O N D O N   R E V I E W   O F   B O O K S
>
>28 Little Russell St
>
>London WC1A 2HN
>
>Tel: +44 (0)20 7209 1101
>
>Fax: +44 (0)20 7209 1102
>
>edit@lrb.co.uk
>
>www.lrb.co.uk
>
>
>Dear Terry,
>
>MK's away, but would be very pleased if you wrote about Susan Sontag.
>I'm sure I don't need to (or perhaps shouldn't) say this, but remember
>that as well as being squeamish about poo we (collectively) are
>squeamish about sentiment. Would you be able to deliver early next week?
>
>Best wishes,
>Jean
>
>
>-----Original Message-----
>From: Terry Castle ▓▓▓▓▓▓▓▓▓▓▓▓▓▓▓▓▓▓
>Sent: 28 January 2005 03:09
>To: LRB (editorial)
>Subject: to Mary-Kay W.
>
>Dear Mary-Kay,
>
>   Occurred to me to ask if you might be interested in a short personal
>piece about Sontag. I had a 10-yr. on-again-off-again friendship (?)
>with her, rather like the relationship between Dame
>Edna Everidge and her little side-kick Madge.   (I don't need to
>explain who was Madge.)   The piece would have its funny moments but
>would be in the end a (fairly profound) appreciation .   I find I am
>pretty sad about her death and keep finding myself wondering what it is
>all about.
>
>   Guaranteed no-poo clause.
>
>   Best wishes, Terry

1

Email from Terry Castle to the editors,
28 January 2005

EXTRACT FROM VOL. 27 NO. 6 · 17 MARCH 2005

Desperately Seeking Susan

Terry Castle

THE last two times I saw Sontag I managed to blow it – horrendously – both times. The first debacle occurred after one of the films at a festival she was curating at the Japan Society. I'd been hanging nervously around in the lobby, like a groupie, waiting for her: Sontag yanked me into a taxi with her and an art curator she knew named Klaus. (He was hip and bald and dressed in the sort of all-black outfit worn by the fictional German talk-show host, Dieter Sprocket, on the old *Saturday Night Live*.) With great excitement she explained she was taking me out for 'a real New York evening' – to a dinner party being hosted by Marina Abramovic, the performance artist, at her loft in Soho. Abramovic had recently been in the news for having lived for 12 days, stark naked, on an exposed wooden platform – fitted with shower and toilet – in the window of the Sean Kelly Gallery. She lived on whatever food spectators donated and never spoke during the entire 12 days. I guess it had all been pretty mesmerising: my friend Nancy happened to be there once when Abramovic took a shower; and one of Nancy's friends hit the jackpot – she got to watch the artist have a bowel movement.

Abramovic – plus hunky sculptor boyfriend – lived in a huge, virtually empty loft, the sole furnishings being a dining table and chairs in the very centre of the room and a spindly old stereo from the 1960s. The space was probably a hundred feet on either side – 'major real estate, of course', as Sontag proudly explained to me. (She loved using *Vanity Fair*-ish clichés.) She and Abramovic smothered one another in hugs and kisses. I meanwhile blanched in fright: I'd just caught sight of two of the other guests, who, alarmingly enough, turned out to be Lou Reed and Laurie Anderson. Reed (O great rock god of my twenties) stood morosely by himself, humming, doing little dance steps and playing air guitar. Periodically he glared at everyone – including me – with apparent hatred.

Everyone crowded into their seats: despite the vast size of the room, we were an *intime* gathering. Yet it wouldn't be quite right merely to say that everyone ignored me. As a non-artist and non-celebrity, I was so 'not there', it seemed – so cognitively unassimilable – I wasn't even registered enough to be ignored. I sat at one end of the table like a piece of anti-matter. I didn't exchange a word the whole night with Lou Reed, who sat kitty-corner across from me. He remained silent and surly. Everyone else gabbled happily on, however, about how they loved to trash hotels when they were younger and how incompetent everybody was at the Pompidou. 'At my show I had to explain things to them a thousand times. They just don't know how to do a major retrospective.'

True, Sontag tried briefly to call the group's attention to me (with the soul-destroying words, 'Terry is an English professor'); and Abramovic kindly gave me a little place card to write my name on. But otherwise I might as well not have been born. At one point I thought I saw Laurie Anderson, at the other end of the table, trying to get my attention: she was smiling sweetly in my direction, as if to undo my pathetic isolation. I smiled in gratitude in return and held up my little place card so she would at least know my name. Annoyed, she gestured back impatiently, with a sharp downward flick of her index finger: she wanted me to pass the wine bottle. I was reduced to a pair of disembodied hands – like the ones that come out of the walls and give people drinks in Cocteau's Beauty and the Beast.

Sontag gave up trying to include me and after a while seemed herself to recede curiously into the background. Maybe she was already starting to get sick again; she seemed oddly undone. Through much of the conversation (dominated by glammy Osric) she looked tired and bored, almost sleepy. She did not react when I finally decided to leave – on my own – just after coffee had been served. I thanked Marina Abramovic, who led me to the grungy metal staircase that went down to the street and back to the world of the Little People. Turning round one last time, I saw Sontag still slumped in her seat, as if she'd fallen into a trance, or somehow just caved in. She'd clearly forgotten all about me.

Deborah Friedell writes: The first sentence of Terry Castle's first piece for the LRB was a provocation: 'How bad are most of the novels produced by English women writers in the decades before Jane Austen?' (The answer: very.) But then the paper hasn't exactly tried to keep her out of trouble. Her review of Jane Austen's letters in 1995 was given the innocuous title 'Sister Sister' on the page – the essay is about Austen's relationship with her older sister, Cassandra – but 'Was Jane Austen Gay?' was the cover strap. Within days, Stanford University, where Castle teaches, sent out a press release to make clear that – no matter what was alleged in the *Daily Telegraph*, the *Independent*, the *Observer*, *Time*, *Newsweek* et al – a member of its faculty had certainly not intended to imply that Aunt Jane was a lesbian. Later, in a letter to the LRB, Castle wrote that her essay had been 'grotesquely, indeed almost comically, distorted', but that the 'hysterical reaction on the part of a number of press commentators' was telling: 'So many people, apparently, still consider the mere suggestion that someone like Austen might have had homosexual feelings such an appalling slur that any hope for a sensitive debate on the matter becomes impossible. It is neither a crime nor a sin to love – in whatever way one is able – a person of one's own sex.'

Ten years later, Castle's essay about her complicated friendship with Susan Sontag immediately caused her to be disinvited from Sontag's memorial service at Carnegie Hall. It turned out that we didn't need to worry about the piece being too sentimental (the poo essay mentioned in her email, which we were too squeamish to publish, can be found in Castle's essay collection *The Professor and Other Writings*).

Exorcising Doubles

'There could never be a good biography of a novelist,' Scott Fitzgerald wrote, 'because a novelist is too many people, if he's any good.' Some of the paper's contributors have taken this to heart, impersonating other writers or other versions of themselves. In the early days, Karl Miller occasionally wrote letters (and one poem) under the name James Darke. The identity was never as dim as the surname suggested: his letters had a style of address that was – for an imitation – inimitable. As Colm Tóibín mentions in his piece here about Oscar Wilde's 'chameleon abilities', Miller also wrote a book called Doubles. In the postcard opposite, Alan Bennett, writing to Mary-Kay Wilmers around the time of his play Kafka's Dick, took it upon himself to become Kafka's friend Max Brod. Tariq Ali sometimes rings up the office pretending to be Robert Mugabe, or sends emails as if from an irate ambassador threatening to sue. There have been times when we've suspected every correspondent of being Tariq in disguise.

EXTRACT FROM VOL. 30 NO. 6 · 20 MARCH 2008

The Art of Being Found Out
Colm Tóibín

As 1895 opened, for example, Oscar Wilde could move between intimate family life and, when he grew bored with that, a life in hotels and foreign places. He could mingle with the great and the good and then pleasurably spend time with young men from a different, mostly a lower, social class. By May, Wilde was in prison, abandoned by most of his friends, his reputation in tatters, his name a byword for corruption and evil. His family life was destroyed, he was declared a bankrupt and was about to serve a sentence of a severity beyond his imagination. He had been found out.

In the years that followed, everybody who wrote about him seemed puzzled by the fact that they had known a different facet of him and yet not seemed to know him at all. Yeats, for example, remembered Wilde the married man towards the end of the 1880s:

> He lived in a little house at Chelsea that the architect Godwin had decorated with an elegance that owed something to Whistler . . . I remember vaguely a white drawing-room with Whistler etchings, 'let in' to white panels, and a dining-room all white: chairs, walls, mantelpiece, carpet, except for a diamond-shaped piece of red cloth in the middle of the table under a terracotta statuette . . . It was perhaps too perfect in its unity . . . and I remember thinking that the perfect harmony of his life there, with his beautiful wife and two young children, suggested some deliberate artistic composition.

Wilde's younger son, Vyvyan, also remembered those years when his father was 'a real companion', with 'so much of the child in his own nature that he delighted in playing our games . . . When he grew tired of playing he would keep us quiet by telling us fairy stories, or tales of adventure, of which he had a never-ending supply.'

Among the writers for children whom Wilde admired, according to his son, was Stevenson, whose The Strange Case of Dr Jekyll and Mr Hyde appeared in 1886, the year of Vyvyan's birth. These were the years, as Karl Miller wrote in Doubles, when 'a hunger for pseudonyms, masks, new identities, new conceptions of human nature, declared itself.' Thus Dr Jekyll could announce with full conviction: 'This, too, was myself' as he became 'a stranger in my own house'. Jekyll 'learned to recognise the thorough and primitive duality of man; I saw that, of the two natures that contended in the field of my consciousness, even if I could rightly be said to be either, it was only because I was radically both.' Thus as Wilde set to work on the creation of both himself and his character Dorian Gray, he was following an example which was embedded in the spirit of the age.

London, in the years around the publication of The Picture of Dorian Gray in 1891, was the site where many artists, including Yeats, George Bernard Shaw, Conrad, James and Ford Madox Ford, allowed their doubled selves, and their work full of masked selves, secret agents, secret sharers and sexual secrets, to flourish and further duplicate. Wilde in London was both an Englishman and an Irishman, an aristocrat and an Irish patriot, a family man and a man who never seemed to be at home, a dilettante and a dedicated artist. Everywhere he went, he left behind in some attic of the mind an opposite self, recently discarded.

Ford, who at one point had the same lawyer as Wilde, knew about his chameleon abilities and admired his ability, when the crisis came, to exude self-pity in enormous quantities while at the same time being able to see his self-pity as a kind of play, or further self-dramatisation. Ford wrote:

> There came a dramatic moment in the lawyer's office. Wilde began to lament his wasted life. He uttered a tremendous diatribe about his great talents thrown away, his brilliant genius dragged in the mud, his early and glorious aspirations come to nothing. He became almost epic. Then he covered his face and wept. His whole body was shaken by his sobs. Humphreys [his solicitor] was extremely moved. He tried to find consolations.
>
> Wilde took his hands down from his face. He winked at Humphreys and exclaimed triumphantly: 'Got you then, old fellow.'

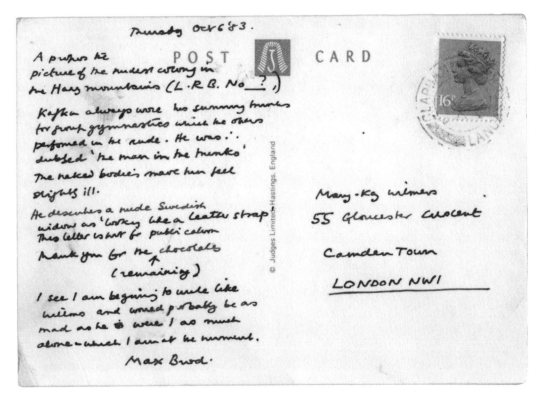

Postcard from Alan Bennett ('Max Brod') to
Mary-Kay Wilmers, 6 October 1983

Transcription:

A propos the picture of the nudist colony in the Harz mountains (L.R.B. No___?)

    Kafka always wore his summery trunks for group gymnastics which the others performed in the nude. He was dubbed 'the man in the trunks'. The naked bodies made him feel slightly ill.

He describes a nude Swedish widow as 'looking like a leather strap'. This letter is not for publication. Thank you for the (remaining) chocolates.

    I see I am beginning to write like Willums and would probably be as mad as he were I as much alone – which I am at the moment.

Max Brod

On what date and by whom?

In 2005 the American poet and translator Eliot Weinberger offered the paper 'a mini-epic on the Iraq war', an extraordinary assembly of quotations and shocking details – the number of bullets purchased, the number of civilians killed – that tells the whole story of that disastrous invasion. 'What I Heard about Iraq' later became a book, a prose poem for radio, and a play that toured the world.

The annotated page proof shown opposite illustrates the kinds of question that come up when pieces are being fact-checked: what precise words were used on what date and by whom? Exactly when the paper started to get serious about fact-checking is a memory lost to time. One junior editor recalls phoning up a well-known novelist in the early 2000s to query an apparent mistake. 'When did you start checking facts?' the novelist asked. 'Oh, about an hour ago,' the editor replied. 'No, I mean when did you start checking writers' facts?' the novelist said, as if it was rather rude to suggest to a contributor that they might have got something wrong.

LRB (editorial)

From:	Eliot Weinberger ████████████████
Sent:	14 January 2005 06:16
To:	LRB (editorial)
Subject:	Re: Marías

Dear Thomas--

Many thanks for asking me to review Marias. I'm afraid it poses a dilemma: I've read all of Marias' books, and like them, and certainly I'd be happy to collaborate with LRB.

But-- I've never written about fiction, and only know a little about what's going on these days. And please understand that, although I have translated some Latin Americans, I am not at all a Hispanist. I know almost nothing about contemporary Iberian Spanish writing, for example, or politics in Spain. (And I gather this new one is about coming to terms with his father's generation.)

I would think that you have far better contributors for this... I could certainly try, but I'm probably better in obscure corners where no one else wants to bother.

In the meantime, for the hell of it, I've sent a mini-epic on the Iraq war which I happened to finish today....

       all best--

       Eliot

----- Original Message -----
From: "LRB (editorial)" <edit@lrb.co.uk>
To: ████████████
Sent: Wednesday, January 12, 2005 1:31 PM
Subject: Marías

Dear Eliot Weinberger,

Would you be interested in writing about the novels of Javier Marías? Tu rostro mañana is shortly to be published in an English translation. I very much hope it's something you'd like to take on.

Best wishes,

Thomas Jones

(I know you've been corresponding with Paul, but it falls to me to distribute fiction.)

LONDON REVIEW OF BOOKS

28 Little Russell St

London WC1A 2HN

       1

Email from Eliot Weinberger to the editors,
14 January 2005

What I Heard about Iraq
Eliot Weinberger

IN 1991, during the first Gulf War, I heard Dick Cheney, then secretary of defense, say that the US would not invade Baghdad, to avoid getting bogged down in the problems of trying to take over and govern Iraq'. I heard him say: 'The question in my mind is how many additional American casualties is Saddam worth? And the answer is: not very damned many.'

In February 2001, I heard Colin Powell say that Saddam Hussein 'has not developed any significant capability with respect to weapons of mass destruction. He is unable to project conventional power against his neighbours.'

That same month, I heard that a CIA report stated: 'We do not have any direct evidence that Iraq has used the period since Desert Fox to reconstitute its weapons of mass destruction programmes.'

Two months later, I heard Condoleezza Rice say: 'We are able to keep his arms from him. His military forces have not been rebuilt.'

On 11 September 2001, six hours after the attacks, I heard that Donald Rumsfeld advised the president to 'hit Iraq. I heard that he said: 'Go massive. Sweep it all up. Things related and not.'

I heard that Condoleezza Rice asked: 'How do you capitalise on these opportunities?'

I heard that on 17 September the president signed a document marked TOP SECRET that directed the Pentagon to begin planning for the invasion and that, a few months later, he secretly and illegally diverted $700 million approved by Congress for operations in Afghanistan into planning for the new battle front.

In February 2002, I heard that an unnamed 'senior military commander' said: 'We are moving military and intelligence personnel and resources out of Afghanistan to get ready for a future war in Iraq.'

I heard the president say that Iraq is 'a threat of unique urgency', and that there is 'no doubt the Iraqi regime continues to possess the most lethal weapons ever devised'.

I heard the vice president say: 'Simply stated, there is no doubt that Saddam Hussein now has weapons of mass destruction.'

I heard the president tell Congress: 'The danger to our country is grave. The danger to our country is growing. The regime is seeking a nuclear bomb, and with fissile material could build one within a year.'

And that same day, I heard him say: 'The dangers we face will only worsen from month to month and from year to year. To ignore these threats is to encourage them. And when they have fully materialised it may be too late to protect ourselves and our friends and our allies. By then the Iraqi dictator would have the means to terrorise and dominate the region. Each passing day could be the one on which the Iraqi regime gives anthrax or VX nerve gas or some day a nuclear weapon to a terrorist ally.'

I heard the president, in the State of the Union Address, say that Iraq was hiding 25,000 litres of anthrax, 38,000 litres of botulinum toxin, and 500 tons of sarin, mustard and nerve gas.

I heard the president say that Iraq had attempted to purchase 'yellowcake' uranium for nuclear weapons from Niger and thousands of aluminum tubes 'suitable for nuclear weapons production'.

I heard the vice president say: 'We know that he's been absolutely devoted to trying to acquire nuclear weapons, and we believe he has, in fact, reconstituted nuclear weapons.'

I heard the president say: 'Imagine those 19 hijackers with other weapons and other plans, this time armed by Saddam Hussein. It would take one vial, one canister, one crate slipped into this country to bring a day of horror like none we have ever known.'

I heard Donald Rumsfeld say: 'Some have argued that the nuclear threat from Iraq is not imminent. I would not be so certain.'

I heard the president say: 'America must not ignore the threat gathering against us. Facing clear evidence of peril, we cannot wait for the final proof – the smoking gun – that could come in the form of a mushroom cloud.'

I heard Condoleezza Rice say: 'We don't want the "smoking gun" to be a mushroom cloud.'

I heard the American ambassador to the European Union tell the Europeans: 'You had Hitler in Europe and no one really did anything about him. The same type of person is in Baghdad.'

I heard Colin Powell at the United Nations say: 'They can produce enough dry biological agent in a single month to kill thousands upon thousands of people. Saddam Hussein has never accounted for vast amounts of chemical weaponry: 550 artillery shells with mustard gas, 30,000 empty munitions, and enough precursors to increase his stockpile to as much as 500 tons of chemical agents. If we consider just one category of missing weaponry: 6500 bombs from the Iran-Iraq war. Our conservative estimate is that Iraq today has a stockpile of between 100 and 500 tons of chemical-weapons agent. Even the low end of 100 tons of agent would enable Saddam Hussein to cause mass casualties across more than 100 square miles of territory, an area nearly five times the size of Manhattan.'

I heard him say: 'Every statement I make today is backed up by sources, solid sources. These are not assertions. What we're giving you are facts and conclusions based on solid intelligence.'

I heard the president say: 'Iraq has a growing fleet of manned and unmanned aerial vehicles that could be used to disperse chemical or biological weapons across broad areas.' I heard him say that Iraq 'could launch a biological or chemical attack in as little as 45 minutes after the order is given.'

I heard Tony Blair say: 'We are asked to accept Saddam decided to destroy those weapons. I say that such a claim is palpably absurd.'

I heard the president say: 'We know that Iraq and al-Qaida have had high-level contacts that go back a decade. We've learned that Iraq has trained al-Qaida members in bomb-making and poisons and deadly gases. Alliance with terrorists could allow the Iraq regime to attack America without leaving any fingerprints.'

I heard the vice president say: 'There's overwhelming evidence there was a connection between al-Qaida and the Iraqi government. I am very confident there was an established relationship there.'

I heard Colin Powell say: 'Iraqi officials deny accusations of ties with al-Qaida. These denials are simply not credible.'

I heard Condoleezza Rice say: 'There clearly are contacts between al-Qaida and Saddam Hussein that can be documented.'

I heard the president say: 'You can't distinguish between al-Qaida and Saddam.'

I heard Donald Rumsfeld say: 'Imagine a September 11th with weapons of mass destruction. It's not three thousand – it's tens of thousands of innocent men, women and children.'

I heard Colin Powell tell the Senate that 'a moment of truth is coming': 'This is not just an academic exercise or the United States being in a fit of pique. We're talking about real weapons. We're talking about anthrax. We're talking about botulinum toxin. We're talking about nuclear weapons programmes.'

I heard Senator Hillary Clinton say: 'Iraq poses a continuing threat to the national security of the United States.'

I heard Donald Rumsfeld say: 'No terrorist state poses a greater or more immediate threat to the security of our people.'

I heard the president, bristling with irritation, say: 'This business about time, how much time do we need to see clearly that he's not disarming? He is delaying. He is deceiving. He is asking for time. He's playing hide-and-seek with inspectors. One thing for sure is, he's not disarming. Surely our friends have learned lessons from the past. This looks like a rerun of a bad movie and I'm not interested in watching it.'

I heard that, a few days before authorising the invasion of Iraq, the Senate was told in a

Blackwell
Mono

Handwritten editorial annotations:

after / 2 / m / that

the first time it was specified that 'yellowcake'; the first time it specified Niger was IAEA.

[biological weapons] materials sufficient to produce

if state of U, no 'yellowcake' no Niger

L Saddam

In July 2001

x

ten / x

preparing

...and 'conceal some of'

...

3 for certain / you know, more first

I don't know. Plus the text of the congressional resolution authorising war on Iraq

you know

...

[... [[[]]]

* not the president: he told aides at National Military Command Center in the Pentagon. Aides' notes read: 'Judge whether good enough hit SH @ same time. Not only UBL. Go massive....' [FIRST REPORTED BY CBS NEWS]

? And: ''

? And: ''

emphasis questionable: the 17 September document was mostly abt planning for Afghanistan, with a few lines abt Iraq at end [FIRST REPORTED BY WASH. POST]

* money had been approved for Afghanistan and the general war on terror
* on the plus side, money was for more than planning [FIRST REPORTED IN BOB WOODWARD]

x this all from same speech in Rose Garden, to press, after addressing congress

second statement out of chronology (if it matters): 17 March 2003

The L-Word

John Mearsheimer and Stephen Walt's piece discussing the influence on US foreign policy of the Israel lobby – an umbrella term for such organisations as the American-Israel Public Affairs Committee (Aipac) – had been commissioned by the *Atlantic Monthly*. After the *Atlantic* turned it down, Perry Anderson suggested they send it to the LRB. 'This sounds excellent,' Mearsheimer wrote. 'All it needs is a link and it will get an enormous amount of attention'. He was right. After its publication in 2006, it was for several years, and by some distance, the most read piece on the LRB website.

The paper received a great many letters in response, though no death threats, despite the fears of one correspondent from New Jersey. There were a number of accusations of antisemitism, as Mearsheimer and Walt predicted, and some very unpleasant remarks about Arabs, but also a great many messages praising the article. Most readers understood that Mearsheimer and Walt were writing about US foreign policy and its effects on the Middle East, though there were also a few congratulatory messages of an antisemitic nature. The letters accusing Mearsheimer and Walt of having written an 'antisemitic rant' and those congratulating them for having exposed a 'secret Jewish' – or, as one individual felt the need to spell it, 'J E W I S H' – 'conspiracy' had something in common: they came from people who appeared not to have read the piece, and who seemed incapable of distinguishing between criticism of Israeli or US government policy and antisemitism. We don't usually publish letters of simple praise, which meant that only letters putting the case against Mearsheimer and Walt appeared in the following issue. This led one correspondent to write: 'Your obvious slant in the

letters you have chosen to publish regarding the Israel lobby establishes, once again, that Israeli apologists are alive and well and living at the *London Review of Books*.'

Six months after the piece came out, the paper organised a debate – 'The Israel Lobby: Does it Have Too Much Influence on American Foreign Policy?' – at the Cooper Union in New York. The panellists were Mearsheimer, Shlomo Ben-Ami, Martin Indyk, Tony Judt, Rashid Khalidi and Dennis Ross. It was moderated by Anne-Marie Slaughter. A book-length version of Mearsheimer and Walt's thesis, *The Israel Lobby and US Foreign Policy*, was published by Farrar, Straus in 2007.

Thomas Jones

12 October

Dear John,

Very good to get your message. I've shown the text to Mary-Kay Wilmers, the editor of the LRB, and they are very interested.

On your and Steve Walt's concerns:

Length: not a problem. They readily go above their average maxima on special occasions.

Extending the essay to include the Israeli lobby: this is what they themselves would want. On seeing the text, MKW commented, indeed, that this was the missing piece of the puzzle.

Updating, and timing: no difficulties..

Fee: yes, they pay for articles.

Editing: in my experience, they work carefully with authors on texts, without trying to make everything they publish politically or tonally uniform, unlike many other periodicals. They are not into censorship.

They would like to see the uncut, or pre-cut version, of the essay. If you could send that to them, you should get a quick overall response. If you need to consult me about anything, don't hesitate. I am currently in London, will be in Berlin next week, but easily contactable.

I entirely agree with you about the importance of this text. Nothing quite like it has ever been written before.

Best,

Perry

Perry, This sounds excellent. Thanx very much. Steve and I, as you can imagine, would love to get the piece published and the London Review of Books would be a fine place to do it. Once the piece appears in a prestigious place like that, all it needs is a link and it will get an enormous amount of attention. We can tell you from lots of conversations that the interest in this subject is great.

Email from Perry Anderson to John Mearsheimer
and Stephen Walt, 12 October 2005

Bad Character

Jean McNicol writes: These pages come from a Festschrift, *Bad Character*, published to celebrate Mary-Kay Wilmers's seventieth birthday. I was told I had to contribute something, but couldn't imagine writing a piece of continuous prose that wouldn't exhibit some of the faults mentioned here (mealy-mouthed, trite, emetic etc). I fretted over this, worried that I was displaying the typical unreliability of the female contributor. At the time, I was compiling the glossary for Andrew O'Hagan's *A Night out with Robert Burns*, and woke suddenly at 4 a.m. with the idea of doing a glossary for Mary-Kay. It's the only notion I've ever had at that time of night that hasn't seemed a terrible mistake in the morning.

YOU AND NON-YOU

JEAN MCNICOL

A

accents unnecessary, left out if at all possible, see **middle initials**
Alzheimer's what MK says she's about to get
any news? the constant question from **Goult**
aria conspicuous singing of one's woes, see **men**
Arsenal MK's team, but not **Sam's**
autistic bubble occupied by **men** and their **computers**

B

bad character what MK says she has
bags at least two, both capacious (and filled with pieces because she works all weekend unlike the rest of us **part-timers**)
beef complain
Belgium where she lived as a child; not popular
bicker what MK and I do
bog off get lost
book about her dodgy relatives, the **Eitingons**. Written mostly in **Goult**, very slowly ('I've only done two paragraphs this week'), with much **wailing** and many **computer** problems
bus 'You can read it on the bus'
busted flush contributor we no longer want to publish

C

capricious something MK says she is
cavalier the paper's behaviour on occasion
cheese brings on migraines, so not to be included in too many canapés at the Christmas **party**
chi-chi pretentious and trendy

68

First two pages of Jean McNicol's glossary for Mary-Kay Wilmers

chicken always for **supper**, at least when John Sturrock is **cooking**

cigarettes much missed: 'Let me smell it'

classics at least classicists understand grammar and don't litter pieces with hanging participles

clotted what some pieces are, also congested, content-free, interminable, mealy-mouthed, trite . . .

computers quickly develop mysterious faults, as do printers, fax machines, email accounts etc

cooking claims to be bad at and will avoid if she can; quite likes doing the shopping in **Goult**

covers much fretted over, see **order of pieces**. Things to avoid: present participles ('they're too inactive'); definite or indefinite articles; having to talk to her about the cover if you've done it and she's in **Goult** and trying to be helpful. 'It's not the Trade Descriptions Act'

cross people climb up on it, see **men**

D

disgrace what one finds oneself in

ditty poem

doctors she thinks she should have been one, like her Aunt Mats

E

Edinburgh 'that terrible rock', see **Venice**

Eitingons written about in the **book**

emetic used of people or their pieces, or both

F

Faber where she worked in the 1960s; Eliot didn't like her swearing

fall apart pieces sometimes do this when edited

female contributors tend to be unreliable: too many other commitments, unlike **men**

EXTRACT FROM VOL. 30 NO. 20 · 23 OCTOBER 2008

One about the Banks

John Lanchester writes: In the middle of 2007 I was part-way through a sequence of pieces about companies that I was (and indeed still am) thinking of turning into a book. Mary-Kay rang up and in her deceptively casual style suggested 'doing one about the banks'. I duly set to work and was in the middle of writing the piece when Northern Rock collapsed. I'm still writing about economics and finance and the aftermath of the credit crunch today, because, unfortunately, we are still living through its after-effects. This piece, 'Cityphobia', was mostly written before the Global Financial Crisis and austerity, but appeared in October 2008 when the crisis was at its most frighteningly intense. As we now know, no less of an insider than George W. Bush was privately saying that 'this sucker could go down.' It was only afterwards that I found out that the insiders who really knew what was happening were even more scared than we outsiders looking in.

Cityphobia

John Lanchester

ONE OF the structural problems which brought us to this pass is that our big banks aren't just big, they're huge: the four biggest each have a capital value of more than a trillion pounds. Add the five biggest together, and the sum is four times the value of Britain's GDP. Our (remaining) banks have less exposure to the famous toxic debt than their US counterparts, but while the wholesale money markets aren't functioning, normal banking life is impossible. They are highly leveraged, too. It was this combination of size and leverage that did for Iceland's banks. The ratio of Barclays' assets to its equity in June hit 61.3 to 1. Imagine that for a moment translated to your own finances, so that you could stretch what you actually, unequivocally own to borrow more than sixty times the amount. (I'd have an island. What about you?) It sounds sensible to reduce that leverage, and indeed it is, except that the process of reducing it is the dreaded 'deleveraging' which is causing the banking system and the wider economy to grind to a halt. The scale of bank leveraging is one of the things that must be targeted by regulators if/when the crisis has passed; we can't let the banks get this far out of control ever again. For a start, there must be a tight limit on the relationship between banks' debt and their equity, and much greater transparency about the nature of banks' 'assets'.

So: a huge unregulated boom in which almost all the upside went directly into private hands, followed by a gigantic bust in which the losses were socialised. That is literally nobody's idea of how the financial system is supposed to work. It is just as much an abomination to the free marketeer as it is to the social democrat or outright leftist. But the models and alternatives don't seem to be forthcoming: there is an ideological and theoretical vacuum where the challenge from the left used to be. Capitalism no longer has a global antagonist, just at the moment when it has never needed one more – if only to clarify thinking and values, and to provide the chorus of jeering and Schadenfreude which at this moment is deeply appropriate. I would be providing it myself if I weren't so frightened.

Having fully indulged their greed on the way up, and created the risks, the bankers are now fully indulging their fear on the way down, and allowing the system to seize up. But it wasn't just the banks. One thing which has been lacking in public discourse about the crisis is someone to point out that we did this to ourselves, because we allowed our governments to do it, and because we were greedy and stupid. It's not just bankers who have been indulging in greed, short-termism and fantasy economics. In addition to our stretched mortgage borrowing, Britain has half of the total European credit-card debt. That is a horrible fact, and although it's nice to reserve the blame for banks who made lending too easy, the great British public is just as much to blame. We grew obsessed with the price of our houses, felt richer than we should, borrowed money we didn't have, spent it on tat, and now that the downturn has happened – as it was bound to do – we want someone else to blame. Well boo fucking hoo. Bankers are to blame, but we're to blame too. That's just as well, because we're the ones who are going to have to pay.

Other than that, it's too early to draw general conclusions from this amazing crisis. What will, what must, die is the mystical belief in the power of the markets that has dominated political and economic discourse in most of the Western world for the last several decades. The markets have so manifestly, so flagrantly malfunctioned that we can't go back to the idea of unfettered liberal capitalism as a talisman, template or magic wand. The unquestioned Cityphilia I wrote about earlier this year is gone, I hope for ever.

Unfortunately, we have no current model of where to go from here, apart from a more heavily regulated form of growth-based liberal capitalism.

John Lanchester: The Crash

London Review
OF BOOKS

VOLUME 30 NUMBER 20   23 OCTOBER 2008   £3.20 US & CANADA $5.95

Murray Sayle: Mao in Vietnam

London Review
OF BOOKS

VOLUME 24 NUMBER 4   21 FEBRUARY 2002   £2.95 US & CANADA $3.95

Ian Hamilton: Megalomania
Eric Hobsbawm: Epidemic of War
Mary Beard: Astérix Redux

Alan Bennett's Review of the Year

London Review
OF BOOKS

VOLUME 23 NUMBER 2   25 JANUARY 2001   £2.95 US & CANADA $3.95

David Trotter:
Wyndham Lewis

Lorna Sage:
Henry Green

Andrew O'Hagan:
A Story

Malcolm Bull:
Judas Saves

Glen Newey:
Chomsky

Andy Beckett
in Santiago

Conor Gearty:
Watch the
Judges

Tom Paulin: The Rain on Crusoe's Island

London Review
OF BOOKS

VOLUME 23 NUMBER 14   19 JULY 2001   £2.95 US & CANADA $3.95

Keith Thomas: John Evelyn's Virtual Garden
Peter Clarke: The Failings of Keith Joseph
Inga Clendinnen: Liver Transplant No. 108
Edward Said: Homage to J.S. Bach

Linda Colley: Britain's Empires
Adam Phillips: Extermination-Camp Man
David Runciman: What constitutes a superstate?

Thomas Laqueur: The Illustrious Dead

London Review
OF BOOKS

VOLUME 23 NUMBER 18   20 SEPTEMBER 2001   £2.95 US & CANADA $3.95

Colm Tóibín: The Talents of James Baldwin
Julian Bell: Sickert lays about him
August Kleinzahler: Too Bad about Mrs Ferri
R.W. Johnson: Hey, hey, Henry K.

Elizabeth Lowry: Alistair MacLeod's Family Legends
Thomas Nagel: Are lemons really yellow?
Tom Shippey: Icelanders go viking
Alison Jolly: Proud to be a Primate

Andrew O'Hagan: Versions of Pastoral

London Review
OF BOOKS

VOLUME 23 NUMBER 6   22 MARCH 2001   £2.95 US & CANADA $3.95

'We are responsible for keeping the landscape the way
people say they are proud to have it – but who pays for it?
The people down the road selling postcards of
the Lake District are making much more than the
farmers who keep the land so photogenic.'
Will Cockbain, hill farmer

Murray Sayle goes back to Bloody Sunday

London Review
OF BOOKS

VOLUME 24 NUMBER 13   11 JULY 2002   £2.95 US & CANADA $3.95

John Lanchester: My Sporting Life
Hermione Lee: Coetzee in London
Christopher Hitchens: Crimes against Allende

Edward Said studies the Road Map

London Review
OF BOOKS

VOLUME 25 NUMBER 12   19 JUNE 2003   £2.95 US & CANADA $3.95

Terry Eagleton: For and Against Orwell
James Hamilton-Paterson on the Tasaday

Sean Wilsey: Life on a Skateboard

Nina Auerbach: The Cult of Zelda
Frank Kermode on Privacy

T.J. Clark: A Savonarolan Bonfire

London Review
OF BOOKS

VOLUME 27 NUMBER 18   22 SEPTEMBER 2005   £2.95 US & CANADA $3.95

Frank Kermode:
Lowell's Letters

David Runciman:
Beyond the Ashes

Daniel Greenberg:
Bush's Scientists

Ferdinand Mount:
Little Rosebery

Jacqueline Rose:
'Specimen Days'

Pankaj Mishra on the Maoists of Nepal

London Review
OF BOOKS

VOLUME 27 NUMBER 12   23 JUNE 2005   £2.95 US & CANADA $3.95

Frank Kermode: Snobbery and John Carey
Patrick Wright: The Art of Camouflage
David A. Bell: Bonapartism

Eliot Weinberger:
The Terrible Tale of Gu Cheng

Mary Douglas:
Sadducees v. Pharisees

Hugh Pennington: Planning for Bird Flu

Perry Anderson: The Divisions of Cyprus

London Review
OF BOOKS

James Wood on Adam Mars-Jones

Patrick Cockburn: Shi'a v. Shi'a
John Burnside: 'Losing Helen'

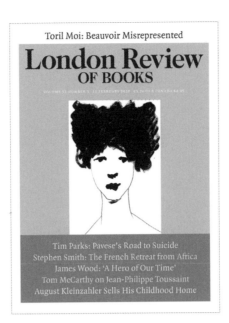

Toril Moi: Beauvoir Misrepresented

London Review
OF BOOKS

Tim Parks: Pavese's Road to Suicide
Stephen Smith: The French Retreat from Africa
James Wood: 'A Hero of Our Time'
Tom McCarthy on Jean-Philippe Toussaint
August Kleinzahler Sells His Childhood Home

Gareth Peirce: The War on British Muslims

London Review
OF BOOKS

Elif Batuman: Superheroes David Bromwich: President-Speak
Jeremy Waldron: The One Per Cent Doctrine Lewis Siegelbaum:
Communist Morality Wendy Doniger: Ekwos, Equus, Aśva, Eoh

Thomas Laqueur buries the 20th century

London Review
OF BOOKS

Neal Ascherson: The German War on Nature
Slavoj Žižek: The Philanthropic Enemy
Patrick Cockburn: The End of Iraq
Anne Hollander: Women in White
Paul Ginsborg: Is Berlusconi done for?
Nicholas Guyatt: Simon Schama's Chauvinism

Sanjay Subrahmanyam: Placing V.S. Naipaul

London Review
OF BOOKS

Malcolm Bull: The Apostasies of John Gray
Elizabeth Lowry on Malcolm Lowry
Ian Hacking: The Colour Red
Jenny Diski among the Handbags
Yitzhak Laor on the Never-Ending War
Bee Wilson: Falling for Michael Moore

Jonathan Raban: Sarah Palin's Cunning

London Review
OF BOOKS

Alan
Hollinghurst:
Sissiness

Jenny Diski:
Jews & Shoes

Clancy Sigal:
Among the
Draft-Dodgers

David
Runciman:
Why Vote?

Responses to Gaza

London Review
OF BOOKS

When does an invasion become a
massacre? If self-defence includes the
bombing of ambulances and feeling no
qualms at killing such an astonishing
number of children, then we have
entered a moral territory from which
there may be no return. Unless of
course we have merely returned to the
imperial 19th century, a world of brutal
and unapologetic conquest, where force
was the only argument that mattered
and our only choice was whether to be
hypocritical about it or not.

Michael Wood

Tony Judt: Bush's Useful Idiots

London Review
OF BOOKS

T.J. Clark:
Re-Imagined Communities

Andrew O'Hagan:
Fathers and Sons

Jerry Fodor:
When is a cow not a cow?

David Edgar:
Shaw's Surprises

Gabriel Piterberg:
Travels in Israel

David Matthews:
How to Write a Fugue

Agnieszka Kolakowska:
My Wife-Murderer

Jenny Turner: The Institute of Ideas

London Review
OF BOOKS

Michael Wood:
Borges
Thomas Laqueur:
Trauma
Jenny Diski:
Arsenic
David Kaiser:
Aliens

2010-19

What have we done?

John Lanchester: Marx at 193

London Review
OF BOOKS

VOLUME 34 NUMBER 7   5 APRIL 2012   £3.50 US & CANADA $4.95

ROSS MCKIBBIN:
Is that it for the
Lib Dems?

SEAMUS PERRY:
Half-Visionary Art

THOMAS JONES:
Eternal Bowie

ADAM SHATZ:
Claude Lanzmann

EVGENY MOROZOV:
Reading It off Your Face

JEREMY HARDING:
Sarcophagi in
Bordeaux

Argumentation

It's sometimes hard to anticipate the pieces that will provoke violent disagreement. An often bad-tempered argument about Shakespeare ('James Wood doesn't know what he's talking about'; 'John Drakakis's hysterical onslaught'; 'Alan Sinfield's angry defence'), under the heading 'Bardbiz', kept the letters page lively for two years in the early 1990s. Taking on the 'evangelist-cum-historian of empire' Niall Ferguson, Pankaj Mishra offered a polemic that Ferguson saw as a libellous 'character assassination' printed by a paper 'notorious for its left-leaning politics'. Their argument continued in the letters pages.

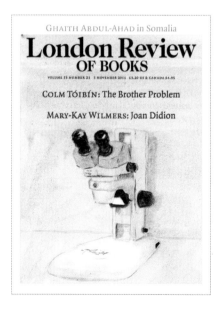

Watch this man

Pankaj Mishra

FREQUENTLY accused since *Empire* of underplaying the dark side of imperialism, Ferguson seems to have come up with a rhetorical strategy: to describe vividly one spectacular instance of brutality – he expends some moral indignation of his own on the slave trade – and then to use this exception to the general rule of imperial benevolence to absolve himself from admitting to the role of imperialism's structural violence in the making of the modern world.

The slave-trading, self-commemorating European conquerors of Asia and Africa, Naipaul writes, 'could do one thing and say something quite different because they had an idea of what they owed to their civilisation'. Ferguson, a retro rather than revisionist historian, tries to summon up some of that old imperial insouciance here. Consequently, his book is immune to the broadly tragic view – that every document of civilisation is also a document of barbarism – just as it is to humour and irony.

Even as he deplores the West's decay and dereliction, he sees signs everywhere of its victory: the Resterners are now paying Westerners the ultimate compliment by imitating them. Gratified by the fact that 'more and more human beings eat a Western diet' and 'wear Western clothes', Ferguson is hardly likely to bemoan the cultural homogeneity, or the other Trojan viruses – uneven development, environmental degradation – built into the West's operating software. Like his biographical subject, Henry Kissinger, he is mesmerised by the Chinese – in his eyes a thrifty, shrewd people who, in colonising remote African lands and building up massive reserves of capital, seem to borrow from the grand narrative of the West's own ascent. For Kissinger and Ferguson, China is, simultaneously, a serious threat to Western dominance and an opportunity for self-affirmation as it downloads – some might say, pirates or hacks – the West's killer apps.

'The Chinese have got capitalism,' Ferguson exults towards the end of the book. At this point, one hardly expects him to explain whether this is an adequate description of an economy on whose commanding heights a one-party state perches, controlling the movement of capital and running the biggest banks and companies. Writing in 1920, Theodore Lothrop Stoddard was more insightful: Asian peoples are 'not merely adopting', he wrote, 'but adapting, white ideas and methods'. Today these include, in both China and India, some of the harshest aspects of American-style capitalism: the truncation of public services, deunionisation, the fragmenting and lumpenisation of urban working classes, plus the ruthless suppression of the rural poor. But in populous countries you can always find what you seek and Ferguson can't be too worried about these killer apps imported from the contemporary West. He must move on quickly to his next intellectual firework. Did we know that there are more practising Christians in China than in Europe? Ferguson has met many Chinese ready to attest to Protestant Christianity's inexorable rise and its intimate link to China's economic growth. In Wenzhou, the 'Asian Manchester', he comes across a Christian CEO, who strikes him as 'the living embodiment of the link between the spirit of capitalism and the Protestant ethic'.

The reheated Weberism – a sign of Ferguson's nostalgia for the intellectual certainties of the summer of 1914 – turns into another lament for Western civilisation, whose decline is proclaimed everywhere by the fact that the churches are empty, taxes on our wealth are high, the 'thrifty asceticism' of Protestants of yore has been lost, and 'empire has become a dirty word.' 'All we risk being left with,' he writes, 'are a vacuous consumer society and a culture of relativism.' And it is with some dark pseudo-Gibbonian speculations about the imminent collapse of the West that *Civilisation* ends.

to London's West End" was scarcely intended as unalloyed praise. And the irony was surely un-missable in the line about my membership of the "neoimperialist gang". Or does Mishra seriously imagine that Max Boot and I meet in New York to compare pith helmets?

The *London Review of Books* is notorious for its left-leaning politics. I do not expect to find warm affection in its pages. Much of what I write is simply too threatening to the ideological biases of your coterie. Nevertheless, this journal used, once, to have a reputation for intellectual integrity and serious scholarship. Pankaj Mishra's libelous and dishonest article brings the *LRB* as well as himself into grave disrepute.

I am, I repeat, owed an apology.

Yours,

Niall Ferguson.

End of a letter to the editor from Niall Ferguson,
published in the issue of 17 November 2011

'I know it. And'

Joanna Biggs writes: 'A Part Song' won the Forward Prize for Best Single Poem, and became the centre of Denise Riley's next collection, *Say Something Back*. I spoke to her recently about the poem, and she reminded me how hard it can be to have made something beautiful out of something you wish had never happened.

LONDON REVIEW BOOKSHOP SAMPLERS, NO. 1

DENISE RILEY

Above, cover of the first in a series of poetry samplers published by Face Press in association with the London Review Bookshop, 2019; opposite, page 14, 9 February 2012

A Part Song
Denise Riley

i

You principle of song, what are you for now
Perking up under any spasmodic light
To trot out your shadowed warblings?

Mince, slight pillar. And sleek down
Your furriness. Slim as a whippy wire
Shall be your hope, and ultraflexible.

Flap thinly, sheet of beaten tin
That won't affectionately plump up
More cushioned and receptive lays.

But little song, don't so instruct yourself
For none are hanging around to hear you.
They have gone bustling or stumbling well away.

ii

What is the first duty of a mother to a child?
At least to keep the wretched thing alive – Band
Of fierce cicadas, stop this shrilling.

My daughter lightly leaves our house.
The thought rears up: *fix in your mind this*
Maybe final glimpse of her. Yes, lightning could.

I make this note of dread, I register it.
Neither my note nor my critique of it
Will save us one iota. I know it. And.

iii

Maybe a retouched photograph or memory,
This beaming one with his striped snake-belt
And eczema scabs, but either way it's framed
Glassed in, breathed hard on, and curated.
It's odd how boys live so much in their knees.
Then both of us had nothing. You lacked guile
And were transparent, easy, which felt natural.

iv

Each child gets cannibalised by its years.
It was a man who died, and in him died
The large-eyed boy, then the teen peacock
In the unremarked placid self-devouring
That makes up being alive. But all at once
Those natural overlaps got cut, then shuffled
Tight in a block, their layers patted square.

v

It's late. And it always will be late.
Your small monument's atop its hillock
Set with pennants that slap, slap, over the soil.
Here's a denatured thing, whose one eye rummages
Into the mound, her other eye swivelled straight up:
A short while only, then I come, she carols – but is only
A fat-lot-of-good mother with a pointless alibi: 'I didn't
Know.' Yet might there still be some part for me
To play upon this lovely earth? Say. Or
Say *No*, earth at my inner ear.

vi

A wardrobe gapes, a mourner tries
Her several styles of howling-guise:

You'd rather not, yet you must go
Briskly around on beaming show.

A soft black gown with pearl corsage
Won't assuage your smashed ménage.

It suits you as you are so pale.
Still, do not get that saffron veil.

Your dead don't want you lying flat.
There'll soon be time enough for that.

vii

Oh my dead son you daft bugger
This is one glum mum. Come home I tell you
And end this tasteless melodrama – quit
Playing dead at all, by now it's well beyond
A joke, but your humour never got cruel
Like this. Give over, you indifferent lad,
Take pity on your two bruised sisters. For
Didn't we love you. As we do. But by now
We're bored with our unproductive love,
And infinitely more bored by your staying dead
Which can hardly interest you much, either.

viii

Here I sit poleaxed, stunned by your vanishing
As you practise your charm in the underworld
Airily flirting with Persephone. Not *so* hard
To *imagine* what her mother *had gone through*
To be ferreting around those dark sweet halls.

ix

They'd sworn to stay for ever but they went
Or else I went – then concentrated hard
On the puzzle of what it ever truly *meant*
For someone to be here then, just like that
To not. Training in mild loss was useless
Given the final thing. And me lamentably
Slow to 'take it in' – far better toss it out,
How should I take in such a bad idea. No,
I'll stick it out instead for presence. If my
Exquisite hope can wrench you right back
Here, resigned boy, do let it as I'm waiting.

x

I can't get sold on reincarnating you
As those bloody 'gentle showers of rain'
Or in 'fields of ripening grain' – oooh
Anodyne – nor yet on shadowing you
In the hope of eventually pinpointing
You bemused among the *flocking souls*
Clustered like bats, as all thronged gibbering
Dusk-veiled – nor in modern creepiness.
Lighthearted presence, be bodied forth
Straightforwardly. Lounge again under
The sturdy sun you'd loved to bake in.
Even ten seconds' worth of a sighting
Of you would help me get through
This better. With a camera running.

xi

Ardent bee, still you go blundering
With downy saddlebags stuffed tight
All over the fuchsia's drop earrings.
I'll cry 'Oh bee!' to you, instead –
Since my own dead, apostrophised,
Keep mute as this clear garnet glaze
You're bumping into. Blind diligence,
Bee, or idiocy – this banging on and on
Against such shiny crimson unresponse.

xii

Outgoing soul, I try to catch
You calling over the distances
Though your voice is echoey,

Maybe tuned out by the noise
Rolling through me – or is it
You orchestrating that now,

Who'd laugh at the thought
Of me being sung in by you
And being kindly dictated to.

It's not like hearing you live was.
It is what you're saying in me
Of what is left, gaily affirming.

xiii

Flat on a cliff I inch toward its edge
Then scrutinise the chopped-up sea
Where gannets' ivory helmet skulls
Crash down in tiny plumes of white
To vivify the languid afternoon –
Pressed round my fingertips are spikes
And papery calyx frills of fading thrift
That men call sea pinks – so I can take
A studied joy in natural separateness.
And I shan't fabricate some nodding:
'She's off again somewhere, a good sign
By now, she must have got over it.'

xiv

Dun blur of this evening's lurch to
Eventual navy night. Yet another
Night, day, night over and over.
I so want to join you.

xv

The flaws in suicide are clear
Apart from causing bother
To those alive who hold us dear
We could miss one another
We might be trapped eternally
Oblivious to each other
One crying *Where are you, my child*
The other calling *Mother.*

xvi

Dead, keep me company
That sears like titanium
Compacted in the pale
Blaze of living on alone.

xvii

Suspended in unsparing light
The sloping gull arrests its curl
The glassy sea is hardened waves
Its waters lean through shining air
Yet never crash but hold their arc
Hung rigidly in glaucous ropes
Muscled and gleaming. All that
Should flow is sealed, is poised
In implacable stillness. Joined in
Non-time and halted in free fall.

xviii

It's all a resurrection song.
Would it ever be got right
The dead could rush home
Keen to press their chinos.

xix

She do the bereaved in different voices
For the point of this address is to prod
And shepherd you back within range
Of my strained ears; extort your reply
By finding any device to hack through
The thickening shades to you, you now
Strangely unresponsive son, who were
Such reliably kind and easy company,
Won't you be summoned up once more
By my prancing and writhing in a dozen
Mawkish modes of reedy piping to you
– Still no? Then let me rest, my dear.

xx

My sisters and my mother
Weep dark tears for me
I drift as lightest ashes
Under a southern sea

O let me be, my mother
In no unquiet grave
My bone-dust is faint coral
Under the fretful wave

A Showcase for Quadraat

In 1990 the LRB began to use a desktop publishing system –
Ventura Publisher – on a Windows PC. It seems implausible,
but I think at first there was just one workstation to do the
whole paper. It was in what was essentially a large cupboard/
storeroom where all the back issues were kept. Files were
sent off on floppy disks for photosetting, then complete text
pages were returned to the office, and adverts and images
pasted in. A couple of years later, we got a modern laser
printer (600 dpi) and found that using this to print on heavy
Mellotex paper was nearly as good as photosetting, so moved
to producing camera-ready copy in house (except images,
which still had to be screened at a repro house).

In 1997 the paper was redesigned. Peter Campbell
presented two designs, both using the typeface Quadraat in
a text size half a point larger than the Times typeface used in
the original design and with a whole extra point of inter-line
space, and shrinking the size of the page slightly. The
rejected version was set over three columns. The editors
didn't like the way the headlines worked (they had to be
ranged left over two columns, as one column wasn't wide
enough and centring them over all three columns ate up too
much space); Peter quite liked it because it made the reading
line more generous and reduced the need for hyphenation.
That same year we launched our first website, in a bold red
and white colour scheme. It was relaunched in 2009 with an
archive containing everything the paper has ever published
– a huge digitisation project. Shown opposite are some of
Peter's roughs for the design.

In recent years we've switched from PCs to Macs, from
Quark XPress (Ventura's replacement) to InDesign – and
everything is digital (though Bryony, who has done our
paste-up since the beginning, still keeps a scalpel in her desk
drawer). Our new website will be the first big project Peter,
who died in 2011, hasn't worked on. The LRB is essentially
austere in design and the font and style settings are its most
distinctive feature. It is a showcase for Quadraat, devised by
the Dutch designer Fred Smeijers. The cover shown here
provides a good example. Unlike the paper's staff, Smeijers
is happy to come across an issue where adverts are thin on
the ground. 'I have said this many times in lectures – the
most faithful user of Quadraat is the LRB . . . I show the public
some slides of the LRB, [including] a slide of a page with four
columns of just Quadraat, no illustrations whatsoever,
stating . . . that this is one of the most beautiful pages of text
you can get these days, and it comes every two weeks!'

Ben Campbell

Ross McKibbin: The Great Education Disaster

London Review
OF BOOKS

VOLUME 24 NUMBER 23   28 NOVEMBER 2002   £2.95 US & CANADA $3.95

Martin Jay: Where are you coming from?
Carl Elliott: The Ethics of Bioethics ▮▮▮
▮▮▮▮▮▮▮▮ George O'Brien: The Sniper
Neal Ascherson: Berlin 1945 ▮▮▮▮▮
Frank Kermode: Angry Young Men ▮▮▮
▮▮▮▮▮ Joseph Frank: 'Natasha's Dance'
▮▮▮ Brendan Simms: Wrotizla, Breslau,
Wrocław ▮▮▮▮▮▮▮▮
Michael Hofmann: Hjalmar Söderberg
▮▮▮ Paul Laity: Are the English human?
Ruth Bernard Yeazell: A.S. Byatt's Novels
Thomas Jones goes back to school ▮▮▮
David Reynolds: The 'Lusitania' Effect
▮▮▮▮▮▮▮▮▮ Stephen O'Shea:
Should Turkey be worried? ▮▮▮▮▮

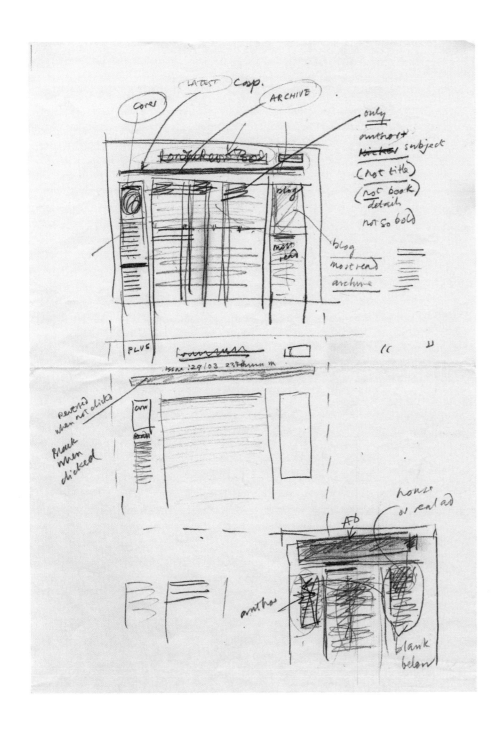

Sketches by Peter Campbell for the new website, 2009

Anna Swan writes: When I started at the paper in 1992, we keyed in most pieces from hard copy. We still do (Alan Bennett, Adam Phillips) occasionally. It may seem old-school but the LRB edits on the page, not on the screen, and for much of the last thirty years the setting has been done by three of us – Brenda Morris, Sue Barrett and me. A typesetting trio. We take in the editors' marks in Word, then set the piece in InDesign. House style is a hybrid of standard copy-editing and proofreading symbols and individual made-up style. As a result of varying standards of legibility and penmanship, some editors' marks are easier on the eye than others, whether in blue, red or pencil, and an edit in two or three different hands can be a nightmare. And then there are those who insist on marking insertions of a hyphen or colon in pencil (not naming any names). At the end of a press week an excess of spacing marks – kerning, takeovers, takebacks – can also be vexing.

Studying Depravity

Boris Johnson was first mentioned in the LRB in January 2001, not long before he became an MP. Thomas Jones made fun of his hair and criticised the *Spectator*, of which Johnson was then editor, for its racism. Reviewing *The Wit and Wisdom of Boris Johnson* in 2013, Jonathan Coe argued that political satire, especially when it takes the form of sniggering at those in power, may be not only ineffective but counterproductive. He quoted Peter Cook: 'Britain is in danger of sinking giggling into the sea.' Heathcote Williams wrote his broadside against Johnson, *The Blond Beast of Brexit – A Study in Depravity*, shortly before the EU referendum in 2016. It's ferocious, and often funny, though not much given to sniggering or giggling. After the pamphlet was mentioned on the LRB blog, quite a few readers wrote in to ask how they could get hold of a copy, so the paper reprinted it. It still sells well at the London Review Bookshop. Heathcote Williams died in July 2017.

Stephen Holmes: The Drone Presidency

London Review
OF BOOKS

VOLUME 35 NUMBER 14 · 18 JULY 2013   £3.50 US & CANADA $4.95

John Lanchester:
Can We Tame the Banks?

Slavoj Žižek:
The Global Protest

Jonathan Coe:
Giggling along with Boris

Neal Ascherson:
At the Hôtel Splendide

Lavinia Greenlaw:
'Bedsit Disco Queen'

Will Self in Battersea Power Station

Sinking Giggling into the Sea
Jonathan Coe

IF anti-establishment comedy allows the public to 'disclaim with laughter' any responsibility for injustice, the sticking point is not really satire itself (for satire can take the gravest of forms) but laughter (or 'sniggering', to use Peter Cook's term) in the face of political problems. *Have I Got News for You* presents thousands of practical demonstrations of this, so let's look at just one of them, from the edition of 24 April 1998. It was Boris Johnson's first appearance as a guest on the programme, and Ian Hislop was tormenting him on the subject of his notorious phone call with Darius Guppy, when they are alleged to have discussed the possibility of beating up an unfriendly journalist. Hislop was doing what he does best, remaining genial but suddenly toning down the humour and confronting the guest with chapter and verse for a past misdemeanour. As the exchange develops, Johnson looks distinctly uncomfortable, describing Hislop's intervention as 'richly comic' and protesting: 'I don't want to be totally stitched up here.' He calls Guppy a 'great chap', to which Hislop answers: 'And a convicted fraudster.' Johnson concedes this, and admits that Guppy made a 'major goof', and then begins to ramble and bumble in his characteristic way, groping for a way out of the corner; sensing, visibly, that Hislop has got him on the ropes, he mentions some of the other things that he and Guppy discussed during that conversation, including their military heroes. And suddenly, Paul Merton interjects with the line: 'Hence Major Goof that you mentioned just now.'

It's a lovely joke, which gets a terrific laugh and a round of applause. But its effect on the exchange is noticeable. An uncomfortable situation is suddenly defused: Johnson relaxes, the audience laughter gives him room to breathe and gather his thoughts. When he next speaks he is back on track, and says winningly: 'Since you choose to bring up this unhappy episode I won't deny a word of it. I'm not ashamed of it' – and off he goes, into one of those endearing, self-deprecatory apologies of which he is now, 15 years later, a consummate master.

It was the same Darius Guppy incident, brought up by Eddie Mair in his television interview with Johnson this March [2013], that produced one of his most cunning apologies. 'I fully concede it wasn't my most blistering performance,' he admitted the next day, acknowledging that 'Eddie Mair did a splendid job. He was perfectly within his rights to have a bash at me – in fact it would have been shocking if he hadn't. If a BBC presenter can't attack a nasty Tory politician, what's the world coming to?' The marked note of sarcasm in that last question suggests, all the same, that Johnson was rattled. As indeed he should have been: the interview, conducted in the cold ambience of a daytime news studio, was truly uncomfortable and damaging. On *Have I Got News for You*, by contrast – in what we might call the anti-establishment comedy version of the same exchange – it was laughter, more than anything else, that let Johnson off the hook. Hislop had been doing his job – bringing *Private Eye*'s brand of sceptical journalism to bear on a politician – and Merton had been doing his: making brilliant jokes. But that moment showed that the two approaches don't necessarily meld. In fact, more often than not, they work against each other.

A number of influences inform Boris Johnson's persona. One of them, undoubtedly, is Hugh Grant. Johnson's sister Rachel wrote a comic novel called *Notting Hell*: her brother has learned a lot about how to charm the socks off people by imitating the star of *Notting Hill*. But he has also learned a good deal from the anti-establishment comedy of the last fifty years (it's possible to imagine him turning, in later years, into Peter Cook's befuddled old aristo Sir Arthur Streeb-Greebling), and he understands that the laughter it generates, correctly harnessed, can be very useful to a politician who knows what to do with it. And one certainly shouldn't underestimate the role played by *Have I Got News for You* in that process.

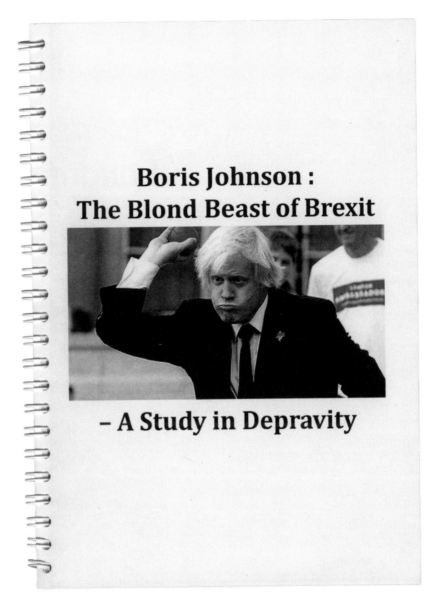

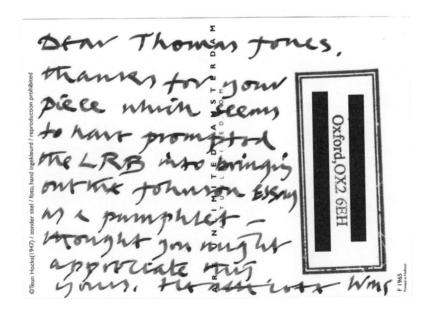

Top, first edition of 'Boris Johnson: The Blond Beast
of Brexit – A Study in Depravity' by Heathcote
Williams, 2016; above, postcard from Heathcote
Williams to Thomas Jones, 2016

Transcription:

Dear Thomas Jones,

Thanks for your piece which seems to have
prompted the *LRB* into bringing out the
Johnson essay as a pamphlet – thought you
might appreciate this.

Yours, Heathcote Wms

Duties of Confidence

Julian Assange needed a ghostwriter and he asked me to come and help him. But I don't think he had any real idea of what a writer is about. He was under house-arrest in Norfolk and I went to see him. We got on well so I said yes, thinking it would tell me something about the age of disclosure that any writer ought to know. My first suggested title for his memoir was *Disclosure*. He said he didn't like it. He thought it would create an expectation in readers that he was about to tell them something. The book deals he'd signed amounted to slightly more than $1.6 million, so it seemed to me that readers *might* want him to tell them something, but I let him say whatever he wanted and then I watched him wriggle to get out of the deal with his publishers and turn me, as he put it, into his 'chief of staff'.

The thing that had become obvious, even before he moved into the Ecuadorian Embassy and began consorting with darker forces, was that Assange loved revealing everybody's secrets except his own. There had been other indications of that: I'd never met a freedom fighter with so many lawyers. And I'd never met a freedom-of-speech advocate with such a liking for NDAs. In any event, I didn't sign one. A couple of years later, I wrote the story of my time with him. At first he tried to persuade me not to. Then he threatened me with lawyers. Standard practice, I knew, for this particular fighter for journalistic freedoms. While insisting on the legal nature of my obligations to him, Assange was ripping up every contract he'd ever been party to, breaking every agreement. One set of rules for him, another set for everybody else. Here was the narcissism I would write about in my long piece in the *London Review*.

A person can be bright while not being bright about themselves; he can be interested in fairness while behaving unfairly; and he can care about humanity but not about people. The lawyer's letters were grandiose and naive – much like Assange's dealings with secret agencies – and I tried to remember the person behind all this, the boy who hated being told lies by the authorities. Assange was a lonely man in whose mind everybody, in the end, became a bastard, a parent, a government.

Andrew O'Hagan

Andrew O'Hagan on Julian Assange

London Review OF BOOKS

VOLUME 36 NUMBER 5   6 MARCH 2014   £3.75 US & CANADA $5.95

At the police station,
Sarah stopped and said:
'Shall I do the honours?'
I watched as she went
out and searched the
bushes.
   'Is she checking for
paparazzi?' I asked.
   'I wish,' said Julian.
   'What then?'
   'Assassins.'

Andrew O'Hagan

10 March 2014

Dear Julian:

Further to your latest legal challenge, I insist
that I will not be gagged. I know you like
secrets to be released, unless they're yours,
but if WikiLeaks is ever interested in posting
my nearly 70 hours of taped interviews with
you, let me know.   all the best,

Andrew O'Hagan

30 September 2014

Dear Julian —
Surely you know that a reporter's material,
carefully gathered in pursuit of the truth,
should be freely available.

                    As ever,

Notes from Andrew O'Hagan to Julian Assange,
10 March and 30 September 2014

'Please do not hesitate'

Seymour Hersh – 'Sy' to his friends, and to the editors at the *LRB* whom he harangued on the phone – was a latecomer to the paper. In his long career he had had fights with everyone – the Associated Press, the *New York Times*, the *New Yorker* – and by 2013 he was pretty much unpublishable in America: it was not thought politic to criticise Obama's foreign campaigns, even when they involved deadlier force, and more summary justice, than the actions of most of his predecessors. So after a working lifetime exposing US abuses abroad – from My Lai to Abu Ghraib – Hersh came to the *LRB* with a counter-narrative about the use of the nerve agent sarin in Syria: not everything could necessarily be pinned on Bashar al-Assad. Stories followed on Erdoğan's support of Islamist rebels and on the killing of Osama bin Laden. There was one piece the paper couldn't publish: another counter-narrative, about what actually happened in the Syrian town of Khan Sheikhoun, when a chemical weapon attack – by whom? – led to the deaths of ninety people. There wasn't quite enough measurable proof for the paper to corroborate Hersh's account; it eventually appeared in *Die Welt*. Indicated opposite with a pink highlighter are some of the questions we wanted to ask about a later piece – on George H.W. Bush's secret wars – which Hersh and his sources irrefutably answered and the *LRB* duly published.

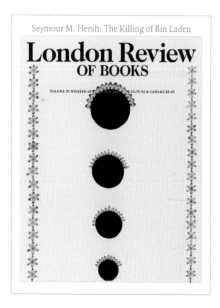

The Killing of Osama bin Laden
Seymour M. Hersh

IT's been four years since a group of US Navy Seals assassinated Osama bin Laden in a night raid on a high-walled compound in Abbottabad, Pakistan. The killing was the high point of Obama's first term, and a major factor in his re-election. The White House still maintains that the mission was an all-American affair, and that the senior generals of Pakistan's army and Inter-Services Intelligence agency (ISI) were not told of the raid in advance. This is false, as are many other elements of the Obama administration's account. The White House's story might have been written by Lewis Carroll: would bin Laden, target of a massive international manhunt, really decide that a resort town forty miles from Islamabad would be the safest place to live and command al-Qaida's operations? He was hiding in the open. So America said.

The most blatant lie was that Pakistan's two most senior military leaders – General Ashfaq Parvez Kayani, chief of the army staff, and General Ahmed Shuja Pasha, director general of the ISI – were never informed of the US mission. This remains the White House position despite an array of reports that have raised questions, including one by Carlotta Gall in the *New York Times Magazine* of 19 March 2014. Gall, who spent 12 years as the *Times* correspondent in Afghanistan, wrote that she'd been told by a 'Pakistani official' that Pasha had known before the raid that bin Laden was in Abbottabad. The story was denied by US and Pakistani officials, and went no further. In his book *Pakistan: Before and after Osama* (2012), Imtiaz Gul, executive director of the Centre for Research and Security Studies, a think tank in Islamabad, wrote that he'd spoken to four undercover intelligence officers who – reflecting a widely held local view – asserted that the Pakistani military must have had knowledge of the operation. The issue was raised again in February, when a retired general, Asad Durrani, who was head of the ISI in the early 1990s, told an al-Jazeera interviewer that it was 'quite possible' that the senior officers of the ISI did not know where bin

Laden had been hiding, 'but it was more probable that they did [know]. And the idea was that, at the right time, his location would be revealed. And the right time would have been when you can get the necessary quid pro quo – if you have someone like Osama bin Laden, you are not going to simply hand him over to the United States.'

This spring I contacted Durrani and told him in detail what I had learned about the bin Laden assault from American sources: that bin Laden had been a prisoner of the ISI at the Abbottabad compound since 2006; that Kayani and Pasha knew of the raid in advance and had made sure that the two helicopters delivering the Seals to Abbottabad could cross Pakistani airspace without triggering any alarms; that the CIA did not learn of bin Laden's whereabouts by tracking his couriers, as the White House has claimed since May 2011, but from a former senior Pakistani intelligence officer who betrayed the secret in return for much of the $25 million re-ward offered by the US, and that, while Obama did order the raid and the Seal team did carry it out, many other aspects of the administration's account were false.

'When your version comes out – if you do it – people in Pakistan will be tremendously grateful,' Durrani told me. 'For a long time people have stopped trusting what comes out about bin Laden from the official mouths. There will be some negative political comment and some anger, but people like to be told the truth, and what you've told me is essentially what I have heard from former colleagues who have been on a fact-finding mission since this episode.' As a former ISI head, he said, he had been told shortly after the raid by 'people in the "strategic community" who would know' that there had been an informant who had alerted the US to bin Laden's presence in Abbottabad, and that after his killing the US's betrayed promises left Kayani and Pasha exposed.

The Vice President's Men
Seymour Hersh

WHEN George H.W. Bush arrived in Washington as vice president in January 1981 he seemed little more than a sideshow to Ronald Reagan, the one-time leading man who had been overwhelmingly elected to the greatest stage in the world. Biography after inconclusive biography would be written about Reagan's two terms, as their authors tried to square the many gaps in his knowledge with his seemingly acute political instincts and the ease with which he appeared to handle the presidency. Bush was invariably written off as a cautious politician who followed the lead of his glamorous boss – perhaps because he assumed that his reward would be a clear shot at the presidency in 1988. He would be the first former CIA director to make it to the top.

There was another view of Bush: the one held by the military men and civilian professionals who worked for him on national security issues. Unlike the president, he knew what was going on and how to get things done. For them, Reagan was 'a dimwit' who didn't get it, or even try to get it. A former senior official of the Office of Management and Budget described the president to me as 'lazy, just lazy'. Reagan, she explained, insisted on being presented with a three-line summary of significant budget decisions, and had office concluded that the easiest way to cope was to present him with three figures – one very high, one very low and one in the middle, which Reagan invariably signed off on. I was later told that the process was known inside the White House as the 'Goldilocks option'. He was also bored by complicated intelligence estimates. Forever courteous and gracious, he would doodle during national security briefings or simply not listen. It would have been natural to turn instead to the director of the CIA, but this was William Casey, a former businessman and Nixon aide, who had been controversially appointed by Reagan. As the intelligence professionals working with the executive saw it, Casey was reckless, uninformed and said far too much to the press.

Bush was different: he got it. At his direction, a team of operatives was set up that bypassed the national security establishment – including the CIA – and wasn't answerable to congressional oversight. The team was led by Admiral Arthur Moreau, a brilliant navy officer who would be known to those on the inside as 'M'. Over the next couple of years, his secret team conducted at least 35 covert operations against drug trafficking, terrorism and, most important, perceived Soviet expansionism in more than twenty countries, including Peru, Honduras, Guatemala, Brazil, Argentina, Libya, Senegal, Chad, Algeria, Tunisia, the Congo, Kenya, Egypt, Yemen, Syria, Hungary, East Germany, Czechoslovakia, Bulgaria, Romania, Georgia and Vietnam.

From May 1983 Moreau's official job was assistant to the chairman of the Joint Chiefs of Staff, General John Vessey, but he was also running a small, off-the-record team primarily made up of navy officers, tasked with foreign operations deemed necessary by the vice president. The group's link to Bush was indirect. There were two go-betweens, known for their closeness to the vice

president and their ability to keep secrets: Daniel Murphy, Bush's chief of staff, a retired admiral who had served as deputy director of the CIA; and, to a lesser extent, Donald Gregg, Bush's national security adviser and another veteran of CIA covert operations. Moreau's team mostly worked out of a small office in a secure area near the National Military Command Centre in the Pentagon basement. They could also unobtrusively man a desk or two, when necessary, in a corner of Murphy's office in the Old Executive Office Building next to the White House.

The Reagan administration had been rattled by a wave of Soviet expansionism and international aggression even before it took office. In 1979 the Soviets had taken over the old air base at Cam Ranh Bay in the former South Vietnam which had been extensively rebuilt and updated by the US during its losing war. It was a base heavy with symbolism for the American and British navies – in December 1941, three days after Pearl Harbor, Japanese dive bombers operating from Cam Ranh sank two of Britain's premier battleships – and the Soviet decision to expand there was seen by some senior admirals as an alarming affront. A revolutionary increase in America's capacity to intercept and decode Soviet signal traffic just as Reagan came to power, meanwhile, but eventually to the discovery by analysts at the National Security Agency of Soviet sleeper agents inside the United States, many of them working in federal jobs with – the Carter White House feared – access to national security data.

A former military officer who worked closely with Moreau recalled the early tensions that prompted Bush to increase the targeting of Soviet operations. Moreau's actions were aimed at limiting Soviet influence without provoking a confrontation. 'We saw the Russians sorting out their internal politics and expanding economically,' the officer recalled. 'Its military had become much more competent, with advances in technology, nuclear engineering and in space. They were feeling good about their planned economy and believed that their state control of education from cradle to grave was working, and it seemed as if the Russians were expanding everywhere. We were in descent; our army was in shambles; morale was at rock bottom, and the American people had an anti-militarist attitude. There was a sense of general weakness, and the Russians were taking advantage of it. They had developed the MIRV' – the multiple independently targetable re-entry vehicle, a missile carrying several nuclear warheads – 'and were putting ICBMs on mobile trains and hardening nuclear silos. This was at the time when it became clear that the president was drifting, and was not an effective leader.'

In 1982, when it was clear that Reagan wouldn't engage in oversight of intelligence and counterintelligence activities, and Bush took charge. He had emerged, by default and very much in private, as the

most important decision-maker in America's intelligence world. 'He controlled the strings,' the officer said. 'We ran small, limited operations that were discreet, with a military chain of command. These were not long-term programmes. We thought we could redouble our efforts against the Soviets and nobody would interfere. And do it in such a way that no one could see what we were doing – or realise that there was a masterplan. For example, the published stories about our Star Wars programme were replete with misinformation and forced the Russians to expose their sleeper agents inside the American government by ordering them to make a desperate attempt to find out what the US was doing. But we could not risk exposure of the administration's role and take the chance of another McCarthy period. So there were no prosecutions. We dried up and eliminated their access and left the spies withering on the vine.' Once identified, the Soviet sleepers who worked inside the federal bureaucracy were gradually dismissed or moved to less important jobs, in the hope that the low-key counterintelligence operation would mask the improvements in the US's capacity to read sensitive Soviet communications. 'Nobody on the Joint Chiefs of Staff ever believed we were going to build Star Wars,' the officer said, 'but if we could convince the Russians that we could sur-

vive a first strike, we win the game.' The aim of the game was to find a way to change the nuclear status quo of Mutual Assured Destruction, or seem to do so. 'We wanted the Russians to believe that we had removed the M from MAD.'

In the beginning, the officer told me, 'there was a great fear that the Russians were ten feet tall. What we found was total incompetence.' Moreau's team were amazed to find how easy it was to reverse Soviet influence. 'The Russians simply were not liked abroad,' the officer said. 'They were boors with shoddy clothing and shoes made out of paper. Their weapons were inoperative. It was a Potemkin village. But every time we found total incompetence on the part of a Soviet mission, the American intelligence community would assume that it was Soviet "deception". The only problem was that it was not deception. We came to realise that the American intelligence community needed the threat from Russia to get their money. Those of us who were running the operations were also amazed that the American press was so incompetent. You could do this kind of stuff all over the world and nobody would ask any questions.'

Congress, and the constitution, were no more of an obstacle to Bush and Moreau's covert operations than the press. The one member of Congress who knew what was going on was Dick Cheney, a close friend and confidant of Bush's from their days together in the Ford administration. In 1976, in the aftermath of the Church Committee's inquiry into CIA abuses, standing intelligence committees had been set up in

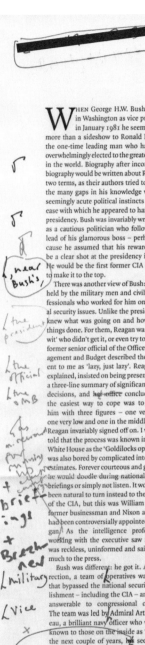

Proof of page 9, 24 January 2019,
with editorial annotations

Women's Issues

From her second contribution to the LRB in October 1989, which talks about the marginalisation of women and of 'women's issues', to her pair of pieces about women in power, both first delivered as LRB Winter Lectures, Mary Beard has more than borne out the preference stated in her letter, opposite. 'Women who claim a public voice get treated as freakish androgynes,' she told the audience at the British Museum in February 2014; she'd experienced this herself after, for example, she wrote about being raped as a graduate student 22 years earlier, and when, in October 2001, she received threats for simply imagining the reasons a person might have for attacking the US. 'So should we be optimistic about change when we think about what power is and what it can do, and women's engagement with it?' Beard asked in February 2017. 'Maybe, we should be a little. I'm struck, for example, that one of the most influential political movements of the last few years, Black Lives Matter, was founded by three women; few of us, I suspect, would recognise any of their names, but together they had the power to get things done in a different way.'

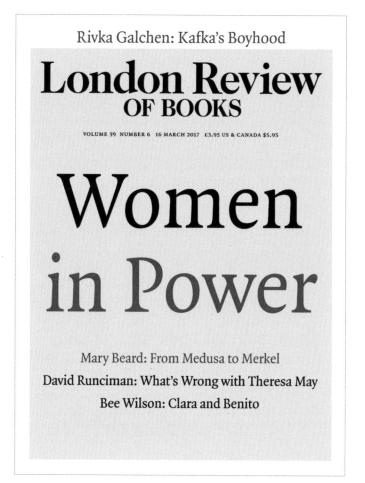

'That's an ecellent suggestion Miss Triggs.
Perhaps one of the men here would like to make it.'

Cartoon by Riana Duncan, first published in 'Punch', reproduced to accompany 'The Public Voice of Women' by Mary Beard, 20 March 2014

NEWNHAM COLLEGE
CAMBRIDGE
CB3 9DF
TELEPHONE (0223) 62273
335712
335700
(messages)

23.5.89

Dear Mrs Wilmers,

Thank you for your kind note.
In fact, I'd love to write for the London
Review.

I teach Classics (mostly Roman history,
culture etc) and would quite enjoy
doing something in this area. But I
suppose I prefer writing about women's
issues, politics, not aggressively technical
sociology. The upmarket/general reader
range. Does that make sense?

Yours

Mary Beard.

Letter from Mary Beard to Mary-Kay Wilmers,
23 May 1989

No Sunny Beaches in Winter

As well as designing the paper, Peter Campbell drew or painted more than five hundred covers between 1993 and 2012. The process was simple, or simple-ish. As Mary-Kay Wilmers wrote in the *LRB* of 17 November 2011, a month after his death, 'From time to time Peter would come into the office with a batch of watercolours under his arm, three or four in a big folder – "I've got some covers for you" – and go away before we looked at them.' That hasn't changed: today a number of artists send us covers, usually a few at a time, and we mock up the ones we like with words to see how they might look. Every other Thursday we choose the image for the new issue. There are considerations – no sunny beaches in winter, no teapots when the pieces are especially serious. On the whole the connection between the cover and the pieces isn't straightforward. Sometimes it's a practical decision: the cover has to accommodate the right number of words, or none at all. It has to be something we think people will want to pick up and look at. Yellow covers sell especially well, we're told.

Sometimes we keep images for a long time, and one day they find favour. Who can say what changed? Occasionally – whether by serendipity or design – a cover says something very direct about the contents of an issue. Anne Rothenstein's image of a woman, hand to head in exasperation, summed up our feelings – and those of most of the contributors to the issue – after the EU referendum in 2016. A Trump-like figure (not originally Trump) seems to emerge from the shadows of another design. As Rothenstein says: 'I am a great believer in the power of irrepressible images. As with writers going where they're led, things will surface in the most surprising ways.'

Of the many things we took for granted when Peter did the covers, what strikes us the most now is his ability to think in terms of the paper's format (it must have helped that he designed it). Not everyone, it turns out, can work in rectangles. Peter knew how to use space, and thought (sometimes grudgingly) about where the words would go. But he was also an artist and he cared about the look of the whole thing and what people would see when it was folded in half (the way it often appears on the newsstand); he knew what sort of effects reproduced well and which didn't. Anne Rothenstein has made most of the covers since Peter's death, many of them collages, and she shares his ability to invent in a limited field. Her covers – like all the best ones – become complete once we add words to them. Thanks to Cressida Bell, Jon McNaught, Alexander Gorlizki, Naomi Frears and Beth Holgate, we continue to have watercolour scenes in Peter's tradition, as well as computer-manipulated images, prints, gouache, delicate miniatures. It is a happy day in the office when new covers arrive.

Alice Spawls

Covers from the issues of 20 October 2016, 2 August 2018 and 6 June 2019, designed by Anne Rothenstein

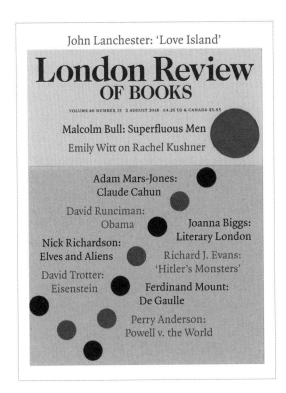

John Lanchester: 'Love Island'

London Review
OF BOOKS

VOLUME 40 NUMBER 15   2 AUGUST 2018   £4.25 US & CANADA $5.95

Malcolm Bull: Superfluous Men

Emily Witt on Rachel Kushner

Adam Mars-Jones:
Claude Cahun

David Runciman:
Obama

Joanna Biggs:
Literary London

Nick Richardson:
Elves and Aliens

Richard J. Evans:
'Hitler's Monsters'

David Trotter:
Eisenstein

Ferdinand Mount:
De Gaulle

Perry Anderson:
Powell v. the World

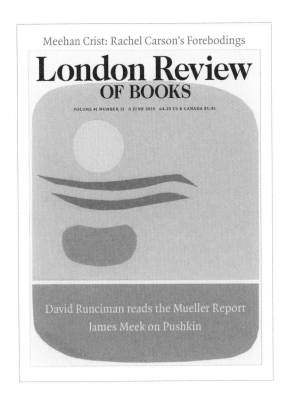

Meehan Crist: Rachel Carson's Forebodings

London Review
OF BOOKS

VOLUME 41 NUMBER 11   6 JUNE 2019   £4.25 US & CANADA $5.95

David Runciman reads the Mueller Report
James Meek on Pushkin

Black Cloud

Tom Crewe writes: It's hard to remember the time when 'Brexit' wasn't really a word; much less of a word, in fact, than 'Grexit', which was once common currency but now feels clumsy on the tongue. 'Brexit' first appeared in the LRB in February 2016, only four months before the referendum, in an essay by Colin Kidd – and has featured in around 170 articles since then. The referendum result prompted one of the paper's rare collections of its contributors' thoughts on an issue. Rereading them three years on, I'm reminded that the implications of the vote were grasped instantaneously: Neal Ascherson dreaded being 'locked in a dark, stuffy nursery cupboard with Boris, Michael, Nigel and their pals'; James Butler saw that there was 'a knot at the centre of British politics'; Sionaidh Douglas-Scott highlighted the problem of the Irish border; Susan Pedersen the problem of the generational divide; James Meek noted what has become the defining paradox of the Brexit process, that a vote which was supposed to be so definitive . . . hasn't settled anything'. For succinctness, David Runciman's verdict hasn't been surpassed: 'It was the wrong question, put at the wrong time, in the wrong way.' J.G.A. Pocock contributed a similarly concise, if rather more gnomic, utterance: 'Avoid further referendums and act for yourselves as you know how to act and be.'

Since then, the LRB has attempted to cover Brexit from all angles: there have been essays on England and Englishness, Britain and Britishness, devolution, law, Theresa May, the Leaver mentality, trade deals and no deal. Julian Barnes revealed that, the day after the vote, an exultant Leaver greeted him with a shout of 'Oi, Flaubert, where are you now?' As Brexit has come to dominate our thoughts, so it has surfaced in unexpected places: in pieces about Eimear McBride, Heidegger, Caravaggio, the mystery of sleep and the travails of the Huguenots. Many of us have come to share Jonathan Coe's feelings as he expressed them in those first responses: 'I understand my country a little better now than I did . . . But I love it a good deal less.'

EXTRACT FROM VOL. 38 NO. 22 · 17 NOVEMBER 2016

England prepares to leave the world
Neal Ascherson

I NEVER thought I would see this opera again. 'Rule Britannia!' peals, the curtain parts, and there is a mad queen poling her island raft away into the Atlantic. Her shrieks grow slowly fainter, as the mainland falls behind. The first performance was in the 1980s. Who could forget Margaret Thatcher's ear-splitting arias? But she never took the raft to the horizon, and never finally cast off the cross-Channel hawser mooring her to Europe. This revival is different. Theresa May says she's bound for the ocean, and she means it.

Or rather, she means it because she doesn't mean it. Nothing in British history resembles this spectacle of men and women ramming through policies everyone knows they don't believe in. Never mind the few genuine Brexiteers. Amber Rudd, Philip Hammond and Theresa May – among others in government – all tried to keep the UK in the European Union. Now they are trying to take it out again, apparently on the terms that will do their country most damage.

There's a kind explanation, a white-coated one and a coarse one. The kind account says that they feel democratically obliged to carry out the wishes of the English people, whatever their private opinions. (A variant suggests that they think themselves duty-bound to save the country from the worst consequences of a disastrous decision, but their recklessness over Brexit doesn't support that.) The white-coated shrink account is that they are pathologically over-compensating out of guilt for backing the wrong side. And the coarse explanation is that they just want to stay in power.

This is a government that stamps and shouts in order to hide its inner weakness. Its majority in the House of Commons is tiny; the Conservative Party is noisily divided; the quarrelling cabinet – despite the 'no running commentary' proclamation – leaks and briefs daily about Brexit. And it's led by a politician whose show of flinty determination conceals – I increasingly suspect – awful fears about her own ability to control her party and something close to panic as she leads Britain into the black cloud of unknowing that covers Brexit negotiations, the trembling economy and the future of the United Kingdom itself.

It's insecurity, not complacency, which is prompting such Little England deafness and blindness to the outside world. May stowed Boris away in the Foreign Office as if it were a scullery cupboard: nothing in there mattered to her. She and the other Tory leaders simply didn't notice that Amber Rudd's plan to name and shame British firms that didn't list their foreign employees provoked days of horrified media coverage all over Europe and America. When the outside world asked if the country that wanted to 'anglify' the NHS, block European students and use EU residents as bargaining chips was really the Britain they had known and loved, May's ministers shrugged.

At the EU Bratislava summit, the defence secretary, Michael Fallon, proclaimed that he would veto European plans to co-ordinate national armies – even though Britain would be long out of the EU by the time anything of the sort could take place. More recently, May told EU leaders in Brussels that Britain intended to use its right to interfere up to the last hour of its membership. When Jean-Claude Juncker commented on May's performance with a loud raspberry, British journalists, accustomed to reporting every EU meeting as if Britain were the only item on the agenda, pretended to be shocked. But the other 27 nations must be wondering when they can tell May to mind her own business.

England is dragging the other nations of the United Kingdom with it as it leaves not only the European Union but the world. Does anyone think seriously that Canada or Australia, comfortably embedded in the American and Asian trade regions, will turn back towards 'the mother country'? Somebody commented that Theresa May was the best person to build a better yesterday (many would say the same about Jeremy Corbyn). It's the way back to a bedraggled exceptionalism, the 1970s pretence that Britain was still at the top table of the Big Three or Four.

What have we done?

London Review
OF BOOKS

VOLUME 38 NUMBER 14   14 JULY 2016   £3.95 US & CANADA $5.95

'Stuzz'

I first heard of John in the late 1960s when I was working at Faber and we were thinking whether or not to publish a translation of one of Alejo Carpentier's magical realist novels. My boss told me to get in touch with someone called John Sturrock, who worked at the *TLS* and knew Spanish and knew about magical realism; he would advise us. I think John said we should and I know we decided not to. Faber was quite stick in the mud in those days.

John's good fortune, he wrote in *The Word from Paris*, a collection of his essays on postwar French intellectuals, was to have entered on his professional life in the mid-1960s when Sartre was ceding the territory to Roland Barthes; when, as John put it, 'the first rustlings of Literary Theory' – he gave it capital letters – 'were to be heard', and the quarrel between those who took to theory and those who took against it was just starting up. John had no doubts about which side he was on – I'm not sure he ever had doubts: he had questions – and the argument for theory was all the more enjoyable (his word) because it had to be made, as he described it, in a country such as Britain, 'so gruffly unreceptive to anything even faintly theoretical'; or foreign.

John's working life divides neatly: a little more than thirty years on the *TLS*, a little less than thirty years at the *LRB*. Among his colleagues he was known and admired above all for two things: the severity of his judgment and the playfulness of his intellect, and I can't think of a more likeable combination. Sadly, it's a combination one is more likely to find on the political right, in the *Spectator*, for example. John's version was staunchly of the left. Not the wild left or the utopian left so much as the dissenting left. Here he is, in August 2003, on one (minor) aspect of the war in Iraq:

The delusional cast of mind of those who ordered our armed services into action on a false prospectus appears to be spreading, no doubt being seen in high places as a sound qualification for anyone who may now be angling to land a job sorting things out in Iraq itself. The man who has been put in charge of a body called the Iraq Industry Working Group was quoted last week as saying that within quite a short time – as little as three years, he thought – Iraq could be turned from the unhappy scene of murderous disorder and deprivation it currently is into a tourist venue, containing . . . such recently overlooked destinations as the 'birthplace of Abraham' and the Hanging Gardens of Babylon, even if these particular sites might need a spot of making over by the people you see on television doing that sort of thing in the English suburbs. Why, on the other hand, wait even three years to open the country up to tourists, when you could start easyJetting them in straightaway and offer them their own weight in air miles if they manage while they're there to do what no one else has done and finger the missing weapons.

The *LRB* piece that caused the most hoo-ha among the paper's readers, and elicited the largest number of indignant letters, was written by John. Alan Sokal, a professor of mathematics at UCL and physics at NYU, had gone into battle against the postmodern theorists whom he accused – I'm simplifying but not greatly – of having no understanding of the concepts they borrowed from science, and no respect for truth either. John's response was to call Sokal a 'bigot'; far better, he said, 'wild and contentious theses' than the 'stultifying rigour' which Sokal 'inappropriately' demanded. Rigour of course has its place. John himself was rigorous and often demanded more rigour from others. But unlike any editor I've known, he saw it as his obligation to 'encourage adventurism in ideas as the way to keep the intellectual pot boiling'.

Mary-Kay Wilmers, writing in 2017

The London Bombs

John Sturrock

TODAY is Thursday 7 July, a date which is likely, by the time this issue of the LRB is read, to have been abbreviated to 7/7, even if the atrocity in London proved a lot less horrific in its consequences than 9/11. Thursday being this paper's day for going to press, I'd written for 'Short Cuts' a few hundred mildly disobliging words about London's having been awarded the 2012 Olympics. I was more pleased than I'd expected to be, but the overjoy of some people was hard to fathom; was that excessively jubilant crowd in Trafalgar Square, I asked myself, a gathering of Balfour Beatty shareholders? If the Olympics coming to London means that rundown bits of the city are going to be 're-generated', all well and good, but you have to wonder why it takes the Olympics to bring about that thoroughly desirable change.

I was getting ready to bring my words to that effect into the Bloomsbury offices of the LRB when I heard about the blasts on the Underground. 'Short Cuts' could clearly no longer be about the Olympics, even though my first thought was that there might be a connection. Could whoever had let off the bombs – and the only group to have claimed responsibility at the time of writing is something called, naively, the Secret Organisation of al-Qaida in Europe – have been so incensed by London's success as to want to put a quick and murderous end to the jollifications? Hardly. This attack couldn't have been planned in 24 hours, though the dark hints we're always hearing that planning such terrorist coups de théâtre takes long months or even years, have to be nonsense, as though the length of time spent in silent preparation has somehow to be commensurate with the severity of the outcome. London might well not have won the IOC vote in any case, as it mightn't indeed had the bombs gone off two days earlier. If they were timed to coincide with an event, it could only be with the G8 meeting in Scotland, to which it so happens significant numbers of London policemen had been sent, to help stop the balaclavaed anarchists.

Tony Blair, taking time off from the feasting and shoulder-rubbing at Gleneagles, said that the summit would continue, that the terrorists were 'trying to use the slaughter of innocent people to cow us, to frighten us out of doing the things that we want to do': words that might not have been so well received in downtown Baghdad. It might have been better if George Bush hadn't been hovering behind Blair's right shoulder. The sight of the two of them together did a lot to clear the mind of thoughts of the Olympics or even the G8 meeting itself as the motive behind the London bombs, which certainly weren't let off to show solidarity with the African poor. Far and away the most rational motive was the one that in the immediate aftermath seemed barely able to speak its name: Iraq.

Which gives one to reflect that if the bombs had gone off at the end of April, instead of early July, i.e. shortly before the general election, the pattern of voting might well have been significantly altered, and the connection with Iraq aired instantly and to beneficial effect. Bear in mind what happened in Spain, where the Aznar government was bundled out of office by an electorate that had been twice outraged by it, first when it supported the war at a time when opinion polls showed the majority against the war to be larger in Spain than anywhere else in Europe, and then by Aznar's breathtakingly squalid attempts to pin the blame for the Madrid bombings on the Basque separatists.

The mayor of London, Ken Livingstone, did a lot better than the prime minister. Instead of coming out with airy and pious abstractions about 'the British way of life', or about our 'civilisation' and their 'barbarism', he spoke specifically and concretely of London. He may also have been making a veiled appeal to the government not to use the attacks as an excuse to tighten even further its rules on immigration and asylum.

Some hope is all I can say.

Joanna Biggs writes: It can be easy to forget what exceptional people your colleagues are. I sat next to John Sturrock for years and I remember small things mostly: the round sunshine-yellow lemon tart he usually ate for dessert at lunchtime, while he read that week's TLS; the time he told me about Albert Camus's honeymoon (not spent with his new wife); the story that he calmly stepped over a collapsed colleague who had broken her ankle falling down the office stairs; the charming, lightly suppressed smile he wore after coming up with a particularly witty pun for the cover; the curly 'r' and 'g's of his red-biroed handwriting; the half-inch of black tea he habitually left in his cup.

But John was a link back to literary journalism proper: he started at the TLS in the 1960s, commissioning the first reviews of Derrida et al; he translated Victor Hugo and Proust; he attacked the mendaciousness of the Blair government in the paper with a fury many younger commentators couldn't summon. In his last email to me, he scolded me for reading the Scott Moncrieff translation of *A la recherche du temps perdu* – 'I truly believe SM overall gives quite a misleading impression of what Proust was doing' – instead of the French. After he died, we found a cache of letters in his desk drawer: one from Iris Murdoch, one from Borges, one from Calvino. I sometimes think of John as the last man of letters.

London Review of Beasts

Certain subjects seem to lend themselves to good pieces. The description of day-to-day lives (Diaries by doctors, postmen etc), or the way something operates (Peter Campbell on escalators), or is organised (Keith Thomas on his working methods). Animals satisfy all of the above. How do they live? How do they behave? How do they organise themselves? The danger is that the contributor, as Ted Hughes did, finds the subject so fascinating they want to keep it to themselves (though we did publish his poem 'Sing the Rat'). In writing about animals we are, of course, thinking about ourselves, and as Amia Srinivasan demonstrates in her piece on octopuses, animals can provide a way of thinking about the limitations of our own thinking. Katherine Rundell's ongoing series, 'Consider the . . .', which has so far taken in the lemur, the wombat, the pangolin, the narwhal and the golden mole, considers the animals' histories, habits and relations with people, as when she writes of the lemurs floating on rafts of vegetation towards Madagascar, 'sailing across the sea to what looked, until the arrival of humans, like safety'.

The Sucker, the Sucker!

Amia Srinivasan

THE OCTOPUS threatens boundaries. Its body, a boneless mass of soft tissue, has no fixed shape. Even large octopuses – the largest species, the Giant Pacific, has an arm span of more than six metres and weighs a hundred pounds – can fit through an opening an inch wide, or about the size of its eye. This, combined with their considerable strength – a mature male Giant Pacific can lift thirty pounds with each of its 1600 suckers – means that octopuses are difficult to keep in captivity. Many octopuses have escaped their aquarium tanks through small holes; some have been known to lift the lid of their tank, making their way, sometimes across stretches of dry floor, to a neighbouring tank for a snack, or to the nearest drain, and maybe from there back home to the sea.

Octopuses do not have any stable colour or texture, changing at will to match their surroundings: a camouflaged octopus can be invisible from just a few feet away. Like humans, they have centralised nervous systems, but in their case there is no clear distinction between brain and body. An octopus's neurons are dispersed throughout its body, and two-thirds of them are in its arms: each arm can act intelligently on its own, grasping, manipulating and hunting. (Octopuses have arms, not tentacles: tentacles have suckers only at their tips. Squid and cuttlefish have a combination of arms and tentacles.) In evolutionary terms, the intelligence of octopuses is an anomaly. Other creatures that are so evolutionarily distant from humans – lobsters, snails, slugs, clams – rate pretty low on the cognitive scale. But octopuses – and to some extent their cephalopod cousins, cuttlefish and squid – frustrate the neat evolutionary division between clever vertebrates and simple-minded invertebrates. They are sophisticated problem solvers; they learn, and can use tools; and they show a capacity for mimicry, deception and, some think, humour. Just how refined their abilities are is a matter of scientific debate: their very strangeness makes octopuses hard to study. Their intelligence is like ours, and utterly unlike ours. Octopuses are the closest we can come, on earth, to knowing what it might be like to encounter intelligent aliens.

What does it feel like to be an octopus? Does it feel like anything at all? Or are octopuses, as Peter Godfrey-Smith puts it in *Other Minds: The Octopus and the Evolution of Intelligent Life*, 'just biochemical machines for which all is dark inside'? This form of question – 'What is it like to be a bat?' Thomas Nagel asked in a hugely influential paper in 1974 – is philosophical shorthand for asking whether a creature is conscious. Many philosophers think consciousness is an all or nothing phenomenon: you either have it or you don't. Humans have it, as do perhaps chimps and dolphins. Mice, ants and amoebas presumably do not. Part of the motivation for the all or nothing view is that it is difficult to imagine consciousness being possessed in degrees. Godfrey-Smith suggests that the octopus is, phenomenologically speaking, in a hybrid situation: its arms are partly self, and partly other.

Earlier this summer, on a drive from San Francisco to Los Angeles, I went to see the octopuses at Monterey Bay Aquarium. At the time Monterey's permanent octopus exhibit housed two Giant Pacifics, though there were more octopuses in its temporary show *Tentacles*, the largest ever exhibition of cephalopods. This was my second encounter with a live octopus. (I have had more encounters with dead octopuses at the dinner table than I care to recall. They make excellent carpaccio. Never again.) The first was off a beach in Mykonos, where I was snorkelling. There wasn't much on the sea floor, just small crustaceans and darting silver fish, until I saw a red mass a few feet away, about the size of a cat, watching me with a single eye. I stayed still, watching it back. The octopus made small, unhurried movements, curling and uncurling its arms, snuffling along the floor. Eventually it crawled to a sunken rope some feet away and wrapped itself around it. Its body became a brown, barnacled coil, and then there was only a single white eye with a black dash of pupil. The eye closed, and the octopus vanished.

Court Green
North Tawton
Devon

Dear Karl,

Yes, I felt guilty about the Rat book. I conned myself for a while – saying I really would like to review it. Truth was – I didn't want to give it all away (I've found that when I review a book I somehow lose it – hand it over to National Trust, with a public speech, something like that – and also lose interest in it). And I didn't want to pass the book to somebody else – I knew I'd never see it again.

So it didn't get reviewed because I liked it too much!

But if you feel somebody might review it – I'll send them the copy on. It really is a curious book – it's so interesting it's nearly comical.

Very glad you'll print my poems. Happy New Year to yourself & Jane
Ted

Letter from Ted Hughes to Karl Miller, 1983

Transcription:

Dear Karl,

Yes, I felt guilty about the Rat book. I conned myself for a while – saying I really would like to review it. Truth was – I didn't want to give it all away (I've found that when I review a book I somehow lose it – hand it over to National Trust with a public speech, something like that – and also lose interest in it). And I didn't want to pass the book to somebody else – I knew I'd never see it again.

So it didn't get reviewed because I liked it too much!

But if you feel somebody might review it – I'll send them the copy on. It really is a curious book – it's so interesting it's nearly comical.

Very glad you'll print my poems.

Happy New Year to yourself and Jane

Ted

Breaking the Internet

For ten winters, the paper has invited three of its contributors to give a lecture at the British Museum. The text is generally printed afterwards for those who can't make it to London. We have heard Frank Kermode define the shudder T.S. Eliot felt when reading Tennyson's *In Memoriam*; Judith Butler lay out the consequences of Max Brod's publication of the novels Kafka told him to burn; Rosemary Hill on clothes, and whether it's an advantage to have that extra sense Virginia Woolf called 'frock consciousness'; John Lanchester consider what Marx might think of us, post financial crisis; Marina Warner document her disillusionment with the higher education system.

In 2013, Hilary Mantel delivered a lecture that considered the plight of Kate Middleton, the duchess of Cambridge, then pregnant with her first child, as well as considering the ways that the bodies of female royals, from Princess Diana to Anne Boleyn, become 'public property'. As Mantel later told the BBC, 'my whole theme was the way we maltreat royal persons, making them at once superhuman, and yet less than human.' A week later, her face was blown up on the cover of the *Daily Mail*: 'Booker prize-winner's venomous attack on Kate'. David Cameron, on a trade mission to India, was asked to comment: 'I think she writes great books, but I think what she's said about Kate Middleton is completely misguided and completely wrong.' Mantel explained that the passages the *Mail* objected to were 'describing the perception of her which has been set up in the tabloid press' – which may explain the real reason for the outrage.

In 2019, Patricia Lockwood attempted to define the internet during the 'days of its snowy white disintegration'. Her lecture, 'The Communal Mind', gave rise to a memorable PowerPoint presentation: the first slide was the one shown here. Joanne O'Leary, one of the editors at the paper, set off a mise en abyme effect when she tweeted a snap of Lockwood standing in front of the slide at the British Museum soundcheck, and then we printed an image of that tweet in the text of the lecture that was going to press as Lockwood was speaking in Bloomsbury. When the lecture finally appeared online, the *LRB* came as close as it ever has to breaking the internet.

She was asked to give a lecture at the British Museum. This was hardly deserved. Still, she stood there, and locked them in her mind for an hour. Her face was the fresh imprint of her age. She spoke the words that were there for her to speak; she wore the only kind of shirt available at that time. It was not possible to see where she had gone wrong, where she would go wrong. She said: *garfield is a body-positivity icon.* She said: *abraham lincoln is daddy.* She said: *the eels in London are on cocaine.* It was fitting finally to appear in that place, an exhibit herself from far away, collaged together in body and mind, monstrous in the eyes of the future, an imbecile before the Rosetta Stone, disturber of the deadest tombs, butterfly catcher and butterfly killer, soon to be folded between two pages herself, and speak about the liftedness of little and large things. ☐

Right, detail from page 14, 21 February 2019;
opposite, drawing of Anne Enright's lecture,
23 February 2018, by Jennifer Lambert

2010
Frank Kermode: Eliot and the Shudder
Neil MacGregor: The Purpose and Politics of the British Museum
Rory Stewart: The Rhetoric of War and Intervention

2011
Judith Butler: Who owns Kafka?
T.J. Clark: Picasso's *Guernica* Revisited
Elif Batuman: Cervantes, Balzac and Double-Entry Bookkeeping

2012
Neal Ascherson: Europe
John Lanchester: Marx at 193
Jacqueline Rose: Marilyn Monroe

2013
Hilary Mantel: Royal Bodies
David Runciman: The Crisis of American Democracy
Nicholas Spice: Is Wagner bad for us?

2014
James Wood: On Not Going Home
Mary Beard: The Public Voice of Women
Andrew O'Hagan: Ghosting Julian Assange

2015
Tariq Ali: The New World Disorder
Adam Phillips: Against Self-Criticism
Marina Warner: The Betrayal of Higher Education

2016
James Meek: Robin Hood in a Time of Austerity
Frances Stonor Saunders: Borders
Colm Tóibín: The 1916 Rebellion

2017
Iain Sinclair: The Last London
Michael Wood: Fritz Lang and the Life of Crime
Mary Beard: Women in Power

2018
Anne Enright: Adam and Eve, the Genesis of Blame
Linda Colley: Can history help?
Rosemary Hill: What does she think she looks like?

2019
Patricia Lockwood: The Communal Mind
Christopher Clark: 1848
Adam Tooze: Is this the end of the American century?

Three Words a Day

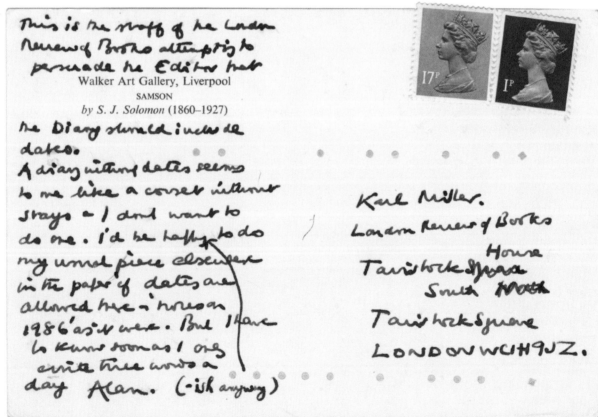

Postcard from Alan Bennett to Karl Miller, 1986

Diary for 2018

Alan Bennett

20 December 2017. Nick Hytner rings saying he hopes to put on the hospital play at the Bridge next year and had I had any thoughts about the title? Off the cuff I suggest *Past Caring*, which I'm sure has been used, but will serve, if only for the announcement of the season in the New Year.

As an early Christmas present Bridget has given us a cow creamer she has made. Unglazed, it is chunky and solid and striped black and white like a bovine zebra. It's a delightful object, a convict cow, and could she be bothered to make more and market them I'm sure they would sell for a substantial price. As it is, it stands on the kitchen table waiting to find its – or her – place. A lovely thing.

11 January. The partridges have landed. I once had to give a talk at Hawthornden, the writers' colony near Edinburgh run by Drue Heinz. Thereafter, every Christmas Drue sends us a box of partridges or venison which, not being especially carnivorous, we find it hard to dispose of. This year, though, Inigo Thomas, having been brought up on such fare, has offered to take them off our hands (and later sends round a brace in a delicious casserole).

7 February. Nick H. rings this morning to say they'd been talking over the play at the theatre and the general feeling is that *Allelujah!* (my original title) makes more of an impact than *Past Caring* and will look better on the posters. I haven't looked it up, but I imagine 'Allelujah' is a godly way of saying 'Hooray!

14 February, Yorkshire. When we had the central heating overhauled a slightly larger radiator was put in the downstairs loo. It's a small room – the smallest room indeed – and now it's become the cosiest room in the house. Used to the lav not being over-warm, I now find it luxurious. In Nancy Mitford's *The Pursuit of Love* the Radlett children in their arctic house used to foregather in its warmest spot, the airing cupboard. With us it would have to be the loo.

7 April. One drawback of my new hearing aid is that it enables me to catch how much I shuffle so that 'Pick your feet up' and 'Don't slur' come back to me from childhood.

9 April. A dream in which a young man with ginger hair picks me up by the novel method of sticking a large stamp-collecting hinge on my back. Whether I end up in his collection I don't recall.

28 May, Yorkshire. I collect the paper from the village shop where, seeing a headline about yesterday's lightning strikes in London, a woman says: 'I love it when they have it nasty down south.'

11 July. Odd coincidence today. I am doing the *Guardian* quick crossword while watching Parliament on TV. I am nearly finished, with one clue left that I can't do: '15 Down: Two-wheeled transport – was in low spirits.' At which point some MP asks the minister (Lidington) about street crime, particularly criminals on mopeds. Which is, of course, the answer.

20 October. A letter from my publisher at Profile, Andrew Franklin. His son lives in Greenwich Village and has a friend (of a friend) who has my face tattooed on his arm, of which Andrew sends me a picture. I'm inordinately pleased by this and as he strolls down Bleecker Street I'm more than happy to be on this young man's arm. (Later it transpires that the friend actually lives in Dartmouth Park Hill so he's more likely to be strolling down Kentish Town Road. Still, you can't have everything.)

30 November. Now that Brexit is upon us I don't find my views have changed at all since the referendum or been modified by anything that has happened or been said since. It's nothing to do with the economic consequences of the pull-out, which are debatable to say the least. But all across Europe the forces of the far right are gathering strength . . . With all our shortcomings we are still a liberal society and if there is to be a struggle with the far right our place is alongside the liberal and social democratic parties in Europe. The flight into Brexit is still being presented as courageous. It isn't. It's cowardice.

The first diary entry by Alan Bennett to appear in the LRB was for 8 February 1983: 'A day off from filming *An Englishman Abroad* and I go to Edinburgh with Alan Bates.' The paper has published extracts from his diaries every year since then, as well as a few from before the paper was founded. From 11 January 1978 (published in 1984): 'Lindsay [Anderson] comes to the door in a plastic apron in the middle of preparing leeks or parsnips. He makes me some coffee, then we sit at the kitchen table and work on the script. He looks at me inquiringly, then puts a straight line through half a page . . . it is like having one's homework marked, and there is a lot of the schoolmaster about him, and some of wanting to please the teacher about me.' Forty years on, from 11 January 2018: 'The partridges have landed. I once had to give a talk at Hawthornden, the writers' colony near Edinburgh run by Drue Heinz. Thereafter, every Christmas Drue sends us a box of partridges or venison which, not being especially carnivorous, we find it hard to dispose of.'

Alan Bennett on a Young Man's Arm

London Review
OF BOOKS

VOLUME 41 NUMBER 1 · 3 JANUARY 2019 £3.95 US & CANADA $5.95

WHAT HAVE WE DONE?
Responses from Europe
Belgium · Bulgaria · Croatia
Denmark · France · Germany
Greece · Hungary · Ireland
Italy · Norway · Poland
Portugal · Spain · Sweden

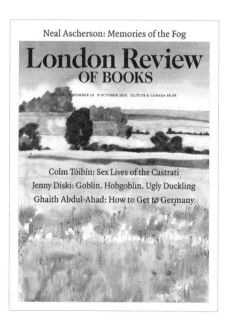

Benedict Anderson: The Frog under the Coconut Shell

London Review
OF BOOKS

James Meek on Farms and Farmers

London Review
OF BOOKS

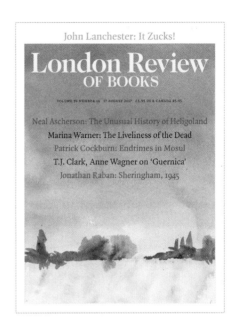

John Lanchester: It Zucks!

London Review
OF BOOKS

Neal Ascherson: The Unusual History of Heligoland
Marina Warner: The Liveliness of the Dead
Patrick Cockburn: Endtimes in Mosul
T.J. Clark, Anne Wagner on 'Guernica'
Jonathan Raban: Sheringham, 1945

Marina Warner: My Mother's Shoes, and Other Tales

London Review
OF BOOKS

David Runciman: A Failed State?

London Review
OF BOOKS

Jan-Werner Müller: The Populist Moment
Charles Nicholl: Dylan's Decade
Frederick Wilmot-Smith: Brexit in Court
Joanna Biggs taps with Zadie Smith

DAVID BROMWICH: DON'T RESIST, OPPOSE

London Review
OF BOOKS

Sidney Blumenthal: The First Family
John Barrell: Hogarth at His Best

James Meek: The Shock of the News

London Review
OF BOOKS

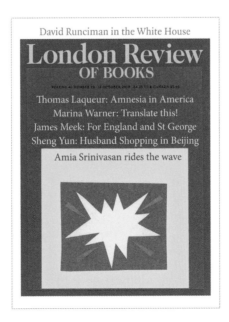

David Runciman in the White House

London Review
OF BOOKS

Thomas Laqueur: Amnesia in America
Marina Warner: Translate this!
James Meek: For England and St George
Sheng Yun: Husband Shopping in Beijing

Amia Srinivasan rides the wave

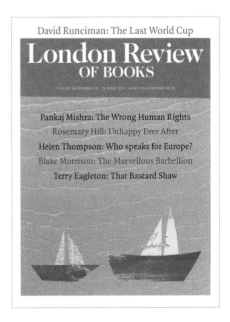

David Runciman: The Last World Cup

London Review
OF BOOKS

Pankaj Mishra: The Wrong Human Rights
Rosemary Hill: Unhappy Ever After
Helen Thompson: Who speaks for Europe?
Blake Morrison: The Marvellous Barbellion
Terry Eagleton: That Bastard Shaw

Acknowledgments

Compiled by Sam Kinchin-Smith
Designed by Christopher G. Thompson
Edited by Jean McNicol and Alice Spawls
Images: Ben Walker
Research: Nancy Gryspeerdt

This book was supported by a Harry Ransom Center
Research Fellowship in the Humanities.

Thanks to Ella Griffiths, Lee Brackstone, Jack Murphy and
Hannah Styles at Faber & Faber; Elizabeth Garver and
Stephen Enniss at the Harry Ransom Center; Courtney
Chartier and Kathy Shoemaker at Emory; R.L. Goldberg
at Princeton; Nick Deschamps at Wings; Sam Sheldon at
the Wylie Agency; Win Campbell, Rea Hederman,
Jane Miller, Sam Miller, Oliver Pritchett, Julian Rothenstein,
Martin Soames, Francène G. Thompson and Alexandra
Tzirkoti.

Isn't the
indistinct
often exactly
what we
need